Where the Mountain Stands Alone

Where the Mountain

Published in Cooperation with

the Monadnock Institute of Nature, Place and Culture

by University Press of New England   Hanover and London

Stands Alone

Stories of Place in the Monadnock Region

Howard Mansfield, editor

Published in Cooperation with the Monadnock Institute of Nature,

Place and Culture at Franklin Pierce College

by University Press of New England,

One Court Street, Lebanon, NH 03766

www.upne.com

© 2006 by Monadnock Institute of Nature, Place and Culture

Printed in China

5   4   3   2   1

Library of Congress Cataloging-in-Publication Data

Where the mountain stands alone : stories of place in the Monadnock Region / Howard Mansfield, editor.

    p.   cm.

"Published in Cooperation with the Monadnock Institute of Nature, Place and Culture."

Includes bibliographical references and index.

ISBN-13: 978–1–58465–555–8 (cloth : alk. paper)

ISBN-10: 1–58465–555–0 (cloth : alk. paper)

ISBN-13: 978–1–58465–556–5 (pbk. : alk. paper)

ISBN-10: 1–58465–556–9 (pbk. : alk. paper)

1. Monadnock, Mount, Region (N.H.)—History. 2. Monadnock, Mount, Region (N.H.)—Description and travel. 3. Monadnock, Mount, Region (N.H.)—Social life and customs. I. Mansfield, Howard. II. Monadnock Institute of Nature, Place and Culture.

F42.C5W48   2006

974.2'9—dc22

2005028682

"Beyond the hills it looked almost as if the blue ocean might be seen. Monadnock was visible, like a sapphire cloud against the sky."

—NATHANIEL HAWTHORNE, 1838

"But that New Hampshire bluff—that promontory of a State—lowering day and night on this our State of Massachusetts, will longest haunt our dreams."

—HENRY DAVID THOREAU, 1842

CONTENTS

Contents

MAPS

Where the Mountain Stands Alone

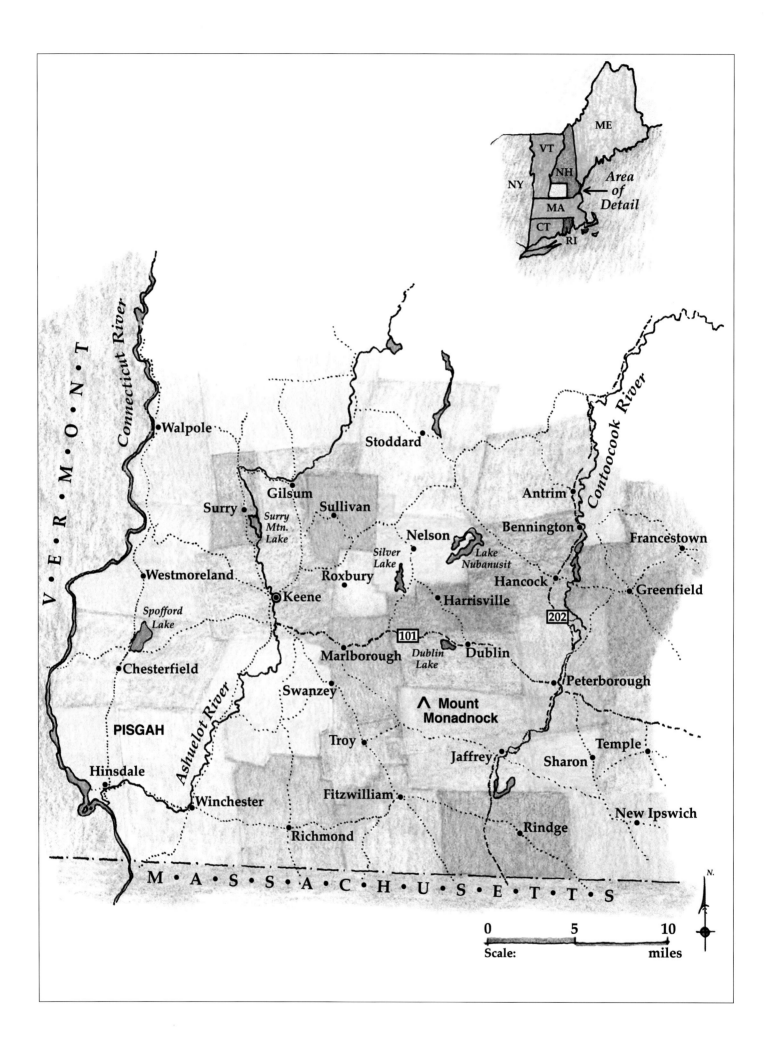

Introduction

HOWARD MANSFIELD

The American Quest for Placelessness

I. Annihilating Space

A few years ago, a small town around here got a McDonald's. The town rejoiced. They greeted the opening day with the high school marching band. They had arrived—in America. Fifty years after drive-in fast food began to remake the diet and landscape, this town of five thousand was at last on the map. Never mind that in the boom years for McDonald's the company wouldn't have bothered with such small towns, and never mind that by now the criticism of fast food can be recited by rote, even by those in line to "supersize" their fries. And never mind that a local, family-owned restaurant was soon extinguished. In the nineteenth century, a town would fight to have a railroad; in our time it's national franchises. We call it sprawl and big-box tyranny, and we're there on opening day, sometimes with a marching band. This is an American tradition.

One part of American history has been a quest for placelessness, a quest to make one place like another. We may sing of "spacious skies" and shower praise on family farms and small towns, but we have been hard at work for centuries to level all local distinctions. From the earliest days, Americans have struggled to build a nation—this phrase "to build a nation" has the mildewed smell of discarded 1950s textbooks for high school "civics." But this was the project: create one people, create one national market. *E Pluribus Unum*, as it says on the greenback: Out of many, one. Out of many places, one standard place. New cities began by laying out a grid, willfully pushing streets through steep hills, cliffs, and ponds. The hills were leveled to fill the ponds and build land out into the harbor.

"To the pleasantness of American life there is one, and perhaps only one, seri-

The B. & M. Railroad Station in Keene. From the earliest days, Americans have worked to create one national market. *E Pluribus Unum*: Out of many, one. Out of many places, one standard place.

ous drawback—its uniformity. Those who have been struck by the size of America, and by what they have heard of its restless excitement, may be surprised at the word," wrote James Bryce in his classic work of 1888, *The American Commonwealth*. Bryce was a British ambassador to the United States (and for several years summered in Dublin, New Hampshire).

The uniformity of American cities was "remarkable." "With eight or nine exceptions . . . American cities differ from one another only herein, that some of them are built more with brick than with wood, and others more with wood than with brick. In all else they are alike, both great and small. In all the same wide streets, crossing at right angles, ill-paved, but planted . . . with maple-trees whose autumnal scarlet surpasses the brilliance of any European foliage. In all the same shops, arranged on the same plan, the same Chinese laundries . . . the same ice-cream stores, the same large hotels with seedy men hovering about in the cheerless entrance-hall, the same street cars passing to and fro with passengers clinging to the door-step, the same locomotives ringing their great bells as they clank slowly down the middle of the street." In the Monadnock region, Bryce would have found Keene—more wood than brick—with a skyline of factory smokestacks shooting up dark geysers. And he would have found mill villages like Jaffrey, Peterborough, and Harrisville—more brick than wood—a little Lowell.

Bryce admitted that England's larger towns had a "sad monotony," but the dreariness of cities on the American plan frightened him. "Their monotony haunts one like a nightmare," he said some thirty years in advance of Edward Hopper's lonely city scenes like the late-night coffee shop in *Nighthawks*. "Even the irksomeness of finding the streets named by numbers becomes insufferable. . . . There is something wearisomely hard and bare in such a system."

He ascribed this bleakness to the lack of a long history, the old complaint of European visitors. "In pacing their busy streets and admiring their handsome city halls and churches, one's heart sinks at the feeling that nothing historically interesting ever has happened here, perhaps ever will happen." (This had become a set form: America is not like Europe. Therefore it is [A] wonderful, [B] awful, [C] both—and pay no attention if I contradict myself in the same breath. Some later critics in the early twentieth century were disappointed because America was too much like Europe.) In San Francisco, Bryce thinks it strange to find the mansions of railroad barons crowning the hills, rather than a proper feudal castle or the ruins of the Acropolis. San Francisco has a spectacular setting, but it turns out to be just a hilly Cleveland. "Travel where you will, you feel that what you have found in one place that you will find in another," he wrote, anticipating today's genre of books lamenting Nowhereville, USA.

Bryce had overlooked the great dedication it had taken to build these bland cities in such a short time. At the start of the nineteenth century, all but 500,000 of the five million Americans lived within fifty miles of the seacoast. Yet "each group of states lived a life apart," wrote Henry Adams. There was little interstate commerce. Shipping a ton of goods thirty miles inland was as costly as shipping the same cargo to England. The mail between Boston and New York took

"To the pleasantness of American life there is one, and perhaps only one, serious drawback—its uniformity," wrote the Englishman James Bryce in 1888. "Travel where you will, you feel that what you have found in one place that you will find in another."

three days (using the better roads). A letter from Portland, Maine, to Louisville, Georgia, took twenty days. The stagecoach from Boston to New Ipswich, New Hampshire, took a wearying fourteen hours to cover fifty miles, departing Boston before first light at 4 a.m. and arriving in time for dinner at 6 p.m. When Thomas Jefferson, on horseback, traveled from Monticello to Washington, D.C., he had to cross eight rivers, five of which had no bridges or boats.

"The union of New England with New York and Pennsylvania was not an easy task," wrote Adams, "but the union of New England with the Carolinas, and of the seacoast with the interior, promised to be a hopeless undertaking. . . . If Americans agreed in any opinion, they were united in wishing for roads."

The young republic built turnpikes, national roads, and canals in fits and starts. When the railroad came along, it was adopted with a religious fervor. European engineers were astonished at the pace of construction and the steep inclines, tight turns, and large locomotives. The railroad was the river that ran uphill, said the Americans, "the river produced by modern science." Railroads were doing God's work, preached Thomas Starr King, a Unitarian minister popular on the lecture circuit. "Railroads are talismanic wands," said one Chicagoan. "They have a charming power. They do wonders—they work miracles. They are better than laws, they are essentially—politically and religiously—the pioneer and vanguard of civilization." Their "iron bands" were looked upon as the savior of a union of distant states. Railroads "annihilated space and time," they nullified distance. The old measures were thrown out: days of travel by horse or oxen, days under sail or on a narrow canal boat.

At a New Hampshire railroad convention in 1834, Charles B. Haddock praised the shrinking distances: "Concord shall be taken up and carried ten hours toward the setting sun. The capital of the State shall be virtually transferred from the banks of the Merrimack to the banks of the Connecticut. The fertile intervals of these beautiful New Hampshire streams shall unite; the intervening mountains shall disappear; the verdant edges of meadows shall knit together; and these glad rivers flow on, side by side, towards the sea."

"Here" was merging with "there." "All local attachments will be at an end," said one observer. In 1883 the railroads standardized time. Four standard time zones replaced more than fifty local or "sun" times. It's as if the railroads had commanded the sun to stand still, said the *Chicago Tribune*. The *Cincinnati Commercial Gazette* protested: Why should our days be thrown off by as much as a half hour "to harmonize with an imaginary line through Pittsburgh"? "Let the people of Cincinnati stick to the truth as it is written by the sun, moon and stars." But local time was too small to be a good commodity. It was another hometown business losing out to a national brand.

The local "truth" was overthrown. Americans had an overabundance of localness, of what we call "place." They worked to "make land." The land as it had existed for ten thousand years—since the last glacier—was an obstacle. The pioneers cleared trees as fast as they could, sometimes in chopping bees, sometimes by one man "driving": cutting through each tree two-thirds of the way, then knocking them down like dominoes by felling one tree into the next. One man could fell an acre of trees in a day by driving. The fallen trees would be left to dry and then burned. The ash was sold as potash and charcoal. The fires frequently spread through the forest, at times eclipsing the sun at noon, as on the "Dark Day" of May 19, 1780, in northern New England. Nearly a year later Antrim, New Hampshire, voted at its town meeting to commemorate the Dark Day with fasting and prayer. Travelers have left us descriptions of acres of charred land, smoldering stumps, and the muddy rush of rivers after a storm. Some of Henry David Thoreau's accounts in *The Maine Woods* read like the destruction that continues today in the Amazon and Indonesia.

"Our dense forests are falling under the ax of the hardy woodsman," Andrew Carnegie wrote to a cousin in Scotland. "The Wolf and the Buffalo are startled by the shrill scream of the Iron Horse where a few years ago they roamed undisturbed. Towns and cities spring up as if by magic. . . . This country is completely cut up with Railroad Tracks, Telegraphs and Canals. . . . Everything around us is in motion."

Another way to understand the quest for placelessness is to consider American cheese. I was once at a dinner in Paris with expatriate Americans who, over the "cheese course," were extolling the virtues of the strong, distinctive local cheeses that one of the guests had procured from a little market in his neighborhood. Why can't we have cheese like this in America, they asked, instead of that awful American cheese? It doesn't even taste like anything. I defended the orange cheese of our childhood. American cheese isn't about taste; it's about uniformity. It's about having the same piece of cheese in Chicago or New York, Duluth or Oakland. Each slice is like the next, no matter where or when you buy it, no matter if it has been shipped thousands of miles in refrigerated railroad cars, trucked through the desert, or bought at the factory store. Everyone gets the same cheese every time. American cheese is a triumph of shipping. The cheese manufacturers, like the railroad, have "annihilated space." Apply that to hamburgers, hotel rooms, automobiles, books, and you can see why Lord Bryce was disappointed to spend days rattling across a huge country only to find "no there there." Americans had worked tirelessly to shrink the continent. My point was lost among the many empty bottles of wine. You can't tell expats anything. (And, yes, the French cheeses were extraordinary. But you couldn't ship them over the mountains to Boxmart in Sacramento.)

II. Mountain Island

In 1935 a small, awkward magazine introducing its first issue made a stand against a New England "about to be sold, to be 'swallered inter' a sea of chain stores, national releases, and nationwide hookups." The editors of the new magazine, *Yankee*, had set up in Dublin, a New Hampshire town with a year-round population of 506. Nearby, 38 people lived in Sharon, 53 in Roxbury, 512 in Harrisville, 561 in Hancock, 394 in Greenfield, and about 2,500 each in Peterborough and Jaffrey. The population of many of these towns had peaked before the Civil War. The towns in sight of Mount Monadnock had failed. They had failed as farmers; failed as manufacturers. They had failed in the quest for placelessness. They couldn't "annihilate" space. It cost too much to ship what could be grown or manufactured. Rural New England was a dead-end street in the national market. In the dreary days of the Great Depression, many of its towns would have offered themselves up to be "'swallered inter' a sea of chainstores."

This failure created a refuge. Resorts are shelters against time—standard time (even if they rely on railroads for visitors). Resorts in the mountains, or at the sea, run on "sun time." Freed from schedules, people can step into the day, into a kind of free-flowing time they remember from childhood, or a sun-drenched boredom. Monadnock—*the mountain that stands alone, mountain island,* in the Algonquin languages—offered a refuge.

The Monadnock towns were rediscovered by waves of summer people, back-to-the-landers, artists, Massachusetts tax refugees, retirees swimming back to their summer camp memories, and believers in the image that New England had created for itself (the small town: white-steepled home of America's pious and better angels). Old-timers found themselves facing a legion of "flatland-ers" or "new natives," who were quick to call New Hampshire's "Quiet Corner" home. Some of these people were dissenters from the drive to make every place look alike; others just wanted that product in a smaller package. In the failure of upright Yankee toil, they found freedom. The farms had failed and left a for-ested land; the mills had failed and left a bounty of water in the dammed ponds, lakes, and brooks. The towns the early settlers had built by common consent were much better than today's most earnest work. The southwestern corner of New Hampshire was, true to its namesake, a mountain island.

This book is a chronicle of that failure and its aftermath in the region where the mountain stands alone. The anthology takes its five-part outline from the shape of human settlement in northern New England: "First Encounters," "Mak-ing Land," "Emptying Out," "Returning," and "Here and Now in the Global Market."

With essays, recollections, historical documents, and photos, *Where the Mountain Stands Alone* portrays life as it was once lived, and as it is lived today. We do not present a straight history, a recitation of dates and facts, but rather the stories that capture the life of a place, the habits and hopes of a community. "Sense of place" is the overworked phrase. The anthology mixes history, memoir, geology, and geography. The elusive feel of one place exists in that intersection of political and family history, landscape, destiny, expectations, weather, and time.

All good place-essays are about close observation, being tourists of the near-at-hand, looking close to home at changes in the land. In this way we avoid being what the national park rangers call "windshield visitors"—taking quick snap-shots of vast places. The criteria we applied when deciding if an essay belongs in the book is this: Does the essay have dirt under its nails? Is the writer working from a specific place? Is he or she studying this place? In this book we are work-ing the land to examine our perceptions, overturn our expectations—working to see the place as clearly as possible. Or, to put it another way, to record how one small corner of America has faced the forces that work to destroy what's local.

In the winter of 2004 Peterborough debated the merits of allowing the sale of town land to a big-box supermarket. The debate was another page from the pattern book of placelessness. The supermarket's supporters wanted to send out the marching band; the opponents argued for preserving the town's distinctive characteristics. They didn't want to be "'swallered inter' a sea of chain stores." The supporters promised great things. This big-box store will have a "wellness section," a bakery, a florist, a bank, they said. The parking lot will be landscaped. There will be 150 new jobs, $200,000 in taxes. We have to spend thousands on groceries elsewhere. We need this big store because others have big stores. Peterborough, they argued, was being left behind. They could have been making the case for the railroad to come to town. Each political season has its own railroad—the technology or business that promises prosperity. Each year will bring something else. There is a global push to make all places as similar as possible, to make one global market. Commerce, Lord Bryce implied, is a one-size-fits-all condition.

In every town within sight of Monadnock you can find a similar debate about accommodating the scale and pace of our protodigital age in eighteenth-century town centers and nineteenth-century mill villages: Widen the road? Build a bypass? Rezone for an industrial park? Stick another cell phone tower on the mountain? Build more houses on four-acre lots, or cluster them on fewer acres, saving the rest of the land? In short: How much is enough?

We have inherited the benefits of failure. Failure bestows a second chance. In failure there are opportunities. Economic stagnation preserved much of what we love of Boston, for example, saving Back Bay, Beacon Hill, and other neighborhoods. Boston's essential cityscape—its *Bostonness*—survived to be appreciated and protected. The same lessons can be applied to the land in sight of Monadnock. The once-bypassed Monadnock region has arrived in the twenty-first century with its rich inheritance of failure, which has saved forest lands, a few farms, and villages. How do we manage prosperity without being leveled by the quest for placelessness?

Today, the fate of this beautiful land seesaws on the cheery slogan of the Monadnock Travel Council: "So near, yet away from it all!" I was on a hike one summer up Mount Monadnock with Tom Wessels, an Antioch professor who is a master reader of the forested landscape. He can see the history from the trees—where sheep grazed 150 years ago, exactly how the hurricane of 1938 hit where you now stand—or (as he does in this book) point out the changes in the land from the Great Gale of 1815. On this day, not long after we had set out up the mountain, we stopped by a stand of red spruce. These trees are in serious decline, weakening from the last harsh winters and DDE, a breakdown product of DDT. We don't use DDT in this country. DDE falls out of pollution from Asia. So near, yet half a world away. No place is isolated. Mountain Island no more.

Part One

FIRST ENCOUNTERS

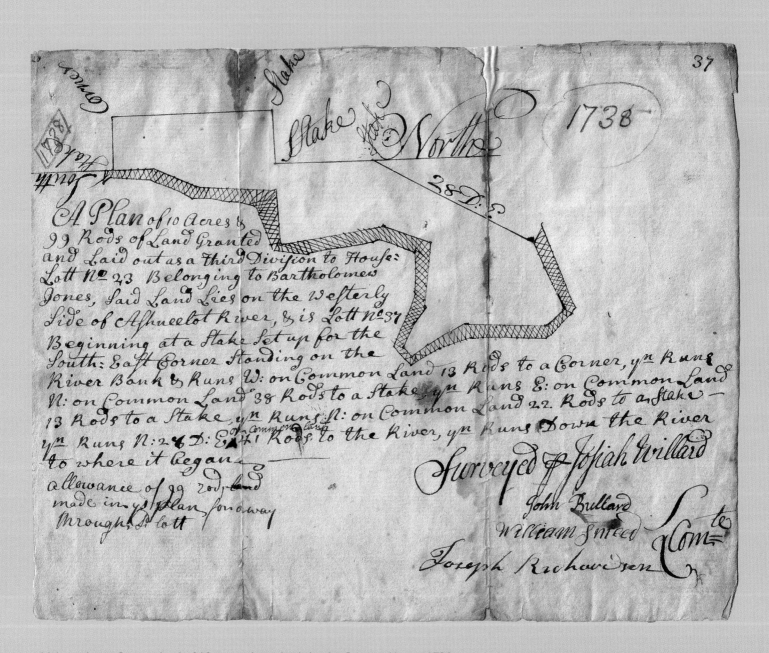

Making claims. Survey deed of 10 acres along the Ashuelot River in Keene, 1738.

Introduction

The Middle Ages stop sixty miles west of the Atlantic Ocean. In 1629 Captain John Mason claimed a sweep of land he named after the English county Hampshire. Mason's land was granted by a council chartered by King James I. This land was bounded by a curve, and this curve and this claim would afflict the province in each generation for 150 years. Captain Mason wanted to establish a lordship for himself and collect rents on these lands. New Hampshire would be like feudal Hampshire. Mason's Curve was the last wash of an ancient feudal sea. The lone curve can be seen on maps today looking like a ripple on a pond. The boundaries of thirty-three towns and three counties curve. Many other town boundaries were drawn in reference to the curve, so that on a map they seem to be tilting.

"The Council Established at Plymouth in the County of Devon for planting, ruling, ordering and governing of New England in America" was chartered by the king in 1620 "to stretch out the bounds of our Dominions." The forty men of the council were granted possession of all the land lying between the 40th and 48th degree of northern latitude, from the St. Lawrence River to present-day Philadelphia, reaching from the Atlantic Ocean to the South Seas. Captain John Smith had named this place New England in 1614, but the English lacked even one settlement north of Plymouth. When Captain Smith showed his map of New England to Prince Charles, the fourteen-year-old Charles wrote in the names of the English places he fancied. Smith kept a separate list of the Indian place-names he had learned, but most of these were already off the English map.

"There is no other Subject of any Christian King or state by any authority from their sovereign Lords or princes actually in Possession of any of the Lands," said the charter. "We have been further given Certainly to know that within these late years there hath by Gods visitation reign'd a wonderfull pleague together with Many Terrible slaughters & Murders committed against the savage & brutish people heretofore Inhabiting in a manner to the utter devastation destruction & depopulation of that whole Territory." The Indians' first contact and trade with the fleets of ships that fished off the coast had also brought them new diseases. Their communities were devastated by epidemics, but they had not vanished as the charter claimed. And some, such as the Narragansetts, were not harmed. "Almighty God in Great goodness & bounty towards us & our people have Thought fit & determined that those Large & goodly Territories deserted as it were by their natural Inhabitants should be possessed & Enjoyed by such of our subjects & people...."

The council set about granting lands. They granted Mason and Sir Fernando Gorges land the two men called Maine. They granted Mason land he called Mariana, which bordered the "Great River Naumkeek," a mythical river recorded in

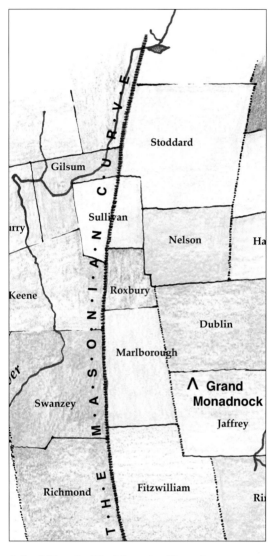

A feudal border. The Masonian Curve is one of the strangest lines drawn on the continent. Delaware has the only other curving boundary like this in the United States.

only one English map. They leased land for three thousand years, and reserved all gold and silver that might be found there for themselves and the king. The deeds were vague, and sometimes they deeded the same land to different people. The forty men of the council did not know this land and had never been there. They were Englishmen. There were no maps as we know them. Before they knew which way the rivers ran, and if the mountains were more than rumors, they claimed it all.

Part one puts the Native Abenaki on those cryptic early maps.

READINGS

Indians and Wolves

Early spellings of the name used by the Abenaki:
Manadnuck, Manadnock, Manudnock, Manadnach, Manadnack, Monadnock, Monadnuck, Monadnick, Monodnock, Monadnoc, Menorgnuck, Menadnak, Menadnick, Menagnick, Menadnuck, Menadnock, Menadnack, Wanadnock, Wannadnack, Wenadnack, Wahmodmaulk.

—Compiled by Allen Chamberlain,
The Annals of the Grand Monadnock, 1936

Thursday [July] 29. We marched north and by west about nine miles and crossed several branches of Miller's River and camped and sent out scouts, which found where the Indians had lived last year and made a canoe, at the north end of the long pond [Lake Monomonac, Rindge, N.H.].

Friday 30. We marched north in the forenoon and came to a pond which run[s] into Contoocook River. In the afternoon we marched northwest in all about 12 miles and camped at Peewunseun [Contoocook] pond and sent out scouts four miles and they found two wigwams made last year. They also found a paddle and some squash shells in one of them, which we suppose they carried from Rutland.

Saturday 31. We marched 12 miles and I with fourteen men camped on the top of Wannadnack Mountain [the first recorded ascent of Monadnock] and discovered 26 ponds. Saw Pigwackett lying one point from said mountain and Cusagee [Kearsarge] Mountain and Winnepeseockey lying northeast from said Wannadnack. The same day we found several old signs which the Indians had made the last year and where they camped when they killed the people at Rutland, as we imagine.

Sabbath day, August the 1st. We marched from the west side of Wenadnack [Monadnock] and crossed three streams that run into Contocook and then camped and sent out our scouts and found two wigwams made in June or July, as we suppose, and found sixteen of their spits which they roast their meat with, all in said wigwam, and one of our scouts went so far that they could not return that same night.

Monday 2. We marched about seven miles and crossed a great branch of Contoocook River and sent out our scouts up and down the river. Each scout traveled about 8 miles.

Tuesday 3. We marched N. E. about sixteen miles and camped and sent out our scouts, who found many old signs of Indians.

Sabbath 8. We returned homeward by reason of our Indians having no provision and several of our English but little. We came to a stream that run[s] into Merimack. We traveled about 24 miles south and by east.

—Captain Samuel Willard, 1725

About the year of our Lord 1739 [the petition records], in consequence of a grant of a tract of land had and obtained from the Great and General Court or Assembly of the Province of the Massachusetts Bay by Samuel Haywood and others his associates . . . a number of people immediately went on to said tract of land and began a settlement (though then very far from any other inhabitants) which we have continued increasing ever since the year 1739, except sometimes when we left the said township for fear of being destroyed by the enemy, who several times drove us from our settlement soon after we began, and almost ruined many of us. Yet what little we had in the world lay there. We, having no whither else to go, returned to our settlement as soon as prudence would admit, where we have continued since and have cultivated a rough part of the wilderness to a fruitful field. The inhabitants of said tract of land are increased to the number of forty-five or fifty families.

—*History of the Town of Peterborough, N.H.*, 1876

The Caleb Howe grave, Hooker Cemetery, Hinsdale. Howe was killed by "Indeans" in 1755. (The epitaph has been chalked for contrast.)

The territorial limits of the town [of Jaffrey] . . . were in 1787 threatened by certain designing men of Sliptown (afterward Sharon), who petitioned the General Court for the annexation of a strip of land one mile in width from the east side of Jaffrey. In a vigorous remonstrance the inhabitants of Jaffrey represented to the law makers of the state that they had no territory to spare. . . . "Moreover there is a very great Mountain in this town and a great number of large ponds which renders about the fourth part thereof not habitable, besides a great deal of other waste land which makes the habitable part of this town but barely sufficient to maintain our minister and support our public privileges."

—Albert Annett, *Granite Monthly*, 1899

Near the close of the last century [about 1795], the bears seem to have left the town [Fitzwilliam] mostly or to have been destroyed; but they were succeeded by wolves in greater numbers and, if possible, more destructive than ever before, and wolf hunts were for some years a necessity, if not a pastime.

The elder Mr. Forristall, Mr. Silas Angier, and Deacon Griffin lost sheep and lambs in considerable numbers, while in a single night sixteen of the flock of Mr. Spaulding, of Jaffrey, were destroyed. The whole community was now aroused, every gun was put in order, and every able-bodied man and boy enlisted to fight the common enemy.

Knowing that Monadnock was the stronghold of the wolves, a company of men from this and the adjoining towns chose Phineas Reed, Esq., as their leader, and surrounding the mountain a few rods apart they simultaneously worked their way to the top, only to find that the game secured consisted of an old bear with her two cubs, and four foxes. All except one of the cubs were shot, but the one saved repaid the kindness of the young man who was carrying it home by biting off one of his thumbs.

After descending the mountain Captain Reed's men heard the barking of a wolf in the woods not far off, and so they surrounded the woods and stood at their posts all night, determined that their foe should not escape. In the morning the wolf was driven out into a piece of cleared land. At least fifty bullets were now fired at him, but he broke the ring and made his way east into a meadow belonging to Rev. Mr. Ainsworth, where he was shot by a young man named Nathaniel Stanley. His weapon was one of the old "Queen's Arms," and he fired two balls and a slug before he finished his work.

As usual on such occasions, the bounty of twenty dollars which was to be received was spent at the nearest tavern.

—History of Fitzwilliam, 1888

From Mount Holyoke, on the southern side of this township [Hadley], at the distance of three miles from the church, is seen the richest prospect in New England, and not improbably in the United States. The mountain is about one thousand one hundred feet above the surface of the [Connecticut] River, but in the place of ascent is of so gradual an acclivity that two-thirds of the elevation may be easily gained on horseback. On the highest part of the summit the inhabitants have cleared away the trees and shrubs, so as to open the prospect in the most advantageous manner. . . .

When the eye traces this majestic stream, meandering with a singular course through these delightful fields, wandering in one place five miles to gain one, and in another four to gain seventy yards; enclosing, almost immediately beneath, an island of twenty acres exquisite in its form and verdure, and adorned on the northern end with a beautiful grove; when it marks the sprightly towns which rise upon its banks, and the numerous churches which gem the whole landscape in its neighborhood; when it explores the lofty forests, wildly contrasted with the rich scene of cultivation which it has just examined, and presenting all the varieties of woodland vegetation; when it ascends higher and marks the perpetually varying and undulating arches of the hills, the points and crowns of the nearer and detached mountains, and the long continued ranges of the more distant ones, particularly of the Green Mountains receding northward beyond the reach of the eye; when, last of all, it fastens upon the Monadnoc in the northeast, and in the northwest upon Saddle Mountain, ascending, each, at the distance of fifty miles, in dim and misty grandeur, far above all the other objects in view; it will be difficult not to say that, with these exquisite varieties of beauty and grandeur, the relish for landscape is filled, neither a wish for higher perfection nor an idea of what it is, remaining in the mind.

—Timothy Dwight, *Travels in New England and New York*, 1796

At the settlement of the township of Jaffrey, Monadnock must have been covered nearly to its summit with a dense forest. Some of my earliest recollections are of fires on its sides, which furnished pillars of smoke by day and fire by night, sufficient to have guided the children of Israel, if their path to the Promised Land had lain in this vicinity. These fires [circa 1800] left a tangled windfall, and a bald rock, as it was called, at the top, which was perhaps bare before that time.

—Joel Parker, "Jaffrey Centennial Address," 1873

A single wolf was still left that alternated between Monadnock and Watatic, and committed great depredations among the flocks wherever it went. In the winter of 1819–20 a number of hunters with their hounds started in pursuit, but day after day the crafty beast rendered all their efforts fruitless. They followed the wolf through Jaffrey, Fitzwilliam, Winchendon and Rindge, and even into the towns of Templeton and Gardner. Meanwhile storms came on, the snow became deep, and two of the original hunters becoming discouraged retired, though their places were at once supplied by more courageous and persevering men.

At no time did the wolf neglect his nightly repast, but while the hunters were resting he took his meal in the nearest barnyard. Phineas Whitney entertained the weary men one night but while they were sleeping the wolf killed several of Mr. Whitney's sheep, drinking the blood as it flowed from the opened veins and taking a little of the most delicate meat, apparently not because it was hungry, but for the purpose of a pleasant entertainment. Then it lay down under some bushes and rested till it was time to start in the morning. For nine or ten days this warfare was kept up, and the wolf, though often seen and fired at, seemed as fresh as at the beginning. Colonel Jewett's bloodhounds were now put upon the track, and followed in close pursuit, but night came on and the wolf was safe.

On the morning of the next day (the Sabbath), the people in Fitzwilliam village, having learned that the wolf was approaching Monadnock, turned out and formed lines of men along the roads to Rindge and Jaffrey. The hounds drove the wolf into the Scott meadow, where it was shot first by Shubael Plympton and then by Lewis Robbins, two or three bullets passing through its body and leaving it dead. The prey was at once brought to Fitzwilliam Common amid the cheers of the people. There was no religious service in the meeting house on the morning of that Sabbath.

This is said to have been the last wolf-hunt in the region about Monadnock.

—*History of Fitzwilliam*, 1888

Here, too, we have the Monadnock, rising in cold, proud, isolated grandeur, an emblem at once of the essential stability and the superficial changes in nature. Its rugged sides, now compact of bald, cragged rock, were formerly covered with trees almost to its summit. But, years ago [circa 1800], the ravening fire, kindled whether by accident or design, spread over a great part of the superior portion of the mountain, killing every tree and shrub wherever it went. The dead trees, decaying and falling, furnished materials for another conflagration [circa 1820], which occurred within the memory of many of us. Some thirty years ago, in the latter part of a dry summer, the fire from a clearing on the side of the mountain made its way to the higher regions, where, feeding upon the decaying wood, and nourished by the wind and the drought, it extended itself over almost the entire northern side. As the daylight paled, giving place to the darkness of night, there might be seen from out the dense sea of livid, flame-tinged smoke, in which the mountain was enveloped by day, countless fires lighting up all along the extended range, glowing with a more vivid brightness as the darkness thickened, until the whole mountain-side blazed with its myriad tongues of waving flame. It was a spectacle beautiful and grand in itself, but rendered sublime and awful by the thought of the dread power of the devouring element, and of the terrible destruction that must ensue, if, the wind and the drought continuing, it should burst its mountain barrier and invade the domains of man. But fortunately, before such a catastrophe was reached, a drenching rain extinguished the fire, and thus put an end at once to the grandeur and terror of the scene.

—Charles Mason, "Dublin Centennial Address," 1852

The subscriber will be ready to wait on who shall visit Monadnock this season after Tuesday next at the brook about one-half hour's walk southeast of the pinnacle where he is erecting a sufficient building as shelter from sun, rain or the chills of night. Tea and coffee, with suitable meats and drinks will be provided. Horses may be left at his house on the turnpike. Spirituous liquids may at all times be had at either place.

—John Fife, *New Hampshire Sentinel*, August 6, 1824

Travel to Monadnock is unprecedented this season. On one day recently there were four hundred people on the mountain.

—*Keene Sentinel*, August 23, 1860

Sokoki Homeland from Monadnock

K'namitobena Sokwaki

MARGE BRUCHAC

Nidôba chiga k'pozibena?
Friend, when shall we embark? . . .
O'da n'wawaldomowen. Nôwatga n'noji tolin.
I don't know. It is a long time since I have made canoes.
—"On Travelling by water in the Indian country,"
  from an 1884 Abenaki dictionary

The Path to Monadnock, from Surry, New Hampshire

On a mountaintop in Surry, New Hampshire, above the Ashuelot River, a large flat boulder sits in a clearing. Pecked and hammered into the surface of the stone is the image of a curved bow, with the bowstring drawn back into a sharp V and a three-feathered arrow at the ready, aiming southeast. Below the bow is a grid

Mali Keating holding her grandmother's wedding photograph from 1872. Keating's family represents the region's unbroken Abenaki presence.

Carved on a flat stone in Surry, a curved bow with an arrow points southeast toward Mount Monadnock.

of three long horizontal lines, crossed by three short vertical lines, tilting in the direction of the arrow.

In 1932, historian Samuel Wadsworth testified to the antiquity of this carving: "The bow is about twenty inches long and the arrow points toward Central Square in Keene and Monadnock Mountain and nearly in the direction of the old Indian village just south of the covered highway bridge at Sawyer's Crossing and on the east side of the Ashuelot River. . . . Mr. C. M. Scovell said that his father knew of it as early as 1845, or before the railroad was built, and that it was known to the oldest inhabitants who supposed it to be of Indian origin. . . . Dr. Josiah Seward suggests that it may have been cut by the St. Francis Indians."

The arrow points to Mount Monadnock, a location from which one can see clearly in every direction: eastward to the Atlantic Ocean, southward toward Long Island Sound, west to the Connecticut River and the mountains beyond, and north to the peaks of the White Mountains. This mountain has witnessed more than ten thousand years of Native presence, situated as it is in the midst of Western Abenaki lands affectionately called Ndakinna, meaning "my homeland."

In geological parlance, the mountain's Indian name now signifies its form. A monadnock is a "hill of resistant rock standing in the midst of a peneplain." Nineteenth-century philosophers remarked on the similarity to the Latin monad, signifying a single unit that reflects the universe. The *U.S. Geological Survey Bulletin* No. 258 says the name originated with the Native words "m'an meaning 'surpassing,' adn 'mountain,' and ock 'place'—place of the surpassing (unexcelled) mountain." Some find its origin in the word manitou, "spirit." One Native dictionary of alnobaôdwa—the Abenaki language—suggests that the name is môniadenak, literally "money mountain." The most likely origin may be found in the word menahan, "island," or the root men-, "separate, apart or distinct," combined with aden, "mountain," to form menahadenock, "the mountain which stands alone."

The Abenaki name for this section of Ndakinna is Sokoki, also spelled Sokwaki, or Squakheag, for the Sokwakiak, "the southern people who are set apart," referring to the southernmost branch of the Wôbanakiak, "people of the dawn." From Monadnock, one can look down on meadows where Sokoki people once planted corn, and where New Hampshire farmers now graze their cattle. Old Indian trails crisscross the countryside, many of them now transformed into highways. Most archaeologists can tell, by the lay of the land, where Native homesites, fishing weirs, and tool caches may be found.

The Native history of the region is not so clear on paper as it is on land. Part of the problem is perspective. The non-Native residents of every town within sight of the mountain have gleaned much of their knowledge of Indians, not from Native people, but from two interrelated Yankee traditions: town histories and local historical memoirs. The town histories offer the usual cast of characters in a frontier morality play spun from the European imagination: savage Indians, peaceful settlers, brave soldiers, and daring explorers, with the requisite number of beautiful maidens thrown in for romantic diversion. Most of the Indian warriors are fierce fighters, and some of the Indian maidens can be found casting themselves over waterfalls in a lovesick swoon. Local memoirs reinforce these stereotypes, with first-person accounts of the fears of the wilderness, the horrors of Indian captivity, the derring-do of Indian fighters, and the exploits of soldiers and settlers, memorialized on local historical plaques for easy reading.

Three centuries' worth of Euro-American references to the mountain called Monadnock offer few insights into intercultural contact. One of the earliest accounts relates how, in May of 1704, Caleb Lyman of Northampton, Massachusetts, passed by Monadnock on his way to ambush and scalp seven Indians at a homesite on the Connecticut River, in consequence of which the Cowass people "forsook their fort and corn at Cowassuck and never returned to this day." In 1724, Lieutenant Jabez Fairbanks led a scout to "the Grand Wanadnock Hill," identifying it as one of those "places as the Indians are most likely to haunt." In the same year, Pequot mercenaries working for the English expressed their willingness to "try for a scalp about Manadnuck."

Reading the Pages of Town Histories, 1704–1988

The town histories of the villages surrounding Monadnock seem reluctant to consider Native peoples as the rightful residents of local lands, and do not even attempt to cloak their racism. Indians, according to most of these histories, simply do not belong here. In July of 1735, Samuel Willard was hailed as the "first" to ascend the mountain, after discovering Native canoes at Lake Monomonac, wigwams at Contoocook, and camping places on Monadnock, in the heart of what he considered an untracked wilderness. In 1937, the author of the *History of Jaffrey* wrote that Monadnock was simply a stopping point for "savage forays upon the Massachusetts frontier in the old French and Indian wars." The 1921 *History of the Town of Sullivan* states flatly that, although Indian relics are often found in the local fields, "Sullivan has no prehistoric history."

Most of the Native people who appear in these town histories are nameless and faceless, apart from a few prominent warriors, chiefs, or individuals who are romantically labeled as "the last of their kind." One exception is the Native man named "Philip," who was a familiar visitor to the cabin of John Kilburn of Walpole, in the midst of contested territory. In August of 1755, when Kilburn's cabin was surrounded by an Abenaki war party, Philip offered safety to his Yan-

Creating Indian history: The Degree of Pochantas in Jaffrey, c. 1940s. This was a local chapter of the national women's auxiliary to the Tribe of Red Men (founded in 1834 and claiming to be America's oldest fraternal organization). Officers in the Jaffrey "council" held titles of Pochantas, Powhatan, Prophetess, Collector of Wampum, First Scout, First Runner, First Warrior, Guard of Tepee, Guard of the Forest, and others. At the time of this photo, the Degree of Pochantas had 500,000 members nationally. Today membership is below 40,000 and "Native American regalia" are worn only "with discretion," says the organization.

kee friend, shouting out "Old John, young John, I know you; come out here; we will give you quarter." Kilburn, who is now held up as a hero in all the histories of Walpole, replied "Quarter, you black rascals! Begone, or we will quarter you!"

Native people were depicted as closer to beasts than humans, "more elusive than the wild animals of the forest." Writers like Albert Annett of Jaffrey intoned that Indians were not skilled hunters, gatherers, or farmers, but mere opportunists who "in their marauding expeditions" randomly "take advantage of every opportunity to obtain game." In 1921, the historian of Hillsborough concluded that the red man's lack of intelligence, not colonial settlement, was the chief cause of strife on the frontier, since "his untutored mind embittered with real and fancied wrongs, was the uncertain and disturbing element hovering over the scenes like a shadowy nemesis." His chief contribution to English culture was fighting strategy—the best woods rangers, one history tells us, "had acquired the tricks and cunning, as well as the ruthlessness, of their savage foes."

Apart from the obvious racial bias in these accounts, eighteenth-century settlers and nineteenth-century historians struggled with their own linguistic confusion about place-names and tribal names. They failed to grasp the far-reaching connections, alliances, and trading networks among different tribes. They saw small, seasonally inhabited, seemingly scattered village sites where Native people saw large, widely traveled, familiar homelands full of resources for hunting and fishing. Europeans assumed that every time Native persons changed location, they changed their tribal identity. As a case in point, during the eighteenth century, some Sokoki families started circulating farther afield, relocating homesites, forming new alliances, or even taking up residence in Canada for a generation or more. That led to their being identified, not by their actual tribal names, but by their location at any given point in time, as "Schaghticoke," "River," "North," "French," and/or "St. Francis Indians."

Modern town historians do not seem to have grown past the biases of their forebears. David Proper, the twentieth-century historian of Keene, tells us that the entire region "was populated only by wild animals and roving bands of Indians." Helen Frinck, author of *These Acworth Hills*, in 1989 painted a romantic picture of the ecological Indian leaving scant evidence. "Because their food and shelter demanded little of nature, and because their religious philosophy taught them to seek harmony with all living beings, they left a minimal imprint on the environment." She accounts for population losses to plague and colonial warfare by noting that "clearly they were no match for the newly arrived white men." Her all too brief summary of Native history in Acworth ends abruptly with an account of the town's "last surviving Indian, Amasa Lawrence," who "moved away, leaving nothing behind, nor any trace of where they had gone."

The 1882 *History of Chesterfield* notes that some evidence of Native intervention and long occupation was clearly visible in places like "Poplar Hill," so named "because portions of it were covered with a vigorous growth of young poplars, which sprang up after the Indians had ceased to set their annual fires, as was their custom." George Aldrich, in his 1886 *History of Walpole*, recorded the abundance of the annual fish runs, the sacred carvings at the falls, and the medicinal spring near Cold River. But lest any reader think Indian life too enticing, he describes the "offensive . . . taste and smell" of the healing water, and paints a disagreeable picture of "the Indian, naturally sullen, morose and mercenary in disposition," with "squaws . . . doing their drudgery," and "papooses wallowing in the filth around the wigwams." White Yankee children had to be taught to fear Native peoples, since "The red man was . . . as wild as the savage beasts around him—a predatory vagabond, in constant warfare . . . his morals not much above the instinct of intelligent animals." If there were any signs of attraction to the lifeways of Native peoples, one needed only recount the history to chase such dangerous thoughts out of a small child's head:

"The tales of those atrocities were the first lessons taught the children of the early settlers. The grey haired veteran with his grandson upon his knee recounted to him, the hundredth time, the Indian tales of by-gone times. The child drank in every word, and became so much excited that his thoughts by day and his dreams by night were but one continued picture of murder and pillage. Thus he became thoroughly schooled, at manhood, with all the wiles of Indian warfare."

Some historians devoted entire chapters to descriptions of Native lifeways, based on information clearly gleaned from firsthand experience, while simultaneously complaining about the persistence of Native people and traditions. Jeremy Belknap, writing in 1791, was particularly disturbed by "the idea that lonely mountains and rocks are inhabited by departed spirits."

Many have attempted to revive the departed spirits of Indians past, from the spiritualist who imagines Indian spirits guiding his thoughts, to the archaeologist who reconstructs a sense of history from what has been left behind. Many stories have been spun from the bones, pottery, and projectiles of the past, but few have included the perspective of the Native people who created those remains. Archaeologists and anthropologists claim to be scientific mediators of the past, but even they have been influenced by the discourse of disappearance.

So how do we read past, and through, the pages of those town histories that teach us so much about prejudice, and so little about Indians? One option is to turn to the first-person accounts of colonists who lived with the Native peoples, rather than relying on the words of those who tried to exterminate them. Another way is to interview contemporary Native peoples, although many are understandably reluctant to talk about their family history to strangers. Another is to take a closer look at events that we think we know, while honestly considering which images are missing, and which perspectives have been intentionally silenced. I invite you to stand beside me, atop Mount Monadnock, and observe, through Native eyes, just a few of the moments and events that have been so imperfectly interpreted in the pages of the town histories.

Walma wajônokza miguen
Perhaps I had no pen.
Walma wajonemôza pilaskw.
Perhaps I had no paper.

—"Dubitative conjugations
of the inanimate verb
wajônôzik, to have," from an
1884 Abenaki dictionary

Looking toward Peskeompskut, May 1676: The Native Perspective

The trail up the mountain is icy still, but the days are beginning to lengthen. The year begins with sogali kisos, the "sugar moon," when the sap in the maple trees starts thrumming with the ebb and flow of warm days and cold nights. From here, one can see the ice breaking up in the smaller rivers, and soon, the Kwini-tewk, the "long river," will be clear traveling. Soon, the land will transform, from soft, cold, shifting mud to firmer ground, and the way south will become clear. Throughout Ndakinna, the families are already breaking up winter camp, and birchbark canoes are being patched and sealed for travel. After the snowmelt, one can count at least one full span of the moon before the shadbush blooms, the shad and salmon start their long run upriver to spawn, and people begin to prepare for the spring fishing.

Many different tribes, even during times of war, come together to fish at each of the falls. During this year, 1676 by English reckoning, at namassak kisos, the "fishing moon," a particularly large group of Sokoki people has decided to travel, not north to the falls at Ktsipontegu with their neighbors, but south to the falls at Peskeompskut. There, they will help the lower valley peoples catch and dry enough fish to feed their allies. This year, Wampanoag, Nimpuc, and Narragansett people from the south have sent many young children, women, and old ones north into Pocumtuck and Sokoki territory, to winter over at the falls, where they have been eagerly awaiting spring. The people at Peskeompskut will catch and dry enough fish to feed thousands.

Peskeompskut: Understanding the Historical Records

The histories record that by the late morning of May 19, 1676, more than four hundred Native people were found lying dead at Peskeompskut, the Connecticut River running thick with their blood. Captain William Turner had led his English militia north to the falls to slaughter the elderly men, women, and children who took refuge here. In English memories, the event was recalled as a great battle, the first major victory in Metacom's Rebellion, otherwise known as King Philip's War. The massacre at the fishing falls was the first attack in memory to be made on Native people at this place that was considered an intertribal safe zone. This devastating event caused many of the Native peoples living in the Connecticut River Valley to begin seeking refuge in places far out of reach of encroaching European settlers.

Scouting for Fort Dummer, July 1735: The Native Perspective

Now that war has come to Sokoki territory, the trick is keeping it at the edges. Most of the inland trails are, as yet, unknown to the white people. The way from Merrimack to Winnepesaukee, following the river, was once haunted by Mohawk war parties, but now they keep their distance. Many Native families camped this spring at Winnisquam, and others once again set up the fish weirs at Aguadacton. The way north to Pemigewasset and all through the Wôbiadanak (White Mountains) is clear. To the northwest, there is likewise no trouble around Msquamchumaki (Squam Lake). From Cowass (Newbury, Vt.), north to Nebizonbik (Brunswick Springs), and across to Missisquoi (Swanton, Vt.), Ndakinna is safe.

The English are scouting for land here, but we have assured them that the soil is far richer and less rocky in the south. One of the Sokoki women, Nechehoosqua, and her husband, Massequnt, are considering signing an agreement with some of the English to allow them to settle a town just south of the fort, in the hopes that they will stay there. The former captive who is now a translator, Joseph Kellogg, has offered to arrange the words on paper for them, and promises them much trading credit at the truck house. Woolauootaumesqua is encouraging her sons Pinewans and Wallenas to do the same with the land from Pocumtuck to Wachusett.

At Fort Dummer, the English are paying us good silver to keep the peace in all directions, and warn them when we see any hostiles approaching. Given that many of the so-called hostiles are our friends and allies, those of us who scout for the awanigiak (strangers) find this to be very entertaining work. Periodic reports of hostilities help keep the English close to home. Colonel Partridge has asked all of us scouts to wear green branches on our heads, so that the English, who cannot tell us apart from enemy Indians, will not shoot us by mistake.

Scouting for Fort Dummer: Understanding the Historical Records
When Fort Dummer was constructed at present-day Brattleboro, Vermont, a number of different Indians—Mohawks, Mohicans, and Sokokis—were hired as scouts for the fort. The Mohawk and Sokoki had been enemies at times, but they were now allies, and used the English forts on the Connecticut River as tools to check further English incursions into Indian territory. English soldiers depended on Indian guides, but: "The employment of Indian scouts was attended to with some peculiar difficulties. It was not easy for our men to distinguish between friend and foe when they met them; and no foresight could prevent serious mistakes. When the Scaticook Indians came to the valley on their hunting excursions, it was customary for them to adopt some signal—the wearing of a green bough on the head—and inform the commanding officers of the towns what it was." Historian Josiah Temple observed that Native people had no difficulty distinguishing among the white inhabitants since "Indians . . . were free to hunt and rove at pleasure. They lived in all the towns, and went in and out of the houses of settlers . . . and thus were perfectly acquainted with the state of the forts, fields, and habits of the people."

If it was difficult for soldiers to distinguish Native people they knew by name, it has been even more difficult for later historians to tell tribes apart. Much of the confusion traces to the tumultuous half century between 1670 and 1720, and the movements of Native peoples across the region. Some historians confused the Sokoki people around Monadnock with their Nipmuc neighbors to the south; others mistakenly thought the Sokoki came from the Saco River in Maine; still others identified them as Scaticook, assuming they were Schaghticoke Indians from Connecticut.

After 1676, there were several large-scale movements of Native people from the middle Connecticut River Valley to Schaghticoke, on the Hoosic River in New York, and to Odanak, on the St. Francis River in Quebec. Neither move, however, emptied Sokoki territory of people. To add to the confusion, there were actually three Native places named "Schaghticoke," from the Algonkian word Pishgoch-ti-goch, meaning "where the waters meet." One is still the central village of the Schaghticoke Tribe in northwestern Connecticut, one was in Sheffield, Massachusetts, and one was on the Hoosic River in New York State. Although the Sokoki people living at Hoosic were called "Schaghticokes" by the English, they did not cease being Sokoki.

By 1735, several Sokoki families made the strategic choice to deed over part of their traditional lands. It is not clear whether they intended these deeds to be quitclaims, but the availability of land in northern Massachusetts did, for a time, lessen the demand for land in New Hampshire. Five Sokoki Indians, "Francois Son of Nepuscauteusqua Deceased, and Ompontinnuwa, Penewanse, Cockiyouwah and Wallenas Sons to Woolauootaumesqua deceased Sister to the Said Nepuscauteusqua," deeded land in the present-day towns of Athol, Barre, Dana, Gardner, Hubbardston, Petersham, Phillipston, Princeton, Rutland, Templeton, and Westminster, Massachusetts. At a September confirmation hearing, the signers insisted, "We do further declare to Our certain knowledge that no Indian or Indians of what name or nation Soever has any just right Challenge or interest to or in the abovesaid Tract of Land."

Two of the names on these deeds—Penewanse (also spelled Pinewans, Capinawans, and Capino) and Wallenas (also spelled Wonlinase or Wanlinas)—have persisted as Abenaki family names to the present day. Penewanse derives from "kepinawos," "the person who takes care of someone," and Wallenas, from "wolhanas," has been interpreted as "valley person." The Sokoki men who agreed to scout for Fort Dummer, Fort No. 4, and all the other forts on the long river may have been paid by the English, but they also tried to take care of their families and protect their traditional territory.

Overlooking Upper Ashuelot, April 1746: The Native Perspective

Pinewans, Old Town, Chee Hose, Prik Fore, and the others are standing near tônbiseneca—the stone bow—on a cold day in early 1746, when, far in the distance, they sight a small party of Englishmen descending Monadnock to follow the trail north. The man kneeling over the stone sets aside the hammer, and the others start to break camp. The carving in the stone had seemed incomplete, so a mark was added—three lines horizontal, and three vertical—representing the woven strands of wampum that sealed the alliance between Pennacook, Sokoki, and Cowass. The three tribes had never been at odds with one another, but it was always a good thing to reinforce one's friendships with gifts, and wampum and stone both have particularly long memories.

After a span of time, the Native men slowly descend the mountain, and track the English scouting party northward, listening to every twig crack, every snort, and every curse. After a few days, the English lose their way and turn back. For their own amusement, the Abenaki silently track them home again. When the white men come within sight of the settlement at Upper Ashuelot, they fire their guns, which alarms the inhabitants, and people run in every direction to hide. The discovery that this is a false alarm puts the English at ease too soon.

As they are breaking camp a few weeks later, and cleaning their muskets, Pinewans thinks on how the French have been such reliable friends, offering fair trade, powder and shot, and refuge in the villages near the missions. But the Jesuit religion is too stern for many, and already this spring more than twenty Sokoki families have been to St. Francis and back again. The English forts on the Kwinitewk have proved to be useful supply stations, but they also encourage new settlements, like the one at Upper Ashuelot. English people feel safe near the forts, but they forget that they are living in Sokoki territory. Pinewans crushes a bit of red ocher into the grease in his hands, and then draws a little ash from the fire pit before they set out.

On the morning of April 23, 1746, Captain Simons is reading the Bible aloud when a painted face streaks past his window, and he hears the screams from outside the fort. The town history recounts that "Nathan Blake was at his barn. . . . Hearing the cry of Indians, and presuming his barn would be burnt, he determined that his cattle should not be burnt with it. Throwing open his stable door, he let them out. . . . He had gone but a few steps when he was hailed by a party of Indians . . . feeling himself in their power, he gave himself up. They shook hands with him; and to the remark he made that he had not yet breakfasted, they smiling replied, 'that it must be a poor Englishman who could not go to Canada without his breakfast.' Passing a cord around his arms above the elbows, and fastening close to his body, they . . . conducted him to the woods."

An estimated hundred or more Indians attack Upper Ashuelot that day, and during the following weeks. One night, young Mr. McKenny is on watch when he hears movement at the picket gate and fires through the wood with ball and buckshot. In the morning, the Indians are gone, but he finds blood and wampum beads, mingled together on the ground. By the next week, twenty Sokoki families have shifted their wigwams farther upriver to Cowass.

During the following winter, after the English fort at No. 2 has been abandoned, the four sachems sign their names to a piece of parchment, and nail it to the door of the fort. The document reads, in part, as follows: "Gentlemen, Whereas there have been many grievous complaints in the province . . . with respect to the support and maintenance of your frontiers in a time of war, we . . . have undertaken to free you from this extraordinary charge by killing & taking captive the people & driving them off & firing their fortifications. And so successful have we been in this affair that we have broke up almost all the old settlements in your western frontiers . . . we humbly request . . . whither it be more acceptable to you that we man your defeated garrisons our selves . . . or whither we burn up the forts with the provisions, for we assure you we find much more in them than we want for our own support."

Upper Ashuelot: Understanding the Historical Records

During the "French and Indian Wars," in the eighteenth century, the Massachusetts colonial authorities continued sending scouting parties and militia into Ndakinna, despite negotiations to check English expansion. The Western Abenaki had no recourse but to resort to desperate actions to protect their homes. The French in Canada were more than willing to make alliances with New England's Native peoples, offering military support, building Catholic missions at St. Francis and Norridgewock, and welcoming Native refugees.

Written documentation of Native communities in the inner territory is scarce, however, given the lack of European observers. The names of a few prominent individuals—men like Pinewans and Grey Lock/Wawanowalet—do surface in the historical records, and their stories are also preserved as family names and oral traditions even today. The document found nailed to the door of Fort No. 2, complete with its Indian signatures, currently resides in the Ayer Collection at the Newbury Library in Chicago.

In July of 1752, the Abenaki sachem Atiwaneto sent an even stronger message to Phineas Stevens, at Fort No. 4, during a council meeting in Montreal: "We hear on all sides that this Governor and the Bostonians say that the Abenakis are bad people. 'Tis in vain that we are taxed with having a bad heart. It is you, brother, that always attack us. . . . Brothers, we tell you that we seek not war, we ask nothing better than to be quiet, and it depends, brothers, only on you English, to have peace with us. We have not yet sold the lands we inhabit, we wish to keep the possession of them . . . we will not cede one single inch of lands we inhabit beyond what has been decided formerly by our fathers. . . . We acknowledge no other boundaries of yours than your settlements whereon you have built, and we will not, under any pretext whatsoever, that you pass beyond them. The lands we possess have been given to us by the Master of Life. We acknowledge to hold only from him."

Despite widespread warfare, most of Vermont and New Hampshire remained exclusively Abenaki Indian territory until well into the nineteenth century.

Hunting Pigeons on Monadnock, June 1858: The Native Perspective

Although the English have taken over many of the ancient village sites, turned the trails into roads, dammed the rivers, and scattered their names across the landscape, there is still enough land to support many Native families in Ndakinna. The ash trees still produce good splint for baskets, the fish are still abundant every spring, and the medicine plants can still be found in the usual places. The English have taken to grazing cattle and sheep on many of the lower mountainsides, and planting corn in the old fields, but few of them venture far outside their towns. If one chooses the old trails, there is still good hunting in all the northern forests.

Monadnock is still a good place to hunt, even though some days it is covered with more tourists than birds. Early on a June morning in 1858, a Sokoki man named Kobin and his son are standing on a hill in Surry, looking southeast. The man kneels down to place his hand on the bow and arrow carved into the stone.

When he raises his hand, the eyes of his young son follow the gesture toward the lone mountain. "Alosada k'nadialowôgena wôbipelazak," says the man to his son. "Let us go hunt some pigeons."

Hunting Pigeons on Monadnock: Understanding the Historical Records

By the nineteenth century, Abenaki families were still to be found all across Nda-kinna—the frequency of their travels back and forth across the border allowed some to pass for French Canadian and some to be mistaken for foreign Indians, while others were well known as local Indian doctors, guides, and basket makers. For much of this time, Native American Indian people in New Hampshire were literally "hiding in plain sight," within full view, but of little interest to their white neighbors.

Even the keenest observers exhibited a curious blindness to Native people who crossed their field of vision. Henry David Thoreau, for example, described plants, animals, weather, and his own sensations in excruciating detail, but made only passing mention of the Native people he met while he was out communing with nature. As just one example, his journals record a trip to Monadnock from Troy Station, on June 2, 1858. "We had the mountain in sight before us, — its sublime gray mass — that antique, brownish-gray . . . that gray color of antiquity, which nature loves . . . hard, enduring gray; a terrene sky-color; solidified air with a tinge of earth." He observed "Tiarella cordifoli, abundant and apparently in its prime . . . the leaves of Geranium Robertianum, emitting their peculiar scent," and watercress, "good to eat fresh with bread." During the afternoon, he "met a man (apparently an Indian or Canadian half-breed) and a boy, with guns, who had been up after pigeons but only killed five crows." In that entire entry, Thoreau devoted three pages to plants, more than five hundred words to describing the particular shade of gray on the mountain, and but one sentence to Indians, who were apparently less interesting than rock.

**From St. Francis to Keene, New Hampshire, Spring 1883:
The Native Perspective**

It is spring of 1883, and Mary Watso has just finished unloading the canoe. She and her two young daughters are resting inside the tent at the camp they've set up near Ktsipontegu, now called Bellows Falls. It's been a long journey, from St. Francis all the way down to Quinnipiac territory, at the mouth of the Connecticut River, and back north again. They were visited by Native families from Mohegan and Schaghticoke and Paugusset at each of the campsites on their way to winter over beside the ocean. Mary collected and traded for many different varieties of nebisonsizak, plant medicines, but none of them could cure her of the wheezing sickness brought on by the salt air. Now that they are back near the mountains, she can breathe easier.

Mary's husband, Israel M'Sadoques, is checking through his bundle of furs, and thinking over how comfortable the home territory feels, after so many generations away, when he sees a pair of scruffy-looking white men walking up the bank. "We want your woman," they tell him, gesturing lewdly toward the tent.

Israel M'Sadoques' wedding photo taken at Odanak, Quebec, 1872.

The Sadoques family with their eight surviving children. Israel and his wife, Mary
(Watso) Sadoques, are at center.

Israel bows his head, goes into the tent, and comes back out with his rifle in
hand. He calmly offers them a "ball in the teeth if you don't leave."

By the time the men are out of sight, the family has already dismantled the
camp. The girls are stumbling, still half asleep, but Mary and Israel are rushing,
trying to fit their loosely packed gear into the canoe. At that moment, a kindly
soap salesman shows up with an empty wagon, seemingly out of nowhere, and
offers the family a ride to Keene.

Years later, Mary Watso's granddaughter, Mali Keating, recalled how the family "settled there and my grandfather made his living with traditional Indian
skills . . . he took the horse and wagon and went back to Odanak (St. Francis)
and filled his wagon with baskets . . . having this woodlot, he was able to furnish
ash splints for the Keene Chair Factory. . . . So he had the subsistence farm, he
furnished ash splints, he sold baskets, and he had a tanning business. . . . So
my grandmother . . . besides cleaning and making clothing for eight children,
she was also cooking for hired men and taking care of half the neighbors as an
Indian doctor. So they lived a very busy life."

From St. Francis to Keene: Understanding the Historical Records

Over the course of several hundred years, various family bands from Pennacook,
Pequawket, Pocumtuck, Sokoki, the Schaghticoke village at Hoosic, and elsewhere in New England periodically shifted in and out of Canadian villages for a
few seasons or more. For most Abenaki people, the village site at St. Francis was
just one of many village sites across a broad expanse of traditional homeland;
for some, it became a permanent home. The movement of so many different
bands through Lower Canada, at so many different points in time, led to the
widespread, but erroneous, belief that all the Abenaki in New England originally came from the village of "St. Francis Indians." To add to the confusion, the
term "St. Francis" even today is often synonymous with Western Abenaki. The

shortsightedness of white colonists living on the edge of Abenaki territory made it possible for the large number of family bands who never moved to Canada to keep a relatively low profile.

Israel M'Sadoques, like his father Thomas, was a trapper for the Hudson's Bay Company in Canada. Mary Watso's grandfather, Louis Watso, was a famous Indian doctor who treated Indians and whites throughout the Connnecticut River Valley. Both of these skills—trapping and doctoring—helped the family survive in nineteenth-century New England.

The M'Sadoques family name originated with Shattookquis, a Pocumtuck and Quaboag sachem who, in the 1670s, was one of the first to lead a band of Connecticut River Valley people north to Canada. In Keene, the name was shortened to Sadoques, and their descendants can now be found living across central and northern New England. Although the Sadoques employed a number of people, owned several houses, kept a millinery business on Main Street, educated two daughters to be registered nurses, and were well known in town, not a word about them can be found in any history book of Keene.

Mapping Native Memories in Ndakinna

Incidents like these in the historical records have generally been interpreted as distinctly separate events, happening to unrelated people in separate places and times. But that sense of separation, like the sense of Indian disappearance, is an illusion. Each of these encounters is but a brief snapshot, out of a Western Abenaki family scrapbook holding vast numbers of such moments. The cross-cultural conflicts dramatized in each of these five examples influenced the survival strategies of Native families across the North Country, and still resonate in contemporary Native lives today.

In conclusion, let it be said that the map of Ndakinna, sighting along the arrow at Surry toward Monadnock, or viewed from any other perspective, should never be interpreted as though pockets of white civilization have been set in the midst of an untracked wilderness. Instead, imagine a vast, rich homeland, supporting many extended families, marked by navigable rivers and clear trails, and celebrated in story and song. Over the past few hundred years, this ancient Sokoki homeland has been shot through by violent events, disrupted by colonial settlements and international warfare, and treated as through it were uninhabited, inanimate dirt and rock. But plants spread new seeds, animals return, trees regrow, rivers flow, and Native people remember.

Now stand at the top of Monadnock, and look out at the green forests and rivers, and see how this land is still alive. Despite the efforts of nineteenth-century local historians to write Native peoples out of the region's history, Native stories, memories, and culture have persisted. Native people in the Monadnock region today may be outnumbered by the newcomers, but they can still be found, in small but strong family bands and interconnected communities, living not only in the forest but also in the midst of the most populous towns. The general public may think the Native history of this region ended long ago, but Native people know full well that their story continues.

Nidôbak, u pita wlitebi nôguad sôghebaigamigw.
My friends, here is a respectable looking inn.
K'nawadosanana nawa u?
Shall we alight here?
—"On arriving at the hotel," from an 1884 Abenaki dictionary

Pozoldinaj. Pita wlawiben. . . . Ni k'polowanana.
Let us embark. It is very calm. . . . Now we are out of danger.
—"On Travelling by water in the Indian country," from an 1884 Abenaki dictionary

DAVID STEWART-SMITH

Phineas Stevens at the Threshold of the Frontier

Spring, 1747. It was the second day of what had seemed an endless string of hours. The fort at Number 4, in present-day Charlestown, New Hampshire, had been under siege since early the previous morning. The fort had been abandoned all winter, and the returning frontier militia had only been at the fort for three or four days when the attack came. Every man had been on alert way past his point of fatigue; ditches had been dug, water had been fetched under fire from the well in the parade ground within the fort. In the past twenty-four hours the French and Indians had tried to burn the fort down repeatedly with flaming arrows and a cart full of burning hay. Just past noon on the second day, when the white flag went up from the French and Indians, two individuals stepped into the clearing beyond the thick tree line. Phineas Stevens squinted closely and discerned that they were Indians, walking closer now that the firing had stopped. During Indian warfare it was traditional for there to be several breaks for discussion and an exchange of terms. This was going to be different from yesterday's session with the French commander, who had blustered about how many men he had and how he would destroy everything and everyone at the fort.

The two Indians came to the gates of the fort and were let in to enjoy the hospitality of the parley. They were offered food and drink, and tobacco was shared. Stevens knew these two Indians; he knew their purpose would be stated directly. The conversation was probably in Abenaki, which Stevens spoke and understood. Even though they were surrounded by anxious and exhausted militiamen and rangers from the fort's troop, the conversation was quite private. There would be no face-saving, no puffed up pride. Food was shared and probably a posset of warm rum passed around. With the formalities of the hospitality done, a pipe was lit and passed between the three men. The pipe was passed to signify amity and well-being to all in the circle. The smoke was seen as truth and prayer made visible. Truth would be shared in this parley between the two Indian leaders and the frontier captain of the fort.

Stevens invited the Abenakis to speak freely with him. With eyes carefully averted, the elder of the pair explained that they needed supplies from the fort. They were willing to purchase these supplies—they had furs or currency that could meet the price. Some of Stevens's men, the raw recruits, were impatient, wanting Stevens to explain the gist of the conversation. But he motioned for quiet, listening as the elder explained their condition and predicament. Another silent round of the pipe. Stevens worded his response carefully, thanking the elder for this opportunity to talk and listen. In respectful tones, Stevens explained that he could not sell the Indians any goods from the fort, that it was policy not to sell any goods while French and Indians held the fort under siege, threatening the lives of his men and the structure of the fort.

And then, what is most unusual, Stevens offered to advance the Indians a payment of corn for any hostage that the raiding party would leave at the fort; the hostage could be recovered from the fort at a later time. He offered them five bushels of corn for every man they might leave. What is so surprising about his offer is the code of honor and necessity it implies. First that Stevens, unilaterally, could make such an offer—the fort was holding well during the siege, even though the French and Indians had sent burning arrows into the stockade and buildings. And yet something moved Stevens to provide an offer whereby the war party could be fed, even though he was proscribed by the nature of the attack and the policy of his orders. Further, in offering to receive hostages, he guaranteed their safety and well-being while in custody; there was no distinction made between French or Indian. All this was offered in spite of the fact that for the previous twenty-four hours the French and Indians had done their damnedest to burn the fort down and kill its militia. The French general had threatened to put everyone at the fort "to the sword." And yet Stevens offered a humanitarian end to the encounter, a means by which this starving war party could be fed and leave to fight another day. Stevens, it seems, knew these Indians to be men of their word and the risk they took by exposing their condition to him, but also, perhaps, he understood that the Indians could not accept such an exchange while they were under French command. No explanation in the historical record is offered.

Diagram of the original fort on New England's frontier drawn by John Maynard, July 4, 1746. The small hamlet was the northernmost British settlement along the Connecticut River, 30 miles from its nearest neighbor.

Behind a 10-foot-high stockade, settlers built a fortified town by moving five houses, constructing a sixth one, and linking them together with log lean-tos. On the fort's southern side, by Phineas Stevens's home, they constructed a large, two-story building to act as the town's church and barracks. Here also was the fort's only gate and a wooden watchtower.

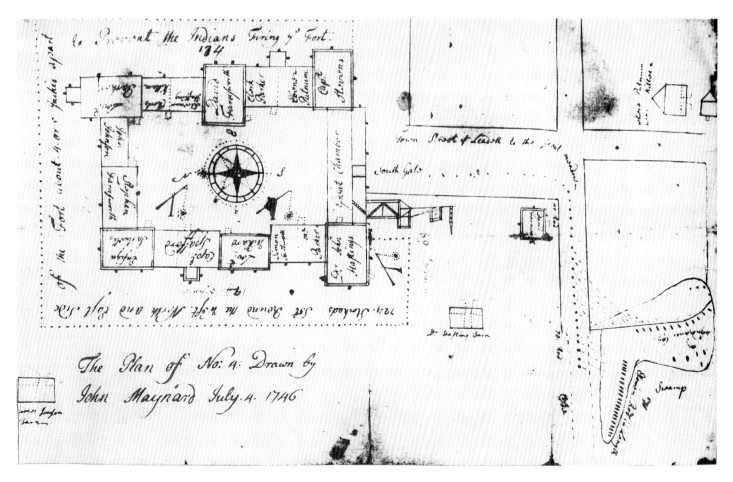

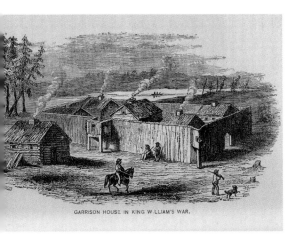

GARRISON HOUSE IN KING WILLIAM'S WAR.

Garrison house and houses within a stockade similar to the Fort at No. 4.

Stevens's account of the incident, a letter to his superiors, makes it clear that the starving condition of the war party perhaps should have outweighed any considerations of military victory. The Indians' leaders had approached to acquire provisions and withdraw. "You may form some idea of the distressed circumstances we were under, to have such an army of starved creatures around us, whose necessity obliged them to be the more earnest," he reported in 1747. "They seemed every minute as if they were going to swallow us up, using all the threatening language they could invent, with shouting and firing, as if the heavens and earth were coming together."

Phineas Stevens was known to the Indians as a man of his word. He had been captured as a young man of sixteen and saved his younger brother's life by signaling with gestures to his Indian captors that he would carry his brother on his back, if necessary, all the way to Canada. That kind of grit certainly won him some respect. He was third-generation frontier born and bred. His grandfather was the famous Simon Willard, who had established the Indian community at Musketaquid (Concord, Mass.) and later brought John Eliot up the Merrimack to meet the Pennacook chiefs to establish the first Indian mission village at Wamesit (Chelmsford). When Stevens was redeemed from his captivity some years later, he spoke fluent Abenaki, could track anything in the woods, and had a knowledge of the northern frontier of New England like no other white man of his time. During his time at Charlestown, from 1740 to 1755, Stevens personally schooled and sent out just about every ranger in New England. Fort Number 4 was the threshold to the frontier and was a place where, under Stevens's leadership, Indians and settlers could meet, trade, and raise families.

A young white settler, Susanna Johnson, noted her first impressions of the frontier in 1744: "When I approached the town of Charlestown, the first object that met my eyes was a party of Indians holding a war dance, a cask of rum which the inhabitants had suffered them to partake of, had raised their spirits to all the horrid yells, and feats of distortion which characterize the nation. I was chilled at the sight and passed tremblingly by. At this time Charlestown contained nine or ten [white] families, who lived in huts not far distant from each other. The Indians were numerous, and associated in a friendly manner with the whites. It was the most northerly settlement on the Connecticut River, and the adjacent country was terribly wild."

This raid on the fort at Number 4 took place in 1747 and was part of a series of events in what is known as the Five Years War, part of the French and Indian wars, between the English colonies of New England and New France in Canada. Only three years earlier, the fort had been a gathering place for settlers and Indians where, according to Susanna Johnson, there seemed to be no laws about how whites and Indians intermixed and lived. One can only speculate as to how many frontiersmen chose Indian women to be their companions and mothers of their children. The frontier was a hard place, and most colonial women were not conditioned for that existence.

"In those days there was such a mixture on the frontiers, of savages and settlers, without established laws to govern them, that the state of society cannot be easily described, and the impending dangers of war, where it was known that the savages would join the enemies of our country, retarded the progress of refinement and cultivation," wrote Johnson. "The inhabitants of Charlestown began to erect a fort, and took some steps toward clearing their farms; but war soon checked their industry."

Stevens was self-educated, yet in reading his journals and letters one sees a thoughtful and patient mind at work. While his journals and letters are a bit formal and stilted in their language, there is nothing clumsy or uneducated about them. He also appreciated the presence of the Indians along the Connecticut River Valley. He knew that this was their homeland. He knew that they loved this wild and grand landscape deeply. According to Stevens, "Were it not for ye French it would be Easy to Live at peace with ye Indians." Later in the wars, the leaders of the Abenaki from upriver came to ask Stevens to stop any colonial military plans for taking over their village at Cowassuck (Newbury, Vt.). This was during the beginning of the next war in the French and Indians wars. The colonials aimed to eradicate as many of the Abenaki as possible from the territory. However, Stevens knew that the Indians valued their trade with the "English" of New England. Fort Number 4 had been repeatedly spared destruction because of its importance in trade with the Indians.

By 1753 the Abenaki stated that no further settlements beyond Charlestown would be allowed and that the settlers would have to trade with the Indians for timber and fur from the region. Stevens's defense of Cowassuck was another unilateral position: he held that the Cowassuck Abenaki would live peaceably with the settlers so long as the New Englanders did not violate the stated boundaries of Abenaki territory and kept the fort open for trade. Given the gathering storms of the French and Indian wars, Stevens's vision of the frontier demonstrates an unusual understanding of the Indians and the integrity of the frontier. Many years later, during the American Revolution, the New Englanders came to value the neutrality of the Abenaki and relied on the Indians of the Upper Connecticut Valley to keep them apprised of any major British troop movements coming out of Canada.

Such was Stevens's role on the frontier that he could quell the colonial desire for conquest of the territory and eradication of the Indians. He frequently traveled to Quebec Province to negotiate for captives, using his skills as negotiator and his knowledge of tribal protocol. He even brought John Stark out of captivity, a man destined to become a great hero during the Revolution. One has to wonder what the history of this region might have been without Phineas Stevens's steadfast and courageous defense of the frontier and his friendship and honor among the Abenaki.

In one of those terrible ironies of history, after his career spent along the Connecticut River Valley frontier, Stevens was posted to Chinecto, Nova Scotia. There he caught a fever and died at the age of fifty-one in 1756. As the eighteenth century careened into the events of the American Revolution and the establishment of a new nation, Stevens and his legacy were eclipsed in history. His life is not recorded in *The Dictionary of American Biography*. Today he is rightly remembered at Fort Number 4, but beyond this region the name of Phineas Stevens casts few echoes. In Indian country, among the Abenaki, he is still well remembered as friend, counselor, and fierce warrior. It is a remarkable thing to be held as a formidable enemy, fair negotiator, and trusted friend all in the same period of history. Stevens was all that to the Abenaki people in the region. We still wonder what it could have been like to fulfill his vision of a new nation that included Indians and Indian territories.

Travel well, friend, Phineas. *Wli'bamkani.*

11,000 Years on the Ashuelot

ROBERT GOODBY

On a sunny morning in late June, the Newport High School van turned off the paved road into a small clearing carved out of the forest. The teacher, a young man with a wrestler's physique and a single braid on his shaved scalp, got out. His students gathered around him, and he led them down a path, walking over the place where, according to the archaeologists, his ancestors had lived some 11,000 years before. The path led down and off this ancient site, and rose again to a high terrace at a hairpin bend in the slow-moving Ashuelot River. Here was a campsite from 7,000 years ago, and continuing south along the west bank of the river, he walked over other campsites: 4,000 years old, 1,500 years old, 500 years old. On this day and in this place the past and future of the Abenaki people came together, and while his students listened to the archaeologist explain about stone tools, layers of soil, and the action of glaciers, the young teacher thought briefly of the creator Odzihozo, and how Ndakinnah, the Abenaki homeland, had come to be.

Twenty thousand years ago, the area of Swanzey known as Sawyer's Crossing was covered with an immense sheet of glacial ice, part of the Laurentide ice sheet that extended to southern New England. The ice sheet was melting and its leading edge retreating northward as the ice age was coming to an end, and by 13,000 years ago Sawyer's Crossing was ice-free, with a cold, unstable climate and a shifting environment of grassland and open spruce forest. Large lakes of glacial meltwater, clear, cold, and lifeless, covered the Connecticut River valley, extending into what would become the valley of the Ashuelot. Shortly after they formed, these lakes began to drain, swiftly and deeply downcutting through the fine sandy outwash soils deposited by the glacier and forming the channel of the Ashuelot River.

By 11,000 years ago, the river had, in this location, assumed its modern course, flowing north before turning sharply to the southwest. This hairpin bend was lined on all sides by high sandy terraces, which, on the west bank, gradually declined in elevation until reaching the small, easterly flowing Beaver Brook. A small pond, later reduced to a bog, lay to the east, and a mixed woodland of spruce, pine, and a few hardwoods covered the land. Herds of caribou moved through this region, which had recently been home to the rapidly disappearing ice-age giants, mammoths and mastodons. The ice-covered tip of Mount Monadnock was visible to the east, unobscured by the mature forests that would later hide it from view.

Into this setting came the first people, called Paleoindians by archaeologists, and they camped on the high terrace to the north of the river's bend. These early people hunted the caribou, perhaps keeping an eye out for one of the larger

Screening history. Student archeologists dig test pits at the Whipple Site in Swanzey. Most evidence from 11,000 years of native history will be found about 20 inches below the surface.

animals of whom their elders still told stories, and they carefully selected high, dry terraces from which they could watch the movements of game. They lived in small family groups, building shelters around small hearths, staying for short periods of time, perhaps returning again the next year or in a generation. Long after their departure, burned fragments of wood from their fires, a few pieces of burned bone, broken stone tools, and chips from toolmaking lay scattered about the ground, eventually to work their way a few inches into the soil. Master hunters, these people prized high-quality stone for their tools, and there was none to be had in this region. Despite this, many of their tools were made of smooth, lustrous cherts and jasper, acquired through extensive networks of kin that stretched over hundreds of miles. Their spears were tipped with beautifully made points with deep channels running down their faces, a style used by Paleoindian people across North America that the archaeologists would name Clovis.

The artifacts of these people lay in the loose sands above the Ashuelot for millennia, disturbed only slightly by the trespasses of tree roots and burrowing animals, before they would be seen by the students and their Abenaki teacher. By the nineteenth century, land clearing, plowing, and logging were regular occurrences, and the twentieth century brought the construction of a line of massive utility poles that cut through the heart of the site. In 1973 Arthur Whipple, a lifelong Swanzey resident and avocational archaeologist, discovered the site that would eventually be named for him. He notified archaeologists from the University of Massachusetts of his find; one of these, a graduate student named Mary Lou Curran, wrote her dissertation on and devoted much of her career to the study of the site. At the same time, however, relic hunters from the neighborhood and from other neighboring states began an episodic campaign of looting at the site that would last for years, bracketing the careful excavations of the archaeologists with gaping craters—reckless violations for the sake of private avarice.

In the late 1970s and early 1980s, a team of archaeologists worked painstakingly, with the help of Arthur Whipple, to excavate limited portions of the ancient site and try to salvage some of what the looters had plundered. This work revealed three concentrations of artifacts, each representing, perhaps, a single episode of occupation, the encampment of individual families, or areas where particular tasks like tool production or animal butchering had taken place. Fluted points, scrapers, thousands of stone flakes, and a few fragments of caribou bone were recovered. Radiocarbon dating of burned wood from the site placed the occupation between 10,000 and 11,000 years ago, and for two decades the site would remain the oldest reliably dated site in New Hampshire.

As part of their research, the UMass archaeologists tested downstream from the Whipple site, digging small 25 cm square (10 inches square) test pits placed at wide intervals. Aside from a thin scattering of artifacts at one point along Beaver Brook, this testing did not yield any artifacts. A few artifacts from the vicinity of the Paleoindian site, and from local collectors, suggested there were the remains of more recent Native occupations from the Archaic and Woodland periods (10,000 to 3,000 and 3,000 to 500 years ago respectively) in this loca-

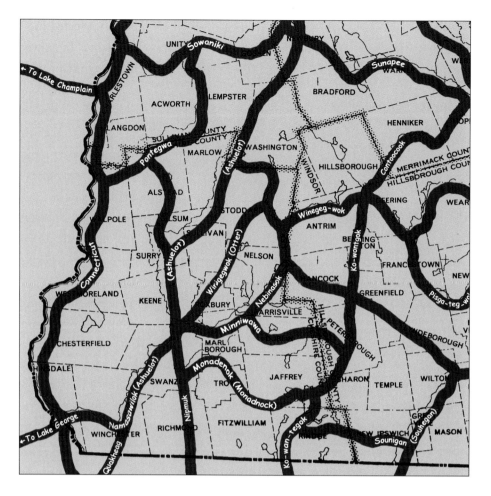

Many trails converged in present-day Swanzey, near the 11,000-year-old Native site.

tion. Art Whipple continued to watch over the site, trying to deter looters, and occasionally recovered artifacts eroding from the riverbank or in the ruts left by dirt bikes under the power lines, carefully noting their locations for the use of other archaeologists.

Well before archaeologists began working here, white people associated the area of Swanzey around Sawyer's Crossing with Indians. In the 1800s, children combed the area around the covered bridge, collecting the arrowheads and other relics turned up by their fathers' plows. On a few occasions burials were uncovered and their bones scattered and lost, leaving only a mention in the history books of how the bodies had been curled in a "seated" position. The remains of an "Indian fort" from the seventeenth century could also be seen in the low embankments, all that remained of the wooden palisade testifying to the violence that swept this region with the coming of the white people. In the 1960s, using the hints in town histories and oral traditions, a historian would re-create the network of Indian trails that crossed New Hampshire, four of which met at Sawyer's Crossing. These trails bore some of the Abenaki names that still define the region, including Namasawilok (Ashuelot) and Monadenok (Monadnock).

A ten-minute walk downstream from the Paleoindian site is the Swanzey fish dam. The dam consists of a V-shaped alignment of boulders pointing downstream at the point where Beaver Brook flows from the west to join the Ashuelot. The east bank at this location rises steeply from the river, while the west bank is lower, sloping gently to the water's edge. The dam is covered with a thick layer of silt, deposited when historic dams and modern flood controls slowed the flow of the river. One of the best descriptions of the dam comes from the *New England Observer* in 1888, where a Mr. Wheelock wrote:

> The low water in the Ashuelot, occasioned by the repairs at the Swanzey mill has exposed the old traditional Indian dam . . . it is less than a hundred feet wide, but the dam being in the shape of a harrow pointing downstream is more than that distance. . . . It is made of stones such as a man could lift. . . . It varies from six to twelve feet in thickness, according to the depth of the water. It looks like a tumbled down wall mixed with gravel, but it must have cost weeks of labor.

Low water on the Ashuelot River in 1950 revealed the V-shaped "Indian fish dam."

The dam has been exposed a few times since, including once in the 1950s when an aerial photograph was recorded.

It isn't certain how the dam was used. Although Wheelock offered a romanticized nineteenth-century vision, in which "Here stood the young brave and watched the silver-bellied salmon, and struck at him with his flint-pointed spear," it is more likely that a variety of other, more numerous fish were caught here. Other anadromous species might have included shad or alewives, the latter of which swim upstream in large schools during the late spring. The fact that the tip of the V is pointing downstream suggests it was designed to force fish swimming upstream closer to shore, where they could be netted or speared.

Skepticism about such substantial structures abounds in archaeological circles, where it has long been doubted that the Native people of New England built in stone. Wheelock's account is significant in this respect, as he notes: "Near by the old dam lives Jonas L. Moore. Here lived his father and grandfather before him. For one hundred and thirty years this has been called the Indian dam." The written histories and oral traditions of Swanzey consistently refer to this as the "Indian Dam," and historic accounts document the discovery of "a half a peck of arrow and spearheads, all in one pocket . . . [and] some twenty Indian fire places" when the area by the dam was plowed. Despite this, and despite the absence of any historic mills, roads, or settlements at this location, some archaeologists have insisted that the dam is only the remnants of a historic wing dam, or is perhaps an "eel dam" constructed by the first white settlers of Swanzey and left unmentioned and unremembered in subsequent histories.

The reluctance of twenty-first-century archaeologists to accept the dam as a creation of the Abenaki exhibits a curious continuity with eighteenth- and nineteenth-century stereotypes of Native people. Wheelock himself noted of the dam that "Indians were lazy, and this work of theirs is the more surprising on this account; perhaps there is nothing like it in the state." Only in 2002 would a combination of archaeological and historical research begin to provide the sort of evidence white people insisted on before setting these stereotypes aside, and confirm the accuracy of the early historic accounts.

While the archaeologist led the students south to the fish dam, the teacher trailed behind, content to temporarily put his charges in another's hands. A red-tailed hawk (siOmo in the Abenaki language) floated high over the power lines, turning a wide, graceful circle and causing time to slow to match the pace of the river. He watched the hawk, seeing its beauty and power but feeling his thoughts tugged in other directions. He had to make sure he returned the students to the high school in time to meet their bus. He had to stop at the bank. He needed to talk to a woman at the computer store, and get home in time for his wife to get to work, leaving him some precious time with their baby daughter. He thought about his daughter, the care they had put into choosing her traditional Abenaki name, and the argument he'd had with the nurse when his wife put down "Native American" on the birth certificate. There would be time tonight for him to play his flute for the baby, making the sounds that widened her eyes and stilled her crying as they floated through their log home deep in the woods of Sullivan County. He turned his eyes away from his watch and back to the hawk, not caring that he'd fallen even farther behind his students, because it gave him time to reflect on the powerful symbol of siOmo. The bird flew high above the question of whether the Abenaki had been on this land, and above the question of whether they are there still. The hawk soared into a place where a thing exists simply by being itself, without having to justify or explain its existence and how it lives between two worlds.

In the summer of 2002, another archaeological survey was begun along the Ashuelot. Fifteen students from Franklin Pierce College, under the direction of the author, spent a month at this place. The Paleoindian site would be avoided; instead, the survey focused on discovering more recent archaeological sites along the terraces to the south and, finally, conducting a thorough survey of the fish dam area to settle the question of its alleged Native origin. There was the possibility, too, of discovering yet more Paleoindian sites, as it was well known that throughout the Northeast these sites occurred in clusters. While this survey would build on the efforts of the UMass archaeologists, it would differ in some respects. Testing would be conducted along both sides of the river, and would involve larger test pits (50 cm square) placed at closer intervals of eight and four meters. Continuity with the earlier archaeological effort was provided by Art Whipple, who shared his extensive knowledge of the area, his recollections of the earlier survey, and his own small collection of artifacts patiently collected from the surface of the site over many years.

Assessing the historical claims that the Swanzey fish dam was built by Native Americans and not by white people would require many forms of archaeological evidence. The dam itself was inaccessible, hidden by silt and eelgrass under six feet of water, visible only in the shadows cast by a handful of the larger boulders. Testing along the banks would need to show that Native people were present at this location, and that there was no significant European presence. That alone, however, would not prove that Native people had built the dam. To do this, there would need to be evidence that large quantities of fish were processed here. This was based on four assumptions: (1) that the effort required to build the dam would be undertaken only if it yielded large quantities of fish, presumably the anadromous fish or eels that ran up the river in schools in the spring; (2) that

Stark points dating to the Middle Archaic, some 7,000 years before present.

with such a dam more fish would be caught than could be consumed at one time; (3) to prevent the surplus fish from spoiling, they would have to be cleaned, smoked, and/or dried, and (4) that human nature being what it is, the choice would be made to do this processing close to where they were caught, avoiding the chore of carrying large quantities of fish and keeping the waste products at some remove from actual habitation sites.

Fish-processing sites, in turn, could be expected to have evidence of the substantial fires used in smoking and drying, clusters of cracked and fire-reddened rocks, and innumerable small pieces of wood charcoal. The remains of the fish themselves would be less likely to survive; it is very possible that only the guts were left on the ground, to be eaten by the Indians' dogs. Even if bony portions of the fish were left behind after the dogs were finished, they would have decayed quickly in the acidic soil. The soil of New England typically leaves little of the rich material culture the Native people had; tools of wood and bone, wigwams on wood frames with bark coverings, and artwork in such perishable media as porcupine quills and birchbark rapidly disappear. It is also possible that, after processing, the fish remains were placed back in the river as an offering of thanks, a practice still remembered by some Abenaki people today. Occasionally, when burned, small bone fragments may be preserved as well as even smaller remains such as fish scales, and these can be extracted from soil samples taken from a site and analyzed in the laboratory.

The survey began on a June afternoon on the high terrace overlooking the hairpin bend in the river. Parallel lines of test pit locations were established with a surveyor's transit, and each test pit was carefully dug, with each distinct layer of soil removed separately and screened through one-quarter-inch wire mesh. Soil stratigraphy was simple, with a thin layer of undisturbed topsoil or a thicker layer of plowed sandy loam overlying a stratum of fine yellow brown glacial sand. Sites in such settings are shallow, as little soil has accumulated over the layers of glacial sand, and almost all the artifacts were recovered from these first two layers, typically no more than 50 cm (20 inches) below ground surface. Even the artifacts from the Paleoindian site had been recovered near ground surface, many in the thin upper zone of historically plowed soil.

Four teams of students began excavating four test pits, and fears that the survey would be unprofitable (this was, after all, the area where UMass had surveyed twenty years earlier and found nothing) were quickly dispelled when telltale flakes and worked chunks, or cores, of rhyolite and quartz were found in all four test pits. Art Whipple produced artifacts he had discovered on this terrace: tiny fragments of pottery from the Late Woodland period (c. 1,000 to 500 years ago) and a well-made stemmed point of blue gray volcanic stone. Known as Stark points to archaeologists, points of this style date to the Middle Archaic, some 7,000 years before present.

The survey continued southward along the broad open terrace on the west side of the river, encountering clusters of flakes, rough, broken fragments of tools, and exhausted stone cores from which no more flakes could be struck. Each of these clusters could represent a moment in time, an hour in which, on a spring morning, a boy and his uncle, or a girl and her mother, sat, talked, and made tools for the work that would be done in the coming days and weeks, watching the meltwater-swollen river move quickly toward the dam and listening to the shouts of those struggling with a net full of panicked alewives. Toolmaking was also an opportunity for education, reflected in the discarded, awkwardly shaped fragments left behind by a seven-year-old apprentice knapper, each with the steep step fractures left by inexpert blows. Millennia later, apprentice archaeologists would marvel that such crude tools were made and used by the Indians, not stopping to think that their makers, like themselves, were only in the first stages of learning a craft.

As the survey moved south, the land dropped as it approached Beaver Brook. Here the archaeologists turned east, extending their grid into the woods and toward the fish dam. For the next two weeks, their work would focus along a 300-foot stretch on both banks of the river, the low western bank and the high bank on the opposite shore. When they were done, and the artifacts were washed, counted, weighed, and cataloged, and their locations were marked on the site map, the resulting patterns were clear. On both banks there were Native artifacts, with the greatest number occurring immediately adjacent to the fish dam. Evidence of Euroamerican presence was limited to a stone wall on the high east bank and traces of plowing and land clearing on both sides. There were no roads that led to this location, no foundations, and only a sparse scattering of nails, brick fragments, and broken glazed pottery far outnumbered by the Native artifacts recovered from the same spot. If one were to measure presence by the materials left behind, this was first and foremost a Native place, with only a few pieces of refuse and a layer of plowed topsoil to tell that the invading culture had ever been here.

The Native artifacts included hundreds of flakes of stone from toolmaking, by far the most common artifact encountered on almost any Native sites. With scores or hundreds of flakes left behind for every tool finished and taken elsewhere, these are the most obvious marker of an ancient Native presence on the land, surviving all the ravages of time and soil, lying close below the surface to rear up in the roots of an overturned tree, the entrance to a fox den, or in the wire mesh screens of archaeologists. Flakes from the terrace next to the fish dam reflected a reliance on, and knowledge of, local and regional geology, including rhyolites from volcanic outcrops, quartz cobbles from the bed of the Ashuelot, and quartzite from west of the Connecticut River. The rhyolite and quartzite may have been moved from their sources down and up the Connecticut River and its tributaries, the highways of the Abenaki, who built and used both light birchbark and heavier dugout canoes made from large white pines.

Other native artifacts included the kind of stone tools generations of white people would reflexively identify as arrowheads. In reality, many of these were probably spear points or, mounted on short wooden handles, multipurpose knives. Their distinctive forms, changing through time in consistent ways across much of northeastern North America, allow archaeologists to date sites by their presence. All six of the "arrowhead"-type tools recovered from the banks by the fish dam date to the Late Archaic period, between 3,000 and 5,000 years before present.

The most finely worked of these is a Normanskill point, first defined by archaeologists in the Hudson River Valley. It is the lone artifact from the site made of an exotic stone, a fine-grained black chert that may originate in the upper reaches of the Hudson. A second point, a quartz triangle, belongs to the Small Stem tradition, named by archaeologists to describe a widespread technological tradition found across much of the northeastern United States. The remaining four tools are of styles associated with the Susquehanna tradition, considered by some archaeologists to have been brought into New England by an immigrant population from the mid-Atlantic region beginning 3,800 years ago. Although

Stone tools. *A:* Normanskill point. *B:* Quartz triangular point. *C through F:* Susquehanna tradition points.

an external influence may account for the appearance of these styles at this time, at the fish dam as at most New England sites these Susquehanna points are made of local material, suggesting their makers were not strangers to this land.

One final stone tool was found on the last day of fieldwork in 2002. The broken bit end of a stone gouge was recovered ten feet from the edge of the river immediately next to the fish dam. The edge of the concave bit is symmetrical, highly polished, and still sharp. Stone tools such as these were used to make the dugout canoes favored by the Abenaki for travel on slow-moving rivers and on lakes. To make such a gouge required dozens of hours of patient pecking, grinding, and polishing of a hard volcanic stone such as diorite or andesite, and its breaking was likely accompanied by a string of Abenaki expletives.

Other artifacts encountered at the fish dam included small shards of Native pottery. Native ceramics were of unglazed earthenware, manufactured by mixing clay with small particles of crushed stone. The vessels were formed with coils of clay piled one upon another and paddled to form a single wall, then fired in an open fire. First appearing some 3,300 years ago, ceramics changed slowly in form over time, gradually acquiring zones of decoration created by incising or stamping the still-wet vessels with wooden or bone tools. By the time of the European invasion, most ceramic vessels were made with thin, hard walls and elaborately decorated rims or collars, an art form that continued well into the seventeenth century, only to disappear with the defeat of a broad alliance of Native people in King Philip's War, from 1675 to 1676. Typically discarded after they were broken in use, ceramic vessels are further reduced to small fragments by the trampling of humans and animals and the actions of frost.

On the east bank, a single small shard of a ceramic vessel was recovered from the high bluff overlooking the fish dam. Decorated by rocking a toothed implement on its outer surface, this shard dates to the Middle Woodland period, between 1,300 and 1,700 years ago. On the opposite bank, on the low terrace right next to the dam, a scattering of hard, thin-walled shards were found, including

Stone gouge. The broken end of a stone gouge was found 10 feet from the edge of the river, right next to the fish dam.

Ceramic shards. *A:* Rocker-dentate stamped, Middle Woodland period, between 1,300 and 1,700 years ago. *B through D:* Incised rim shards dating to the last centuries of Native independence, or the first decades of European contact.

41

Hearths. While direct evidence of large-scale fish processing by the dam proved elusive, three hearths of fire-cracked stone were discovered on the west bank.

three with elaborately decorated rims. These shards, from at least three separate vessels, date to the last centuries of Native independence or, perhaps, the first decades of the period of European contact.

While direct evidence of large-scale fish processing by the dam proved elusive, three hearths of fire-cracked stone were discovered on the west bank. Pieces of wood charcoal from two of these hearths were radiocarbon dated to a span between 3,300 and 3,800 years before present, contemporaneous with the stone points. The few small fragments of bone recovered during the excavation of the hearth were identified as deer and turtle. Many pieces of fire-altered stone were recovered from the upper layer of plowed soil on the west bank, recalling the observation by Wheelock that "twenty Indian fireplaces" had been plowed up at this location. Perhaps the evidence for fish processing was already scattered before our excavation, or perhaps it awaits more archaeological work. There is little doubt, though, who lived by this dam, and how long they were there.

For years historians, and even some early archaeologists, depicted the Native people of the Connecticut River Valley as mere nomads, or (in the case of Vermont) as utterly absent for much of the pre–contact period. Simon Griffin, in his *History of the Town of Keene* (1904), states that this area was "a wilderness" inhabited only occasionally by "roving bands of Indians [who] prowled these forests for game, or threaded through them . . . on habitual trails to and from their more permanent abodes." The denial of a long-term Native presence in the region had obvious utility in weakening any potential claims to land or to reparations, and it echoes down to the present as a revitalized Abenaki people assert their presence and growing aspirations for recognition and autonomy.

The archaeology and history of the Sawyer's Crossing neighborhood have produced a vivid and undeniable account of a deep presence of the Abenaki and their ancestors. From the end of the ice age over 11,000 years ago, people came here again and again for over four hundred generations, fishing, hunting and gathering, building canoes, raising their children, and listening to the tales of their elders. This was a significant place, where the deep presence of the Abenaki resulted in an accumulation of memories and stories that became as attached to the land as the tools and the bodies of their ancestors lying in the fine sandy soil. A few seasons of archaeological work, excavating only a tiny percentage of this site, places these people here at 11,000, 7,000, 4,000, 3,440, 1,800, and 500 years ago. With more excavation, the gaps would almost certainly narrow and perhaps even disappear. From the first arrival of the caribou hunters to the seventeenth century, when they built a palisaded fort to defend this place and hold the growing numbers of their enemy at bay, this was a place of significance, imbued with meaning and history by the resilient people who called this part of Ndakinnah, their homeland and place of creation.

By the end of their last afternoon at the site, the archaeologists, dirty and tired, had hauled away their equipment and bits of history, each in its own plastic bag with an identifying label. A white woman in a kayak streaked over the fish dam, not knowing it was there, heading south. Dusk came, and the waters of the Ashuelot continued to flow slowly over the ancient dam, making the eelgrass wave and bestowing even more of its protective silts. To the east, a pickup truck rumbled across the covered bridge, its fading sounds audible to those Old Ones still buried nearby, if they were listening. Perhaps they were not. Perhaps, instead, they were preoccupied with thoughts of the young teacher, and what his visit had meant, and when, but not if, he would return.

JOHN R. HARRIS

Borders and Boundaries

The human region is a complex of geographic, economic, and cultural elements. Not found as a finished product in nature, not solely the creation of human will and fantasy, the region, like its corresponding artifact, the city, is a collective work of art.
—Lewis Mumford

Regions are often defined by their watersheds; however, in the Monadnock region this approach doesn't work. As Ezra Stearns's *History of the Town of Rindge* reports, "here are several dwelling-houses, the water from one side of the roof of which finds its way into the Connecticut, and from the other side into the Merrimack River." In place of a watershed, our region looks to Mount Monadnock, a 3,165-foot eminence located fifteen miles east of Keene, for identification. The Monadnock region today encompasses roughly one thousand square miles and includes approximately 100,000 inhabitants located in some thirty-six towns.

Geography plays a critical role in the settlement patterns of any region. In the Monadnock region, Massachusetts men primarily, most of whom were second and third sons, followed game trails, rivers, and the contours of the land northward beginning in the 1740s. Some, like Nehemiah Howe of Deerfield, plied the Connecticut River in search of fertile land along its eastern bank, while others, like Abel Platts of Rowley, traveled shorter distances overland in search of hay meadows or plateaus tucked among the hills to the east. The claims that these men staked were tenuous, for Native people remained reluctant to abandon their most productive lands, and at the same time, provincial governors argued over the legitimacy of earlier English grants. Thus, Abel Platts in 1754 was required to appear in court to verify his occupancy of land in Rindge, and Nehemiah Howe was forced from his log structure in Westmoreland in 1745, taken captive by Abenaki people, and marched to Montreal, where he died a decade later.

The boundaries of the Monadnock region have been contested for more than three hundred years, and the legacy of these disputes remains evident in the outlook and attitudes of its inhabitants to this day. The earliest and most convoluted border controversy involved the establishment of a line separating the provinces of Massachusetts and New Hampshire. When in 1629 King James I granted to Captain John Mason a vast expanse of land in the New World, neither man was familiar with the territory. As a consequence, the original Masonian grant was filled with geographical inaccuracies, the most serious of which was the supposition that an upstream voyage on the Merrimack River would follow a straight westerly course inward from the so-called Black Rocks at its mouth. When in the 1660s it became evident that such a journey up the Merrimack in fact curves south and then turns sharply northward toward Lake Winnipesaukee, the royal governors of both provinces began to stake out competing claims. Finally, after attempts to settle the boundary dispute in 1693, 1695, 1705, 1715, 1719, and 1737 all failed, representatives of both parties appealed directly to George II. In 1740 the King ruled that a straight line would be drawn due west from the point at which the Merrimack River begins its northward curve. When a permanent line was surveyed the following year, virtually all of the Massachusetts claims to the Monadnock region became invalid.

The boundary decision of 1740, severing the inhabitants of this region from their base of support in Massachusetts, had the practical effect of creating a constellation of sovereign and independent towns. For the next twenty-seven years most of these communities had almost nothing to do with the province of New Hampshire. Town lines were redrawn in deference to the Masonian curve (see map, p. 000). Settlers who were threatened with eviction from homesteads they had established under earlier colonial military grants in Jaffrey, Peterborough, New Ipswich, and Rindge prosecuted their claims in court, while most residents went about their business and appealed to Massachusetts to provide security. This original spirit of independence and autonomy from New Hampshire's sphere of economic and political influence remains in effect today.

The colonists' urge to unify against Britain after 1776 provoked a second set of border disputes for inhabitants of Monadnock towns. This time the controversy involved the Connecticut River being designated as a boundary separating New Hampshire from territory that eventually became the state of Vermont. Massachusetts men like Nehemiah Howe had once relied on the river as their transportation corridor, along which neighbors or even members of the same early families selected sites on either bank. During the period of Indian unrest in the 1740s, farmers in Putney and Westminster, on the west bank, and in Westmoreland and Walpole, on the eastern side of the river, had joined forces for protection and defense. Therefore, although the Crown in 1764 designated the Connecticut River as the western boundary of New Hampshire, residents of Cheshire County continued to communicate and trade frequently with farmers across the river, with whom they shared a common heritage.

The Vermont controversy, as the dispute became known, further alienated the Monadnock region from the remainder of New Hampshire. At a convention held in Cornish in 1781, representatives from thirty-three of the thirty-six towns in the region voted to cast their fate with Vermont. Passions grew particularly heated in towns like Swanzey, Winchester, and Keene, which contained a mix of mercantile and agrarian interests. Keene voters actually organized separate town meetings in 1781, where they adopted articles authorizing two competing court systems and separate militias, and elected representatives to serve in two state legislatures. Tempers flared later that year when competing sheriffs arrested and incarcerated one another in an attempt to enforce contradictory laws. Like the earlier boundary dispute, this conflict was ultimately resolved by executive decree rather than by democratic action. Newly elected president George Washington wrote a letter in 1782 admonishing Vermont governor Thomas Chitten-

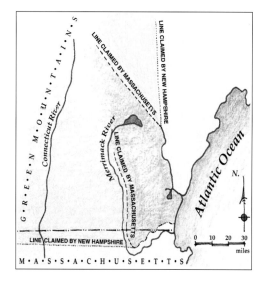

The border between New Hampshire and Massachusetts was contested from the earliest settlement.

Although the Crown initially designated the Connecticut River as the border between New Hampshire and the lands that later became Vermont, representatives of 33 New Hampshire towns voted to join Vermont in 1781.

den to give up all claims to land east of the Connecticut River if he hoped to secure his application for statehood.

The resolution of these boundary conflicts continues to cast a shadow. Voting records and survey results indicate that inhabitants of the Monadnock region remain more closely aligned in outlook and attitude with residents of Massachusetts or citizens of Vermont when compared with their own New Hampshire brethren. Thus, while George W. Bush carried the state of New Hampshire in 2000, he was defeated in thirty-one of thirty-six Monadnock towns. And a 2003 survey conducted by the New Hampshire Charitable Foundation measuring "community giving effort" across the state concluded that the communities with the highest scores were clustered in the Monadnock, Connecticut River Valley, and Lakes regions.

The topography along the region's eastern border serves to reinforce this cultural isolation, for a ridge of relatively steep hills runs north-south from Hillsborough through Temple. As a result, hill towns like Dublin and Harrisville record elevations of 1,493 and 1,299 feet above sea level respectively, while towns like Milford and Amherst lying downslope are situated only 263 and 268 feet above sea level. In winter months especially such contrasts in elevation continue to act as a barrier isolating the Monadnock region from its economic and political counterparts to the east.

The northern reaches of the Monadnock region were from the start the most inaccessible, and they remain the most sparsely populated today. The town of Marlow, for example, contains only 29 persons per square mile of land area, and its neighbor Stoddard has managed to protect over twelve thousand acres of forest. Precisely delineating a northern boundary is itself a challenge, for inhabitants of a town like Alstead send their children to nearby Fall Mountain Regional High School, purchase gas and groceries in Bellows Falls, Vermont, and transport their sick to a hospital in Keene.

The Disorderly Origins of the Granite State

MAPS AND ESSAY
BY PETER SAUER

The terrain of the Monadnock region, and of the White Mountains and their adjacent uplands, is unique in North America. It is among the continent's most unpredictably variable topographies. To the west, the Green Mountains rise as a range of massive, regular ridges, marching in orderly Appalachian ranks all the way to Georgia. But to the east, north, and south, New Hampshire's horizons are boisterous, disorderly, and everywhere surprising.

New Hampshire is a relatively new addition to North America. The Green Mountains, and the Appalachians west of the Connecticut River, were already more than 160 million years old and neatly folded in place when New Hampshire arrived. The forces of continental drift pushed three or four large landmasses together and sent them crashing toward the Green Mountains' shores.

Each impact raised a new series of folded mountains, and each mountain-raising was preceded and accompanied by massive volcanic upwelling. The geological tumult continued for more than 350 million years. Then, 100 million years ago, glacial ice—enough frozen water to lower the world's oceans by 350 feet—moved across New Hampshire. The landscapes that emerged from under that ice, ten to twelve millennia ago, are the products of the interactions of rock, ice, and water.

Three sets of contrasting landscape features illustrate the forces that created this region's surprising and distinctive landscapes and influenced its human history.

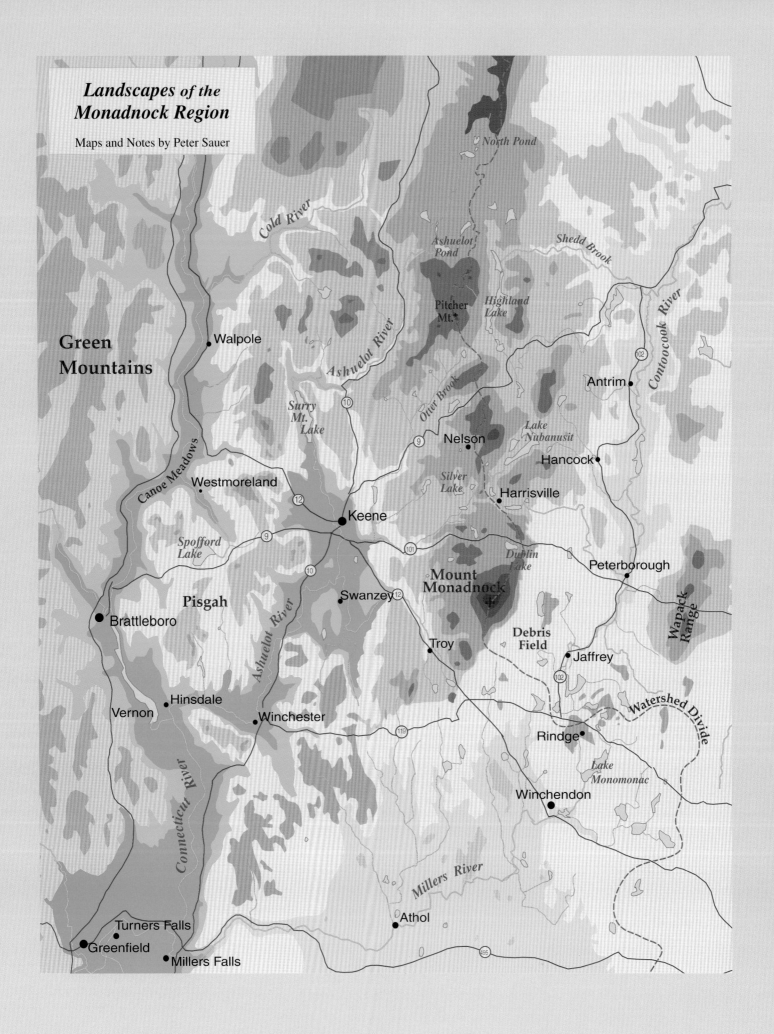

Landscapes of the Monadnock Region

Maps and Notes by Peter Sauer

North Pond

Cold River

Shedd Brook

Ashuelot Pond

Contoocook River

Green Mountains

Walpole

Pitcher Mt.

Highland Lake

Ashuelot River

Antrim

102

Surry Mt. Lake

Otter Brook

Nelson

Lake Nubanusit

10

9

Hancock

Canoe Meadows

Westmoreland

Silver Lake

Harrisville

12

Keene

9

Spofford Lake

10

Dublin Lake

101

Peterborough

Pisgah

Swanzey

12

Mount Monadnock

Wapack Range

Brattleboro

Debris Field

Jaffrey

Ashuelot River

Troy

102

Hinsdale

Watershed Divide

Vernon

Winchester

Rindge

119

Connecticut River

Lake Monomonac

Winchendon

Millers River

Athol

Turners Falls

495

Greenfield

Millers Falls

The Disorderly Origins of the Granite State

The terrain of the Monadnock region, and of the White Mountains and their adjacent uplands, is unique in North America. It is among the continent's most unpredictably variable topographies. To the west, the Green Mountains rise as a range of massive, regular ridges, marching in orderly Appalachian ranks all the way to Georgia. But to the east, north and south, New Hampshire's horizons are boisterous, disorderly, and everywhere surprising.

New Hampshire is a relatively new addition to North America. The Green Mountains, and the Appalachians west of the Connecticut River, were already more than 160 million years old and neatly folded in place when New Hampshire arrived. The forces of Continental Drift pushed three or four large land masses together and sent them crashing toward the Green Mountain's shores. Each impact raised a new series of folded mountains, and each mountain-raising was preceded and accompanied by massive volcanic upwelling. The geological tumult continued for more than 350 million years. Then, one hundred million years ago, glacial ice — enough frozen water to lower the world's oceans by 350 feet — moved across New Hampshire. The landscapes that emerged from under that ice, ten to twelve millennia ago, are the products of the interactions of rock, ice and water.

Three sets of contrasting landscape features illustrate the forces that created this region's surprising and distinctive landscapes and influenced its human history.

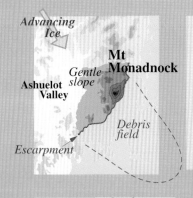

Mountain Slopes and Glacial Debris

The region's pre-glacial terrain was rugged with steep mountaintops and deep "V" shaped valleys. The glacial ice approached from the northwest, widening valleys and reshaping ridge and mountain slopes and summits.

The ice made northwest facing slopes less steep and smoother. Monadnock's slope east of Keene and Swanzey is an example. As the ice passed over the mountain, it plucked and pulled the rock from the summit and the southwestern slopes, creating a steep western slope and scattering mountain stones and boulders along a debris field, which southeast of Mount Monadnock extends into Massachusetts.

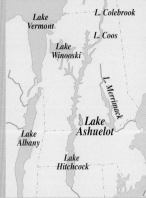

Post - Glacial Lakebeds and Terraces

Twelve thousand years ago, as the glacial ice withdrew, torrents of sediment- and ice-laden meltwater created high, glacial lakes. The lakes drained slowly, often over a thousand years. As their water levels dropped, seasonal flooding created a series of descending terraces.

The three major terraces that rise above Ashuelot River were formed when its water flowed into Lake Hitchcock through a gap downstream from Winchester.

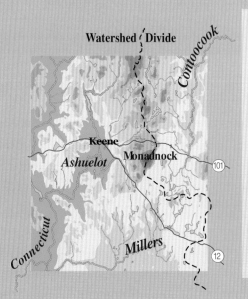

Watersheds and River Valleys

Mt. Monadnock marks the southern end of the high watershed divide that isolates the western third of New Hampshire that lies along the south flowing Connecticut River. East of this divide, the Merrimack and all of New Hampshire's other streams and rivers flow into the Atlantic.

In the Monadnock Region the divide separates the watersheds of the Ashuelot and Millers Rivers from the Contoocook's, which flows to the Merrimack. North of Mt. Monadnock, were it crosses Rt. 101, for example, the divide runs along the spine of the upland.

Just south of Monadnock's summit, the divide bends to the southeast and drops to cross Monadnock's glacial debris field (Map 1.). Route 12 traces one of the state's few lowland passages across the divide.

Where they meet on this rolling lowland, the young headwaters of the Contoocook and Millers Rivers are vying to expand their watersheds up-stream through the glacial debris field. Their rocky and boulder-strewn valleys stand in sharp contrast to the neatly terraced, stone-free, former lakebeds of the Connecticut and Ashuelot.

NATHANIEL HAWTHORNE **Journal: The Lost Child**

Monday, September 17, 1849

This part of the country is but thinly inhabited, and the dwellings are generally small. It is said that, in the town of Temple, there are more old cellars, where dwellings have formerly been, than there are houses now inhabited. The town is not far from a hundred years old, but contains now only five or six hundred inhabitants. The enterprising young men migrate elsewhere, leaving only the least energetic portion to carry on business at home. There appear to be but few new improvements; the cultivated fields being of old date, smooth with long cultivation; —here and there, however, a tract newly burned over, or a few acres with the stumps still extant. The farmhouses all looked very lonesome and deserted, today, the inhabitants having gone to the regimental-muster at New Ipswich.

As we rode home, Ephraim told a story of a child who was lost, seventy or eighty years ago, among these woods and hills. He was about five years old, and had gone with some work-people to a clearing in the woods, where there was a rye-field, at a considerable distance from the farmhouse. Getting tired, he started for home alone, but did not arrive. They made what search for him they could, that night; and the next day the whole town turned out, but without success. The next day, many people from the neighboring towns took up the search; and on this day, I believe, they found the child's shoes and stockings, but nothing else. After a while, they gave up the search in despair; but, for a long time afterwards, (a fortnight, or three weeks, or more,) his mother fancied that she heard the boy's voice in the night, crying "Father! Father!" One of his little sisters also heard this voice; but people supposed that the sounds must be those of some wild animal. No more search was made, and the boy was never found.

But, (it is not known whether it was the next autumn, or a year or two after) some hunters came upon some trace of the child's wanderings among the hills, in a different direction from their previous search, and farther than it was supposed he could have gone. They found some little houses, such as children build of twigs and sticks of wood; and these the little fellow had probably built for amusement, in his lonesome travels. Nothing, it seems to me, was ever more strangely touching than this incident—his finding time for childish-play, while wandering to his death in these desolate woods; and then pursuing his way again, till at last he lay down to die on the dark mountain-side. Finally, on a hill which Ephraim pointed out to me, they found a portion of the child's hair, adhering to the overthrown trunk of a tree; and this is all that was ever found of him. But it was supposed that the child had subsisted, perhaps for weeks, on the berries and other sustenance, such as a forest-child knew how to find in the woods. I forgot to say, above, that a piece of birch, or other bark, was found, which he appeared to have gnawed. It was thought, that the cry of "Father! Father!" which the mother and little sister heard in the night-time, was really the little fellow's voice, then within hearing of his home. But he wandered away again, and at last, sank down at the foot of some tree; and there death found him, and carried him up to God. His bones were never found; and it was thought that the foxes and other wild animals had taken his little corpse, and scattered the bones; and that, dragging the body along, one lock of his flaxen hair had adhered to a tree.

I asked a physician whether it was possible that a child could live so long in the woods; and he thought it was, and said that children often show themselves more tenacious of life than grown people, and live longer in a famine. This is, to me, a very affecting story; and it seems to be felt as such by the people of the country. The little boy's parents, and his brothers and sisters, who probably lived to maturity or old age, are all forgotten; but he lives in tradition, and still causes wet eyes to strangers—as he did to me.

Part Two

MAKING LAND

Sheep at pasture on Pitcher Mountain in Stoddard.

Introduction

"Esq. Stiles can remember when (1786, or thereabout) there were but four time-pieces in town. These were old-fashioned box-clocks, which, together with the chimney, took up no small part of a house in those days," reports *The History of Temple, New Hampshire* (1860). "Most people used the hour-glass. ... Some people used sun-dials, and all had their 'noon-marks.'" The hour and the minute were not important. Time was kept in other ways, marked in the terse entries of farmers' diaries:

> April ye 4th 1803. Fair; began ploughing in earnest; sowed peas.
>
> April ye 5th 1803. Cloudy; wind [from] N. Sowed 1 Bushel wheat.
>
> April ye 8th 1803. Cloudy; raw and chilly wind from S.E. to S.W. alternately; small rain at evening; sowed 1 bushel of rye & ½ bushel of wheat. Set cabbage stumps.
>
> April ye 13th 1803. Warm & Hazy; wind [from] South-west. Sowed 1 Peck wheat—sowed peas for early use.
>
> April ye 27th 1803. Cloudy & chilly wind N.E. Sowed 12 qts F. seed & peas and turnip seed.
>
> April ye 29th 1803. Planted 4 Bush of Potatoes.
>
> May ye 17th 1803. Warm & pleasant, wind W. Did but little. Caught 1 shad.
>
> May ye 26th 1803. Fair & warm; wind S.E. planted squashes, cucumbers, water-melons and muskmelons.
>
> June ye 29th 1803. Finished hoeing corn ye 2d time.
>
> July ye 4th 1803. Fair & pleasant wind [from] N. Began haying in earnest.
>
> July ye 10th 1803. Sunday, fair & warm wind W. Dined on green peas. Mr. Farrar preached with us.
>
> Aug. ye 2d 1803. Fair and warm wind N.W. put in 2 Load Rye.
>
> Aug. ye 14th 1803. Had roasted corn.
>
> Sept. ye 12th 1803. Fair & pleasant, wind [from] E. Gathered onions & Beans & began to dig potatoes.
>
> Oct ye 21st 1803. Fair and pleasant. Wind [from] W.: finished gathering apples.

These are Ebenezer Edwards's diaries. Edwards was a representative man of the early period, coming to Temple in 1780. Originally from Acton, Massachusetts, he had served with the Acton Company of Minute Men at Concord Bridge in April 1775. Edwards represented Temple in the state legislature for fourteen years, and was a "fluent and dignified" town meeting moderator for twenty years. He ran a store in what is today the General Miller house and built a "pearl ashery." Pearl ash, a refined potash (which is made from wood ash), was used for making soap. "Trade was carried on upon credit altogether. The store-keeper collected all the country produce and sent it to market by ox-teams; sometimes five or six ox-teams filed along the road," according to the Temple history. "The main articles were butter, '3 or 4 tons potash, and 3000 or 4000 yards tow cloth.'" The Temple of Edwards's era counted these enterprises: carpenters, plough makers, blacksmiths, cider makers, maple sugar makers, tanners, and shoemakers. ("If you wanted a pair of shoes . . . you would get your leather at the tanner's and carry it to the shoemaker.") By 1817, Temple had four grain mills, three sawmills, and one fulling mill.

Edwards also made shingles, and by this work, too, he counted his days:

> 1803, April ye 20th: Cut pine timber for shingles & left one log to see if ye worms will injure it: it being the day before the moon changes.
> April ye 22d. Sawed & butted shingle-timber.
> July ye 26: Cut two pine trees precisely on the 1st quarter of the moon.

Part two looks at some working days on the farms and in the mills, and the marks they left on the land.

The New Road to Keene, 1839

The late Gov. Hill's journey to Keene; visit to "The Gentleman Farmer" in Jaffrey; ascent of Monadnock, &c. &c.

From the *Farmer's Monthly Visitor*:

Another Journey!

Stronger and stronger grows our attachment for the mountains and high hills of New England! Every journey we take, every inquiry we make, raises their value on our estimation. We used to pass them, covered and pitted all over with crags and isolated rocks, as sterile and desolate regions of little or no use to the world. On more minute examination and inquiry, we find the most valuable pasture grounds far up the sides of the mountains and to the tops of the highest hills.

New Road to Keene

A late journey to Keene was performed one way over a new road, shortening the distance between Concord and that town nearly ten miles. This road pursuing the North branch of the Contoocook beyond Hillsborough, passes through Antrim, Stoddard, Nelson and Sullivan, through ravines in a mountain region no less romantic than other parts of New-Hampshire. Crossing this road nearly

Making land. Labor crew in Westmoreland, c. 1890.

at right angles is the "Forest road," leading from Charlestown, N.H. to Nashua on the way to Boston. Both the Branch road and Forest road have been made at a great expense to the towns through which they pass; and it would have staggered the belief of the first settlers of the back bone ridge of New-Hampshire, who clambered over many steep hills to get to and from the rivers either East or West, had they been told that means would be successfully used to pass from town to town in almost any direction, with roads having nowhere a rise greater than four or five degrees. Yankee ingenuity has discovered the method of making such roads in such a country; and Yankee enterprise is found sufficient to construct and complete them over streams and through gullies and clefts of rock, and over swamps where it would seem impossible for man or beast to make their way, before the smooth track for carriage and horses had been cut out and covered with loam and gravel.

Low Lands in the Mountains

The town of Stoddard divides the waters of the two great rivers. This town from its elevation may be called a mountain town, although within its limits there is no rise of land so precipitous as to give it the name of a mountain on the map. Strange it is that we find out so little of what we consider familiar until we personally visit the localities. We had no idea, for instance, that the North branch of the Contoocook could extend more than half a dozen miles beyond Wallace's hill in Antrim, which stands in the point of land separating the two branches, until on inquiry we find on the East side of a declivity at the highest elevation, running nearly North and South, a series of ponds and swamps extending nearly twenty miles North through the towns of Stoddard and Washington, to the very base of the Sunapee mountain. These swamps and lakes are on a table of land so level that a dam of a very few feet elevation overflows for the whole distance; and the owners of thousands of acres are liable to suffer injury and in some cases ruin to their lands from the circumstance that this flowage has existed more than twenty years, giving legal title to the right.

The highest isolated elevation is between the towns of Stoddard and Antrim. The fattest beeves of all the vicinity are pastured annually upon this hill. The whole of this back bone region is excellent for rearing and fattening oxen and sheep. Myriads of grasshoppers the present year cover the pastures, and in some instances these take more of the green feed than the cattle themselves; yet despite of these vermin the oxen and horses ranging the hills are in better condition than those kept in stalls and stables.

A Beautiful Amphitheatre in the Hills

In a few miles from the intersection of the Keene and Forest roads in Stoddard, we come to a pond of some two miles in extent, being the base of a most beautiful amphitheatre among the high hills. The scenery of this amphitheatre, presenting a surface of enclosed pastures and fields, of shrubs, trees and rocks, upon the unequal sides of the hills, is truly magnificent. At the outlet of the pond is a village including several brick edifices and a factory. This is in the town of Nelson on the North side; and it is worthy of notice that in this mountain town on the South side is another very considerable village which has grown up from water power furnished from the ponds which are the feeders of the Contoocook river, running in a direction opposite from the waters of the North village, being one of the heads of the Ashuelot, running into the Connecticut near the Southwest line of the State. Down this stream in a valley extremely narrow the whole way for ten miles, the new road has been constructed.

We have remarked as one advantage of new roads constructed in ravines and valleys of steep ascent, that they frequently bring into use quantities of fine timber which until these avenues were opened was inaccessible. The land growing this timber, which is frequented, soon comes into cultivation. On the Ashuelot road passing the latter part of the way in the evening, the bright fires of the clearings in some cases seemed to be almost directly over our heads.

The "Gentleman Farmer"

The day after the agricultural exhibition at the elegant and prospering village of Keene, we visited our friend Conant at Jaffrey, fifteen miles easterly of Keene, who well deserves the appellation of *gentleman farmer*, because he has made himself more truly independent than any king, prince or potentate upon the habitable globe by the labor of his own hands. Twenty-three years ago he purchased the Thorndike farm in that town, consisting of some three hundred acres, for the sum of $4,500. This farm with its additions is now worth about $10,000; and while constantly increasing its value, Mr. C. has contrived to gather a capital in money even greater than the value of his landed estate; so that while he lives at his ease without even the necessity of labor, on the income of a moiety of his property, he has it in his power to do great good with the income which flows from other sources. We say he has no necessity to labor: yet it would be impossible for him to live without daily labor of some kind when about the premises; and the ease with which he accomplishes much in a little time, the economical arrangement of his cultivated grounds, the order and neatness of his house and barns and other buildings, explain to us how with the aid of an accomplished "better half," no less competent than himself, he had contrived, from the product of his own industry, to grow rich without oppressing his neighbor.

Ascent of the Monadnock. View of Many Villages.

Free to go out of our way to visit such a man, we took the freedom to ask him to accompany us to the top of the mountain, Monadnock. Mr. Conant's farm is directly under this mountain on the easterly side, and in a direct line is not over three miles from the top. He had sometimes taken the direct route to the mountain with friends; but he concluded on this occasion it would be easier to travel back on the old Marlborough turnpike about four miles towards Keene to the ridge or spur which divides the waters of the height of land. The ascent upon the mountain is on the southerly side, and the distance from the road over the spur is three miles; the travel was much less steep than that upon Mount Washington, in which latter case in a travel of about the same distance the ascent is nearly double. We were two hours in ascending Monadnock, and one hour in descending from the highest point to the road. We tarried at the top of the mountain one hour, and had the aid of an excellent glass. The atmosphere was hazy, so that objects at a great distance could not be so distinctly descried. The White Mountains were not visible, but their location was distinct from the shape of the clouds which envelop them at this season of the year. To the North and East the higher elevations within the distance of a hundred miles in New-Hampshire and Maine were easily identified. All along the back bone of Vermont and Western Massachusetts the Green Mountain range was distinct. Mount Holyoke and Mount Tom near Northampton, the Wachusett near Worcester, and the Blue Hill south of Boston, were readily pointed out. All the meeting houses and villages, East, West, North and South, situated on the hills and many in the open valleys for twenty and thirty miles were prominent.

Sources of Ample Water Power

But the most gratifying object presented from the top of this mountain was the many ponds lying round about it, the feeders of the abundant water power which is so extensively useful in propelling all the varieties of labor saving machinery. The quantity of water flowing from the highlands toward the sea, and the furnishing the incessant flow of the rivers, seems to be almost incredible. These waters in the hill towns cover much of the land: formerly they covered much more than they now do, as it is evident that the hundreds and thousands of fresh meadows, which abound much more at the higher than the lower elevations, were formerly ponds of water, which in the lapse of ages have gradually drained off.

Town of Jaffrey

From the top of Monadnock we look towards the south east and east, immediately down upon the town of Jaffrey, inhabited principally by a race of wealthy, intelligent farmers, whose ample and well finished barns are the standing proof of the substantial thrift which follows industry. The farmers of this town not only own their farms, but a majority of them have money at use in other towns. When the New-Ipswich bank went into operation some eight or ten years ago, a few farmers in Jaffrey at once took one third of its capital of one hundred thousand dollars: every dollar was paid in, and neither of these stockholders ever have occasion to take out a dollar for his own use. If all banks had been constituted in the same way—If the stockholders of banks were simply men who had spare money to invest, and not those who want the use of more money than they own—we would not have witnessed the sad spectacle of failing and swindling banks that the country has exhibited at different times during the last thirty years.

Good and generous living is evident by every appearance in the town of Jaffrey: the roads are kept in the best repairs, and their location changed wherever a sharp hill can be avoided. Carriages of pleasure are kept by most of the farmers; and for these the fat horses pastured upon the hills are trained as sure of foot when rapidly descending the steepest roads and pathways. Some of the dwellings in taste equal the best of the city houses, with the addition, which the city cannot furnish, of ample yards of ornamental shrubbery and fruit trees. We noticed one farm house erected simply for the accommodation of one family, at one and the same time, which extended, as we were told, one hundred by forty-eight feet on the ground, and two stories besides the attick—all finished, and the outside painted white. The barns and outhouses beside this great dwelling appeared from a distance to be in good trim, and the lands productive. It was located near the foot of the magnificent Monadnock, on a stream, which has its sources near the foot of that mountain.

Granite Roads and Bridges

Our journey for the first time through the towns of Jaffrey and Rindge was richly paid in the satisfaction we took while witnessing the substantial prosperity of the yeomanry of these towns. A single improvement on the Rindge turnpike, now a free road, in the distance of a few rods, could not have been made the present fall at an expense much less than a thousand dollars. The roads in this region are constructed on the true principle: hills, over which the travel has passed ever since the first settlement, are ingeniously avoided. That most valuable of all kinds of rock, the Granite, which is the foundation and superstructure of the majestic mountain Monadnock, and which is as easily rived as a log of oak or maple, is now extensively used in the construction of bridges and causeways. Arches over the Contoocook and other considerable streams are constructed of pure split granite, which fixed on a foundation of the same material will stand forever. The splendid bridge erected two or three years ago by the town of Henniker which cost about $3300, and is actually worth much beyond that sum, has been already noticed in the *Visitor*. Another granite arched bridge over a branch of the Contoocook running from the north, was erecting when we passed, the expense of which paid in cash by the town was from seven to eight hundred dollars. We are glad that our fellow citizens of Henniker are abundantly able to build and support these noble structures: such a generous public spirit as they evince richly merits and is generally accompanied by such prosperity as attends them. The town of Hillsborough, in imitation of its sister on the river below, is also completing the structure of a beautiful granite bridge over the main river at the village denominated Hillsborough Bridge.

There is no stream of water in the State presenting more abundant water power than the Contoocook: near its confluence with the Merrimack it receives the Blackwater, and at a short distance further the Warner river: on the way from thence to Hillsborough it has several tributaries whose sources are a few miles distant in the hills; but near the Hillsborough Bridge village, thirty miles from its mouth, it unites the two main upper stems coming from the north-west and south-west. The southern stem at Peterborough again unites two other stems, on each of which are several factories and villages. The northern branch again branches off in two or more directions, all having much water power not yet used, and several saw, lumber and grist mills already erected. A road constructed from near the mouth of this river to the Jaffrey factory village might be made with little other rise than the natural fall of the river; it could probably be constructed so that a carriage horse need hardly be interrupted in a trot all the way. Portions of that road have already been made. In the course of ten years the towns through which this stream passes, abundantly able to build and support such a road, will find it to their greatest interest to have the whole distance completed.

Connecticut River Ferry, 1900

The New England Magazine

A man in a buggy drove down the steep sandy road which leads to the river on the New Hampshire side. The ferryman came down from the house to meet him, passed the time of day, and stepped on board the big, shallow scow in which teams are ferried across. The traveller drove his team on to the boat. The ferryman, standing at the end of the boat farthest from the shore, took firm hold of the stout wire rope to which the big craft hung, through pulleys raised at its side, and, walking slowly from that end of the boat to the other, started it and its load across the stream. When he had walked the length of the boat he went back, took a new hold, and walked again. . . . The passenger was sitting calmly in his buggy,

From the mid-nineteenth century to 1930, traffic crossed the Connecticut River at Britton's Ferry between Westmoreland, N.H., and Putney, Vt.

talking crops, the horse quite heedless of the fact that the waters of the Connecticut were rippling within a few inches of him on every side, for the ferryboat at its deepest place is only twenty inches deep. The ferryman, with his gray hair and patriarchal beard, might have been Charon, except for his genial blue eyes. For pulling the heavy boat and its load across the river and then pulling it back again to his interrupted work, the ferryman is paid ten cents. . . .

The ferry . . . leads from Westmoreland, in New Hampshire, to East Putney, in Vermont. It is typical of all those on the river, and more picturesque than most of them. It has been established there for very many years. The ferryman of today has been there since 1858. Twice, early in this century, corporations built a toll bridge across the river at or near this point, and the ferry was discontinued; but each bridge was carried away by ice and high water after a short life, and now for many years the ferryboat has had no rival to its claims. . . .

I have crossed the ferry . . . very many times, at all seasons of the year, and under almost every possible condition of water and weather. Only one who has summered and wintered with New England's noblest river can understand how many these conditions may be. In summer the Connecticut is a beautiful picture of brown water between green banks. During the almost half a century that the present ferryman has watched it, there has been one winter when the river at this point did not freeze over so as to interrupt crossing with the boats; but usually its surface forms a natural bridge of ice for three or four months every winter. With the coming of spring, the rise and fall of the water and the warm sun on the banks weaken the ice at each side, and there are open places to be crossed with care, and sometimes danger, on temporary bridges of planks. When the weather eye of the ferryman sees the final "freeze-up" coming, the big boat is drawn out of the water and hauled up the bank to a point where it will be above high water, no small distance on the banks of a river which rises, as the Connecticut sometimes does here, to a height of thirty feet above low-water mark. Years ago this annual drawing out of the heavy boat meant an all day's "bee," at which the help of ten yoke of oxen and as many drivers was required; but now a "tackle block" and one pair of horses do the work in a few hours.

Before the final closing of the river, and after the solid ice goes out in the spring, floating ice and "snow-broth" make crossing difficult. The last named obstacle is saturated snow, filling the water of the river on the surface to a depth of from six inches to two feet, and almost impossible to make progress through. Blocks of floating ice must be dodged or pushed away from the boat's path. Even then the ice will sometimes block suddenly below the boat's crossing and set back so suddenly that the boat will be caught amidstream. Once, in 1864, an ice gorge formed below the ferry so massive that it dammed the river, and the water, setting back, rose so rapidly that it flooded the ferryman's house and drove him and his wife to take their two little children at one o'clock in the morning and flee to safer quarters on higher ground.

"When I start out to go across, when the ice is running," said the boatman,

Looking from Vermont toward Britton's Ferry landing and the ferryman's house. The entire family was on call for the ferry.

"I never know when I am going to get back." Then he told of one winter experience, when a passenger blew the horn before breakfast. "I went over after him. We got caught in the ice and the rope broke, letting the boat be carried down the stream, but not out of sight of the house. We couldn't get anywhere, and it was noon before we landed. The worst of it was that every little while some of the folks would come out and shout to me that breakfast was ready."

"Yes," said his daughter, who was listening to the story, "seems as if any trouble was sure to come just at meal time, so as to make us women here in the house all the more work."

How much work does fall to the wife and daughters of a ferryman, one must live with them to really understand. At many crossings they help to run the boats. Here they have not often had to do that, since a family of stout boys has grown up, one after the other, to be the father's helpers; but many is the meal of victuals the women have set for belated and hungry travellers, many the drunken man they have taken in and cared for until he was sober enough so that it was safe for him to go over in the boat. Time and again they have left their work to go out and reassure some nervous woman who is afraid to cross; while more than once they have sheltered and dried, cleaned, brushed and ironed out people whom carelessness or accident has plunged into the water. Most accidents occur from people taking chances when the ice is breaking up at the edge of the river in the spring. Sometimes a horse is nervous, and prudence requires that he be unhitched from the wagon before he is taken on to the boat, and the wagon be drawn on and off the boat by hand. Once in a great while a horse is found with such an unconquerable aversion to the boat that he can never be made to cross in it. Some men cover a nervous horse's head with a blanket. The ferryman says that more trouble comes from the nervousness of the driver than that of the horse. Only one horse ever plunged off amidstream here during the life of this ferryman, and he was a blind horse ill managed by a careless driver.

Parables of Place

TOM WESSELS

To really know a place is not possible. Each landscape is a combination of multiple events that stretch far back in time—various cultural histories, climatic and geological transformations that reach beyond the tenure of our species. But it is possible to become acquainted with a landscape in a more intimate way, and through this growing familiarity develop a fulfilling connection to place. This possibility resides in the stories that are etched into every landscape—stories that go back centuries, millennia, and even into deep geological time. The following vignettes explore just a few of these stories that have transpired in the last two centuries. Each is related to a specific location, although all of them are representative of the region.

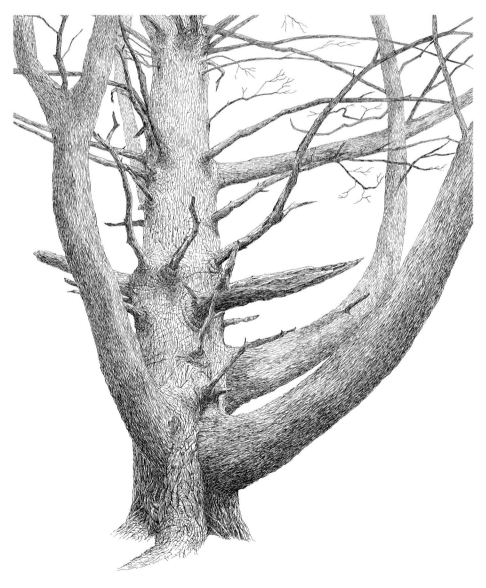

The branches of a magnificent white pine at Stonewall Farm in Keene were shaped by growing in an open pasture.

The Great September Gale

The most well-known hurricane to strike the Monadnock region is the 1938 hurricane—the most costly storm worldwide, in terms of property damage, of its time. It arrived late in the afternoon of the autumnal equinox. Cities like Keene were devastated by winds exceeding one hundred miles an hour that toppled the vaulted elms that lined their streets. Some residents still remember driving through a maze of fallen elm trunks. But most of those who witnessed the 1938 hurricane or live in the region today are probably unaware of another storm—one that was probably displaced from our collective memory by the 1938 hurricane—the Great September Gale of 1815. This powerful hurricane tracked right through the Monadnock region with its eye cutting a path from Gardner, Massachusetts, through Jaffrey and Hillsborough. Mount Monadnock received the full brunt of the storm. Raked first by winds out of the east and then by winds out of the west, the summit forest of red spruce was leveled.

Many people know of the early 1820s fire that exposed Monadnock's summit, but don't realize the important role that the Great September Gale played in that fire. Without the preceding gale, it's possible that the fire would have spared portions of the summit forest. But the fallen red spruce logs, drying for years, were waiting fuel when the fires reached the summit. They burned with an intense ferocity that killed all existing plant life. Erosion by wind and rain did the rest to create a hiker's magnet that today attracts over 100,000 individuals annually.

A landscape remade by sheep. On the exposed summit of Gap Mountain, a sea of shrubs including juniper and blueberry, and exposed bedrock, are a legacy of the nineteenth-century "sheep fever."

Sheep Fever on Gap Mountain

To the southwest of Mount Monadnock rises Gap Mountain at 1,700 feet. Approaching this summit from the west brings me up a moderate to steep slope sectioned off by lichen-encrusted stone walls. These walls are solely constructed with large boulders. When I encounter walls like these I can't help but ponder their builders: how did they deal with chronic back ailments? Within the walls are mats of ancient, ground-hugging juniper, some with trunks more than six inches in diameter. Poking through the juniper are various species of young trees—maple, birch, pine, and cherry. Upon reaching the exposed summit, with a breathtaking view of Monadnock, I find a sea of shrubs including juniper, highbush blueberry, spirea, plus exposed outcroppings of bedrock everywhere. This open summit, as well as the fence-bound, west-facing slope proclaim their origins to "sheep fever." Sheep fever did not infect the mammal it is named after but rather the human inhabitants of central New England.

The "fever" was a wool-growing mania, often described as similar to religious fanaticism. Within three short decades, sheep fever completely transformed the central New England landscape from one that supported self-reliant farms to one dominated by market farms that produced wool.

To gain an understanding of just how dramatic the changes were between 1810 and 1840, the following facts may help put things into perspective. In 1810 30 percent of central New England was open agricultural land. By 1840 it was 80 percent open. In just thirty years, one-half of the forest that covered northern and western portions of Massachusetts, the bulk of Vermont, all of New Hampshire south of the White Mountains, and the southwestern quarter of Maine was removed and the cleared land put into sheep pasturage. With this massive deforestation the preferred fencing material—wooden split rails—was no longer available. So stone replaced wood. If we consider that about 120,000 miles of stone fencing transects our central New England forests, that more than 90 percent of this stonework was constructed between 1800 and 1840, and that if we piled all that stone it would be five times as massive as the Gaza Pyramids in Egypt, we find the eighth wonder of the world within walking distance of our doorsteps.

When I look over the summit of Gap Mountain I realize how powerful was the fevered desire to grow wool. Of all places, why would this bedrock-ridden summit have been cleared? How much forage could it have produced? Such questions probably never surfaced through the delirium of this period.

Luckily, there was a quick recovery from sheep fever. In their zeal to grow as much wool as possible, farmers allowed severe overgrazing, and the sheep pastures that covered the region quickly became degraded. Also the Erie Canal and the railroad opened the Ohio Valley and its rich, untouched soils. So commencing in 1840 many central New Englanders turned their backs on their hill farms and, with their sheep in tow, headed west. Most of the Monadnock region's rural communities, towns like Acworth and Marlow, have fewer human residents today than they did in 1840. The wool was then brought back to central New England via rail and canal to be processed in all the mill towns—like Harrisville,

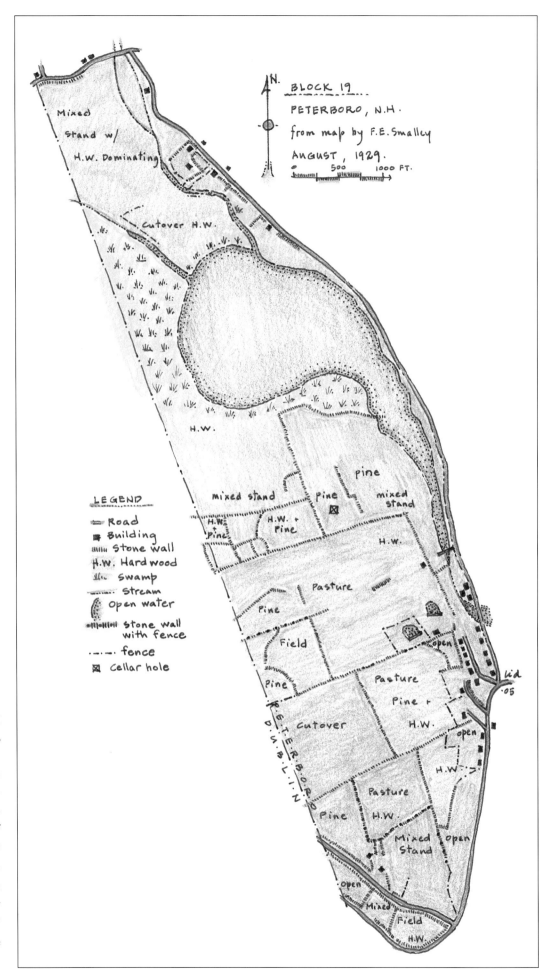

N.

BLOCK 19
PETERBORO, N.H.
from map by F.E. Smalley
AUGUST, 1929.
500   1000 FT.

Mixed
Stand w/
H.W. Dominating

Cutover H.W.

H.W.

LEGEND
Road
Building
Stone wall
H.W. Hardwood
Swamp
Stream
Open water
Stone wall
with fence
fence
Cellar hole

mixed stand   Pine   pine   mixed stand

H.W. + Pine   H.W. + Pine   H.W.

Pasture

Pine   Field

Pine   Cutover

Pasture   Pine + H.W.   open   open

H.W.

Pasture

Pine   H.W.   Mixed Stand   open

open   Mixed Field   H.W.

P.E.T.E.R.B.O.R.O. S.L.I.N.

Wd .05

For almost 50 years, starting in the late 1920s, New Hampshire's foresters mapped every stone wall in the state south of the White Mountains. They were pursuing white pine blister rust, which spread through currant and gooseberry bushes that grow along stone walls. On these maps, showing land shorn of trees once more, New Hampshire looks like Ireland, with thousands of small fields: a landscape ordered into rooms of three or four acres. This 1929 map shows West Peterborough by a reservoir and dam that was replaced in 1950 by the Army Corps of Engineers' flood control project, the Edward MacDowell Dam.

Manchester, Lawrence, and Lowell—that were spawned during the sheep fever period.

Stone Walls and Flax

Stonewall Farm in Keene has one of the most impressive open-grown white pine trees in the region. This tree grew by itself in a pasture that certainly predated the nineteenth century. I call wide-spreading trees like this one "pasture trees," since they were intentionally left to provide shade for livestock on hot summer afternoons. Adjacent to this magnificent tree is an old beaver pond that can be crossed, via a boardwalk leading to a forest dominated by a fine stand of white pine. As one enters the forest, a stone wall parallels the path to the right. This wall, and the forest floor on both sides of it, tell this tale: By the path, the forest floor is flat and even. But on the other side of the wall the ground undulates with pillow-and-cradle topography—evidence of long-decayed trees that were toppled by windthrow or snow and ice loading. As a falling tree's roots ripped out of the ground, they excavated a cradle. When the roots decayed, they dropped the excavated earth as a pillow—a rounded mound directly adjacent to the cradle. The lack of pillow-and-cradle topography on the path side of the wall indicates that this area was plowed at one time, either to grow crops or to be put into a hay field. The stone wall itself also tells us that this area was once cultivated, since numerous small stones are found within the wall and dumped next to it on the path side.

Cultivation is the only process that both generates and necessitates the removal of small stones. Most who have gardens in this region know that each spring when they turn the soil a whole new host of rocks will have migrated toward the surface, the product of freezing and thawing. Since even small stones get in the way of turning the soil, gardeners pick them out. But in lawns or hay fields, such rocks never surface. They are held in place by the perennial roots of the grass. So stone walls with lots of small, fist-size stones indicate that adjacent land was once cultivated to grow crops—not mowed to produce hay. But the crops that once grew here at Stonewall Farm are seldom grown in New England any more.

Although the majority of the region's agricultural land was in pasturage for sheep during the first half of the nineteenth century, a substantial portion was also cultivated for grains such as barley, wheat, rye, and flax. Flax had two uses: the seed could be ground for its oil, and the stalks were processed to produce linen. I was shocked when I first learned that it took about two acres of flax to produce enough fiber to make one linen bedsheet. Hence, far more land was in cultivation in central New England's hill towns during the early 1800s than we see being farmed today. The linking of all the mill towns by rail in the mid-nineteenth century killed New England's farms, for now many crops could be imported by rail from more productive regions outside New England.

If we were traveling through the region in 1840, we would see a landscape almost completely deforested, inscribed by stone walls that kept sheep in their pastures and out of adjacent fields of cultivated grains. This site at Stonewall Farm is a nice remnant of that historic early nineteenth-century landscape.

White Pine

As mentioned above, the white pine forest at Stonewall Farm is a fine stand of trees, but a five-minute walk from Route 114 in Bradford, New Hampshire, brings you to one even more glorious. There you will find a stand of pine that hosts about a dozen trees that reach over 150 feet in height, the largest being about five feet in diameter. Yet impressive as these trees are, they would appear to be of only adolescent stature next to some of the presettlement pines that grew in this region.

Appalled at the wanton cutting of these majestic trees, Timothy Dwight wrote in 1821, "There is reason to fear that this noblest of all vegetable productions will be unknown in its proper size and splendor to future inhabitants of New England." How prophetic his warning has become. It is not easy to imagine trees that would fit well in an old-growth forest of the Pacific Northwest growing right here in New England, but once they did.

Two hundred and fifty years ago it was still possible to find white pines in New Hampshire that were greater than seven feet in diameter and rose to over two hundred feet in height. But to find such trees, one would need to travel to the steep-sided ravines of tributaries that flowed into major rivers such as the Connecticut or Merrimack. Since the big pines could grow more than one hundred feet taller than the surrounding forest, they needed to be tucked into the landscape in places where they would find protection from lightning strikes or windthrow. They found this protection within the confines of the steep-sided riverine ravines—sites that exist because of the retreat of the Laurentide Ice Sheet from New England.

For close to fifteen thousand years New England was cloaked by glacial ice more than a mile thick. Its weight pushed the continental crust of the region down into the plastic mantle of the earth. When the glacier melted out of southern New England fourteen thousand years ago, the continental crust in that region rose back up out of the mantle a few hundred feet. The uplift backed up New England's major drainages into what are called pro-glacial lakes. The old beds of Lake Hitchcock (which filled the Connecticut River valley, Lake Ashuelot in Keene and Swanzey, and Lake Merrimack north of Concord) can still be seen as the flat valley floors that border these rivers today. Eventually the glacier melted out of central New England, allowing this land, also, to rise up out of the mantle, draining the pro-glacial lakes and exposing their flat lakebeds. The downcutting of the rivers and their tributaries in the old lakebeds created steep ravines where the huge white pines eventually sheltered.

Wantastiquet

Another stand of impressive white pines can be found on the lower slopes of Wantastiquet Mountain across the Connecticut River from Brattleboro, Vermont. Pines in this forest tower over 130 feet and dwarf the understory hardwood trees. Henry David Thoreau climbed Wantastiquet and wrote of its impressive forest—another landscape that was never cleared for agriculture. Yet this forest is not free from disturbance. It tells a dramatic, more recent tale.

The pines and some very large specimens of white oak and black birch are scattered through a forest of much younger, multiple-trunked red maple. Multiple-trunked trees are the result of either logging or fire. It's hard to imagine a logger passing up the dramatic pine and oak to cut red maple, so fire makes more sense, and traces of past fires abound on this mountain.

The most convincing evidence of fire is the numerous basal scars that lie on the uphill sides of many of the large trees. Knowing that fire burns up a slope, many people think that scarring should occur on the downhill side of trees. But on a slope, leaf litter, branches, and fallen logs are all slowly pulled downhill by gravity. Each standing tree acts like a dam to this flow, causing forest litter and downed wood to collect on the uphill side of the tree. This material forms what is called a fuel pocket. When fire reaches it, the fuel pocket burns intensely, damaging the uphill side of the tree.

The last big fire on Wantastiquet took place not long after World War II began and consumed the whole mountainside from the Route 9 bridge to well south of the Route 119 bridges. One can only wonder what it must have looked like from the streets of Brattleboro as the fire raged up the mountain. But the Wantastiquet fire wasn't the only big fire at that time. Stoddard and Marlow witnessed a fire that consumed over twenty thousand acres of forest in late April 1941. Fires burning at the same time in Hancock, Harrisville, and Spofford consumed thousands of acres. In total more than forty thousand acres of forest in the Monadnock region were torched that year due to a combination of a very droughty summer and lots of dry slash left from the 1938 hurricane. A similar situation developed during the summer of 2002 in areas where large amounts of slash generated by the 1998 ice storm coincided with a very dry summer. Early September rains that year dampened what could have been another dramatic fire season.

Pisgah Old Growth

To forest ecologists, Pisgah State Park is famous for its documented Harvard Tract of white pine–hemlock old-growth forest that was decimated by the 1938 hurricane. This was one of the few tracts of old growth that had been quantitatively studied in New England. It served as a reference point until the 1990s, when scientists started to discover various tracts of old growth throughout New England. Why had all these old-growth forests not been recognized for more than half a century? They often lacked trees of large stature. It was thought that old-growth trees must be big. But a tree whose trunk does not exceed a couple of feet in diameter can be more than three hundred years of age. Once one has developed an eye for bark textures and canopy shapes, seeing this antiquity becomes possible.

A fine April day not long ago found me exploring Pisgah with my close friend Rich Thompson. The previous fall I had encountered two small stands of old-growth forest on the Pisgah Mountain ridgeline. It seems most people, including me, thought that Pisgah lost all its old growth in 1938. I wanted to show Rich the two stands that were ten to fifteen acres each. During the afternoon, while circling back to the Pisgah ridgeline, we started approaching North Round

Pond from the south. All around us were black birches less than eighteen inches in diameter with coarse-ridged bark—very different in appearance from the smoother bark I'd expect to see on trees of this size. I mentioned to Rich how old they looked. Then we came across a sixteen-inch-diameter downed beech that had been cut and cleared from the trail. We stopped to count the rings. The beech had just shy of two hundred. When we reached the southeast side of the pond we were greeted by a wonderful stand of old-growth hemlock with remnant snags of American chestnut—never salvaged following the fungal blight of the early 1900s. The hemlocks ranged up to three feet in diameter and didn't spread limbs until fifty feet above ground. Their deeply furrowed, rusty-red bark spoke of their antiquity. This was old growth that many might have recognized.

On subsequent visits, coring of the trees revealed that the largest hemlocks reach 325 years old with many beech, black birch, and red oak reaching 250 years old in the uplands to the south of the pond. The entire tract looks to be close to a hundred acres in size.

The area lies in a section of forest—thousands of acres in extent—that was never opened for agriculture. Any sites not protected by west-facing slopes were leveled by the 1938 hurricane. I believe that prior to that date much of this area held old-growth forest, not just the Harvard Tract on the east slope of Mount Pisgah. It's surprising and encouraging to see that portions of our presettlement forest continue to exist.

These events—fire and wind, farming booms, and logging—have left their marks on the land. Each is a story, a parable, with this lesson: to begin to know a place, we should do it the honor of studying it closely.

Journal: Thoreau on Monadnock, 1860 HENRY DAVID THOREAU

Henry David Thoreau climbed Mount Monadnock four times. On his last visit in August 1860 he camped on the mountain with his friend the poet William Ellery Channing.

Aug. 4. 8.30 A.M.—Start for Monadnock.

Begins to rain at 9 A.M., and rains from time to time thereafter all day, the mountain-top being constantly enveloped in clouds. . . .

There was a little sunshine on our way to the mountain, but the cloud extended far down its sides all day, so that one while we mistook Gap Monadnock for the true mountain, which was more to the north.

According to the guide-board it is two and one fourth miles from Troy to the first fork in the road near the little pond and the schoolhouse, and I should say it was near two miles from there to the summit, —all the way uphill from the meadow.

We crossed the immense rocky and springy pastures, containing at first raspberries, but much more hardhack in flower, reddening them afar, where cattle and horses collected about us sometimes came running to us, as we thought for society, but probably not. I told Bent of it, —how they gathered about us, they were so glad to see a human being, —but he said I might put it in my book so, it would do no harm, but then the fact was they came about me for salt. "Well," said I, "it was probably because I had so much salt in my constitution." Said he, "If you had had a little salt with you [you] could hardly have got away from them."

Hiking to Mount Monadnock from the Troy railroad station, Henry David Thoreau and his friend William Ellery Channing passed Perkins Pond in Troy.

"Well," said I, "[I] had some salt in my pocket." "That's what they smelt," said he. Cattle, young and old, with horns in all stages of growth, —young heifers with budding horns, —and horses with a weak [?] Sleepy-David look, though sleek and handsome. They gathered around us while we took shelter under a black spruce from the rain.

We were wet up to our knees before reaching the woods or steep ascent where we entered the cloud. It was quite dark and wet in the woods, from which we emerged into the lighter cloud about 3 P.M., and proceeded to construct our camp, in the cloud occasionally amounting to rain, where I camped some two years ago.

Choosing a place where the spruce was thick in this sunken rock yard, I cut out with a little hatchet a space for a camp in their midst, leaving two stout ones six feet apart to rest my ridge-pole on, and such limbs of these as would best form the gable ends. I then cut four spruces as rafters for the gable ends, leaving the stub ends of the branches to rest the cross-beams or girders on, of which there were two or three to each slope; and I made the roof very steep. Then cut an abundance of large flat spruce limbs, four or five feet long, and laid them on, shingle-fashion, beginning at the ground and covering the stub ends. This made a foundation for two or three similar layers of smaller twigs. Then made a bed of the same, closed up the ends somewhat, and all was done. All these twigs and boughs, of course, were dripping wet, and we were wet through up to our middles. But we made a good fire at the door, and in an hour or two were completely dried.

Standing and sitting before the fire which we kindled under a shelving rock, we could dry us much quicker than at any fireside below, for, what with stoves and reduced fireplaces, they could not have furnished such blaze or heat on any inn's [?] kitchen or parlor. This fire was exactly on the site of my old camp, and we burned a hole deep into the withered remains of its roof and bed.

It began to clear up and a star appeared at 8 P.M. Lightning was seen far in the south. Cloud, drifting cloud, alternated with moonlight all the rest of the night. At 11.30 P.M. I heard a nighthawk. Maybe it hunted then because prevented by the cloud at evening.

I heard from time to time through the night a distant sound like thunder or a falling of a pile of lumber, and I suspect that this may have been the booming of nighthawks at a distance.

Aug. 5. The wind changed to northerly toward morning, falling down from over the summit and sweeping though our camp, open on that side, and we found it rather cold!

About an hour before sunrise we heard again the nighthawk; also the robin, chewink, song sparrow, *Fringilla hyemalis*; and the wood thrush from the woods below.

Had a grand view of the summit on the north now, it being clear. I set my watch each morning by sunrise, and this morning the lichens on the rocks of the southernmost summit (south of us), just lit by the rising sun, presented a peculiar yellowish or reddish brown light (being wet) which they did not any morning afterward. The rocks of the main summit were olive-brown, and C. [Channing] called it the Mount of Olives.

I had gone out before sunrise to gather blueberries, —fresh, dewy (because wet with yesterday's rain), almost crispy blueberries, just in prime, much cooler and more grateful at this hour, —and was surprised to hear the voice of people rushing up the mountain for berries in the wet, even at this hour. These alternated with bright light-scarlet bunchberries not quite in prime.

The sides and angles of the cliffs, and their rounded brows (but especially their southeast angles, for I saw very little afterward on the north side; indeed, the cliffs or precipices are not on that side), were clothed with these now lively olive-brown lichens (umbilicaria), alike in sun and shade, becoming afterward and generally dark olive-brown when dry. *Vide* my specimens. Many of the names inscribed on the summit were produced by merely rubbing off the lichens, and they are thus distinct for years.

At 7.30 A.M. for the most part in cloud here, but the country below in sunshine. We soon after set out to walk to the lower southern spur of the mountain. It is chiefly a bare gray and extremely diversified rocky surface, with here and there a spruce or other small tree or bush, or patches of them, or a little shallow marsh on the rock; and the whole mountain-top for two miles was covered, on countless little shelves and in hollows between the rocks, with low blueberries of two or more species or varieties, just in their prime. They are said to be later here than below. Beside the kinds (black and blue *Pennsylvanicum*) common with us, there was the downy *Vaccinium Canadense* and a form or forms intermediate between this and the former, *i.e.* of like form but less hairy. The *Vaccinium Canadense* has a larger leaf and more recurved and undulating on its surface, and generally a lighter green than the common. There were the blue with a copious bloom, others simply black (not shiny, as ours commonly) and on largish bushes, and others of a peculiar blue, as if with a skim-coat of blue, hard and thin, as if glazed, such as we also have. The black are scarce with us.

These blueberries grew and bore abundantly almost wherever anything else grew on the rocky part of the mountain, —except perhaps the very wettest of the little swamps and the thickest of the little thickets, —quite up to the summit, and at least thirty or forty people came up from the surrounding country this Sunday to gather them. When we behold this summit at this season of the year, far away and blue in the horizon, we may think of the blueberries as blending their color with the general blueness of the mountain. They grow alike in the midst of the cladonia lichens and of the lambkill and moss of the little swamps. No shelf amid the piled rocks is too high or dry for them, for everywhere they enjoy the cool and moist air of the mountain. They are evidently a little later than in Concord, —say a week or ten days later. Blueberries of every degree of blueness and of bloom. There seemed to be fewer of them on the more abrupt and cold westerly and northwesterly sides of the summit, and most in the hollows and shelves of the plateau just southwest of the summit.

Perhaps the prettiest berry, certainly the most novel and interesting to me, was the mountain cranberry, now grown but yet hard and with only its upper

"There were a great many visitors to the summit," wrote Thoreau. "The young men sat in rows with their legs dangling over the precipice, squinting through spy-glasses and shouting and hallooing to each new party that issued from the woods below."

cheek red. They are quite local, even on the mountain. The vine is most common close to the summit, but we saw very little fruit there; but some twenty rods north of the brow of this low southern spur we found a pretty little dense patch of them between the rocks, where we gathered a pint in order to make a sauce of them. They here formed a dense low flat bed, covering the rocks for a rod or two, some lichens, green mosses, and the mountain potentilla mingled with them; and they rose scarcely more than one inch above the ground. . . .

We stewed these berries for our breakfast the next morning, and thought them the best berry on the mountain, though, not being quite ripe, the berry was a little bitterish—but not the juice of it. It is such an acid as the camper-out craves. They are, then, somewhat earlier than the common cranberry. I do not know that they are ever gathered hereabouts. At present they are very firm berries, of a deep, dark, glossy red. Doubtless there are many more such patches on the mountain.

We heard voices of many berry-pickers and visitors to the summit, but neither this nor the camp we built afterward was seen by any one. . . .

Aug. 6. The last was a clear, cool night. At 4 A.M. see local lake-like fogs in some valleys below, but there is none here.

This forenoon, after a breakfast on cranberries, leaving, as usual, our luggage concealed under a large rock, with other rocks placed over the hole, we moved about a quarter of a mile along the edge of the plateau eastward and built a new camp there. It was [a] place which I had noticed the day before, where, sheltered by a perpendicular ledge some seven feet high and close to the brow of the mountain, grew five spruce trees. Two of these stood four feet from the rock and six or more apart; so, clearing away the superfluous branches, I rested stout rafters from the rock-edge to limbs of the two spruces and placed a plate beam across, and, with two or three cross-beams or girders, soon had a roof which I could climb and shingle. After filling the inequalities with rocks and rubbish, I soon had a sloping floor on which to make our bed. Lying there on that shelf just on the edge of the steep declivity of the mountain, we could look all over the south and southeast world without raising our heads. The rock running east and west was our shelter on the north.

Our huts, being built of spruce entirely, were not noticeable two or three rods off, for we did [not] cut the spruce amid which they were built more than necessary, bending aside their boughs in order to enter. My companion, returning from a short walk, was lost when within two or three rods, the different rocks and clumps of spruce looked so much alike, and in the moonlight we were liable to mistake some dark recess between two neighboring spruce ten feet off for the entrance to our house. We heard this afternoon the tread of a blueberry-picker on the rocks two or three rods north of us, and saw another as near, south, and, stealing out, we came round from another side and had some conversation with them, —two men and a boy, —but they never discovered our house nor suspected it. The surface is so uneven that ten steps will often suffice to conceal the ground you lately stood on, and yet the different shelves and hollows are so much alike that you cannot tell if one is new or not. It is somewhat like traveling over a huge fan. When in a valley the nearest ridge conceals all the others and you cannot tell one from another.

This afternoon, again walked to the larger northeast swamp, going directly, *i.e.* east of the promontories or part way down the slopes. Bathed in the small

Thoreau saw bullfrogs and tadpoles in ponds like the one in these stereoscopic images.

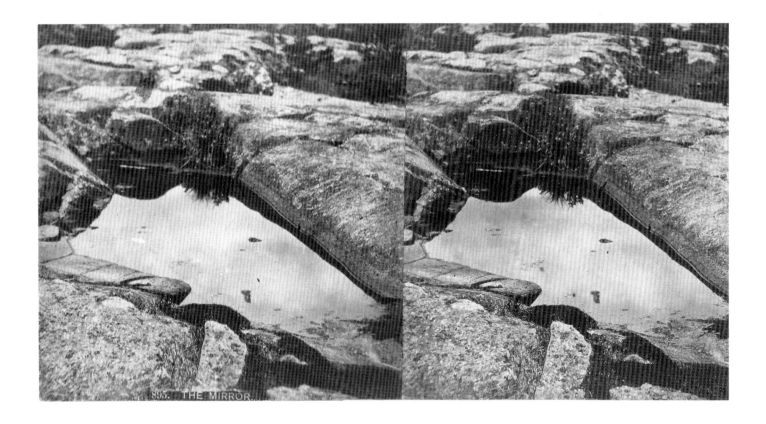

895. THE MIRROR.

rocky basin above the smaller meadow. These two swamps are about the wildest part of the mountain and most interesting to me. The smaller occurs on the northeast side of the main mountain, *i.e.* at the northeast end of the plateau. It is a little roundish meadow a few rods over, with cotton-grass in it, the shallow bottom of a basin of rock, and out the east side there trickles a very slight stream, just moistening the rock at present and collecting enough in one cavity to afford you a drink. This is evidently a source of the Contoocook, the one I noticed two years ago as such. . . .

At 5 P.M. we went to our first camp for our remaining baggage. From this point at this hour the rocks of the precipitous summit (under whose south side that camp is placed), lit by the declining sun, were a very light gray, with reddish-tawny touches from the now drying *Aira flexuosa* on the inaccessible shelves and along the seams. Returned to enjoy the evening at the second camp.

Evening and morning were the most interesting seasons, especially the evening. Each day, about an hour before sunset, I got sight, as it were accidentally, of an elysium beneath me. The smoky haze of the day, suggesting a furnace-like heat, a trivial dustiness, gave place to a clear transparent enamel, through which houses, woods, farms, and lakes were seen as in [a] picture indescribably fair and expressly made to be looked at. At any hour of the day, to be sure, the surrounding country looks flatter than it is. Even the great steep, furrowed, and rocky pastures, red with hardhack and raspberries, which creep so high up the mountain amid the woods, in which you think already that you are half-way up, perchance, seen from the top or brow of the mountain are not for a long time distinguished for elevation above the surrounding country, but they look smooth and tolerably level, and the cattle in them are not noticed or distinguished from rocks unless you search very particularly. At length you notice how the houses and barns keep a respectful, and at first unaccountable, distance from these near pastures and woods, though they *are* seemingly flat, that there is a broad neutral ground between the roads and the mountain; and yet when the truth flashes upon you, you have to imagine the long, ascending path through them.

To speak of the landscape generally, the open or cleared land looks like a thousand little swells or tops of low rounded hills, —tent-like or like a low hay-cap spread, —tawny or green amid the woods. As you look down on this landscape you little think of the hills where the traveller walks his horse. The woods have not this swelling look. The most common color of open land (from apex at 5 P.M.) is tawny brown, the woods dark green. At midday the darker green of evergreens amid the hardwoods is quite discernible half a dozen miles off. But, as the most interesting view is at sunset, so it is the part of [the] landscape nearest to you and most immediately beneath the mountain, where, as usual, there is that invisible gelid haze to glass it.

The nearest house to the mountain which we saw from our camp—one on the Jaffrey road—was in the shadow even of the low southern spur of the mountain which we called the Old South, just an hour before the sun set, while a neighbor on a hill within a quarter of a mile eastward enjoyed the sunlight at least half an hour longer. So much shorter are their days, and so much more artificial light and heat must they obtain, at the former house. It would be a serious loss, methinks, one hour of sunlight every day. *We* saw the sun so much longer. Of course the labors of the day were brought to an end, the sheep began to bleat, the doors were closed, the lamps were lit, and preparations for the night were made there, so much the earlier.

The landscape is shown to be not flat, but hilly, when the sun is half an hour high, by the shadows of the hills. But, above all, from half an hour to two hours before sunset many western mountain-ranges are revealed, as the sun declines, one behind another, by their dark outlines and the intervening haze. . . .

Of course, the last half of these mountain-ridges appeared successively higher and seemed higher, all of them (*i.e.* the last half), than the mountain we were on, as if you had climbed to heights of the sky by a succession of stupendous terraces reaching as far as you could see from north to south. The Connecticut Valley was one broad gulf of haze which you were soon over. They were the Green Mountains that we saw, but there was no greenness, only a bluish mistiness, in what we saw; and all of Vermont that lay between us and their summit was but a succession of parallel ranges of mountains. Of course, almost all that we mean commercially and agriculturally by Vermont was concealed in those long and narrow haze-filled valleys. I never saw a mountain that looked so high and so melted away at last cloud-like into the sky, as Saddleback this eve, when your eye has clomb to it by these eight successive terraces. You had to begin at this end and ascend step by step to recognize it for a mountain at all. If you had first rested your eye on *it*, you would have seen it for a cloud, it was so incredibly high in the sky.

After sunset the ponds are white and distinct. Earlier we could distinguish the reflections of the woods perfectly in ponds three miles off.

I heard a cock crow very shrilly and distinctly early in the evening of the 8th. This was the most distinct sound from the lower world that I heard up there at any time, not excepting even the railroad whistle, which was louder. It reached my ear perfectly, to each note and curl, —from some submontane cock. We also heard at this hour an occasional bleat from a sheep in some mountain pasture, and a lowing of a cow. And at last we saw a light here and there in a farmhouse window. We heard no sound of man except the railroad whistle and, on Sunday, a church-bell. Heard no dog that I remember. Therefore I should say that, of all the sounds of the farmhouse, the crowing of the cock could be heard furthest or most distinctly under these circumstances. It seemed to wind its way through the layers of air as a sharp gimlet through soft wood, and reached our ears with amusing distinctness.

Aug. 7. Morning—dawn and sunrise—was another interesting season. I rose always by four or half past four to observe the signs of it and to correct my watch. From our first camp I could not see the sun rise, but only when its first light (yellowish or, rather, pinkish) was reflected from the lichen-clad rocks of the southern spur. But here, by going eastward some forty rods, I could see the sun rise, though there was invariably a low stratum or bar of cloud in the horizon. The sun rose about five. The tawny or yellowish pastures about the mountain (below the woods; what was the grass?) reflected the auroral light at 4.20 A.M. remarkably, and they were at least as distant as at any hour.

There was every morning more or less solid white fog to be seen on the earth, though none on the mountain. I was struck by the localness of these fogs. For five mornings they occupied the same place and were about the same in extent. It was obvious that certain portions of New Hampshire and Massachusetts were at this season commonly invested with fog in the morning, while others, or the larger part, were free from it. The fog lay on the lower parts only. From our point of view the largest lake of fog lay in Rindge and southward; and southeast of Fitzwilliam, *i.e.* about Winchendon, very large there. In short, the fog lay in great spidery lakes and streams answering to the lakes, streams, and meadows beneath, especially over the sources of Miller's River and the region of primitive wood thereabouts; but it did [not] rest on lakes always, *i.e.,* where they were elevated, as now some in Jaffrey were quite clear. It suggested that there was an important difference, so far as the health and spirits of the inhabitants were concerned, between the town where there was this regular morning fog and that where there was none. I shall always remember the inhabitants of State Line as dwellers in the fog. The geography and statistics of fog have not been ascertained. If we awake into a fog, it does not occur to us that the inhabitants of a neighboring town which lies higher may have none, neither do they, being ignorant of this happiness, inform us of it. Yet, when you come to look down thus on the country every morning, you see that here this thick white veil of fog is spread and not there. It was often several hundred feet thick, soon rising, breaking up, and drifting off, or rather seeming to drift away, as it evaporated. There was commonly such a risen fog drifting through the interval between this mountain and Gap Monadnock.

One morning I noticed clouds as high as the Peterboro Hills, —a lifted fog, —ever drifting easterly but making no progress, being dissipated. Also long rolls and ant-eaters of cloud, at last reduced by the sun to mere vertebrae. That morning (the 8th) the great and general cloud and apparently fog combined over the lowest land running southwest from Rindge was apparently five hundred or more feet deep, but our mountain was above all.

This forenoon I cut and measured a spruce on the north side [of] the mountain, and afterward visited the summit, where one of the coast surveyors had been signalling, as I was told, to a mountain in Laconia, some fifty-five miles off, with a glass reflector.

After dinner, descended into the gulf and swamp beneath our camp. At noon every roof in the southern country sloping toward the north was distinctly revealed, —a lit gray.

In the afternoon, walked to the Great Gulf and meadow, in the midst of the plateau just east of and under the summit.

Aug. 8. Wednesday 8.30 A.M. Walk round the west side of the summit. Bathe in the rocky pool there, collect mountain cranberries on the northwest side, return over the summit, and take the bearings of the different spurs, etc. Return to camp at noon.

Toward night, walk to east edge of the plateau.

Aug. 9. At 6 A.M., leave camp for Troy, where we arrive after long pauses, by 9 A.M., and take the cars at 10.5. I observed these plants on the rocky summit of the mountain, above the forest: —

Raspberry, not common.

Low blueberries of two or three varieties.

Bunchberry.

> *Solidago thyrsoidea.*

Fetid currant, common; leaves beginning to be scarlet; grows amid loose fallen rocks.

Red cherry, some ripe, and handsome.

Black choke-berry.

> *Potentilla tridentata*, still lingering in bloom.

> *Aralia hispida*, still lingering in bloom.

Cow-wheat, common, still in bloom.

Mountain cranberry, not generally abundant; full grown earlier than lowland ditto.

Black spruce.

Lambkill, lingering in flower in cool and moist places.

> *Aster acuminatus*, abundant; not generally open, but fairly begun to bloom.

Red elder, ripe, apparently in prime, not uncommon.

> *Arenaria Groenlandica*, still pretty common in flower.

> *Solidago lanceolata*, not uncommon, just fairly begun.

> *Epilobium angustifolium*, in bloom; not common, however.

> *Epilobium palustre*, some time, common in mosses, small and slender.

Wild holly, common; berries not quite ripe.

> *Viburnum nudum*, common; berries green.

White pine; saw three or four only, mostly very small.

Mountain-ash, abundant; berries not ripe; generally very small, largest in swamps.

Diervilla, not uncommon, still.

Rhondora, abundant; low, *i.e.* short.

Meadow-sweet, abundant, apparently in prime.

Hemlocks; two little ones with rounded tops.

> *Chelone glabra*, not yet; at northeast swamp-side.

Yarrow.

Canoe birch, very small.

> *Clintonia borealis*, with fruit.

Checkerberry.

Gold-thread.

One three-ribbed goldenrod, northwest side (not *Canadense*).

Tall rough goldenrod, not yet; not uncommon.

> *Populus tremuliformis*, not very common.

> *Polygonum cilinode*, in bloom.

Yellow birch, small.

Fir, a little; four or five trees noticed.

Willows, not uncommon, four or five feet high.

Red maple, a very little, small.

Water andromeda, common about the bogs.

Trientalis.

Pearly everlasting, out.

Diplopappus umbellatus, in bloom, not common (?); northeast swamp-side, also
northwest side of mountain.

Juncus trifidus.

Some *Juncus paradoxus?* } about edge of marshes.

Some *Juncus acuminatus?* } about edge of marshes.

CYPERACAE

Eriophorum gracile, abundant, whitening the little swamps.

Eriophorum vaginatum, abundant, little swamps, long done, (this the coarse grass
in tufts, in marshes).

Wool-grass, not uncommon, (common kind).

Carex trisperma (?) or *Deweyana*, with large seed, slender and drooping, by side
of northeast swamp. *Vide* press.

Carex scoparia? or *straminca*? a little.

C. debilis.

Carex, small, rather close-spiked, *C. canescens*-like (?), common.

A fine grass-like plant very common, perhaps *Eleocharis tenuis*; now without heads,
but marks of them.

Grasses

Aira flexuosa.

Glyceria elongata, with appressed branches (some purplish), in swamp.

Blue-joint, apparently in prime, one place.

Festuca ovina, one place.

Cinna arundinacea, one place.

Agrostis scabra (?), at our spring, *q.v.*

Ferns And Lichens, Etc.

A large greenish lichen flat on rocks, of a peculiarly concentric growth, *q.v.*

Some common sulphur lichen.

The very bright handsome crustaceous yellow lichen, as on White Mts., *q.v.*

Two or three umbilicaria lichens, *q.v.*, giving the dark brown to the rocks.

A little, in one place, of the old hat umbilicaria, as at Flint's Pond Rock.

Green moss and sphagnum in the marshes.

Two common cladonias, white and greenish.

Stereocaulon.

Lycopodium complanatum, one place.

Lycopodium annotinum, not very common.

Common polypody.

Dicksonia fern, *q.v.*

Sensitive fern, and various other common ones. . . .

The black spruce is the prevailing tree, commonly six or eight feet high; but
very few, and those only in the most sheltered places, as hollows and swamps,
are of regular outline, on account of the strong and cold winds with which they
have to contend. Fifteen feet high would be unusually large. They cannot grow
here without some kind of lee to start with. They commonly consist of numerous
flat branches close above one another for the first foot or two, spreading close
over the surface and filling and concealing the hollows between the rocks; but
exactly at a level with the top of the rock which shelters them they cease to have

any limbs on the north side. . . . They thus remind you often of masts of vessels with sails set on one side, and sometimes one of these almost bare masts is seen to have been broken short off at ten feet from the ground, such is the violence of the wind there. I saw a spruce, healthy and straight, full sixteen feet without a limb or the trace of a limb on the north side. When building my camp, in order to get rafters six feet long and an inch and a half in diameter at the small end, I was obliged to cut down spruce at least five inches in diameter at one foot from the ground. So stout and tapering do they grow. They spread so close to the rocks that the lower branches are often half worn away for a foot in length by their rubbing on the rocks in the wind, and I sometimes mistook the creaking of such a limb for the note of a bird, for it is just such a note as you would expect to hear there. The two spruce which formed the sides of my second camp had their lower branches behind the rock so thick and close, and, on the outsides of the quadrant, so directly above one another perpendicularly, that they made two upright side walls, as it were, very convenient to interlace and make weather-tight. . . .

Our fuel was the dead spruce—apparently that which escaped the fire some forty years ago!!—which lies spread over the rocks in considerable quantity still, especially at the northeast spur. It makes very good dry fuel, and some of it is quite fat and sound. The spruce twigs were our bed. I observed that, being laid bottom upward in a hot sun, as at the foot of our bed, the leaves turned pale-brown, as if boiled, and fell off very soon. . . .

The bird peculiar to the mountain was the *F. hyemalis*, and perhaps the most common, flitting over the rocks, unless the robin and chewink were as common. These, with the song sparrow and wood thrush, were heard regularly each morning. I saw a robin's nest in one of the little swamps. The wood thrush was regularly heard late in the afternoon, its strain coming up from the woods below as the shadows were lengthening.

But, above all, this was an excellent place to observe the habits of the night-hawks. They were heard and seen regularly at sunset, —one night it was at 7.10, or exactly at sunset—coming upward from the lower and more shaded portion of the rocky surface below our camp, with their *spark spark*, soon answered by a companion, for they seemed always to hunt in pairs, —yet both would dive and boom and according to Wilson, only the male utters this sound. They pursued their game thus a short distance apart and some sixty or one hundred feet above the gray rocky surface, in the twilight, and the constant *spark spark* seemed to be a sort of call-note to advertise each other of their neighborhood. Suddenly one would hover and flutter more stationarily for a moment, somewhat like a king-fisher, and then dive almost perpendicularly downward with a rush, for fifty feet, frequently within three or four rods of us, and the loud booming sound or rip was made just at the curve, as it ceased to fall, but whether voluntary or involuntary I know not. They appeared to be diving for their insect prey. What eyes they must have to be able to discern it *beneath* them against the rocks in the twilight! As I was walking about the camp, one flew low, within two feet of the surface, about me, and lit on the rock within three rods of me, and uttered a harsh note

(For Title, see over.)

"At almost any hour of the day they were seen wending their way single file in various garb up or down the shelving rocks of the peak," wrote Thoreau.

like *c-o-w, c-o-w*, —hard and gritty and allied to their common notes, —which I thought expressive of anxiety, or to alarm me, or for its mate.

I suspect that their booming on a distant part of the mountain was the sound which I heard the first night which was like very distant thunder, or the fall of a pile of lumber. . . .

As for quadrupeds, we saw none on the summit and only one small gray rabbit at the base of the mountain, but we saw the droppings of rabbits all over the mountain. . . . As for insects: There were countless ants, large and middle-sized, which ran over our bed and inside our clothes. They swarmed all over the mountain. . . .

There were a great many visitors to the summit, both by the south and north, *i.e.,* the Jaffrey and Dublin paths, but they did not turn off from the beaten track. One noon, when I was on the top, I counted forty men, women, and children around me, and more were constantly arriving while others were going. Certainly more than one hundred ascended in a day. When you got within thirty rods you saw them seated in a row along the gray parapets, like the inhabitants of a castle on a gala-day; and when you behold Monadnock's blue summit fifty miles off in the horizon, you may imagine it covered with men, women, and children in dresses of all colors, like an observatory on a musterfield. They appeared to be chiefly mechanics and farmers' boys and girls from the neighboring towns. The young men sat in rows with their legs dangling over the precipice, squinting through spy-glasses and shouting and hallooing to each new party that issued from the woods below. Some were playing cards; others were trying to see their houses or their neighbor's. Children were running about and playing as usual. Indeed, this peak in pleasant weather is the most trivial place in New England. There are probably more arrivals daily than at any of the White

Mountain houses. Several were busily engraving their names on the rocks with cold-chisels, whose incessant clink you heard, and they had but little leisure to look off. The mountain was not free of them from sunrise to sunset, though most of them left about 5 P.M. At almost any hour of the day they were seen wending their way single file in various garb up and down the shelving rocks of the peak. These figures on the summit, seen in relief against the sky (from our camp), looked taller than life. I saw some that camped there, by moonlight, one night. On Sunday, twenty or thirty, at least, in addition to the visitors to the peak, came up to pick blueberries, and we heard on all sides the rattling of dishes and their frequent calls to each other. . . .

They who simply climb to the peak of Monadnock have seen but little of the mountain. I came not to look *off from* it, but to look *at* it. The view of the pinnacle itself from the plateau below surpasses any view which you get from the summit. It is indispensable to see the top itself and the sierra of its outline from one side. The great charm is not to look off from a height but to walk over this novel and wonderful rocky surface. Moreover, if you would enjoy the prospect, it is, methinks, most interesting when you look from the edge of the plateau immediately down into the valleys, or where the edge of the lichen-clad rocks, only two or three rods from you, is seen as the lower frame of a picture of green fields, lakes, and woods, suggesting a more stupendous precipice than exists. There are much more surprising effects of this nature along the edge of the plateau than on the summit. It is remarkable what haste the visitors make to get to the top of the mountain and then look away from it.

Northward you see Ascutney and Kearsarge Mountains, and faintly the White Mountains, and others more northeast; but above all, toward night, the Green Mountains. But what a study for rocks does this mountain-top afford! The rocks of the pinnacle have many regular nearly right-angled slants to the southeast, covered with the dark-brown (or olivaceous) umbilicaria. The rocks which you walk over are often not only worn smooth and slippery, but grooved out, as if with some huge rounded tool, or they are much oftener convex. You see huge buttresses or walls put up by Titans, with true joints, only recently loosened by an earthquake as if ready to topple down. Some of the lichen-clad rocks are of a rude brick-loaf form or small cottage form. You see large boulders, left just on the edge of the steep descent of the plateau, commonly resting on a few small stones, as if the Titans were in the very act of transporting them when they were interrupted; some left standing on their ends, and almost the only convenient rocks in whose shade you can sit sometimes. Often you come to a long, thin rock, two or three rods long, which has the appearance of having just been split into underpinning-stone, —perfectly straight-edged and parallel pieces, and lying as it fell, ready for use, just as the mason leaves it. Post-stones, door-stones, etc. There were evidences of recent motion as well as ancient.

I saw on the flat sloping surface of rock a fresher white space exactly the size and form of a rock which was lying by it and which had lately covered it. What had upset it? There were many of these whitish marks where the dead spruce had lain but was now decayed or gone.

"But what a study for rocks does this summit top afford," wrote Thoreau.

The rocks were not only coarsely grooved but finely scratched from northwest to southeast, commonly about S. 10° E. (but between 5° and 20° east, or, by the true meridian, more yet). I could have steered myself in a fog by them.

Piles of stones left as they were split ready for the builder. I saw one perfect triangular hog-trough—except that it wanted one end—and which would have been quite portable and convenient in a farmer's yard. The core, four or five feet long, lay one side.

The rocks are very commonly in terraces with a smooth rounded edge to each. The most remarkable of these terraces that I noticed was between the second camp and the summit, say some forty rods from the camp. These terraces were some six rods long and six to ten feet wide, but the top slanting considerably back into the mountain, and they were about four or five feet high each. There were four such in succession here, running S. 30° E. The edges of these terraces, here and commonly, were rounded and grooved like the rocks at a waterfall, as if water and gravel had long washed over them.

Some rocks were shaped like huge doughnuts. The edges of cliffs were frequently lumpishly rounded, covered with lichens, so that you could not stand near the edge. The extreme east and northeast parts of the plateau, especially near the little meadow, are the most interesting for the forms of rocks. Sometimes you see where a huge oblong square stone has been taken out from the edge of a terrace, leaving a space which looks like a giant's grave unoccupied.

On the west side the summit the strata ran north and south and dipped to east about 60° with the horizon. There were broad veins of white quartz (sometimes one foot wide) running directly many rods.

Near the camp there was a succession of great rocks, their corners rounded semicircularly and grooved at the same time like the capital of a column reversed. The most rugged walking is on the steep westerly slope.

We had a grand view, especially after sunset, as it grew dark, of the *sierra* of the summit's outline west of us, —the teeth of sierra often turned back toward the summit, —when the rocks were uniformly black in the shade and seen against the twilight. . . .

Water stands in shallow pools on almost every rocky shelf. The largest pool of open water which I found was on the south-west side of the summit, and was four rods long by fifteen to twenty feet in width and a foot deep. Wool- and cotton-grass grew around it, and there was a dark green moss and some mud at the bottom. There was a smoother similar pool on the next shelf above it. These were about the same size in June and in August, and apparently never dry up. There was also the one in which I bathed, near the northeast little meadow. I had a delicious bath there, though the water was warm, but there was a pleasant strong and drying wind blowing over the ridge, and when I had bathed, the rock felt like plush to my feet.

The cladonia lichens were so dry at midday, even the day after rain, that they served as tinder to kindle our fire, —indeed, we were somewhat troubled to prevent the fire from spreading amid them, —yet at night, even before sundown, and morning, when we got our supper and breakfast, they would not burn thus, having absorbed moisture. They had then a cool and slightly damp feeling.

Every evening, excepting, perhaps, the Sunday evening after the rain of the day before, we saw not long after sundown a slight scud or mist begin to strike the summit above us, though it was perfectly fair weather generally and there were no clouds over the lower country.

First, perhaps, looking up, we would see a small scud not more than a rod in diameter drifting just over the apex of the mountain. In a few minutes more a somewhat larger one would suddenly make its appearance, and perhaps strike the topmost rocks and invest them for a moment, but as rapidly drift off northeast and disappear. Looking into the southwest sky, which was clear, we would see all at once a small cloud or scud a rod in diameter beginning to form half a mile from the summit, and as it came on it rapidly grew in a mysterious manner, till it was fifty rods or more in diameter, and draped and concealed for a few moments all the summit above us, and then passed off and disappeared northeastward just as it had come. So that it appeared as if the clouds had been attracted by the summit. They also seemed to rise a little as they approached it, and endeavor to go over without striking. I gave this account of it to myself. They were not attracted to the summit, but simply generated there and not elsewhere. There would be a warm southwest wind blowing which was full of moisture, alike over the mountain and all the rest of the country. The summit of the mountain being cool, this warm air began to feel its influence at half a mile distance, and its moisture was rapidly condensed into a small cloud, which expanded as it advanced, and evaporated again as it left the summit. This would go on, apparently, as the coolness of the mountain increased, and generally the cloud or mist reached down as low as our camp from time to time, in the night.

One evening, as I was watching these small clouds forming and dissolving about the summit of our mountain, the sun having just set, I cast my eyes toward the dim bluish outline of the Green Mountains in the clear red evening sky, and, to my delight, I detected exactly over the summit of Saddleback Mountain, some sixty miles distant, its own little cloud, shaped like a parasol and answering to that which capped our mountain, though in this case it did not rest on the mountain, but was considerably above it, and all the rest of the west horizon for forty miles was cloudless. I was convinced that it was the local cloud of that mountain because it was directly over the summit, was of small size and of umbrella form answering to the summit, and there was no other cloud to be seen in that horizon. It was a beautiful and serene object, a sort of fortunate isle, —like any other cloud in the sunset sky. . . .

The voices of those climbing the summit were heard remarkably far. We heard much of the ordinary conversation of those climbing the peak above us at a hundred rods off, and we could hear those on the summit, or a hundred and thirty rods off, when they shouted. I heard a party of ladies and gentlemen laughing and talking there in the night (they were camping there), though I did not hear what they said. We heard, or imagined that we heard, from time to time, as we lay in our camp by day, an occasional chinking or clinking sound as if made by one stone on another. . . .

I carried on this excursion the following articles (beside what I wore), *viz.*: —

One shirt.

One pair socks.

Two pocket-handkerchiefs.

One *thick* waistcoat.

One flannel shirt (had no occasion to use it).

India-rubber coat.

Three bosoms.

Pins, needles, thread.

A blanket (would have been more convenient if stitched up in the form of a bag).

Cap for the night.

Map and compass.

Spy-glass and microscope and tape.

Saw and hatchet.

Plant-book and blotting paper.

Paper and stamps.

Botany.

Insect and lichen boxes.

Jack-knife.

Matches.

Waste paper and twine.

Iron spoon and pint dipper with handle. All in a knapsack.

Umbrella.

N.B. —Add to the above next time a small bag, which may be stuffed with moss or the like for a pillow

For provisions for one, six days, carried

2¼ lbs. of salt beef and tongue.	Take only salt beef next time, 2 to 3 lbs.
18 hard-boiled eggs.	Omit eggs.
2½ lbs. sugar and a little salt.	2 lbs. of sugar would have done.
About ¼ lb. of tea.	⅔ as much would have done.
2 lbs. hard bread.	The right amount of bread, but might have taken more.
¼ loaf of home-made bread and a piece of cake	but home-made and more *solid* sweet cake.

N.B. —Carry salt (or some of it) in a wafer box. Also some sugar in a small box.

N.B. —Observe next time; the source of the stream which crosses the path; what species of swallow flies over mountain; what the grass that gives the pastures a yellowish color seen from the summit.

Thoreau never returned to Monadnock. He died of tuberculosis on May 6, 1862. He was forty-four years old.

Following Thoreau
J. Parker Huber

On September 7, 1852, Thoreau walked from Peterborough, past the Eveleth house, to the summit of Monadnock and down the south side, dashing the last stretch to Troy to catch the 3:00 p.m. train back to Concord.

Impossible, I thought after reading his journal account of this. Impossible. So on the same day one year, I set out to replicate his experience. Leaving Peterborough center at 8:47 a.m. I reached the Eveleth house at 1:20 p.m., where I met the owners, Bruce and Mary Elizabeth McClellan, sipping cocktails on the green with their friends the Griswolds. Bruce informed me that there was no path from here on and suggested going by compass.

"He's going to be in Troy at three like Thoreau," Bruce told his wife, who upon hearing I had no compass, quipped, "three a.m."

She went about serving luncheon, which I fantasized eating as I sweated upward through the woods following stone walls (which signified pastures when Thoreau came), a dry brook, and openings through spruce and striped maple, thinking that her joke may be true, until I happily met the Pumpelly Trail and rose to the top at 4:45 p.m.

Immediately, I descended the White Arrow Trail to Old Toll Road to Route 124 west, and on to Monadnock Street south to Troy. The station is still standing a block southwest of the common, where the town hall clock read 7:15 p.m. My results: seventeen miles in almost ten and a half hours. Thoreau's walk may have been slightly shorter since he moved in a straight line through relatively open terrain. If he left at dawn, 4:30 a.m., which is in character (though his departure time and place are unknown), his travel time was the same. Granted his youth then (he was thirty-five), I gained an appreciation for his integrity and energy.

Marlborough's Granite Quarry
John R. Harris

"A little west of the center of town lies a ledge of fine and beautiful granite, which, for building purposes, is unequalled by any in the state," wrote Charles Bemis, in the *History of the Town of Marlborough* (1881). Stone from this quarry was first removed by Asa Greenwood, a skilled local stonecutter and carpenter, who constructed a number of magnificent granite homes and foundations in town. The Marlborough quarry provided the granite used by the Cheshire Railroad Com-

Marlborough's Webb quarry c. 1905.

pany to construct overpasses, bridge abutments, and culverts between Fitchburg and Bellows Falls. In 1868 A. G. Mann purchased the one-hundred-acre site and began to expand its operation. Records for 1873 indicate that Mann shipped 6,005 tons of granite building stone to Worcester, another 135 tons to Lowell, and 360 tons to Boston. Eighteen years later George D. Webb of Worcester purchased the business and installed a private railroad that connected the quarry to the Boston and Maine line.

Both of Harold Larro's grandfathers worked at the Webb quarry: one immigrated from Finland as a nine-year-old and carried water to the stonecutters at age thirteen; and the other operated the massive stone crusher that provided fill for road construction before the days of concrete and asphalt.

Harold Larro's father, Clarence, worked as an engineer aboard the locomotive specially designed for hauling granite to Webb Depot. Clarence also ran the steam-powered hoists scattered throughout the quarry site. These machines featured a rotating derrick and a cable-operated boom that could pick up and position granite slabs for transport.

Granite quarries, like many other nineteenth-century industrial sites in the Monadnock region, served as mixing bowls for ethnic diversity. At Webb quarry one might hear Finnish, Italian, Irish, and French spoken on any given day. Many of the quarrymen were first-generation immigrants who lived in nearby company housing situated in ghettos with names like Finntown or Little Canada.

John A. Williams, the father of Marlborough resident Alan Williams, worked for many years as a paving cutter in the Webb quarry. John learned his craft in northern Wales and immigrated to America in 1907. He cut stone in seventeen states and Canada before settling down in Marlborough on a farm where he walked to and from the quarry. Workers at the Webb operation are reported to have turned out three million granite paving blocks annually.

When George Webb died, the business was sold to the Hildreth Construction Company, and granite continued to be quarried until 1933. At the outbreak of the Second World War the cutting sheds were dismantled and the locomotive, derricks, and boilers were cut up for scrap. Decades later local teens continued to frequent the quarry site, where they would swing from booms and drop into the clear cold water.

Workers at the Webb quarry.

The stone crusher.

RONALD JAGER

A Mill Girl's Offering

She spent no money on fine clothes nor ornaments. . . . We younger ones were awed by her silence and reserve. But later . . . came to recognize her character as that of one studious, gentle, and self-sacrificing.
—Harriet H. Robinson, *Loom and Spindle* (1898)

In 1883 a local printer in the town of Washington, New Hampshire, turned out a slim volume of homegrown poetry, whose title page reads: *Poems of Sarah Shedd, Founder of the Shedd Free Library, Washington, N. H.* The publication was timed for the dedication of the town's new Shedd Free Library building. The book is handsomely put together, but so far as I know, only two copies of it now exist, both in the Shedd Free Library. The person, the poetry, the local printing with its flowery preface, the occasion, the library—these are all elements in a heartwarming New England nineteenth-century story. Is it more than just a simple local story?

It certainly resonates with other versions of other stories, all with protagonists and plots so recognizable and recurrent that they bear a representative, almost mythic, quality. Sarah was born in Washington to John and Lydia Shedd in 1813, the second of four children. Her mother was a Farnsworth, a name forever associated with the origins—in the same Washington—of the Seventh-Day Adventist denomination. She began teaching school at age fifteen; at seventeen her father died, leaving Sarah, her mother, an older sister, and a younger sister and brother. When Sarah was twenty the younger sister died; then the older sister married and eventually moved to the West. It is now the early 1830s, and Sarah is a young lady living with a widowed mother and a young brother, and the prospects are not bright. Meanwhile, agents for the new textile mills in Lowell, Massachusetts, are fanning out to rural towns, offering farm girls good employment in a chaperoned environment, and all the allure and independence of life in the city. Like thousands of other girls, Sarah is interested. She joins the other farm girls in Lowell for a time, then comes home to teach school, then goes back to the mills to earn money for her mother's living and her brother's education.

And so it goes for decades, year in year out. By the late 1850s, when she is forty-five, Sarah decides to stay home in Washington to take care of her aged mother, who soon dies. Sarah herself dies in 1867 (probably of tuberculosis), when she is fifty-four, and leaves a bequest of twenty-five hundred dollars in her will for a town library. People are amazed at her cheerful self-sacrifice through the years, amazed at the money she had managed to scrape together and save, amazed at her sheer goodness. Saintly, they said.

Such is the story in outline: not myth or fiction, but history and fact. And perhaps more. Poet, teacher, laborer, giver of a library: some lives fit familiar patterns. She represents for her particular rural community what we might call "the higher values," personally enacting its literary, artistic, and moral aspirations. Elements in nineteenth-century social culture sometimes delegated such roles to spinster ladies of high moral standing, and in this climate virtue itself assumed a markedly feminine tone. One thinks of the temperance movement, or of the innumerable improvement societies that sprouted and flourished at this time. History handed Sarah Shedd a role, and she filled it perfectly. But what was such a woman really like?

There exist some widely scattered threads that will help us to weave a fuller story; and there is also a larger framework that will help us see in clearer light the various Sarah Shedds of the world. That framework comes from the rise and early success of the mighty textile mills and their central place in the Industrial Revolution in nineteenth-century New England, and from the armies of farm girls who heard the bells of the mills and marched off to work.

Sarah Shedd: poet, teacher, laborer, and benefactor.

Mill Girl

It is about seventy miles, as the turnpike once ran, from Washington, New Hampshire, to Lowell, Massachusetts. When Sarah Shedd was born in 1813 in Washington, a thriving rural town that would never have a railroad but lay athwart two turnpikes, Lowell did not even exist. But big changes were afoot. The county's first permanent waterpower textile factory for spinning yarn from raw wool or cotton began in 1790 in Pawtucket, Rhode Island, and in the next decades dozens of small waterpower spinning mills sprang up on the rivers of southern New England. Cotton from the slave plantations of the South suddenly had new and growing markets in New England. Although the spinning of wool and cotton soon became mechanized factory work, weaving yarn into cloth long remained within the family, and on a domestic loom. That too began to change about the time Sarah Shedd was born, when Francis Lowell and his partners, the Boston Associates, created a new factory system in Waltham, Massachusetts, with waterpower looms. The integrated textile mill began with raw cotton from the South and used waterpowered machinery to pick, card, spin, dye, and finally weave the cloth. Meanwhile, of course, many a New England farm girl like Sarah Shedd worked by hand on a loom at home, often using woolen yarn also spun at home but, when the family could afford it, increasingly using cotton yarn from the power spinning factories in southern New England.

By 1820 the Boston Associates were on the prowl for a new site, bigger and better and with more power. Attracted to East Chelmsford and the falls on the Merrimack River, they quietly bought up the canal, bought the nearby farmland, bought up a few small mills, bought most of the water rights, and bought nearly everything else in sight. Then they set about constructing from scratch a system of textile mills, new canals for transportation, then worker housing and, indeed, an entire factory city, again on the British model. Fancis Lowell had died by this time, so in 1826 his name was given to the new city that was rising on the farmscape, and Lowell it has remained. It was a thoroughly integrated factory

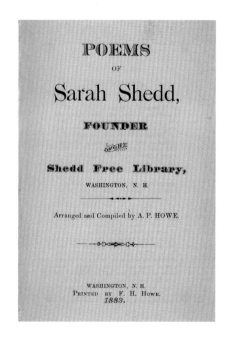

Sarah Shedd's poetry was edited by her friend Ashbury Howe and printed by his son for the library dedication.

system that they created, and it was immediately successful: cotton cloth, gingham and calico, had a huge market, and they knew how to make it cheaply. By the 1830s the only problem was the shortage of workers to tend the machines. Where could they be recruited?

It is likely that Sarah Shedd responded to one of the hundreds of recruiting posters that were spread throughout the towns of northern New England. This may have been about 1832, when she was nineteen, or even earlier. "Her parents were in narrow circumstances," Sarah's mill friend, Harriet Robinson, later wrote, "but they had endowed her with a good mind, and had given her a fair education, which was supplemented by tuition under Mary Lyon, of Holyoke Seminary, one of the first women preceptors of her time." Mary Lyon, in fact, was perhaps the leading female educator of the 1830s and '40s. A well-known teacher in several academies in New Hampshire and Massachusetts, she became famous as the founder of Mount Holyoke Female Seminary, now Mount Holyoke College, in 1837. We don't know just where or when Sarah studied with her, but she certainly chose her mentor well.

Friends testified that Sarah had ardently desired to continue her formal education but had been unable to do so. Perhaps she had studied with Mary Lyon before her father died, and his death may have been the reason she could not continue her education but went to the mills instead. We do know that by 1832 Sarah's brother Joseph was fifteen and eager for academy work, but there wasn't one in Washington, so it would cost money for him to go elsewhere; and we know that Sarah helped to pay for it. For one thing that a mill job promised was a steady paycheck.

A mill job promised other things as well: a regimented life, incredibly long hours, and a working environment that was noisy, hot, and polluted with lint. There were good things too: companionship of friends and peers, nearby shops for stylish clothes, a rich cultural life (lyceums, concerts, lectures, lending libraries, literary circles, theater) better than anything imaginable back home on the farm; also freedom from parents and community, pocket money for new clothes and other fine things, and the thrill of real earnings to take back home. Not a life for everybody—but a life freely chosen by thousands of young New England women.

For about twenty-five years (1830–1855) mill life at Lowell was almost exclusively a female life—with male overseers. Many workers were teenagers and most came, as did Sarah, from northern New England farms. The mill owners desired a predictable and compliant staff of workers (operatives, they were called) that worked together, lived together, and also dined and socialized and worshipped together, and followed the same rules. A perfect role for farm girls—so the Boston Associates and other mill owners thought—who had been born and raised among spinning wheels and hand looms on largely self-sufficient farms. The recruiters visited nearly every sizable rural community, put up posters announcing interviews, hired the young women, and arranged their transportation to Lowell, where they were met and conducted to their boardinghouses, usually four to a room, and shown the rules. In some cases the amenities of the boardinghouses were thought to be so excellent—fine tableware, nice furniture, piano, sitting room, books, periodicals—that the public was invited in to admire the facilities. By 1836 Sarah Shedd was one of about six thousand female workers in Lowell. Ten years later, one of ten thousand; and by the time of the Civil War, Lowell had the heaviest concentration of industry in America.

"Flowers from a Thousand Hillsides"

Gathered in such large numbers, the young women made a striking collection in more ways than one. The poet John Greenleaf Whittier, then living in Lowell, was dazzled by the sudden influx from the countryside: "Acres of girlhood, beauty reckoned by the square rod . . . the young, the graceful, the gay—the flowers gathered from a thousand hillsides and green valleys of New England . . . Sisters of Charity dispensing comfort and hope and happiness around many a hearthstone of your native hills!" Of course it was beauty and charity enacted at a certain price. The summer working day, including short breaks for food, was up to fourteen hours, slightly shorter in winter. Life was run by the factory bells: wake-up bell at 4:30 A.M.; enter the mills at 4:50; machines start at the five o'clock bell; work until the seven o'clock breakfast bell; to the boardinghouse and back at the machines again at 7:35; noon bell at 12:30; thirty-five minutes for lunch and back again by bell; then work with only short breaks until the evening bell at 7:00 P.M. Evenings were for reading, writing, socializing, but the curfew rang at 10:00, and it was lights out at 10:30. Although Saturday was sometimes just a half working day, some of these flowers, surely, had wilted by the weekend. Sunday was a day of rest, and attendance at church was required. For the week's work, seventy hours at least, Sarah received about $3.75, and food and lodging consumed $1.25 of that. This was widely regarded, by parents and operatives alike, as good wages.

Letters from those times testify to the high esprit de corps among these flowers from the hillsides, as they rapidly developed a new sense of companionship and community. An early and vivid example is this: by the mid-1830s the women were united in believing that their hours were too long, the machines running too fast, and the operatives responsible for too many of them at once. What could be done? There was a protest, then the firing of a ringleader, then a bold solidarity march through the city by other mill workers, a workers' rally and fiery speeches, finally a strike by more than eight hundred operatives. It was a brave and communal effort; but it soon fizzled. The women knew they could be dismissed for striking and be blacklisted, making them unemployable.

However, in 1836 when the owners threatened a wage cut, there was a larger strike; and this time the united operatives got a few concessions: wages were not cut, machines were not speeded up. Later, the mill workers formed the Lowell Female Labor Reform Association, and four thousand of them petitioned the Massachusetts legislature for a ten-hour day. Lowell's legislative representative opposed it, so the mill workers (who couldn't themselves vote, of course) lobbied the male voters and got him defeated in the next election. Still, the legislature as a whole was unmoved: there was no ten-hour law until 1874.

Was Sarah Shedd involved in any of this? The available records, which are slim enough, indicate that she was not among the ringleaders, but they don't tell us more. After her death a friend wrote: "She was a good conversationalist, and when she spoke everyone listened." Of course, she too would have found the work hours long and tedious, and the machines too many and too fast and too noisy, but from personal testimony speaking of her dignity and reserve, it appears that leading a raucous factory protest would not have been her style. Surely she would have offered thoughtful and wise counsel to the agitators, and then probably retired to work on her next literary composition.

Writer

This is the place in the tapestry where we must pick up the bright thread of the literary and intellectual efforts of the mill girls. Professor Peabody of Harvard, who lectured regularly at Lowell lyceums, reported in the *Atlantic Monthly* that four-fifths of his audience were factory girls, each one of them reading a book when he came in! And there were very few, he said, "who did not carry home full notes of what they had heard. I have never seen anywhere so assiduous note taking. No, not even in a college class . . . as in that assembly of young women." The *Lowell Offering*, a literary monthly (from 1841 to 1845) to which Sarah Shedd contributed, was distributed in Boston and Lowell and in other cities of New England, and within the many rural communities from which the girls originated; it was written and edited entirely by the mill workers or, as they called themselves on the title page, "Factory Girls."

Several things were unique here: never before in Europe or America had young women as a class, and in such numbers, been working together in a factory. Moreover, women didn't usually write for publication, and they certainly didn't normally edit publications. And these writers are just self-described factory girls! What is going on here? Charles Dickens, visiting from London, took home copies and then saluted the *Lowell Offering* in his book *American Notes*: "Putting out of sight the fact of the articles having been written by these girls after the arduous hours of the day—it will compare advantageously with a great many English annuals." President Felton of Harvard was in France and wrote that he had heard an entire lecture at the University of Paris devoted to—of all things!—the *Lowell Offering*, the point of which was to illustrate what women can do. Then a selection of *Offering* articles was published in book form in England. It may not be too much to say that this periodical made young women as a class historically visible for the first time, and not only as factory girls but also as budding young leaders and writers. In the 1840s there were at least seven self-improvement clubs in Lowell, and the *Lowell Offering* took its themes and its origins from such a society connected with a Lowell Universalist Church. Not surprisingly, some of the *Offering* stories were also thinly disguised critiques of mill life, a system that made the owners rich at heavy cost to young women.

Most alumnae of the *Lowell Offering*—most of Sarah Shedd's circle of friends—left the mills within a few years, and some went on to conspicuous careers: poets, missionaries, novelists, teachers, lecturers, artists. The best known of these was Lucy Larcom, friend of Whittier and author of *A New England Girlhood* (in print today) and other works. Eliza Jane Cate wrote five books, beginning with *The Rights and Duties of Mill Girls*, and Harriott F. Curtis wrote many essays for the *New York Tribune* and also five novels. Margaret Foley became a well-known sculptor, in Boston and Rome, while Harriet Farley wrote and lectured prolifically in New York, and Lydia S. Hall became a missionary among western Indians, keeper of a Temperance Inn, and briefly acting treasurer of the United States. Harriet Hanson Robinson became the author of the well-known mill memoir *Loom and Spindle* (in print today) as well as several other books, including the once-famous poetic drama *The New Pandora*. All this lay far in the future, of course, but such was the circle of friends that surrounded and stimulated Sarah Shedd in Lowell, as she blossomed among Whittier's "flowers gathered from a thousand hillsides."

Harriet Robinson tells us "Miss Shedd was not a prolific writer, and her contributions for *The Offering* were always of a serious nature." Most of the material in *The Offering* was published anonymously, or with a pseudonym, so it is impossible to pick out Sarah Shedd's particular work. This submerging of individual women's voices reflects again, perhaps, the very powerful sense of community among the mill girls; it may also testify to simple modesty on their part, unsure as they were of their reception, unsure of their talents, sometimes insecure about their lack of education.

In Sarah's book of poems, only a few are direct reflections of her life as a mill girl. Rather, many of her poems are centered in Washington, New Hampshire, naming and meditating on particular people, or fields, or lakes, on Draper Hill or Lovell Mountain. Even as she took her mind to Massachusetts, she left her heart in New Hampshire. From her Washington home she could glance northward across the village green, and right there loomed the stately town meeting-house. To that building she devoted the longest poem in the book, including such lyrical lines as these: "Our Pilgrim fathers loved their God; / Their worship was sincere; / So our forefathers knelt to him, / And built this temple here."

Teacher

Many of the young women left the mills before they were out of their twenties, and most of them married; but Sarah Shedd did not marry, and she came back to the mills year after year. By the 1850s the Lowell mills were hiring more and more immigrant families, especially Irish, and the *Lowell Offering* coterie had dispersed; so this was probably the time when Sarah herself moved on to the mills in Salem, New Hampshire, and then to Biddeford, Maine. Perhaps she wanted to enlarge her experience, encounter a new city, make new friends; but in summers she regularly returned to Washington, there to rejoin old friends and often to teach school. Maybe, going back and forth, she really felt she had the best of the only two worlds that were open to her.

Meanwhile, she developed in her hometown a reputation as an outstanding teacher. A Washington native and neighbor, Carroll Wright, who rose to the position of U.S. commissioner of labor (equivalent to secretary of labor today), remembered her as his first teacher. Wright came home to help dedicate the

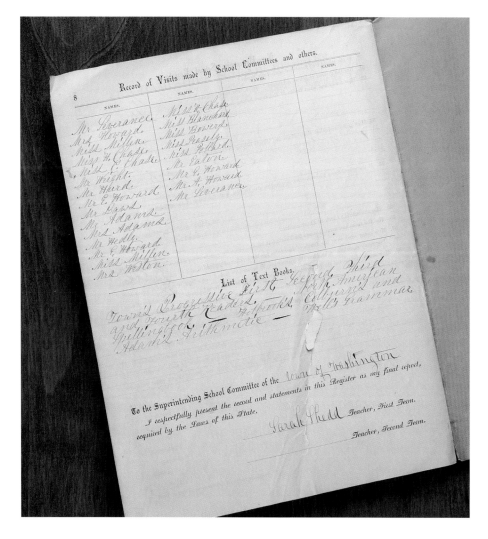

A report by Sarah Shedd on her year's teaching. "Her genial smile won the hearts of the children," said one of Sarah Shedd's students. "We longed for her coming, regretted her going."

new Shedd Free Library building fourteen years after her death and to share his reminiscences. He spoke of his childhood teacher in glowing terms: "The first school I ever attended was kept by her, in the front room of the store opposite the post office. Her genial smile won the hearts of the children. . . . We longed for her coming, regretted her going. . . . She wandered with us over the hills and fields, gave us instruction from her heart and mind, as well as from the books we used. . . . Her genial disposition lighted the pathway of many a boy and girl, and . . . make her memory as fragrant as spring flowers." She first taught school in 1828, and her pupil Carroll Wright, born in 1840, would not have gone to school until at least 1848; so we may conclude that she taught off and on for at least twenty years, and probably more. Wright thus speaks for generations of Washington students whose pathways she lighted.

Home to Stay

In 1858 Sarah finally left the mills for good and returned to Washington to care for her mother. A Ladies' Circle had earlier formed around the Universalist Society in Washington, and since Sarah was clearly someone special in town, it was natural that she be elected to office. Upon her return she was promptly made secretary. According to the constitution of the Ladies' Circle, the members felt "a deep and ardent interest in the cause of universal Grace and love," and believed that "by united effort, much can be accomplished that is not now done to disseminate these great principles abroad." Again the theme: lofty ideals and united effort. Essentially, this too was an improvement society, the sort of organization a Sarah Shedd would join on sight.

The first record book of the Ladies' Circle survives in the Washington town archives, and it shows that Sarah was not a typical secretary. The main activity of the Circle was sewing, knitting, making coats, vests, pants, pillowcases, rugs. Especially rugs. Innumerable meetings were devoted to cutting up rags for rugs! From her minutes: "For work—cut rags. For talk—amused ourselves with our own and others' short-comings." Another: "Cut rags for work. Rags seem to be eternal." Such a life for Sarah to come home to—she who had spent her life in textile mills! Her minutes as secretary show that the chatter and gossip at Circle meetings quickly bored her, and she records of one meeting: "Some useful hints on the medicinal uses of plants. How pleasant to record one useful thought." Then she decided to jot down the topics of conversation so that fifty years later people "might learn if the Circle, if it shall then exist, or the tone of conversation among ladies in general shall have risen, or whether among ladies in all times the world over it is 'chit-chat, laugh and grow fat.'" Undoubtedly, Sarah was thinking back fondly twenty years to her mill town social life and literary friends and to those exciting days when the *Lowell Offering* was first born.

Life in Washington may have been a bit of a trial, but Sarah Shedd was a resolute doer of good works, and after two years as secretary she summarized in her annual report (May 30, 1860) the year's accomplishments. In addition to sewing projects (dozens of coats, vests, and socks), they included refurbishing the Universalist worship space in the town meetinghouse, the removal of the remaining box pews, the installation of new risers. All this, Sarah noted, "will remain to aftertime a standing monument of the Industry and Perseverance of a few Ladies with no 'capital' but their hands to work and their heads to plan," and she felt assured that "that indomitable spirit, will not now leave us . . . but will continue . . . while there is left us anything to perfect or to beautify."

"Anything to perfect or to beautify"—a precise summary of her lifelong aspiration.

Shedd Free Library

It would be fully in character for Sarah Shedd, as she listened to the thin chatter of Circle meetings, to have thought: What this town really needs is not more quilts and vests, but a library. We need an open window and a larger loom, something that points us beyond our little Circle and our tattered rags and our local gossip. Good books, and the habit of discussing them, could be the center of attention in this town. It was a typical Sarah Shedd idea. Something to perfect and beautify—like the very minds and hearts around her.

A town library was so significant a project—and so unlikely—mainly because of the extremely high cost of books. In rural towns like Washington in the mid-nineteenth century, books were not a conspicuous part of the scene, and for good

The town needed not more quilts and vests, but a library, thought Sarah Shedd.

reason. At Sarah's mill wages, with maximum savings of two dollars per week, it would take a week's savings to buy one good book. At that time in Washington, New Hampshire, a man's working wage was a dollar a day, not enough to buy one book—even if the farmer were inclined to spend his cash that way. Accordingly, books were scarce luxuries in this and every other rural town. A public library in town with hundreds of books that could be freely borrowed by anybody was a spectacularly ambitious idea, beyond the dreams of all but the most idealistic, and certainly—the available town resources being so slim—far beyond anything ever contemplated in the town's budget.

Here was a project so bold and idealistic that nobody could expect to mobilize the community to create it from scratch. No, it would require heroic individual effort. Sarah nourished the plan silently and saved her money carefully, and not until a few weeks before she died did she put her design into her will. She left twenty-five hundred dollars to start a town library—not a building, but a collection of books—a sum that in today's terms would be worth at least two hundred thousand dollars.

The library project was launched almost immediately; a Library Committee was appointed whose first act would be to decide "that the library shall be known as the Shedd Free Library." Temporary rooms were found, books purchased, a librarian named, rules drawn up, books lent. In 1881 a former Washington boy who had become a man of means, Lumen Jefts, built and then donated a fine new brick building to house the growing library, and these were the events celebrated in 1883 with the publication of Sarah Shedd's poems. At that time her beloved library was reported to be over two thousand books strong. Since then, and for well over a century now, the library has splendidly served the purpose that Sarah envisioned.

Sarah Shedd was married, not to a man, but to doing good works with and for others. She was certainly in love with high ideals. Was she ever in love with another person? We cannot be sure, and no one has given us any direct evidence, but she may have left some hints. Her book of poems includes a short series of "Valentine Poems," love poems certainly, although the beloved is not identified. Poetic exercises? Or directed to a particular person? One poem begins: "I am still thy Valentine, / Bowing at no other shrine; / Of thy face I'm fondly thinking, / All thy love tones I am drinking; / Soul from soul no force can bar, / Witness I, from thee so far." And it concludes: "Hear me, thou to me most dear, / I have loved thee many a year; / When we sat beneath the willow, / Rested on the self-same pillow; / I have loved thee many a year, / Am I still to thee so dear?" If there is an untold personal story there, it is unlikely that we shall ever know it.

A Hillsborough friend wrote that Sarah "had a mind of great strength and versatility" and that "all snobbery and pretense seemed to retire before this really noble woman." A mill friend wrote that "Miss Shedd may be called the philanthropist par excellence, of the early mill girls. Her whole life was one of self-sacrifice." Ashbury Howe called her writings "brilliant yet modest, reflecting . . . the intrinsic excellence of her mind and character," and he referred to the Shedd Free Library as "the magnificent bequest of this noble, heroic, and truly gifted woman."

Such is the language which those who knew her best were disposed to use—noble, heroic, gifted, sainted. Editor Howe concluded his introduction to her poems by breaking out into his own verse about the Shedd Free Library: "Within these walls her angel form / Shall float on golden wings, / And feed the hungry soul on food / That sweet contentment brings. / O! Breathe her name in accents soft, / With reverence be it said; / We venerate that goodly name, / The sainted Sarah Shedd."

HOWARD MANSFIELD   # The Family History of Water

In hurricane season, Chick Colony pays attention to the weather in the Caribbean. Chick lives in Harrisville, New Hampshire. He's not interested in the local forecast; he's waiting for the end of the forecast when the weatherman sweeps his arm hundreds of miles south down the Atlantic seaboard where he points to a hurricane wheeling toward some small Caribbean island. When a hurricane starts tracking north, Chick heads out to the dam.

Chick's given name is John J. Colony III. No one calls him that, mostly because his father was John J. Colony, Jr., and the name is too formal. Four generations of his family ran the Cheshire Mills in Harrisville before it went out of business in 1970. When his father was in his eighties, Chick became the choreographer of the watershed. He also looks after the mill village of Harrisville, a handsome red-brick ensemble resembling a small liberal arts college. "The factory under the elms," as one historian called it, seems like an idealized picture of itself (even with only one surviving elm).

Whenever I visit I have a feeling of arriving after an evacuation. The tall mill

Waterland: The mill town of Harrisville.

buildings, shaped by technology, have the upright bearing of a thrifty, church-going, laconic New England. The buildings are austere, serious; the bell towers have authority.

It is reassuring to find these poised and graceful buildings calmly reflected in the water. It is like meeting a man of his word. But these mills, now turned to quieter purposes, are deceiving. Though we may not recognize it, Harrisville is a creation of moneymaking. We recognize such sites when we see the mills of Lowell, Ford Motor Company's River Rouge factory, or the cooling towers of a nuclear plant, but here we are fooled—just as we are fooled by Lake Nubanusit.

The outlet dam on Lake Nubanusit is a small thing. The floodgates are only three feet across. The top of the dam is 11.8 feet. Flashboards, old rough lumber, add another six inches. The gatehouse is a wooden shed, home to a few bats and some wasps.

Inside Chick looks down at the top of the dam, the new aluminum gates, and the old flashboards. There is a wheel on top that can be used to open the gates. He looks at a water-level gauge and the water running over the top. He pokes a long rod in and pulls it out. The rod is wet a handspan or more, about six inches. There is plenty of water flowing out. He has already removed a couple of flashboards, so he decides to leave everything alone for a while. He is like a baker testing a cake.

The gatehouse on Lake Nubanusit. One of the thousands of small New England dams, a legacy of the age of waterpower.

The errand and the warning seem mismatched. A storm hundreds of miles across, a thousand miles away, sends Chick a mile out of town over dirt roads to a hut the size of a toolshed where he might turn an old iron wheel as some bats look on. This is not the heroic dam—Hoover stopping the Colorado—that stars in encyclopedias and documentaries. This is just one of thousands of small New England dams, a legacy of the age of waterpower.

The act of adjusting the dam also seems a bit mismatched. Chick moves a board or two, or turns the wheel a little, and adjusts the water level for a watershed that includes hundreds of houses along the shores of several large ponds and lakes. It's as if by adjusting your television reception you were adjusting the world, and not a picture of the world.

Behind this small gatehouse lies a 715-acre lake, and flowing into that, attended by its own dam, a smaller 180-acre pond. These in turn flow a mile and a half through a great meadow toward a third pond and the third Colony dam.

Chick and his family own this water. Or rather they own the legal part of the water—the part of the water that is power, the part that isn't "wetness" or the loons, or the sunsets in the memories of generations of summer people. They own the *measure* of the water, the right to control it. This legal right trumps all other rights on the lake, and this makes some people angry. Everyone has an opinion about the water level on Nubanusit. There are file folders up in Concord at the Dam Bureau bulging with letters of complaint going back to 1938, petitions, and the records of hearings. The homeowners' association on the lake wants the lake's level high so their docks float. But those living at the end of the lake in the town of Nelson want it at a different level than those at the other end of the lake three and a half miles away in Hancock. The Audubon Society wants the water level held steady for the loons. One year the loons laid their eggs late and the Audubon asked Chick to delay lowering the lake.

The Colonys are keenly aware of the many claims on this water, and of what serious weather can do to all this fine-tuning. Chick, like his father, does not just see a lake or a brook—he sees a watershed. He sees water on the move from Spoonwood Pond and Lake Nubanusit to Harrisville Pond to Skatutakee Lake and on to the Goose Brook, which meets the Contoocook in Peterborough and then flows north to the Merrimack and finally the Atlantic. Few people know where the rain that runs off their roof is headed. (About a mile from the Harrisville mills in Nelson, two of the six major watersheds in New Hampshire touch. Parke Hardy Struthers at Merriconn Farm liked to say that a drop of rain falling on one side of the ridgepole was destined for the Connecticut River, and on the other side, the Merrimack. He combined the names for his farm.)

Chick has an eye for waterpower. He once told me that Keene—the "big city" nearby with a population of 22,500—would have been an ideal site for a large reservoir. An industrialist could have flooded twenty square miles of the valley and powered quite a large operation. I doubt that anyone else has ever cast an antediluvian eye on Keene and seen the broad Main Street, the Civil War statue in Central Square, and the white spire of the First Church under water.

But our era values waterfront, not waterpower. When confronted with the idea that someone owns the water of their beloved summer place, ordinary red-meat, free-hand-of-the-marketplace Republicans are befuddled. Who can own the water? Some hidden tree-hugger rises up in them. They think this fine long pond was the work of God, not the Harrises and Colonys, whose dams created the lake they know. They believe it to be Eden. But Lake Nubanusit is an industrial reservoir. Each day they swim or canoe in an early nineteenth-century version of the coal heap and the cooling tower. Water was power, not recreation.

In this small watershed are the echoes of the nineteenth-century fights over water rights. Everyone has a claim. Chick has inherited a waterpower kingdom in the age of the leisure economy. Owning water—three dams in this case—is all liability. That's what sends Chick out to the dam on a sunny fall day—the liability of history: the memories of the great New England Hurricane of 1938.

I. 'Thirty-eight and After

"We get into September, we see any rain at all, we open our gates just as fast as we can," Chick's father, John, told me a few years before he died. There are three large ponds and three smaller ponds "above us," he said, listing, in addition to Spoonwood and Nubanusit, Shadrach, Tenney, Tolman, and Harrisville Ponds. "They all come together in Harrisville. If you fly over this area, you'd be astounded by how many lakes and ponds there are involved. It's a good watershed. It gets a lot of good storage—there's a lot of snowfall. You see, we're at an altitude of seventeen hundred feet and snowfall lasts, builds up all winter. It is quite unusual to see that many lakes in a smaller area."

On its short journey from Lake Nubanusit through Harrisville to Peterborough, nine miles, the Goose Brook falls six hundred feet. (On most maps today it's the Nubanusit Brook, but the Colonys stick to the old name.) In 1870 the brook powered eight mills employing more than nine hundred workers. From the air, the brook is hard to distinguish. You wouldn't select it as a route for a lazy canoe trip, let alone associate it with the word "power." It meanders like a newsboy's paper route. Yet in the time before there were towns and water rights, the brook fell through a steep ravine in a way wild enough to discourage the first white settlers. In the lottery to distribute the land for the town-in-the-making known as Monadnock Number Three, John Usher had the misfortune to draw Range 10, Lots 13 and 14, the ravine's location. There was no place to farm; there was scarcely a level place for a plow. He gave up the wasteland that would become Harrisville.

The Colonys had the waterpower appraised by an expert in 1903. John Humphrey, a turbine builder, considered these highland lakes and ponds to be "perhaps the best and most reliable water power of its size, to be found in New England or elsewhere." With many ponds in a small area, the ratio of land to water is four to one. A typical watershed has a twenty to one ratio. John called it a "flashy" watershed—a sudden storm could catch the Colonys with the reservoirs too full, and the damage downstream could be tremendous. An increase of one foot in the level of Nubanusit will, when released, raise Harrisville Pond three feet. Humphrey issued a warning:

> Permit me to call your attention to the great risk incident to entering upon a season of heavy rainfall with the Nubanusit Lake nearly or quite filled—as by so doing the stream is not only returned to its primitive uncontrollable turbulence, but has an additional element of danger in the probability of a breakage of the dam, which would let loose a body of water likely to do much damage at Harrisville and other places on the stream. . . . For this reason it is much safer and better to have the pond three feet below high water mark in September.

Water has a family history in Harrisville. "Abel Twitchell lived in that white house right over there, the first house in town, just restored. Started a sawmill village and used the waterfall here," said John as he sat in his house on Harrisville Pond. "He and his brother owned all the lots around this lake. So there was no formality of having to buy the water rights from all the others. They owned it all just by owning the whole lake. That was about 1790 that water was first used."

From the back porch of John's house, the view straight up the pond shows no other houses. The porch looks north to where the Goose Brook enters the pond after its trip from the outlet dam on Lake Nubanusit. It's like some deep woods' view—another deception in a state that had once managed to be both industrial and rural. Close by, visible from a side window, is Chick's brick house. "Bethuel Harris, by the way, when he came here from Providence, he married Twitchell's daughter and built that house right there," John said, pointing to Chick's house. "His sons built these other brick houses around. This was Cyrus Harris's house, and he was the oldest brother. Milan Harris is across the street." He finished the tour by noting the houses of the other sons. This was John Colony's neighborhood.

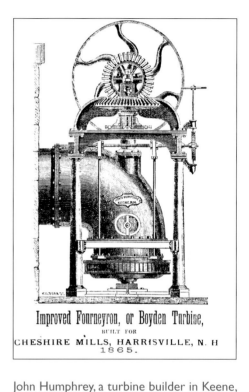

Improved Fourneyron, or Boyden Turbine,
BUILT FOR
CHESHIRE MILLS, HARRISVILLE, N. H
1865.

John Humphrey, a turbine builder in Keene, thought Harrisville fortunate to have "perhaps the best and most reliable water power of its size, to be found in New England, or elsewhere."

On green, eye-ease ledger paper, John had drawn up a corporate flowchart, little rectangular boxes linked with lines to show a true accounting of who owned the water rights, from top to bottom, a cascade of names falling like water.

"These are all the deed references," he said, starting with Breed Batchelder in 1762. "And so it came down through Bethuel Harris to Milan Harris, who had that mill right there, and Cyrus Harris, who lived here and built the stone mill." The chart continues to the Colonys' Cheshire Mills, and after that, John Colony. "These things go right down through the generations like any other piece of property," he said. (And "just like any woodlot or house," dams are taxed.)

"My family was in the textile business in Keene: Faulkner & Colony. That started around 1815. Equal partnership between two families." About thirty-five years later, the Colonys were looking for a new mill. "Cyrus Harris decided to separate from the other Harrises, started another mill. He built the stone mill down here, the Granite mill. And unfortunately, or fortunately for us, I guess, just about the time this brand new empty mill was finished, he died. What they called consumption in those days. Tuberculosis. So my family, independently of their partners in Keene, came over here and bought this brand-new, empty stone mill. Brought new machinery and machined it up.

"When my family came and bought this mill here, everybody needed more power. And so my family, with the covenants of the others, but independently financed, went up and put a dam in Spoonwood. And that added to the storage for the dry month of August. They went around and paid all the farmers around the lake for the privilege of raising the water up to a certain fixed point." The land was mostly meadows and cow pastures.

"Nubanusit was just a series of three smaller lakes. They gradually raised the dams; they needed more power. Of course the more they raised them, the higher the level went and the more the storage was. That was quite an incentive—it was a prospering industry—to develop that capacity and height.

"It was a help to all these other mills. The Harrises still ran that mill and there was another Harris, who had some partners, ran the mill down the hill. At one time there were four or five users right in a row here in Harrisville. Somebody dumped the water from his turbine, it went down to the next guy, and the next guy." In dry times the mills squabbled with each other, sometimes in court; in flood times the mills were sued by farmers for lost pasture, and by the town for submerged roads.

Harrisville ran on water, but the town was created by the railroad. The village that grew up around the mills straddled the town line between Dublin and Nelson. (The line ran right through Chick's house.) When the farmers in those towns refused to subscribe to the new railroad coming through, Milan Harris, with the swift aid of the state legislature, created Harrisville in 1870, taking with him part of the other two towns. Harrisville was "railroaded" into existence.

In John's telling, all of Harrisville's history was contemporary. "My family came over here, to Harrisville, in 1852," he said. "There was one farmer that didn't sell us the water rights in the 1860s. Breed Batchelder, the first owner of the water rights, was a Tory; he didn't last long around here," he said, making it sound as if

Opposite: Water was power; water was wealth. Owning the water was important to mill owners. Eben C. Tolman was one of a dozen who sold the right to build a dam and raise the water level on Long Pond (Nubanusit) to the Cheshire Mills in the late 1860s.

Know all Men by these Presents, That I Eben C. Tolman

of Nelson in the County of Cheshire and State of New-Hampshire, for and in consideration of the sum of Thirty Six Dollars, to me in hand, before the delivery hereof, well and truly paid by The Cheshire Mills a corporation duly established by law the receipt whereof I do hereby acknowledge, have given, granted, bargained, sold, and by these presents do give, grant, bargain, sell, alien, enfeoff, convey, and confirm, unto the said Grantees and their and assigns, forever, the right and privilege of causing and maintaining at the outlet in Nelson of Long Pond, so called a permanent tight dam and flume, the top of which shall be upon a level with an iron driven into a hole drilled in a stone at their present dam, near the gate house, and two irons driven into holes drilled in a large stone on the shore of said pond, about twenty six rods north of the west end of said dam and of flowing by means of such dam so much of the lands here in after described belonging to me as will be flowed in conse- quence of erecting and maintaining said dam, at the height above stated. Viz. a certain tract of land lying in said Nelson and Hancock between land belonging to said Corporation and lands of Benjamin Derby lying on the easterly shore of said Pond —

I also give, grant, bargain, sell and convey, unto the said Cheshire Mills, the right and privilege at any time of drawing off the water from said lands, until the surface of said pond shall be eleven feet and ten inches below the irons above mentioned. —

To HAVE and to HOLD the said granted premises, with all the privileges and appurtenances to the same belonging, to the said Grantees and their and assigns, to _____ and their only proper use and benefit forever. And I the said Grantor my heirs, executors, and administrators, do hereby covenant, grant, and agree, to and with the said Grantees and their and assigns, that until the delivery hereof I am the lawful owner of the said premises; am seized and possessed thereof in my own right, in fee simple; and have full power and lawful authority to grant and convey the same in manner aforesaid; that the said premises are free and clear of all and every incumbrance whatsoever.

And that I the said Grantor my heirs, executors, and administrators, shall and will warrant the same to the said Grantees and their and assigns, against the lawful claims and demands of any person or persons whomsoever.

And I, the subscriber, wife of the Grantor, for the consideration aforesaid, do hereby release to the said Grantees my right of dower in the premises, my homestead right, and all other my right and interest therein.

WITNESS our hands and seals, this twentieth day of August Anno Domini one thousand eight hundred and sixty six

"Operatives" at the Cheshire Mills, c. 1890. Around 150 operatives produced woolens, flannels, suedes, and fleeces at Mill Number One.

a moving van—Tory Vanlines—had come for Batchelder recently. Of some other mill owners who were early partners of the Harrises, he said, "They were strangers around here." In a phrase, John Colony could take you from 1763 and Breed Batchelder to 1970, when his family's mill closed.

He took the long view. Once he was going through a stack of legal deeds with his lawyer. The deeds had been found in an old strongbox.

"When was this deed passed?" the lawyer asked.

"Fifty-three," said John.

"Fifty-three?" asked the lawyer. "Fifty-three—I was your lawyer in '53. I don't remember that."

"Eighteen fifty-three," said John.

When Chick asked him what he thought about Pat Buchanan's run in the 1996 New Hampshire presidential primary, John said, "One President Buchanan is enough." (Back in 1856 the Democratic Colonys had welcomed President James Buchanan's victory. Celebrating mill workers had fired a cannon at rival Republican Milan Harris's mill, breaking some windows. When Milan protested, the "Buchanan boys" punched him, or so went Milan's case in court.)

At the start of the twentieth century, John's father, John, Sr., would take the early morning train from Keene, arriving in Harrisville at 5:45 a.m. On dark winter mornings he would nap on a cot in his office until the waterpower was turned on at 7:00 a.m. A thrifty Yankee wouldn't start the wheels turning just for his own use.

Thrift was a steady habit. As late as 1945, the company did not employ stenographers or bookkeepers. The Colonys did their own paperwork by hand. The

Keene and Harrisville offices had no typewriters. (And there was no telephone in the Harrisville office before 1928.) The mills and the workers' boardinghouse were known for their cleanliness.

John began working in the mill in 1937 after Harvard and a European tour with his friends. He had wanted to go to Harvard's business school for a year, but his father was getting on in years at age seventy-three, and he thought it prudent to stay home and learn the mill business. He spent two months working in the different departments of the woolen mill, including the carding room, the dye house, and the spinning room. "I got to be a pretty good mule spinner," he said. He has a strong affection for the machinery and the cloth. "They were beautiful fabrics. And they were tough, really tough," he said, recalling the cloth they made for major league baseball team uniforms. After his apprenticeship he was put in charge of a payroll of up to 450 employees, which was paid out weekly in cash brought in on the train from Keene.

As a mill owner, John continued the Colonys' practical tradition. He was a "hands-on manager" long before the business schools burdened us with that term, fixing broken machinery and repairing the mills. His sons were required to work summer maintenance jobs at the mills. One summer his son George was painting a building when he saw his father, then sixty years old, way up on the cupola of a mill. John had tied a ladder to one of the posts and climbed up with a paint can tied to his belt. He believed that it was too dangerous for anyone else.

In John's second year at work, the hurricane of September 21, 1938, hit; the Goose Brook flooded Harrisville as Humphrey had warned thirty-five years earlier. All that water "above" the town was coming their way. It had been raining for two weeks before the hurricane. "There were tremendous floods everywhere. We'd been watching Harrisville—the lakes were full, the floodgates were open, and the water was still coming up," said John. Nelson's road agent saw the wind driving twelve-foot waves over the Nubanusit dam. On one side of the lake, 80 percent of the trees were blown down. "We were doing all we could to get the water through. Of course it had to pass under the mill. We used sand bags to bolster up the banks. Water was going around both ends of the Harris mill, it was wiping out the roads down below, and going in the windows of the Granite mill. It was pretty bad."

It was far worse downstream in Peterborough. "Right in the middle of that hurricane they called us up and wanted to know if we could stop the flow of water from Harrisville. Peterborough begged us to close the floodgates because they were having so much trouble." There was nothing John could do.

"What you have to remember first is that nobody expected anything to happen," said Everett S. Allen, who saw the hurricane in New Bedford, Massachusetts. Disasters were something that happened in faraway places where people "built their houses out of straw." The hurricane arrived without preamble, without forecast or hype.

There's never been a hurricane in these latitudes, people said: it's a line storm, a three-days' blow at the equinox. In Rhode Island they had lunch and watched the surf crash, and sent their children back to school. It can't happen here, people said.

Hour by hour, the hurricane remade New England, each town a variation of wind and flood, and occasionally fire. "Keene [New Hampshire] is a shambles. Its elms were its pride. Today they are its sorrow," Ralph G. Page wrote in his diary. Thousands of big trees were down in the city. "Wheelock Park looks like the Argonne forest. Its beautiful pines are piled like huge jackstraws. . . . Cut off from the rest of the world except by short wave radio, Keene is a world by itself tonight."

In Peterborough, the Goose Brook raced into the Contoocook. "I was shocked at the size of the little Contoocook—no longer the gentle, reedy stream where I had fished as a kid, but a veritable Missouri—turgid, yellow, hissing and muttering downstream," said Edwards Park. He had walked into town with his father on errands. His father, too, had thought this was a line storm.

The Contoocook jumped its banks, flooding Main Street, and the town started to burn. The fire began in a granary. "Great clouds of flying debris, all in flame," pushed by the wind, burned down three blocks. Firefighters ran with a slack hose through the flooded street. "Gripping the hose, the gang charged the surging flood. It swept them cleanly off their feet, one by one, and hurled them downstream, and we watched aghast," said Park. They tried and were knocked down again before they got the hose through. The firefighters stood in floodwater up to their hips all night. The fire threatened the entire town.

The day after was sky blue, perfect—like heaven, people said. "I remember on that day how spent one emerged, how quiet people were, as nature was finally

A sudden disaster in a time of great troubles, the 1938 hurricane hit Peterborough hard. Main Street flooded and the town began to burn.

quiet, and how incredible it was, not only that the storm was over, but that it could have occurred at all," said Everett S. Allen.

The world had changed overnight, and it would change again. Hurricanes could invade New England. "We thought we were safe in our cold north from their furies. It will take us a long time to recover our faith in the security of the northland," said Cornelius Weygandt. The 1938 hurricane was one of the worst disasters in American history, surpassing the San Francisco earthquake in death, injury, and destruction.

Three days after the hurricane, the *Keene Evening Sentinel* published an emergency edition, printed on a press rigged to a gas engine. In four pages of news about the wrecked and isolated city, the back page had a bulletin from the Associated Press: "War Appears Inevitable." Prime Minister Neville Chamberlain's appeasement talks with Hitler were failing. "France, Russia, Germany and Czechoslovakia are reported ready to enter the conflict immediately." A week later, Hitler was allowed to seize part of Czechoslovakia; the world would at be war within a year.

II. Leisure Power

After the flood, after the war: peacetime, summertime. More than sixty years gone by, a new century. Two young men in their late twenties were portaging their canoe over the dam at Spoonwood Pond. Their talk turned to the man who owned the dam. "All he talks about is the hurricane of '38," one of them said. "Thirty-eight. Thirty-eight." His friend answered him, "You should've been out in the woods with John," a trapper and tracker. "He was always talking about it: 'In '38 this was all blown down; in '38 nothing was standing. You should've seen this in '38.'" The pond sparkled in the summer morning. They looked around as if to say, what's the big deal?

Waterpower, having changed our entire landscape, is nearly invisible to modern observers. Waterpower created Lake Nubanusit, but leisure power now stakes its claim and the mill legacy is all but forgotten.

After World War I, the Cheshire Mills began to retire its waterpower. Electricity arrived in 1924, but water supplied two-thirds of the mills' power until 1947. The mills closed in 1970, a bleak year for the textile industry; fifty-four other New England mills closed that year. (There were 95,000 broadlooms in the United States at one point. "We figured if it ever got to 20,000, the industry would be stabilized. So we patiently waited," said John. "It got down to 5,000 looms—it wasn't damn hot then.") In March 1971, *Yankee* magazine's usual "House for Sale" article featured Harrisville as a "Town for Sale." The Colonys and their friends began Historic Harrisville, preserving the village not as a museum theme park but by finding compatible businesses for the empty mills.

The Cheshire Mills had closed, but the Colonys still owned the water. (By deed, the Colonys own the right to draw 11 feet 10 inches. The deed defines full pond as 13 feet 1 inch.) This deed was contested in a battle between leisure power and waterpower. It was a kind of civil Hatfield and McCoy feud, with a New England cold defiance substituted for gunfire. Petitioning the state for a hearing on the lake's level in 1977, the Nubanusit Lake Association said: "Our specific complaint is as follows: the level of the water of the lake varies considerably and in an erratic fashion during the months of June through October when the lake is used for recreational purposes and as a water supply for cottages on its shores." Or as one petitioner wrote, "We have been on the lake since 1950 and the water level has been most annoying these 26 years." Add to this letters complaining of John Colony's "seemingly irrational control" of the lake, and suggestions that he was a fading Yankee king holding onto to the dam as his "last vestige of power."

John Colony's answer was patient, direct, and a little biting: "The basic problem is that Spoonwood and Nubanusit are very large lakes in an extremely small watershed, and as such, approach very nearly the function of true reservoirs and not the unchanging lakes of great beauty that all newcomers feel that they have discovered." This was his answer in each decade.

Before the last public hearings about the lake's level in 1993, the lake association surveyed its members, asking them to check one of the following:

—I prefer the seasonal level range from 11'9" to 12'6"
  —Other (Please specify) _____
—I prefer winter level to be 11' or above
  —Other (Please specify) _____
—I would like to see the seasonal level continue until October 15 rather than September 15 [favored by the majority]

The lake association and the Colonys were not living in the same place. They had two different conceptions of the landscape. The map the cottage dwellers along Nubanusit would draw and the one John or Chick would draw were different. For a half century the debate had been the same. I say lake and you say reservoir. I say natural and you say man-made. I say float my boat until Labor Day and you say 1938.

These days peace has broken out. Chick talks weekly with a member of the lake association who monitors the water level. In September 2003, when Hurricane Isabel began to gather in the Caribbean, Chick was regretting his decision to leave the water level at full pond. "I couldn't reach my consultant, who was no doubt out swimming or boating, so I decided to start drawing down the pond in a hurry. Later that night he called, and I braced myself for his question: why was I letting so much water go so fast? I was surprised when he nervously asked if I thought the gates were open enough. Clearly, he had his eye on the Caribbean too. In the end, Hurricane Isabel turned out well for us and poorly for North Carolina."

But Chick knows what his father knew. In 1635, 1815, and 1938 great tropical hurricanes ripped into New England. Historians of hurricanes say that New England can expect five to ten hurricanes a century, and a serious 1938-size storm every 150 years. It won't be the same, of course, but a hurricane with the power of 1938 will happen again.

"Plant Your Apples on the Hills"

JANE BROX

Though no more than a handful of apple orchards still stand in the Monadnock region, they once held familiar ground on the slopes between valley towns and the wild. May blossoms floating in a milky dusk were both a heart-lifting and common sight, as were the laden August branches, and the bare crowns of the January trees glinting in a cold sun. Only fifty years ago there were so many to be seen along the area's back roads that the Monadnock Region Association in Peterborough advertised apple blossom tours in the New York and Boston newspapers, and local papers printed suggested routes: "In Greenville Route 123 from Mason passes right through an apple section. Further north on the same route a tour leaves the main road to wind up the wooded country road to Clover Hill Farms in Wilton. Between Milford and Wilton signs will lead across the Souhegan River to the McLeod orchards in Milford. From here the drive goes up the hills to Parker Farms just over the town line in Lyndeboro, then on to the highest

The first trading in apples was local. "The winter is long and cold; the summer short and uncertain," said an agricultural report. In orchards like this one in Peterborough, farmers pruned and picked their trees and pressed cider.

elevation, turning back down past Hampshire Hills Farm into Wilton. Off Route 101 between West Wilton and Peterboro, another tour leads over a good country road to the Barry Orchards in Temple township. Next suggestion is to drive back over to the village of Temple where a route goes out the Temple-Sharon Road to the Davis Orchards."

The way apple orchards were planted in ordered rows across high slopes, which made for a sea of blossoms in plain view, was surely part of the draw for tourists, though—as befits a New England farm—all that beauty was a consequence of the practical. "If your farm is in a valley I would not advise the apple business," exhorted an early twentieth-century promoter of apple cultivation. "Look to the hills, the hills of New Hampshire, plant your apples on the hills." High land assured good air circulation, which encouraged a healthier tree, and frost comes later to the slopes than to the low places. Even more particularly, thinking farmers preferred not to plant their early varieties on a south- or west-facing slope, which might warm up too early and present a danger of freeze during May blossom time. They chose hills that offered protection from the wind.

Such conscientiousness in the siting of orchards came late to apple culture in the region. The first settlers wouldn't have given the placement of their trees much thought. Apples had been established in the English countryside by the seventeenth century—they are an old crop, thought to have originated in Kazakhstan—and the earliest trees came to the New World with the first settlers who planted them, not for market, but for family use. They'd set a tree or two beside a fence or in a corner where it provided shade for grazing sheep and cattle that often browsed the lower branches. They might plant a small orchard, but not in the precise rows and blocks our modern eye is accustomed to. Henry David Thoreau described them as having "rows so devious that you would think that they not only had grown while the owner was sleeping, but had been set out by him in a somnambulic state."

A farmer would not have pruned his trees in those early years, nor would he have made any attempt to control the many pests that afflict apples. There simply wouldn't have been time on a mostly self-sufficient homestead that depended on the children and women of the household for labor. The fruit would have been indifferent, uneven, nameless. The trees would have been supplied from a neighboring farmer, or grafted or transplanted from the wild. They were growing everywhere in the wild, sprouting up from pomace heaps or from seed dropped by birds, and each seed would produce an unpredictable fruit since apples don't sprout true from seed—a tree must be grafted to be identical to its parent. We would not think much of the quality of those first fruits.

Apples were used primarily to make cider, though not the cider we now buy at farm stands and supermarkets, which is simply juice. Colonial cider was always fermented. A farmer might sell a bit of his store locally, but most of it was consumed by the household, drunk at every meal: men downed a good tall glass of it before beginning the work of the day, and children drank it in a watered-down state. What apples weren't used for cider were dried for winter use. Women painstakingly pared and sliced barrels of apples and strung them by the fire or in drying sheds. In winter neighbors gathered together for evenings of paring apples.

As the eastern colonies became more established, apple growing became a more conscientious enterprise. Farmers began to select seedlings, working over time to produce better-flavored varieties with good keeping qualities. Some set out trees specifically to raise stock for sale, and within a short time innumerable seedling orchards stretched across the eastern United States creating, as one commentator has said, "one of the greatest—though largely unintentional—breeding experiments ever conducted." Legendary varieties, known more self-consciously in our time as "antique apples," came from those orchards, the oldest being the Roxbury Russet, established in 1649. Others, so popular in the eighteenth and nineteenth centuries, are mostly gone from common knowledge today: Ben Davis, Northern Spy, Porter, Rhode Island Greening, Sutton, Sweet Winesap, Tolman Sweet, Twenty Ounce, Wagener, Wealthy, Westfield-Seek-No-Further, Wolf River, Williams-Ladys Apple. Perhaps the most important for the Monadnock region was the Baldwin—a crisp juicy storage apple, tart, flavorful for cider—first developed in Wilmington, Massachusetts, around 1740. In his *History of Peterborough, New Hampshire*, George Morison notes that the first Baldwin tree in town was planted around 1765 by Gustavus Swan on land that is now part of Upland Farms. The Baldwin was to keep its primacy in the region into the twentieth century.

Even as orchards began to be more deliberately set out, trees continued to thrive in the wild and on the old grounds of homesteads that had been abandoned. Though farming was still the common life, by the mid–nineteenth century New England agriculture was already in decline. The West, with its richer soils, had opened up, and the cities were drawing children away from the country. During that time Thoreau, in his corner of New England, encountered "fruit of old trees that have been dying ever since I was a boy and are not yet dead, frequented only by the woodpecker and the squirrel." In his vibrant, enthusiastic essay "Wild Apples," you can feel the significance New England's first—and some might say only—fruit had for the day. Thoreau loved the way apple trees were scattered through the countryside, remnants of a time "when vast straggling cider-orchards were planted, when men both ate and drank apples, when the pomace-heap was the only nursery, and trees cost nothing but the trouble of setting them out. Men could afford then to stick a tree by every wall-side and let it take its chance."

"In 1836," he continues, "there were in the garden of the London Horticultural Society more than fourteen hundred distinct sorts. But here are species which they have not. . . . There is, first of all, the Wood Apple (*Malus sylvatica*); the Blue-Jay Apple; the Apple which grows in Dells in the Woods (*sylvestrivallis*), also in Hollows in Pastures (*campestrivallis*); the Apple that grows in an old Cellar-Hole (*Malus cellaris*); the Meadow Apple; the Partridge Apple; the Truant's Apple (*cessatoris*), which no boy will every go by without knocking off some, however *late* it may be; the Saunterer's Apple, —you must lose yourself before you can find the way to that; the Beauty of the Air (*decus aeris*); December-Eating; the Frozen-

Thawed (*gelato-soluta*), good only in that state." But Thoreau also believed that the day of the wild apple was almost gone. "Now that they have grafted trees, and pay a price for them," he writes, "they collect them into a plat by their houses, and fence them in, —and the end of it all will be that we shall be compelled to look for apples in a barrel."

Wild apples have never entirely disappeared from the Monadnock region, though apples in a barrel were to become an important commodity as agriculture moved away from self-sufficiency and took its place in the market economy of a nation that was steadily becoming more and more industrialized. The first trading in apples was local. In *Transactions of the New Hampshire State Agricultural Society* for the years 1850, 1851, and 1852 it is noted: "In a foreign market New Hampshire has hardly a fair chance. Her soil is for the most part hard and unproductive, save by expensive tillage. The climate is unfavorable for some important crops. The winter is long and cold; the summer short and uncertain. The great hope of the farmer must be in a home market. To accomplish this for himself, he must encourage the mechanical industry around him. He must give his patronage to home manufactures. He must offer inducements to the various branches of trade, and labor to settle around the many waterfalls, that dash and foam among our 'Crystal Hills.'"

The primary early market for apples was cider, the producers of which bought apples from small local farmers. In his Peterborough history George Morison notes that John Quincy Adams built a cider mill at his farm on the Old Dublin Road: "For years the old pomace was dumped along the road into neat piles on the south side and could be seen year after year, as an advertisement of what was done there each fall. . . . Cider was big business in Peterborough in those days. In 1870 there were six cider mills which altogether produced 3,290 barrels of cider. J. Q. Adams was the leader with 940, John Cragin made 750, John H. Vose 600, Charles Barber 425, L. McClenning 350, and E. A. Robbe 225." But the temperance movement that swept across the United States in the nineteenth century was to greatly affect cider production. By 1886 fewer than a thousand barrels of cider were produced in the region.

The end of large-scale cider production did not mean the end of trade. The railroad had opened up more distant markets to New Hampshire farmers, and by the latter nineteenth century Monadnock-region apples were being shipped to St. Paul, Cincinnati, Cleveland, and overseas to England. Morison observes: "Dalphon Osborn was called the Apple King in the 1880s and 1890s and bought direct from the farmers, shipping them in barrels all over the country. In 1888 he shipped from Peterborough over 3,000 barrels which he bought at $1 apiece from the producers. Most of these were shipped by steamer to Liverpool. Four years later over 5,000 barrels were shipped by freight, mostly to western cities."

The Monadnock region, close to Boston and New York, was well positioned to take advantage of closer markets, too, which grew as the urban population on the East Coast swelled. The demand for apples was constant and large—in one late nineteenth-century year the Gloucester fishing fleet alone used thirty-seven tons of dried apples to feed its 4,300 fisherman—and the market seemed bright with promise. The Boston & Maine Railroad, a significant booster for the apple industry, published a pamphlet for prospective growers. "There are no opportunities anywhere in America as bright as the horticultural possibilities of planting the apple on the Hills of New Hampshire," it claims. "In the first place the soil and the climate are at least equal to those of any other section of the country. In a large way they are superior, but on top of that we are right down in the northeastern corner of the United States, where the people live who have got the money."

No matter the market demand, the Monadnock region continued to suffer from a general decline in farming, which became even more rapid in the early twentieth century. In 1860 there were 2,757 farms in Cheshire County. By 1900 2,660 remained; by 1920, 1,625. Paul Gates, in a study of farming in Gilsum, tracked the decline: "In the 1880's thirteen out of the twenty-three towns . . . showed declining population. In the 90's sixteen suffered losses, and in the first two decades of the 20th Century, nineteen towns were similarly affected." He observes how difficult it was to continue in the face of such decline, or to interest new farmers in taking over abandoned holdings that had rapidly fallen into decay, the fields becoming overgrown with brush: "The accumulating effect of a shrinking tax base worsened the plight of those farmers trying to continue their struggle with land that was not returning a fair income. Part time farming was increasingly resorted to. This is clear evidence that many were aware that the pursuit of agriculture in Gilsum offered little promise. Neither was there much promise of selling the farms for anything like the costs in labor and capital that had been put into them."

In the face of such decline, the New Hampshire Department of Agriculture held out hope that large commercial apple culture could keep further abandonment at bay. The New England soil and the climate did produce a fine-flavored apple in general, and apples don't require level loamy soil to thrive; they could occupy the steeper lands of the Monadnock region. The challenge was to bring the apple grower into the modern world, especially as regards the quality of the fruit: the pest-afflicted, indifferent apples that had been adequate for the home and the local cider mill were not adequate for the urban market. The Department urged farmers to prune their trees, which would produce large, more consistent fruit, and to dust them for pests, particularly scab, which was endemic in New Hampshire orchards. Would that they all could have been as conscientious as William Putnam of Hancock: "During the past fifteen years I have planted upwards of twenty acres with apples, part of which was on sprout land that I cleared. A grower can rest assured that New Hampshire apples, grown, graded and packed scientifically and honestly will meet any competition."

But there's evidence that the job of raising the quality of the apple crop was a long and arduous task. In 1910, Frank West Rollins, a former governor of the state, knew the work it would entail, and he addressed it in article on the abandoned farm: "I want to say just one word about fruit, and especially apples. There is no place in the known world where you can raise better flavored apples than in New Hampshire. Mind you, I am not saying we do raise them now, but we can. . . . A tour throughout the state will show you just why we don't raise them. The New Hampshire farmer looks upon the apple as he does upon the blueberry, or the wild raspberry, —as a casual thing that the good Lord has sent along and which He (the Lord) takes care of or not. . . . The farmer . . . never husbands the trees, never trims, never grafts. You can see thousands of these neglected orchards in a day's drive."

Along with specific care, the Department of Agriculture encouraged farmers to concentrate on a few recommended varieties. The broader market was also a more narrow one, and the endless choices of the early years were a liability. Those marketing apples to city dwellers wanted dependable, familiar varieties. In the early twenties, the Baldwin was still the most popular commercial apple, though the McIntosh was gaining favor. The Department also suggested growing Wealthy, Gravenstein, Rhode Island Greening, Delicious, Wagener, and Northern Spy. The broader market soon made its choices, and the Baldwin eventually lost its primacy. It was a fine apple for the local world: it stood up to long storage and was perfect for cooking. But the McIntosh, with its smooth skin and red blush, had greater eye appeal, it ripened early, and its flesh was tender and its skin was crisp, which made it ideal for eating out of hand.

Commercial orchards were firmly established on the hills of the Monadnock region by the early decades of the twentieth century. Upland Farms, where one of the first McIntosh orchards in the state was planted, was considered a commercial orchard by the early 1930s. As for the Baldwin, it had already begun to lose favor when a freeze in 1934 killed many of the New Hampshire trees both in the larger commercial orchards and in the smaller orchards on general farms. Haydn Pearson, whose father had such a farm in Hancock, recollected in his book *That Darned Minister's Son* that until that freeze the orchard had been the backbone of their farm's economy.

Perhaps the most significant moment concerning apples in Pearson's memoir is in this memory of his father pruning: "If I were to choose which mental picture of Father means the most to me (outside of his preaching) I would take the one of a typical winter day when Father was pruning in the orchard. The hills and fields white with snow, the temperature below freezing, blue jay and chickadees calling. I see Father now, standing in the snow, pruning saw in hand, studying the tree so he could prune it to the shape he wanted." How different from the early settlement farmer who set a tree by a wall and let it take its chance. It seems the New Hampshire Department of Agriculture had succeeded; apple growing had become associated with deliberate care and the idea of order. Part-time farmers could become philosophical about the practice. "A man needs to pause occasionally when near the top of his ladder," Pearson writes, "and look across fields and valleys to blue-green mountains rising to the horizon. He needs to savor the sun and to feel the soft touch of the south wind."

In the early 1950s, at the height of the May blossom tours, the apple trees on Upland Farms numbered six thousand. Though commercial apple growing seemed to be thriving, farming in general was still in precipitous decline. By

A Jamaican worker adds to the harvest at Alyson's Orchard in Walpole.

1950 the number of farms in Cheshire County had dropped to 1,045. By 1959 only 488 farms remained; in 1969, 238. Soon enough labor-intensive commercial apple growing joined the downward trend: apples from such farms could no longer compete with apples grown on more expansive orchards in Washington State, New Zealand, and China. The international market kept the price low—the wholesale price in 2003 was the same as it had been forty years earlier. The first years of the twenty-first century saw Upland Farms, the last large orchard in Peterborough, go out of business.

The few orchards that survive from here on will likely do so not only by raising a quality apple but by selling the idea of the New England farm, for though the farms have disappeared the idea of them continues to dwell in our minds, and the small New England holding stretching across the hills is the kind of farm most people imagine, and will flock to on weekends. Alyson's Orchard in Walpole not only grows apples; the owners have an inn on the premises. You can be married there, or take cooking classes. As for the varieties of apples, it's a safe bet that no modern apple, on these hills or anywhere else, will hold the market for as long as the Baldwin did. The McIntosh, so popular in the mid–twentieth century, has been out of favor for decades, overtaken by the Macoun and the Honey Crisp—"a revelation," remarks one commentator. "Its sassy sweetness makes the all-too-common Mac pale in comparison." Those who know a Mac fresh from the tree in late September will always beg to differ.

Though it's unlikely any apple orchard will now be abandoned to the wild—houses will be planted on the land—it's not hard to imagine that at least a few abandoned McIntosh and Baldwin trees are growing in the steep woods of the region, providing feed for the deer and birds, and that on a late October walk you might encounter seedlings sprouting from their drops, bearing apples those beyond the woods will never hear of, kin to the Frozen-Thawed, good only in that state, or the Saunterer's Apple. You must lose yourself before you can find the way to that.

RECOLLECTIONS

Marion Davis, Cattle Drover
Mortimer Peebles

In the early twentieth century, cattle kept the mountains open; it was a countryside of panoramic views. At the beginning of the summer, cattle would be gathered in Concord, Massachusetts, for the three-day drive to pastures in New Ipswich, Sharon, and mountains to the north.

Marion Davis was a cattle drover (and the women's world champion woodchopper in 1936). She lived in New Ipswich with her husband, Frank Robbins. "In the spring along the first of May or the last of April we had to begin to mend fences over on the mountain in Sharon and on Barrett Mountain because we were going after cattle the last of the month," Davis told her niece, Connie Hall.

"May twentieth was what they used to call Pasture Day—go get the cattle from down country. When we got the fence mending pretty well done Frank hitched up Sukie. She was a little horse that he had raised from a colt. Grandpa gave her to him and told him he could break her and she was his. So he'd go down to Concord with Sukie and visit the different farmers, find out how many head of cattle they had to come up over the road for pasture through the summer months. A week's notice from then they would meet with their cattle at Meriam's Corner. There was a big barnyard there. We had to get down there the night before because all of those cattle had to be tagged and the descriptions of them set down in a book with their tag number. It took a good long evening job doing it because we generally had around 125 head. Meriam's Corner was in Concord, Massachusetts, where during the Revolutionary War the men gathered to plan their affairs.

"The next morning we generally left about four o'clock to drive the cattle. We had a man who would go on ahead and take ten or twelve of the cows that had been over the road and knew the route. It was quite a job. Sometimes they'd start ahead and the man that was with them would have to get ahead of them and kind of hold them back a little. It was work keeping them all on the go; it took quite a crew to start us out. We'd wind up at Knops Pond in Groton for the first night's stay. There was a big pasture there that went down to the edge of a pond where the cattle could drink. We'd leave again the next morning and we'd make the Townsend Poor Farm out of West Townsend for the second night. Lots of times when we got there, there'd be another drove of cattle ahead of us that was going up to Stoddard. I remember they had the pasture, and we had to put our cattle in the barnyard, which crowded them some, but we managed all right.

"The next morning we'd make for the mountain. Sometimes we put cattle into the Old Peppermint. That's where there used to be a tavern many years ago. Other times we'd make the top of the hill where the Brown place used to be, where the Wapack Lodge finally wound up. It took us two to three days sorting out the cattle to go to the different pastures. We'd take fifteen to twenty head over to Sharon pasture; there were about two hundred acres there. Some went up onto the north end of Barrett Mountain to the Haines pasture, and the rest over to the Reed and Wheeler near the old Livingston place.

"In 1917 we got a Model T Ford. It was one of those that had the brass trim, brass around the lights and on the front of the car. It was the first time we ever used a car to downcountry with cattle. . . . It wasn't as much pleasure going down with the car. It wasn't like having old Sukie following along behind."

The last of the cattle drives was around 1920. When the cattle were tagged, they also had to be tested by a veterinarian for TB. "That was quite a siege because we had to keep them over there for what was called an ear and tail test. They would take blood from the ear and then the tail, and it wasn't a sure test at that. A lot of the cattle reacted to it. I can remember the last little heifer that I had charge of coming up over the road. She lagged, was tired, and I had to push her and keep at her. We got them into the Peppermint. That night it rained and it poured. When we went over, we went in through the gate and there lay the little heifer. . . . She was dead, apparently reacting to the testing.

"But that was years ago. Once they started bringing the cattle up by truck, things were never the same again."

In 1922 Davis and her husband laid out the Wapack Trail. Working Sundays between farm chores, they cleared a twenty-one-mile ridge trail. (Davis came up with the name, uniting the starting point at Mount Watatic with the end at North Pack Monadnock Mountain.) They later built the Wapack Lodge, which she ran until 1964. She would have as many as seventy for a Sunday dinner, and more than a hundred for Thanksgiving and New Year's.

The ninety-one-year-old Davis was honored in 1985 with a trail named for her on Pack Monadnock. Five generations of her family lined up for a photo that day. She died the next year. The Wapack Lodge, struck by lightning, burned down in 1993. Today, the Friends of the Wapack maintain the trail.

The Grange Votes Down Automobiles

The monthly Grange supper was an anticipated event. It was a hale and hearty, vigorous, enterprising group. The suppers in the downstairs hall and the programs in the upstairs auditorium were high spots of our social life. Each Grange meeting had a different supper committee that provided the baked beans and brown bread as a starter. Then as each family arrived, women brought scalloped potatoes, scalloped oysters, ham, cold roast beef, cold pork, chicken pies, cakes, puddings, cookies, apple, squash, mince, pumpkin, custard, chocolate, cherry, raspberry, or other kinds of pies.

There were varied types of programs in the upstairs hall after supper. Some of them were strictly ritualistic with addresses by outside dignitaries of the order. Periodically Pomona Grange, an area that included several subordinate lodges, met at Hancock. In the same way, every few months we would go to Peterborough, Hillsboro, Jaffrey, Antrim, or Bennington.

The majority of the programs featured home talent. There were evenings of songs, recitations, spelling bees, and debates. The most memorable debate I have ever heard took place in the Grange Hall along about 1912. It was before I was a member, but on many evenings the program was open to the young folks after the first few minutes of ritual governed by the laws that ordain Grange affairs.

Deacon Dabney, a big prosperous farmer and outstanding citizen of the town, opposed Banker Whitaker. The former took the affirmative of the proposition: "Resolved, horses will never be supplanted by automobiles."

Deacon Dabney was a powerful speaker. He had represented the town in several sessions of the state legislature in Concord. He was famous for his beautiful Morgan horses as well as his large herd of purebred Jerseys. He loved horses; each year he took many prizes at Henniker Fair. The deacon gave a condensed history of what horses had meant to mankind down through the ages. He described the debt man owed to his faithful friend. He told how horses had helped to build a new nation in this western wilderness and how he was welcomed by the Morgans as he went to the barn any time of the day or night. He told us you could depend upon horses, that they worked steadily and uncomplainingly. He got a laugh by describing how he had seen an automobile try to pull through the sand near his house.

He had the crowd with him. There was no doubt of that. Most of the listeners had horses and most of the people, adults as well as young people, loved their four-footed friends.

The deacon came to a dramatic, blazing finish with emotion and fervor in his voice. "How can these smelly, noisy, ungodly contraptions ever take the place of our horses?" he demanded. "Perhaps they will serve as playthings for the idle

The automobile arrives. The Hancock Garage, c. 1920. There's a garage there today.

rich. But they will never be practical for everyday, dependable use. Why, think of it. Everyone has horses. What will become of our beloved horses if people buy automobiles?" The applause was rousing and generous.

Then Mr. Whitaker stood up. He wasn't an orator. Quietly he told us that, as far as he could foresee, within a few years many people, perhaps most families, would have a car. The crowd laughed. It was a good-natured laugh. Mr. Whitaker was not a Scrooge. He lent money to many on the strength of character. Farmers knew that he was their friend. But Mr. Whitaker was always looking ahead.

The banker told us that the destiny was riding the roads, that mechanical power was destined to supplant muscles, both of horses and men. He even said, with a smile I can still remember after more than thirty years, that the airplane would someday be as important as automobiles. He told us that planes would fly clear across the United States without stopping. Everyone roared at that. Everyone except Father. "Perhaps," said Mr. Whitaker, "my grandchildren will fly across the ocean in a plane." That was as funny a joke as anyone had heard in ages.

The banker was ahead of us—and knew he was too far out front. When it came time for the vote, the banker took the verdict smilingly, and folks thought he was a good sport. In fact, most of the audience believed the banker talked the way he did just to put up as good an argument as possible for the crowd's entertainment.

The vote was about ninety-nine in favor of horses and one for the coming of the automobile age. Father Pearson gave the banker his vote. Everyone agreed that the elder was a kindly man and such action was to be expected of a minister. No doubt Father really believed in horses, but he didn't want Mr. Whitaker to feel that no one was for him.

Part Three

EMPTYING OUT

Good food for hard times. John Judge in front of his diner, which stood at 92 Main Street in Keene from 1931 to 1937. He advertised "regular forty cent dinners."

Introduction

From her house on Court Street in Keene, Frances Faulkner listened for the train leaving town. "If you stood on the porch on a summer night, with the wind just right, you could hear the train all the way down at the crossing on old Marlboro Street at the stone arch bridge ... there was a whistle-stop there. Then there was one at Eastern Avenue all the way to Keene station. And when it left—Island Street, Pearl Street, West Street—you could hear the train all the way with the whistle, as if it were a symphony for half an hour on its way to Bellows Falls."

By day, the sound of factory whistles shaped time. Each factory was known by the pitch of its whistle. At lunch, Faulkner recalled, "one would go off at noon. Another one would go off at a quarter to one. It got so you knew what time it was by which company's whistle it was." Mill time defined the city.

Erskine Broadley and his father came to Keene in 1929 to work in the mills, at the suggestion of an uncle who was a "boss spinner." They were hired as weavers in the Colony Mill working the night shift, 6:00 p.m. to 6:00 a.m., five nights a week: sixty hours, twenty dollars a week. After a month, they were laid off, and went to Gilsum to work in an old mill. It was October 1929. At the month's end, the stock market crashed and "then everything went." "We'd work a week and we'd loaf a week. And sometimes we'd loaf more than a week. They shared the work and did the best they could to keep us going. Then they decided the only way to keep going was to give us a cut—cut wages." Broadley's salary went from twenty-five dollars a week to ten dollars for part-time work. There was no unemployment pay. Still, he could survive. His rent was ten dollars a month for a furnished apartment with an outhouse in back of the barn. For a dollar he could fill the back of his old Model T with wood to run the two woodstoves in the apartment. "We just went to work once in a while and then we didn't work for a long time." The Gilsum mill folded. He and his father moved on to a West Swanzey mill—"Probably worked about six weeks and bango: laid off." He went to work in mills in Hillsborough. "Prosperity was just around the corner, they used to tell us. We never finally got around that corner."

Part three, "Emptying Out," looks at New England's long decline, which set in after the Civil War.

The Last 113 People

Wilson family historian Edgar V. Wilson wrote of his father Frederic Wilson's boyhood that "the time of his birth (1822) was in Stoddard's golden age. Its farms were all occupied; its virgin soil still yielded abundant crops; large families were the rule and its schools were well attended; its people were happy and content."

This rural hill town at the northeast corner of Cheshire County was indeed a thriving agricultural community of 1,200 residents at the time of Frederic Wilson's birth. Its farms produced sixteen tons of butter, twenty-one tons of hay, and forty-two tons of pork during 1820.

Wilson spent most of his life at or near the farmstead where he was born. As he aged, grayed, and grew feeble, however, so too did his native town. By the time of his death at seventy-five years in 1897, the farms were mostly abandoned, the virgin soil was exhausted, the large families gone, and many of the schools stood empty and exposed to the elements. The population of the town had decreased by more than two-thirds—from 1,208 to 367 residents. During Frederic Wilson's lifetime this once-thriving agricultural community had decayed to the point of near extinction. There were a variety of reasons for this rapid, yet common, demise of a New England hill town.

Stoddard's agricultural problems began thousands of years before man ever set foot on its soil. The topography of the town consisted of uneven hills topped with thin soil crowded with granite boulders left behind when the last glacier retreated northward.

Wilson homestead.

Wilson homestead, 1921.

Although poorly suited for agriculture, that was precisely the reason the town was settled in the late 1760s. The farms succeeded for half a century until the thin soil became depleted. Some farms lasted longer than others, such as the Reed farm near Center Pond, operated by Frederick and Emily Reed and their son George, shown in this 1901 interior photograph. The farmhouse was built by family patriarch Jonas P. Reed in 1839.

Farming in Stoddard rapidly became an unfruitful career, however. The newer, more productive farms to the west began to provide urban markets with the produce that the hill towns could not. The majority of the town's farm families surrendered to the inevitable, or lingered too long and were forced to leave or go hungry.

Stone walls toppled, orchards were neglected, and white pines began to sprout in the fields. Saddest of all was the fate of the farmhouses themselves. These old homes in the dying hills were unmarketable and were simply abandoned to the elements as their owners left to pursue the dream of lush farmland to the west or the comforting hourly wage of the factory worker.

The abandoned homes quickly became forlorn as windows and doors deteriorated or were removed, leaving gaping holes in the walls.

New England's unforgiving seasons shifted foundations and battered unattended roofs and siding. Shockingly little time passed before the houses collapsed into their own cellars, resulting in a tangle of broken beams and shattered boards. The fractured wood disappeared even more quickly under the heavy hand of nature. The fieldstone foundations and bricks from the fireplaces around which the families had warmed themselves remained the longest.

Farming was not the sole livelihood available to the residents of Stoddard, however. Sawmills, gristmills, tanneries, and a variety of woodenware shops were built along the brooks and streams of the town from its earliest days. It was

Emily, George, and Frederick Reed inside the farmhouse built by Jonas Reed.

Stoddard Lumber Company team departing for Hancock Depot, 1896.

in the 1840s that a new industry that would employ hundreds of residents first opened its doors in Stoddard.

Joseph Foster fired the community's first glass furnace at South Stoddard in 1842. He came to town to take advantage of two abundant local raw materials: wood to fire the furnaces and sand from the numerous ponds and lakes to melt in those furnaces for the production of glass bottles. Over the next thirty-one years four firms operated five factories and employed hundreds of townspeople while producing millions of bottles for markets throughout the northeastern United States. The final factory closed its doors in 1873. Several factors played a role in the demise of the glass industry, but perhaps the most important was the cost of transportation.

The development of the railroad not only allowed the influx of western produce and an easy means for discouraged farmers to escape from the region; it also destroyed many manufacturing firms that were unfortunate enough to be

1860s view of hardscrabble farmland bordering Cold Spring Pond.

Log drive on Long Pond.

located miles from the nearest railhead. The railroad was never built through the rugged terrain of Cheshire County's northern hill towns. It was a long, rough, and expensive haul for the wagons full of fragile bottles to reach the nearest depot at Keene, fifteen miles to the southwest. This and other economic factors resulted in a profit margin that could not sustain the industry after the early 1870s.

The woodenware shops fared somewhat better. The abandoned farms were rapidly reverting to white pine forest. Portable sawmills could be transported through the forests and operated wherever the best trees were available. Not only was there an abundance of raw material; the abandoned farms were available inexpensively, often for the cost of unpaid taxes.

The Stoddard Lumber Company soon acquired thousands of acres in several local towns. The company's mills turned out lumber, pails, handles, knobs, shingles, and rocking chairs.

By the time Frederic Wilson died in 1897, his boyhood home near the western

Littlefield's sawmill.

Recitation at the South Stoddard School.

border of Stoddard was in disrepair. It soon disappeared altogether, as did every one of the dozens of farms in the neighborhood. Only sixteen of the more than one hundred farms that had operated in the town when he was born survived in 1897. Ten percent of the population worked for the Stoddard Lumber Company.

Governor Frank W. Rollins initiated New Hampshire's Old Home Week just one year after Frederic Wilson's death. It was painfully clear that not only was Stoddard disintegrating; rural hill towns across the state were equally depressed. Old Home Week was instituted as a means of enticing former residents to return for a few days to their "old home" towns. Maybe nostalgia would make them realize they truly missed the dear old place. Perhaps they would return, buy an old farmhouse, or invest in some property.

Old Home Week was successful, but only in getting some old-timers to return for a few days. Dozens of elderly former residents made the pilgrimage to Stoddard year after year, reminisced about days gone by, commented on the decay of their beloved village, and went away again, leaving the town under a thickening pall of silence. The few locals who still lived in the town dressed up for the weekend and then went back to eking out an existence in the increasingly isolated community.

Marlow stage at the Central House Hotel, 1906.

Some new highways were built along the fringes of the town, but the road through the heart of Stoddard was not an important route to anywhere other than the village itself. Town roads deteriorated or disappeared entirely. The Marlow stage still came through town during the first decade of the 1900s, but most of the passengers continued on to other destinations.

Although the Stoddard Lumber Company was hampered by transportation costs and rumored to be plagued by mismanagement, it was still a blow to the town when the factory burned in 1907 and was not rebuilt. One resident commented that "when the mills went the heart of the town went." The final manufacturing industry was now gone.

A few enterprising residents became cattle and sheep dealers to take advantage of the few remaining open fields. These men would fatten their herds in the temperate hills of Stoddard throughout the summer and then walk their animals to the stock markets at Brighton, Massachusetts, when autumn arrived.

These were typically longtime residents who soon retired from the long hours and forced marches of the cattle drover or shepherd as the brush encroached incessantly into the coarse fields.

Stoddard did have one natural feature that worked to its advantage. The

Campers at Hunt Rock, Center Pond, 1894.

numerous lakes and ponds that speckled the surface of the town began to attract sportsmen and tourists in the late 1890s. Unfortunately, the rugged shores of the lakes, combined with the bad roads and unreliable modes of transportation, kept the summer visitors, and their dollars spent in town, to a minimum.

The government census enumerator found a mere forty-one households harboring 113 people when he toured the rutted roads of Stoddard in 1930. As one of the largest towns in southwestern New Hampshire in physical area, Stoddard now supported fewer than one family per square mile of countryside.

Eight families were still trying to farm the impossible soil, even though their farms housed only twenty-eight cows and four sheep. More than a dozen men worked in the woods building roads, cutting trees, or driving log trucks.

Perhaps most telling, however, were the professions with a single practitioner. There was one housepainter, one blacksmith, one mason, and one storekeeper in the general store, all trying to survive by providing services for a dwindling pool of neighbors. George Randlett earned a few dollars by boating visitors up and down Long Pond. Fred Jennings climbed the Pitcher Mountain fire tower each morning during the summer season to keep watch over the thriving forest to ensure that a single match did not spark a forest fire that might run unabated for miles in any direction. Marion Russell was the sole schoolteacher instructing the

Stoddard Center, 1902.

Stoddard Center, 1920s.

town's fifteen school-age children in the only surviving, one-room school. Half of the residents admitted to the census taker that they had no occupation at all.

The thriving hill town of 1820 had vanished. The farms were gone, the soil exhausted, the fields clogged with brush and trees. The flourishing glass and lumber industries had come and gone. And most of the people were gone as well; what was there to keep them here?

This was more than a temporary downturn. The population of this isolated community had declined an average of ten people every single year for 110 years in a row. The majority of those who remained amidst the rapidly encroaching forces of nature were families whose ancestors had lived there for generations. Most could not bear to leave despite the fraying social and economic fabric of their community. By 1930 it was doubtful if Stoddard's last 113 people could keep their town from disappearing altogether.

Gertrude Tomas surveying the destruction of another old Stoddard homestead.

LETTER

Stoddard Reawakening, 1946
Charles L. Pierce

March 4, 1946

To the editor,

The outlook for Stoddard is better than it has been for many years. The new families who have recently come, or will soon come, to make Stoddard their permanent residence and have entered so heartily into the church, social and educational activities of the town, give great encouragement to those who have labored for its welfare for many years.

We have the nucleus of a typical New England village, among the hills which are not too near to give a shut in feeling. In Stoddard you feel as if you were on top of the world, and that the ocean ought to be in sight over its east range, or Round Mountain, as Bacon Ledge hill was called in 1830.

All the elements of a village are there. The old 1836 church with its box pews, one of the few left. Opposite is the old Central House, which is in process of being restored, by Mr. Lee L. Manley, who has also modernized the house next to the hotel.

The Historical Building comes next with the town library on the lower floor, and the historical exhibition rooms on the second.

The Morse homestead, with its tall pillars is an ancient relic of the old church which stood on the hill back of the present church, for it was built with lumber from the old church, one of the bulkhead doors being one of the old church doors, and the lift up seats in the dance hall on the third story were new seats, in the box pews. Opposite is the old village store built in 1840 by Joe W. Eaton. About 1861 it was occupied by John Nelson who founded the Nelson Stores in Manchester. The parsonage opposite is being modernized by Mr. Higgins, who will make it his home.

Next is the home of Mr. Howard Goodspeed, which he has modernized and made it his home for several years. It was built by Stearns Foster, who had a blacksmith shop opposite.

Down at the corner of the Washington road is the typical Town Hall which has been made very attractive inside for social and business gatherings.

All these with the other village houses make a picture of a real country village from any part of which you can see off a good distance. It is 1430 feet altitude at the hotel corner.

For the first time in many years we have a resident doctor and it gives a great feeling of security to know that Dr. Keim has come to live at the Lawley place. There are times in the summer when there are four doctors in town.

There are two Soldiers' monuments in the village.

Now here is a village of typical form and beauty in the midst of a vast uninhabited tract of beautiful country but cut off from pleasure drives except the two ways to Keene, and we have to go the same old way every time.

If the Washington road was made a black road, or even a good dirt road, it would open up circuits for pleasure driving and would connect with the black road from Washington to Goshen and Newport and would be valuable in case of another great forest fire.

KEVIN GARDNER

Land of Stone

Remnant of a utopia. The stone-enclosed burying ground where J. Warren Wilder's son and other members of the family rest.

All across the Monadnock region, a mutable but lasting journal is written in handmade structures of native stone—a tangible record of working relationships between people and places, compiled over many generations, explaining how we got here from there.

Stonework is also, very often, surprisingly personal testimony. Even the most ruinous bridge or half-collapsed foundation suggests something about the attitudes and aspirations of its makers, inviting us to speculate about everything from its builders' identities to the numerous mysteries in its placement, con-

figuration, and purpose. We accept this invitation as a way of investing the relics bequeathed to us with new value for our own time.

The process can be a tricky one. Reading the slouched stone remnants of a former landscape seems to require two nearly impossible feats. First, one must observe what is no longer there—the buildings, roads, fields, and connective tissue of activity for which the stonework served as skeletal underpinning. Second, one must ignore what has since appeared—the trees, the overgrowth, the layers of abandonment and disturbance that seduce the senses with peculiar blends of remorse, curiosity, bemusement, and admiration. Furthermore, the stone remains of New England's past landscapes are almost always incomplete. Foundations without buildings, walls without livestock, and millraces without machinery are like books from which crucial pages—even entire chapters—have been randomly ripped. Describing someone's feelings about a place by looking at his abandoned stonework is like trying to describe someone's feelings about clothing by looking at the soles of his shoes.

Yet the tension between things that are and things that have been is also an essential prerequisite for understandings that may teach us as much about ourselves as about the objects that attract our attention. This is the "dialogue" that Christopher Woodward describes in his book *In Ruins*. Without it, the Monadnock region's legacy of stonework is worthless. Without it, we who live here have no idea where we really are.

Wilder's Utopia: No Place Like Home

So far as they are known, the facts of Wilder's Utopia are startling enough. In 1882, an eccentric millionaire named Jones Warren Wilder returned to the town of Rindge, where he had failed in the sawmill business years before, and began buying up old farms. Eventually, he acquired more than seven thousand acres, mostly in East Rindge. Then he set out to create an entire town.

Within a dozen years, the forty-room mansion Wilder built for himself was surrounded by a vast array of fields, barns, shops, mills, and dormitories. Cheshire Place, as he called it, employed perhaps five hundred workers, perhaps a thousand. The "town" produced lumber, bricks, bobbins, clothespins, and cider, among other products. It raised enormous quantities of livestock, entered the dairy business, and bottled its own blueberry vinegar for shipment far and wide. It had a veterinary hospital, an underground, wind-powered water system, and a fifty-foot observation tower. Recent scholarship has decided that Cheshire Place was primarily a business venture, but contemporary attitudes saw something more grandiose in Wilder's intentions: an effort to create a self-sustaining agricultural empire. In some quarters, it came to be known—not without prejudice—as Wilder's Utopia.

But when J. Warren Wilder suddenly died in 1894, his Utopia evaporated like an inexplicable dream. Operations dwindled, livestock was sold, and the workers disappeared. Buildings, equipment, and considerable land were auctioned off in 1913. In 1921, Wilder's son George returned and led a modest effort to revive the place, but his own death ten years later ended the dream forever.

In spite of its immensity and its ambition, Cheshire Place has almost utterly disappeared. Of the thirty or more major buildings that once stood there—including what may have been the largest barn in New England—only the mansion and a couple of nearby outbuildings remain, now occupied by a small private school. Gardens, pastures, and the network of roads have largely returned to forest. On the ground, the enormity of Wilder's vision is now represented almost entirely by stonework.

Of this, there is no shortage. Wilder employed at least two full-time crews of Irish stonemasons during the decade or more that it took to build the infrastructure of Cheshire Place, and they produced some remarkable work. The main dam behind the uppermost of Wilder's elaborate system of four turbine-feeding ponds runs to twenty feet high and two hundred feet across, more or less. Easily wide enough to bear a roadway along its top, it is constructed entirely of random and half-cut boulders, laid dry and backed with earth. The complex of sluiceways and supporting walls at the ponds' outflow is unusually deep for a structure of its kind, evidence of the size of the turbines it once contained and the huge timber structure it carried overhead. The gigantic foundation of the main barn, still nearly intact, is expertly constructed, with interior walls more than ten feet high on the uphill side. Butt-ended freestanding buttress walls as tall as the foundation itself jut into the space in several places, beautifully fitted in patterns of one over three stones, standing straight as the day they were laid. Their relatively narrow, slightly tapered widths defy conventional New England wisdom with respect to the height that dry-laid stone can safely reach, testimony to the excellence of their construction and the invisible presence of deep, true footings beneath them.

These are only a sample of Cheshire Place's most arresting stone remains. Of course there are walls—possibly miles of them—running along the roads, retaining some of the steeper slopes, organizing pastures and barnyards, circling the family plot. Gateways are defined with six-foot split granite posts. Ramps climb to the upper floors of long-gone secondary barns. The remnants of a stout, slab-capped retaining wall are still visible around the old mansion.

Wilder's stonemasons favored rough-dressed block work in freestanding walls and support structures, and split or naturally flat-faced boulders in sidewalls, dams, or retaining work. Some of the stone they used was gathered traditionally, in the course of land clearing. More of it was quarried nearby or split from exposed ledge or outcropping. In some cases, particularly along the estate's main approach, they worked in unshaped rubble capped with long, narrow granite slabs. Contrary to some reports, there's nothing unusual about their building styles—they are all common ones in nineteenth-century New England stonework. Nevertheless, something is backward about it all.

A truism of an old New England place is that the care and attention paid to stonework is a consequence of its proximity to the homestead's center. The finest, most careful work on a prosperous, well-developed farm would almost invariably be that which was nearest to the house. Farther out in the surrounding land, walls and other structures tended to become rougher, more strictly utilitarian in style. At Cheshire Place, the opposite is the case. Though the outlying dams, mill-races, and barn foundations largely endure in monumental exactness, there is a faint air of indifference in the laying of the walls along the drive and around the mansion. Placement of individual stones seems hurried and imprecise, the caps less carefully selected. Compared with the finest of what their builders made, these walls are almost careless, and as a result they have not aged well. What they seem to say may be apocryphal, but in the dialogue between incompleteness and imagination, they carry a powerful suggestion.

Wilder's Utopia was a corporation. It was never quite a home, never a loved place. The stony footprints it left in passing mutter a cold story of extreme professional competence practiced without personal engagement, without any pride deeper than that of mere workmanship. That is why the worst stonework at Cheshire Place is the work in sight of J. Warren Wilder's bleak Victorian mansion and the best is scattered far away, resolutely bearing up the ghosts of his barns and mills and holding back the waters of his unemployed ponds. In a larger sense, it is also why Cheshire Place could never endure.

Only one small part of the wreckage of this vast enterprise still retains anything like a sense of wholeness: the stone-enclosed burying ground where Wilder's son and other members of the family rest. Serenely guarded by a tall grove of maples, it occupies the middle of an otherwise useful pasture just down the hill from the mansion. It's somehow appropriate that Wilder himself, the enigmatic instigator of it all, is absent from his own cemetery. In death, the Ozymandias of New Hampshire was relocated to New York City.

Edith Page's Fountain

The stone remains of Edith Page's home speak delicately of an idea: a beautiful and decorous idea of the farm as a place of peace and refuge, such as an ancient vineyard in Tuscany might be to a weary exile. Edith Page set out to make such a place when she came to Dublin and bought the old Derby farm, on what is now Page Road, in 1891.

Miss Page was a Bostonian, a spinster of the Gilded Age. Socially connected to Dublin's literary and aristocratic summer community, she came to the country "an almost helpless invalid," but soon found "health and delight . . . in the management of fields, orchards, and barns." The Dublin town history of 1920 declares that she also raised "dairy stock, upon which she spent considerable sums of money." Day-to-day chores were carried out by a hired manager, of course, who lived in the Derbys' old farmhouse. Miss Page built another dwelling for herself. Her friend and (perhaps) companion, a Miss Minnie Preble, occupied an additional cottage on the property.

There are no buildings on the Page estate today. In fact, it's difficult, at first glance, to read the place as a farm at all. Stone walls and foundations string along both sides of Page Road, but the land is essentially a long hillside looking down on a swamp. It is thickly, messily forested. Far above the cluster of stone remains, the ground begins to level off somewhat. The hilltop is where one would expect to find a homestead, particularly one first settled in 1772, but Edith Page's place is at the bottom. When the buildings stood and the land was clear, that endless, rising hill must have framed the farm magnificently.

The stonework itself is of two distinct styles. One is the old, familiar, dry work in random fieldstone, under what must have been a barn and its (possibly) adjoining farmhouse. This foundation combines large and small stones, split and unsplit, in a typical New England way. Much of it was likely done by the Derby family, who farmed the property for more than a century before Edith Page arrived. Their stonework is sound and functional—though somewhat the worse for wear in spots. They used the stone that came to hand in the best tradition of frugal practicality, and arranged it with an intuitive, not considered, sense of design.

Edith Page had very different ideas. The stonework she added was built by masons, not farmers, and it expresses a vision of rural life that is elegantly civil, European, and romantic beyond anything Samuel Derby's family ever imagined. Above the procession of foundations along the uphill side of Page Road stands a long façade of mortared stones, smaller in average size than the older work, and carefully selected. Contained on either end by roughly triangular sections of

If nothing else remained at Edith Page's ruined farm to testify to her genteel conception of country life, the fountain would still reveal it all.

older retaining wall, it appears to have been an adaptation of one of the Derbys' old foundations. Behind the façade are two small rooms, partly dug into the hillside and enclosed with eight-foot walls in the same carefully mortared style. The rooms are separated by an additional double wall of stone, and the whole structure is level from front to back. It is a fully enclosed, divided foundation. But of what? Just one narrow doorway penetrates the façade, and it gives access to only one of the rooms. There are no interior openings from room to room, so entry to the other one could only have been from above. Finally, only one of the rooms has a window—and it's not the one with the door.

The structure makes no sense as a barn, and hardly much more as a dwelling. But it could have been a lovely milkhouse. The cool, dark, stone-lined rooms below would have been ideal for dairy storage, and the building that sat above it would have opened, on its uphill side, straight into the rising acreage where Edith Page's pastures had to be. Going to and from their barn, her cows would have passed it twice a day.

Compared to the Derbys' rough-and-ready work, the milk house is built in a refined, Old World style that calls attention to its own rusticity. It's conscious of itself in a way that indigenous New England stonework never is. Equally peculiar is the pair of tall, square, mortared pillars that stand nearby, located in a place that could never have been an entrance to the estate but that might well have ushered Miss Page's cows from barnyard to pasture in most elegant style. A small wellhead on the hillside above is built in similar fashion, with a tightly mortared lip and a little shelf around its base to stand on. But the crowning glory of the place is the fountain.

If nothing else remained at Edith Page's ruined farm to testify to her genteel conception of country life, the fountain would still reveal it all. When it was new, a century or so ago, it must have been her pride and joy. If the faint, curling track it stands beside was the main approach to Miss Page's house, it would have been the first thing her visitors saw as their carriage turned into the drive.

The fountain sits against the back wall of a cozy, elevated veranda, bound above and on its sides by low walls of fieldstone. It is a gravestone-sized freestanding niche cut from fine-grained granite, gable-topped, with a vaguely classical open pediment. Its interior is slightly concave, with a scalloped fan carved under the peak. Whatever water-dispensing statuary it was that the niche housed—a spurting cherub, a maiden with a pitcher, the god Poseidon?—is long gone, but the access holes for the fountain's piping are plainly visible. At its base, a small collecting pool is defined by a low, cloverleaf-shaped wall of cast concrete. A necklace of actual scallop shells is pressed into the cement around the curves of its outer face. Cement benches at the veranda's ends and sides invite sitters to rest, and stone steps fall away from it toward the drive. Beside the steps, a little stone waterfall drops down to a reflecting pool, enclosed by more stone and formed concrete. Other low walls wander protectively about, suggesting that the fountain was nestled among informal gardens, some of them partially terraced. The arrangement hybridizes New England methods and materials with elements of continental neoclassicism and formal landscape architecture, yet somehow achieves an unpretentious harmony. It has nothing whatever to do with farming, and everything to do with one woman's love for a particular farm.

Edith Page died at the age of sixty-one, in 1916. That same year, the old Derby farmhouse burned to the ground. Minnie Preble moved into Edith's house, apparently, and stayed on for a time. World War I was ending the Gilded Age, and with it the great era of New England's aristocratic tradition of rural refuge.

Like the rest of the Page estate, the fountain and its surroundings are crumbling away. The whole area has gone to vinca, ferns, and moss, in a state of romantic decay that approaches Ruskinian richness. Yet even in its broken, half-concealed condition, the fountain seems comfortably settled rather than decrepit, its maker's memory of "health and delight" still lingering in the stones and mortar. Until the day it disappears forever, it is a hole in the wall of time, peeking over into another world. It is a place Maxfield Parrish might have been happy to use as the backdrop for a painting populated with his languid, androgynous nymphs. It is Edith Page's tribute to an idyll of country life she imagined, and briefly led.

The Treasure West of London Cut

Somewhere along the now railless bed of the Cheshire Railroad, in East Westmoreland, a buried treasure hides in plain sight. It's a little to the west of the famous London Cut, a mile-long chute precisely excised through solid rock to a depth of as much as thirty feet by crews laying out the road in the late 1840s. A fair amount of the four million cubic yards of material they moved to run the line from Ashburnham, Massachusetts, to Bellows Falls, Vermont, came out of that cut, and most of it went west, where long sections of the line lay on lower, softer ground. Over that stretch they built a causeway, sixty feet high in places, to keep the rail bed level as it emerged from the Cut on its way to Gilboa and the depot in Westmoreland.

The builders of the railroad believed they were making something permanent, a fact to which their work, in thousands of places, still testifies. One of those places is west of the London Cut, where the causeway, close to its most imposing height, finds itself obliged to jump a brook. At other spots where a breach was necessary—and the causeway's altitude more modest—the Cheshire Railroad's engineers would usually place a bridge, timber at first and later steel, between heavy stone abutments. Here they opted for a culvert.

The "culvert" looks like the entrance to King Solomon's Mines. At about sixteen feet wide and fourteen high, it's large enough to drive a UPS truck through. It runs straight under the gigantic earthwork, a distance of about 175 feet, to the streambed's entrance on the other side. The brook is wide and shallow, so in addition to its duties as a culvert, the tunnel is also a useful passageway for people and animals. Composed exclusively of rectangular blocks of granite, it is a perfect arch from end to end.

Its headers—the outer retaining walls encasing each of its openings—are Romanesque in their mass and symmetry. Unlike the roughly split faces of the blocks within the arch—their quarrymen's drill holes still visible along their edges—the header blocks are dressed up with chisel-drafted margins, their edges

Constructed by Irish immigrants in 1846, this culvert near Westmoreland is a monument to the Cheshire Railroad's belief in permanence.

smoothed to straight lines that meet precisely at the joints and set off the mossy, hammer-finished faces of the stone. The headers curl outward, away from the causeway's embankment, stepping down a block at a time as they descend from a height of perhaps eighteen feet over the peaks of the culvert's arches to just two or three blocks high on the outer margins. At the tops of each header, the finishing course of blocks is stepped slightly out over the plane of the header's face, like a molding.

Inside, the arch vaults overhead in a semicircle, springing off a short vertical base about two blocks high. The interior stones of the arch are longer, narrower, and less regular than the dressed stone in the headers, but they are arranged in even courses that run the length of the tunnel. Clearly, each one was split to fit. The streambed underfoot is predictably stony and treacherous much of the way, but it also has flat sections here and there—rigid, nubbly slabs, a kind of floor. They are the broken remains of an artificial watercourse, poured in place to discourage erosion of the archway's footings. The breakup of this concrete streambed seems to have had no significant effect on the structure's integrity, however. It appears quite capable of standing for another 150 years, and maybe another 150 after that.

At least, it did. Sometime during the summer of 2003, after several days of heavy rain, the culvert's downstream header suffered a catastrophic collapse. Were the footings under its inner corners eroded by flash flooding? Did the waterlogged soil above and behind it settle and push just a little too hard? Was the structure's integrity invisibly compromised by the slow, irresistible expansion of tree roots? Any of these things, or all of them together, might have done it. But the orderly grandeur of the culvert's southern face is now a broken, forbidding jumble of random blocks, hastily removed from the streambed by emergency crews and left in piles on either side. Behind the wreckage, the hacked-off interior of the surviving arch pokes unevenly from the gash in the causeway's wall. Exposed now, it will crumble much more quickly.

The culvert was what you might call a common masterpiece. It was certainly far from unique. Hundreds of structures like it were built by the railroads as they blasted, piled, and bridged their way across New England. Yet in an age whose utilitarian public works are routinely characterized by vacancy and ugliness, the culvert's nineteenth-century elegance was almost charming. For all its grand mass and imposing scale, it still looked like something human beings had built. At the same time, it had about it a naïve self-importance that proclaimed the beauty of Progress, a faith in the future prosperity of every corner of the landscape that the railroad's marvelous machines could reach. Like a colonizing missionary unaware of the home country's collapse, the culvert faithfully preached its message of bounty and order until the day its authority at last succumbed to the nameless little brook it governed and adorned.

One of these days, the upstream façade will go. Eventually, deprived of its protective headers, the arch will, too. Then the treasure west of London Cut will disappear forever. Just like the Cheshire Railroad.

The Bridge at the Bottom of the Lake

Gleason's Falls Road isn't much of a thoroughfare. It's a plain gravel track out in the woods a mile or two west of Hillsborough's Lower Village, quiet and narrow as a thousand other Monadnock back roads. It wanders off down a short hill from its junction with Beard's Road, toward the spot where it crosses a rocky brook, also called Beard's. Modest houses are tucked in here and there along the way, and old walls shuffle off into the trees. There isn't the slightest indication that the road leads to anything important. But down in the little hollow where it intersects the brook, hard by the blocky remnants of an old mill foundation, Gleason's Falls Road becomes the unexpected site of a national landmark. It is a mortarless, double-arch stone bridge, one of five such structures still standing within the town's borders. Not long ago, the American Society of Civil Engineers saw fit to include Hillsborough's bridges on its list of historic American construction feats, along with Hoover Dam and the Washington Monument.

Hillsborough got its stone bridges for two principal reasons. The town was prosperous enough to afford them, for one thing, being a particularly fortunate exemplar of New Hampshire's early nineteenth-century agricultural heyday. There was plenty of stone around, too, both random and quarried, and a new technique of splitting—the renowned feather-and-wedge system—had recently come along to greatly increase the accuracy with which granite could be shaped. These advantages might not have been enough by themselves—other towns were prosperous and stony as well, after all—but Hillsborough also had a man named Hiram Monroe, who from his position as selectman argued, cajoled, and convinced his fellow citizens that stone bridges would save them money in the long run by requiring fewer repairs and by resisting the periodic floods that had a tendency to carry away more fragile plank and timber bridges. Besides, hadn't neighboring Henniker successfully erected just such a bridge only recently? The first of Hillsborough's stone arches went up in 1839. After that, it became a habit—over the next thirty-five years or so, the town acquired at least eleven more.

Gleason's Falls Road gets credit only for one bridge, but it really has two, connected by an eighty-foot stone causeway. Beard's Brook divides itself around a little island here. The causeway crosses that, and the bridges jump the channels on either side to connect it to the brook's widely separated banks. The builder's name is unknown, but if the bridges themselves are any indication, he was a man afflicted with multiple personality disorder. Though they are in a sense a unit, these constructions could hardly be more different from one another.

The bridge's western arch is gracefully elfin, sailing lightly over almost thirty feet of water as though it weren't made of stone at all. The outer blocks of its arch (voussoirs) are relatively small, evenly matched, and consistent from end to end. The split granite of its underside follows an even pattern of courses, too. There is hardly more than a foot of additional placed stone between the peak of the arch and the roadbed above—its thinness is one of the reasons the span looks so graceful. Finally, this arch is amazingly shallow—it has a span-to-rise ratio of 4.57, which means it is more than four and a half times longer than it is high. In dry stone construction, an arch this flat places enormous lateral pressure on its abutments, far more than standard semicircular arches. The builder at Gleason's Falls Road solved this problem by jamming one of his arch's ends into the bedrock of a rising hillside on the western stream bank and by backing up the other end with the causeway, which contains something on the order of 425 cubic yards of stone weighing about 950 tons. Engineers shake their heads when they see this thing. Everyone else just thinks it's beautiful.

The eastern arch, however, looks like something thrown together by a gang of trolls. It runs to six feet high and twelve long, which makes it a perfect semicircle, but that's the only perfect thing about it. It is set so low in the causeway's massive wall that it looks more like a hole than a span—five or six feet of stone sidewall rise over it on either side. Moreover, its stones are a mismatched motley of rough split blocks and random, unshaped chunks. The springer (first stone at the base of the arch) on the northeast corner is actually a five-sided lump, somehow placed so that one of its surfaces offers—more or less—the right angle for the next voussoir in the span. Other stones in the arch, on both sides and underneath, are even less shapely. From a builder's standpoint, it resembles a stone-lined well more than an arch—a well that's been cut in half and laid on its side. If it were not for the crushing load of stone overhead, perpetually clamping its misshapen members in place, it would long since have fulfilled its gravitational ambition and crashed into Beard's Brook.

The stylistic schizophrenia of the Gleason's Falls Road bridge is so remarkable that it raises questions. Is the eastern span—the troll hole—original? Or is it a later reconstruction, replacing something more graceful that was lost in a forgotten flood? Was it built to focus the Beard's Brook current for the mill that stood on its side of the stream, or was it patched together when the original millrace washed away or was dismantled?

Nor is the disparity confined to the bridge's pair of arches: it's also visible in the running sidewalls of the structure as a whole. On the downstream side, the line runs relatively straight across. A partially collapsed section on the eastern approach, and an opportunistic young tree that has rooted its way into the wall just above the eastern arch's outflow, are its only signs of deterioration. The upstream side, however, is a different story. The spans themselves are in fairly decent order here, but the connecting causeway is a mess. Huge trees, some of them dead and gone, some not, have distorted its line significantly, and even toppled some sections altogether, notably a sizable one just at the abutment of the western bridge. Elsewhere the sidewall bellies out and staggers over itself with a drunken imprecision in no way reminiscent of the prim rectitude on the other side. The causeway's upstream line bulges sharply outward just past the smaller eastern span, too, further suggesting that the troll bridge is a replacement effort that was never properly lined up with the original structure. The upstream side has also endured the brunt of 150 years' worth of Beard's Brook's occasionally righteous floods, however, and it may be that its current condition is no more than a memento of 1936, or some other notably saturated year. At any rate, there's a very good reason why almost all the pictures taken of the Gleason's Falls Road Bridge are shot from the downstream side.

The petite double arches of Carr Bridge withstood the tremendous 1936 March floods.

Rearing its head above water each March, the bridge at the bottom of Franklin Pierce Lake preserves something central to the character of Monadnock's hill towns.

None of Hillsborough's other extant bridges can quite match the oxymoronic mixture of endurance and ruination on display at Gleason's Falls Road. Farther downhill along Beard's Road, the single span over Gleason's Falls proper (lovers of confusion will note with delight the fact that Gleason's Falls Road neither passes nor leads to Gleason's Falls) arches over the rocky, cascading brook in undamaged splendor, its only visible alteration a shabby set of rails, cobbled together out of white-painted four-by-fours. Still farther on the way back toward town, the toylike Carr Bridge crosses the same stream once more, its identical double arches barely betraying the beating it took during 1936's horrendous March floods. Across town, along the Second New Hampshire Turnpike, the two causeway-connected spans over the North Branch River have been so extensively rehabilitated for modern traffic loads that they barely look like the antiques they are. And at the busy junction of Routes 202 and 9, the double-arched Sawyer Bridge sits in humiliated truncation. Until 1988, it boasted a third vault, a dry land underpass on its southern end, which fell, perhaps in protest, when an anonymous steel and concrete replacement co-opted its longtime job a few yards off to the west.

Reports on Hillsborough's famous stone arch bridges seldom fail to note that five of the original twelve remain (or seven, if you count the causeway-connected spans at Gleason's Falls Road and the Second New Hampshire Turnpike as distinct structures). But this is inaccurate—there are actually six (or eight) still standing. It's just that one of them happens to stand on the bottom of Franklin Pierce Lake, a reservoir created in the 1920s by damming the brook over which it stood. The Tuttle Bridge, as it's known, is a single arch not unlike that over Gleason's Falls. As far as anyone seems to know, it remains in perfectly good condition.

The Tuttle Bridge fascinates because it is immune, in a sense, to any of the variations of place-relationship that Hillsborough's other stone bridges cannot escape. It is exempt from the combination of benign neglect and daily dependence visited on the Gleason's Falls and Gleason's Falls Road spans, unavailable to photographers and fishermen, as Captain Carr's Toy Bridge has always been, not subject to improvements, reconstructions, or embalming, like Sawyer's and the bridges on the Turnpike.

The metaphorical potential of a bridge that obstinately remains standing at the bottom of a lake is almost too tempting even for fiction. Just about any example of ironic interaction between human aspiration and the channel shifts of history's unruly river will light up in the presence of this image, as though it had entered a radiation belt of symbolism. The useless, contrary endurance of the structure is irresistibly endearing, like an old-timer who makes the same disgruntled speech in town meeting year after year whether it's germane to the agenda or not. Every March, when the lake runs low, the bridge pokes its head out of the ice to speak its piece before the rising spring flood rules it out of order and covers it once more. God bless the cranky old thing. When it finally collapses into the mud, something central to the character of the Monadnock's hill towns will lose its voice forever.

Blueberry Planet

History doesn't always make the news. In the summer of 1908, the press described the first Model T automobile rolling off Henry Ford's assembly line in Detroit, and the departure of Commander Robert E. Perry's ship from New York headed for the North Pole. The death of Joel Chandler Harris in Atlanta, the author of *Uncle Remus* and *Br'er Rabbit*, made the news, and so did the appointment in Washington of Gifford Pinchot as chairman of President Roosevelt's new Conservation Commission. But there were no reporters taking notes, no flashbulbs going off on the day that Frederick Vernon Coville, botanist for the U.S. Department of Agriculture, found in Greenfield, New Hampshire, the blueberry bush he'd spent four years seeking. True, the three previous summers his observations had been, by his own testimony, somewhat cursory—principally a matter of noting the size and flavor of the fruit on different wild highbush blueberries as he hiked about the hillsides of southern New Hampshire. That year, though, he'd spent three weeks—nearly all of July—in the town of Greenfield, in a diligent search for the very best blueberry bush of all.

The chance to tramp around in abandoned pastures, wading through waist-high meadowsweet, chokecherry, and young white pines while swatting deerflies and trying not to trip on brambles, was not the sort of project to attract even a cub reporter that hot, dry summer, let alone stop the presses. Diamonds, or oil, would have been newsworthy. Not blueberries. Agriculture in New England was in full retreat, and rock-laden fields were swiftly going back to forest. Of the thousand residents in Greenfield, a century earlier, half that number now remained. It was worse in other towns, of course, a great exodus that left behind only the elderly, the feeble, and those too stubborn to leave.

The one crop that flourished in fields no longer grazed by cattle or sheep was the wild blueberries. Acres and acres of self-sown plants covered the hillsides of the region, both the lowbush *Vaccinium angustifolium* and the much taller highbush species *Vaccinium corymbosum*. Some people called the plants that bore particularly dark fruit huckleberries, misappropriating the name of the stony-seeded fruit of *Gaylussacia*. But whatever you called them, this wild crop needed only picking. Wagons ferried whole families out from the center of town to pick blueberries. So many blueberries, in fact, that for six weeks each summer a steady stream of blue flowed toward the cities of Manchester, Lowell, Worcester, and Boston. The owner of one blueberry-filled pasture in Greenfield kept detailed records for five years. From July 1 to August 16, in the years from 1905 to 1909, he supervised the harvesting and shipping of a total of 12,384 quarts of blueberries. For these he received an average of 10.8 cents per quart.

Two-thirds of this money went to the pickers. Gathering the pea-size wild

All cultivated blueberries are descended from one bush in Greenfield.

fruits was (and is) slow work. Even someone with nimble fingers could spend forty-five minutes filling a single quart. To speed things up, some people resorted to bending the branches of the highbush blueberries over washtubs and beating them with short sections of rubber hose; others used blueberry rakes. The blueberry rake, a dustpan-shaped tool with long, thin wire fingers, worked best on lowbush blueberries. With it someone could harvest as much as three to five bushels a day (equivalent to 160 quarts). But in 1908, the going rate for a quart of raked blueberries was only 1¾ to 2 cents.

You were paid four times that much for a quart of blueberries that you had picked by hand. Those berries in turn—dry, unwrinkled, and still covered with a blue bloom of waxiness—commanded the highest prices. At the start of the season, in the Boston market, handpicked New Hampshire blueberries brought wholesale as much as 20 to 23 cents a quart. The reason for the premium price? Handpicked berries are unbruised and unbroken. Raked berries are fine for blueberry jam, blueberry muffins, or blueberry pie, but they have to be used or processed quickly before they begin to ferment and spoil. All the pickers knew this, except perhaps for the smallest children left sitting in the shade crushing fruit in their chubby fingers.

Had there been a reporter tagging after Coville that July, he or she might have written all this down, grasping the significance of this tall, handsome, somewhat reserved man's quest for the blueberry bush with the biggest fruit. At the very least, we might have a picture of the bush. It turned out to be growing in an abandoned brushy pasture belonging to Fred Brooks, a neighbor, just a short walk away from the Coville family's house. It stood, Coville would note with his characteristic attention for detail, "at an elevation of 950 feet above the sea. . . . in acid and permanently moist but not swampy soil." It wasn't the bush's seven-foot height that made it stand out among the tens of thousands of other highbush blueberries growing wild on the southern flank of Crotched Mountain, or its age. It was the fruit—light blue, sweet, but with a perfect amount of acidity, "decidedly superior," he proclaimed, "to the mild flavor of the lowbush blueberry." And most important of all, each blueberry was big, bigger than all the berries he'd yet seen. Some were more than half an inch across.

Wild blueberry pickers, like nomads in search of better pasture, have always moved on, looking for better bushes, bushes with bigger fruit, berries that will fill a bucket faster. But the 'Brooks' blueberry, as Coville would name it later, was clearly a superior variety. This wasn't according to your know-it-all older sister, either, but by the authority of a scientist from the U.S. government in Washington, D.C. The moment should have been recorded, for with this bush Coville would become the father of the cultivated blueberry. In a few years, blueberries would no longer simply be plucked from wild bushes. Growing them would be big business.

All this is easy to appreciate in retrospect. At the time, what was surprising was that the Coville family was in Greenfield in the first place. The family resided in Washington, D.C., where Frederick had been employed by the USDA ever since 1888, the year after he'd graduated from Cornell (where he'd been the "Best

General Athlete" with four university records in track and field). He'd worked on a geological survey of Arkansas, and coauthored the definitive list of that state's flora. He'd served as the botanist on the Death Valley expedition of 1891, and been a member of the Harriman Expedition to Alaska in 1899 along with John Burroughs, John Muir, and Louis Aggasiz Fuertes. He had played an important part in the establishment of the Desert Botanical Laboratory in Tucson, and was currently serving as the first curator of the National Herbarium at the Smithsonian Institution.

But Coville was worried that his four children, growing up in Washington, would never learn the rural skills that he'd acquired during his childhood in central New York State. And so when a geologist friend of his in Washington named Arthur Keith told him about a farm for sale in Greenfield, right next door to Keith's own parents' place, Coville agreed to visit. He ended up buying the place, the former Alexander farm, on May 2, 1905. The purchase price for the abandoned house and barn and forty acres was four hundred dollars. That summer the whole family—Frederick, his wife Elizabeth, and their four children, Stanley, 11; Katherine, 9; Cabot, 3; and Frederick, 2—came by train from Washington to New York, then by overnight boat to Fall River, Massachusetts, by train again to Boston, then Nashua, New Hampshire, and finally on to Greenfield. Lacking an automobile, they arranged the loan of a horse to serve as transportation, and a single cow to provide the family with the summer's milk. And so it was that the Coville family came to bolster the town's diminishing population, at least for a part of each year. They were summer people.

For Frederick, the town soon afforded a chance to collect plants, although it yielded specimens much less exotic than those collected by some of his colleagues at the USDA. This was a man who back in Washington regularly joined David Fairchild, Walter Swingle, Thomas Kearney, and other plant explorers at their famed "Lunch Mess," provided that one or the other of the men was not off gathering rambutans in Asia, dates in the Near East, or cotton in Africa.

To his colleagues, Coville's interest in the flora of New Hampshire must have seemed a bit provincial—backyard botanizing if you will. We can only imagine what it was about the genus *Vaccinium* that caught the eye of the thirty-nine-year-old botanist. But it may have been simply that everything caught his attention. Years later, his colleague Thomas Kearney would write: "No one who had the privilege of being in the field with Dr. Coville could fail to be impressed with the keenness of observation and his constant appreciation of the beauty and the human appeal as well as the scientific interest of plants." Regarding his attraction to this particular group of plants, Colville said simply that in 1906, less than a year after coming to Greenfield, his "interest was attracted to the subject of blueberry culture."

There had been previous attempts to cultivate blueberries, chiefly by digging up wild bushes and moving them to a garden setting. These had, by and large, ended in failure, with the plants mysteriously going into decline and ceasing to bear fruit. Coville was apparently undeterred. He knew of two venerable bushes growing on the grounds of the Smithsonian Institution and also a group of plants at Harvard University's Arnold Arboretum in Boston that had been transplanted or raised from seed at least thirty years earlier. Convinced that it should be possible to cultivate blueberries instead of simply harvesting wild ones, Coville arranged for George W. Oliver, a colleague of his at the Bureau of Plant Industry, to germinate some blueberry seed for him. In 1907, using the Bureau's greenhouses and nursery beds, Coville began an intensive investigation of the conditions necessary for growing seedling blueberries, experimenting with different soil mixtures, different methods of watering, varying amounts of shade, and day and night temperatures. Within just two years, the experiments in Washington would yield most of the fundamentals of blueberry culture, and in the process Coville would establish the most important condition of all: acid soil. Blueberries transplanted to ordinary garden soil, the sort that has been sweetened with ground limestone, simply fail to thrive. Such soil may be perfect for other garden crops, but it is death to blueberries. Ample moisture and good drainage are important for raising blueberries, too, but it is the soil's acidity that is critical.

Not all of Coville's research was confined to Washington, however. When he returned to Greenfield in 1908, he brought with him 179 seedling blueberries that in early July he confidently planted in a "partially moist natural meadow." Ninety-seven percent of these seedlings, he reported later, survived the hard drought of that summer and the rigors of the following winter. This was not surprising, for they had been returned to their native soil.

All of Coville's experiments with blueberry culture, from the germination of seeds to the rooting of cuttings, were necessary preliminaries for the project he envisioned—the transformation of blueberries from a wild harvest to a cultivated crop. But true domestication, he knew, would require the breeding of superior varieties. His goal: larger, earlier-ripening berries that would not only be easier to pick but would bring the grower the highest prices. This goal had led him to examine wild bushes for the three previous summers, and it finally spurred him, once he'd set out his seedling blueberry plants in the meadow, to devote three weeks to searching for the best breeding stock. When he found 'Brooks', the bush appeared to be perfect in every respect but one. Its only apparent flaw was that it ripened late. It was not until August 2 that Coville picked the bush clean. From the three quarts he harvested that day, he recorded the precise distribution of fruit into various size classes (the largest berry on the bush was 14.02 millimeters in diameter, or 0.552 inches). He discarded all those berries less than 10 mm and carried the remaining two quarts back to Washington for seed.

The next summer, he tried hand-pollinating 'Brooks' with its own pollen, both on the original bush and on plants he'd propagated by grafting and by rooting cuttings. It was a complete failure, producing not a single viable seed. Self-sterility, or a plant's inability to pollinate its own flowers, was to prove characteristic of many varieties of blueberries. Fortunately, that same year, 1909, another neighbor of the Covilles' in Greenfield, Frank Russell, whose land lay in the other direction from Fred Brooks', drew Coville's attention to the best lowbush blueberry on his six-hundred-acre farm. Now shaded by the branches of a young oak tree, it no longer bore fruit, but taken back to the greenhouses in Washington it proved to yield berries that were nine-sixteenths of an inch in diameter. What's more, the light blue berries ripened much earlier than those of 'Brooks', a trait that was to prove valuable.

'Brooks' and 'Russell' became the parents of the first generation of hybrid blueberries; they were first crossed in the spring of 1911. Some of these first-generation hybrids were in turn crossed with each other in 1913, and the results, some three thousand hybrid seedlings, were planted out in Coville's research plots in Washington. Most of the bushes, reflecting their mixed ancestry, were intermediate in height. Back in Greenfield, Coville had heard these plants popularly called half highs, a sign that such interbreeding was a natural occurrence.

Thousands of full-size plants required considerable room to grow and evaluate, and so it was fortunate that a copy of Coville's first paper, the 1910 Bulletin No. 193 of the Bureau of Plant Industry titled "Experiments in Blueberry Culture," came into the hands of Miss Elizabeth C. White of New Lisbon, New Jersey. Her family was in the business of growing cranberries (a congeneric species, *Vaccinium macrocarpon*), and Miss White grasped the significance of blueberries as a potential new crop for the wasteland surrounding her family's bogs. She immediately contacted Coville and the two soon entered into a formal agreement whereby she would provide space in New Jersey to field-test the blueberry hybrids being produced in Washington.

She also provided additional breeding material. 'Sooy', for example, was a select wild highbush blueberry belonging to the mid-Atlantic species *Vaccinium australe* that had fruit five-eighths of an inch in diameter. The particular plant was discovered by a picker by the name of Ezekiel Sooy. Grabbing a piece of the original bush in Coville's presence, Sooy ripped it from the ground, exclaiming to the alarmed Coville, "That root will grow. You can't kill a blueberry bush." Another selection was 'Rubel', a wild plant that is still in cultivation today. ('Rubel' has recently been shown to have one of the highest antioxidant levels of all known varieties of blueberry, which in turn already exceed the antioxidant levels of all other fruits.) As for the name 'Rubel', it comes not from the Russian currency but from Rube Leek, its discoverer. Unwilling to name it either 'Leek' or 'Rube', Coville chose the man's first name and added to it the first initial of his last.

These selections and others would all play a part in the creation of hybrid blueberries. But none was to play as ubiquitous a role as the original 'Brooks'. The first hybrid blueberries, a trio of them, were introduced by the USDA in 1920. The first was appropriately named 'Pioneer' and had light blue berries measuring three-quarters of an inch in diameter. It had 'Brooks' and 'Sooy' as parents, as did the second variety, 'Katherine', named for Coville's daughter, who in one of her high school years had done all the pollinations. The third was a cross between 'Brooks' and 'Chatsworth' (the latter from the New Jersey town of that name). This was named 'Cabot', after Coville's son, who as it turned out was the only one of his three sons not to enter the blueberry business, becoming a diplomat instead.

The year 1926 saw the introduction of 'Rancocas' ('Brooks' × 'Russell' × 'Rubel') and 'Greenfield' ('Brooks' × 'Russell'), which commemorated the town where it all began. In 1930, Stanley Coville, who was married and already growing blueberries in New Jersey, got his namesake, a variety resulting from a cross between 'Katherine' and 'Rubel'. By 1937, the USDA project had fruited sixty-eight thousand seedlings and introduced a total of fifteen varieties. All but two of these varieties had 'Brooks' in their ancestry, and it was Coville's firm conviction that these two would have been tastier if they had had 'Brooks' in their genes. Another fifteen varieties would be introduced in the next twenty years derived from seed and seedlings bred by Coville, but Coville himself died suddenly on January 9, 1937, at the age of sixty-nine. His legacy was already assured: a small but growing number of commercial highbush blueberry plantations, including those owned by his sons Stanley and Frederick. Not until 1949, a dozen years after his death, did the great botanist get a variety named for himself, a very late-ripening variety with highly aromatic, slightly tart berries, of the sort that had always appealed to his palate. Coville would have liked 'Coville' if only because it had 'Stanley' as one of its parents, proving that in blueberry breeding, at least, the child can be father of the man.

Today there are more than 150 named varieties of blueberries, and potential new ones are lined up in breeders' fields. The search is not just for larger berries but also for ones that ripen earlier or later, varieties that will tolerate extreme cold or extreme heat, varieties with built-in resistance to insects and disease. There are now more than fifty thousand acres in production in North America alone, not to mention the plantations springing up in South America, Europe, Asia, New Zealand, and Australia. Pickers still rake wild lowbush blueberries from the barrens of Maine, but almost all the fresh fruit on the shelves of grocery stores and supermarkets comes from cultivated highbush blueberry hybrids—bushes grown in Michigan, New Jersey, North Carolina, and Washington. Only hikers and picnickers have the time to mess with the tiny fruits of wild highbush blueberries.

With the new hybrids, pickers now harvest twelve quarts an hour. That's a quart every five minutes, for which they receive 40 cents. As the minimum wage increases, so no doubt will the size of the blueberry to allow even faster harvesting (until someone comes up with a variety that can be machine-harvested for fresh use). The berries are huge, some more than an inch across. They are easy to pick; they come off the bush cleanly, with a nice, small, dry scar. But if you look closely at these hybrid blueberries, stare deeply enough into their heart, you'll find again and again the large-fruited blueberry from Greenfield, New Hampshire. Its blood is in 'Bluecrop' and 'Blueray', in 'Bluetta', 'Collins', 'Darrow', in 'Earliblue', 'Herbert', 'Northland', and 'Patriot'. The list goes on. At a recent conference of North American blueberry researchers, someone tried to compute the dollar contribution of cultivated blueberries resulting from Coville's efforts, and came up with a number in excess of a billion dollars. 'Brooks' was a parent to most of these varieties. The original bush may be long gone, but its offspring are very much with us.

So too is the family. There are still Covilles in Greenfield. The original house burned in a forest fire that started in May of 1925 and quickly spread, but the house was rebuilt by Coville's son Frederick (the only one of the Coville children not to have a berry named after him, because his father didn't want people to think he'd named a berry after himself). Frederick, or Freck as he was sometimes called, grew blueberries commercially in North Carolina but continued to come to Greenfield every summer until his death a few years ago. He left behind four bushes of 'Coville' that are still flourishing in a row at the west corner of the house. His son Frederick V. Coville, an orthopedic surgeon from Colorado called Rick, and Rick's brother Ned, a forester in Ketchikan, Alaska, have inherited the place.

The 140-acre property now includes the land on which the original 'Brooks' plant stood. That pasture, like most of southern New Hampshire, has long since grown up to mature trees, and would be in forest today except for a freak tornado that touched down a few years ago and cut a neat swath right up the side of the hill. In the wake of the loggers who salvaged the downed wood, there is now a large clearing once again. Fresh ground for blueberries.

Mention Frederick Vernon Coville and you will hear many things: that he was chairman of the Research Committee of the National Geographic Society for seventeen years, that he spent thirty years establishing the National Arboretum, that his real expertise was the flora of Death Valley. But in Greenfield, he is remembered for blueberries. If a monument is ever erected to him, it should be to the man who picked a winner on that July day back in 1908. The discovery of 'Brooks' was his finest hour. Writing in the 1937 *Yearbook of Agriculture*, in an article completed just a few weeks before his death, he once again described the large-berried bush lest anyone miss its importance: "I regard its selection as of fundamental importance to the success of the Department's blueberry-breeding experiments," he said. "Every breeder of race horses or of milk cows understands that the choosing of the individuals to be interbred is of the highest importance. Plant breeders usually select carefully the species they intend to interbreed, but often make the mistake of paying too little attention to the choice of superior individual plants within the species." Picking out one bush from a sea of others was Coville's real gift. No one was there to witness the moment, but it was a moment to behold. From this one bush, growing in an abandoned Greenfield pasture a hundred years ago, has come a bloodline so broad and so blue that by now it has added its own tint to our blue planet.

Debt, drink, and despair plagued "the painter of Monadnock," William Preston Phelps, in his later years. His studio, sometimes mistaken for a chapel, was a big, high-ceilinged place, filled with his paintings and with items he had acquired during his travels.

The Tragic Life of William Preston Phelps

EDIE CLARK

On February 27, 1917, William Preston Phelps, known as "the painter of Monadnock," sat in his kitchen in Chesham, New Hampshire. Through the window, his beloved Mount Monadnock could be seen, cloaked in a froth of snow. He had turned to this mountain so many times throughout his life, for inspiration, for solace, for wonder. Hundreds of his canvases focused on this singular peak, around which the entire region revolved. He had painted it from every aspect, in all kinds of weather, including a day just like this one. But this was not a day when he looked to the mountain. His farm, where he had been born and which had been in his family for three generations, was in disarray as was his studio, where more than two hundred of his paintings had been taken out, photographed, cataloged, titled, and described by others than himself. These paintings were by no means his life's work but they were the ones in his possession, and they included two of his masterpieces: *The Grand Canyon*, thought to be the first painting ever created of that ultimate American landscape—the magnificent work measured seven feet by twelve feet—and *The Tillers of the Soil*, which had been exhibited for many years at the Museum of Fine Arts in Boston. In the studio, aside from his own paintings, were canvases given to him by his teachers Wilhelm Velten and Ernst Meissner, the great German artists who had schooled Phelps in his painstakingly realistic techniques. On shelves, decorating his vast, high-ceilinged studio, were souvenirs from his travels in Scotland, Wales, Germany, France, and England. His art and his passion for his art had taken him and his family far from this homely New Hampshire farm. The sixty-nine-year-old painter had risen from his roots here on the farm to almost international acclaim. Students had come to study with him here from distant places. Nonetheless, since his wife, Anna, had died, debts had piled up and his drinking had increased.

The winter of 1917 had been one of the hardest in memory. The snows had fallen steadily and intensely throughout the months of January and February and bitter, high winds had drifted snow across the roads continually, making travel on these rough dirt roads virtually impossible. Preston, the tall, garrulous painter who had always enjoyed welcoming visitors and students into his studio, had spent many days and nights alone. Along with his finances, his health had been in decline. His tall, slender constitution had become gaunt, his nerves fragile.

That morning, a neighbor, whom Preston had known his entire life, had come to the door, apparently to check on him. In a burst of madness, Preston grabbed his pistol and brandished it at his friend, threatening him. The frightened man ran home and called the authorities.

Calves in the Lane: Phelps was flawless in his rendition of cows and sheep and found early in his career that one way to earn extra income was by painting portraits of prize cattle and horses.

Through the windowpane, Preston saw the sheriff's black car pull into his yard. The excruciating dealings of the last two years were coming to an end. As William Preston Phelps, cuffed in the back seat, was taken away by the sheriff to the asylum in Concord, the mountain receded. What loomed was the auction, long planned, wherein all his paintings and all his earthly possessions, even including his checkerboard and the petrified wood he had picked up on the desert in Arizona, would be sold to the highest bidder.

The son of Jason and Mary Phelps, William Preston was born March 6, 1848, on a farm in the Pottersville section of Dublin, which is now known as Chesham. At the time of Preston's birth, the farm was a busy place, with cows, pigs, sheep, goats, chickens, and all the sundry affairs of a working farm. Jason was a farmer but he was also a painter and a furniture maker. Violins that he made are still being played. In the front room of the farmhouse, he stenciled the walls and decorated the paneling around the fireplace with imitation wood graining. Family diaries indicate that he ground his own paint and that, although he was a hardworking farmer, he was also employed as a housepainter. The two endeavors were not lost on the oldest of his two sons. Preston (as he was known to family and friends) grew up farming. In the records on file at the Smithsonian, his daughter Ina recalled that her father "worked on the farm, doing the usual chores such as milking, feeding and bedding horses and cows, feeding poultry and pigs (always), driving cows to pasture, running the horse rake, treading and mowing the hay and mowing with the scythe."

Preston "always mowed his lawns" (that was the word used, not fields) "with his scythe, barefoot and early before the dew dried, producing an expert piece of work—no holidays in it," noted his granddaughter Hilda Parker.

This work on the farm would serve him later in his art, as one of the star accomplishments of his paintings was his ability to draw animals in such a way as you can almost see the animal move. He was flawless in his rendition of cows and sheep and found early in his career that one way to earn extra income was by painting portraits of prize cattle and horses.

Apparently as a boy, when he was not working on the farm, Preston drew constantly. He went to school in Dublin, both grammar school and high school, and his notebooks were filled with sketches and drawings. When Preston was fourteen, his father, perhaps more interested in the money Preston might be able to earn than in developing his artistic notions, sent him to apprentice with a sign painter, Jeduthan Kittredge, in a shop in downtown Lowell, Massachusetts. The young Preston proved himself to be enterprising. By the time he was twenty, in 1868, he had married Jeduthan's daughter, Anna Marie, and within another year, he owned his own sign-painting business just a few doors down from his father-in-law.

The signs he painted were complex and beautiful—intricate scrollwork and elliptical scenes painted on wagons and sleighs. Patrons were so impressed that they began to ask him to paint the same scenes on canvas to be framed and hung in their homes. In the evenings, Preston took the train to Boston, where he studied a more serious kind of art, and soon he began to paint landscapes and local scenes along the banks of the Merrimack and Concord rivers. He put these paintings up for sale in the window of his sign shop, and in time he was known as Lowell's first landscape painter.

Lowell was an industrial city, on the rise but also interested in cultivating its somewhat sparse cultural climate. Toward that end, a group of prominent Lowell citizens raised the money to send Preston to Germany to further his art education. At the age of twenty-eight, in 1876, he kissed Anna and his two children good-bye and sailed for Europe alone, where he began studies in Munich at the Royal Academy of Art.

In Munich, he met and traveled with many of the up-and-coming artists of that day, most especially including William Merritt Chase, with whom he was to share a long friendship. Preston enjoyed this time, but it ultimately proved too much for him and in less than a year he returned, lonely and homesick for his family. A little more than a year later, he returned to Europe, this time with Anna and the children, Ina and Edward, then aged seven and four respectively.

He continued his studies in Munich with Velten, who bestowed on Preston his lifelong devotion to plein air painting. With his family around him, these years

A Phelps canvas showing winter ice. Phelps was especially fond of painting in winter. He often chose dark, moody days on which to paint. His skies are the color of tarnished silver, and snow appears far more often than green grass.

traveling the valleys of the Rhine and Dussel rivers were possibly Preston's happiest and the least troubled of his life. He sent several paintings home to the National Gallery, and he was able to sell two, one for five hundred dollars and the other for a thousand dollars, excellent money in those days. In 1879, he moved his family to Paris, where, he told his brother years later, "a whole new way of thinking about color was opened to me." He did not elaborate, but it is known that his early paintings are done in a predominantly brown palette, yet his European and post-European work opens out into reds and blues and violets.

From Paris, they traveled to England and Scotland and Wales, where Preston continued to work up new canvases. At the end of 1879, they sailed home from Glasgow to New York and then made their way by coach home to Lowell, where they were greeted like homecoming heroes.

Preston loved Scotland and in 1881 he felt a pull to return to the Highlands, where he created many canvases of the landscape and the native cattle. A newspaper clipping noted: "It is a singular fact that before Mr. Phelps, no American artist ever endeavored to show us what the Scottish Highlands were like."

Soon after, he rejoined his friend William Merritt Chase for a working tour of Italy, Venice, Capri, and once again Germany. In November of 1881 he sailed home to Lowell in a hurricane, which broke the main boom and swept three of

the crewmen overboard. He huddled for safety in the saloon along with all other passengers, and they arrived safely in New York as the winds were dying.

And so, after five years of on-and-off travel through Europe, Preston settled down in Lowell, where he set up a studio. In the summers, he roamed the New England coast, as well as Grand Manan. He also did a series of paintings along the Merrimack River in the mornings and evenings. But he wasn't able to live solely from the sales of these paintings, and he continued to supplement his income by painting portraits of cattle and prize bulls.

In 1886 he went west, where he began a series of paintings, most notably the large one of the Grand Canyon. At the edge of the canyon, Preston built a structure around the painting so that he could work on it continually outdoors—he recounted later to his children and grandchildren that while he was painting, Indians would come up behind him and quietly observe him at work and then silently move off. When he was finished, he rolled the canvas and took it home with him on the train. He considered this painting to be his masterpiece.

Preston's father died in 1888, leaving the family homestead to him. Anna, being a city girl, was reluctant to move, but for Preston the farm was a place to which he had returned frequently throughout his life, and it was a place that gave him respite. They waited for Ina to finish high school and then, in 1890, the family moved to the homestead.

Phelps's painting of the homestead barn interior. His wife, Anna Marie, feeds the chickens as their daughter, Ina, looks on. Late afternoon light streams through the knots and spaces in the barn boards. The look in the eyes of the cattle is of a vast benevolence.

Phelps's canvas of a view looking south to Monadnock. "He studied the mountain with the eye of a lover. In sunshine and shadow, in storm and calm, in all seasons and under all conditions, he watched and noted and painted," Charles E. Hurd wrote in 1898.

What he discovered on his return to Chesham was his love of Mount Monadnock. "Standing one afternoon in the doorway of the little porch, looking southward, [Preston] saw what he had seen with his outer eyes a thousand times before but never saw as he saw it now. In the distance, over the long green slope, across the valley below and the wooded ridge beyond, towered the great mountain, its gray summit of granite shouldering the sky. . . . This was it at last! The commonest things now took on new meaning. The artist had now found and recognized his life work," Charles E. Hurd wrote in 1898. "He studied the mountain with the eye of a lover. In sunshine and shadow, in storm and calm, in all seasons and under all conditions, he watched and noted and painted."

Two years later, Preston bought the land across the road and built his studio. He designed it and built it himself. Sometimes mistaken for a chapel, the studio was a big, high-ceilinged place, filled with his paintings and with items he had acquired during his travels. On one wall, he hung his masterpiece, *The Grand Canyon of the Colorado*, concealed by a great red curtain. When visitors came, he enjoyed dramatically pulling the curtain back to reveal the enormous canvas.

He was especially fond of painting in winter, which was a cold and forbidding endeavor. To make himself comfortable, he built a traveling studio that could be transported on horse-drawn sled or wagon. The shelter was equipped with easel, paints, canvas, and a small oil stove. This enabled him to work outdoors for long periods of time. Though the summer seasons would have permitted him to work outdoors with less of an encumbrance, it's interesting that so many of his

canvases capture the mountain in the winter, in ice, in snow, the afternoon light casting pink shadows onto the bluish snow.

Many of his canvases are undated and unmarked, leaving it to us to guess just where he was when he painted that particular view of the mountain. Although there is a preponderance of scenes from Dublin and Chesham, he did circle the ridge and commit almost every angle of the mountain to canvas. Preston's eye was like a camera. He painted with extreme honesty, so that every blade of grass, every sheep in pasture comes to us just as it was, no embellishment, no changes. This left us with yet another legacy, which he surely could not have predicted. Once forested to the very top, the mountain experienced a raging forest fire two hundred years ago, which bared the peak and created the rock face that is now so familiar to all of us. But time and the edicts of conservation have left the mountain's face to evolve naturally. If we use his images as a gauge, we can see that the tree line has advanced toward the summit—which intimates that it may, once again, become forested to the top.

Once he returned to Chesham, he must have been busy all the time at his easel, whether inside the barn, in the heated wagon, or out in the snow. He was probably a familiar sight, out in the weather, capturing the scenes he was so drawn to. He often chose dark, moody days on which to paint. His skies are the color of tarnished silver and snow appears far more often than green grass. He liked the autumn palette as well, the umbers and the mustards. In various works, the mountain is fox colored, crimson, almost black. Rather than midday,

A Phelps painting of Monadnock with cattle in foreground. His eye was like a camera. He painted with extreme honesty, so that every blade of grass, every sheep in pasture comes to us just as it was, no embellishment, no changes.

he painted most often in the evening or early morning, yielding salmon skies or a peach glow to the snow. Why he worked more in the cold seasons is a question worth pondering. The practical answer would be that he was a farmer and winter was when he had more time on his hands. Or perhaps he was drawn to the darker moods of winter.

The subjects of his paintings are virtually always the mountain or the farm. He likely found that the mountain canvases sold well so he worked to build up that inventory. But from his heart, he painted the farm scenes, the cattle in their stalls, the pigs and hens in the yard. Several of his largest and most impressive canvases capture scenes of mud season, the color of the mud on the canvas so real it seems he might have used the mud itself, rather than mix the paint to match. His scenes are like snapshots of those times: teams of oxen clearing snow and hauling sap sleds, sheep grazing, men scything hay, and even one extraordinary scene of Anna Marie, feeding the chickens inside the barn with little Ina, who looks to be about five in the painting, and the cattle looking on. Late afternoon light streams through the knots and spaces in the barn boards. The look in the eyes of the cattle is of a vast benevolence.

This frenzy of painting activity that surrounded his return to Chesham lasted about ten years, until 1901, a year that perhaps stole the life from him, even though he lived another twenty-two years. Preston's son, Edward, had grown up to become an artist like his father. He was a painter and had taken also to lecturing, which he enjoyed. When he was twenty-seven, he traveled to the West to paint and to prepare a series of lectures. In May of 1901, Edward was in Waco, Texas, waiting for a train when a child tumbled onto the tracks in front of the incoming train. Edward jumped down, grabbed the baby, and was able to toss the child back up to its mother before he was run over and killed.

Anna, who was older than Preston by five years, had not been well, and both she and Preston took the news of their son's death very hard. Within six months, in December of 1901, Anna died, leaving Preston alone on the farm. He began to drink heavily, frequenting the Dublin hotel bar. In 1906, he married again. His new wife apparently felt that she could cure him of his drinking. However, in 1909, she divorced him.

Preston was a frugal man who ate sparingly and carefully—his lunch was always a thick sandwich of chopped onions and hard-boiled eggs with French dressing (he was famous for this recipe, which he had learned to make in France) and a glass of milk. Every Sunday, he made seven of these huge sandwiches, laid them on a platter under a damp cloth, and left them in the cellar for the week's rations.

In 1914, he turned to the auctioneering firm of J. E. Conant and Sons in Lowell for help with his finances, according to papers left to the Smithsonian by his daughter, Ina. Over the years, Preston had already borrowed, one note at a time, until he owed Conant more than $2,500. At that point, J. E. Conant pretty much owned William Preston Phelps, which meant that there would be an auction to sell the farm and all of its contents, including his paintings.

Preston was by then in his sixties and had heart complications. The distress he felt over the prospect of the loss not only of his homestead, which had been in the Phelps family since 1763, but also of his studio and all his paintings, can only be loosely imagined. As the date of the auction loomed, Preston brooded while Ina worked steadily toward the sale. Though the papers do not articulate this, the efforts that Ina put into preparing the site indicate that she very much anticipated a financial gain.

After her father was removed from the house, Ina stepped up her efforts. At that time, she and her husband, the artist Roger Hayward, lived in Marlborough, and her diary entries indicate that many days, from May to August, they walked the seven miles from their home in Marlborough to the Phelps homestead to work on the estate. She scrubbed the farmhouse, polished anything that could be polished, wrote the extensive copy for the auction catalog, and framed and prepared paintings for the sale. Many nights, she recorded that they worked until three or four in the morning on these tasks. It must have been excruciatingly painful work. As she carefully prepared each cherished family object, she knew she would never see these things again. Ina was able to smuggle several paintings home with her so that the family could have a few of her father's works. But Conant caught wind of this and eventually a sheriff was dispatched to watch over the farm and the paintings. Her last days at the farm were under guard.

In an almost cruel twist, the summer of 1917 was one of the hottest in memory. In the days leading up to the August 2 sale, the mercury reached nearly one hundred degrees. In the cities, Boston, New York, and Philadelphia, many deaths were blamed on the relentless heat wave. Additionally the United States was perilously close to joining the war in Europe, which had dominated the news for the past year. Local boys had recently been drafted.

And so, in this wilting heat and with this grim national backdrop, the auction was held. Hundreds gathered on the lawn that Preston had once scythed so perfectly but which now was scattered with his bureaus and tables and chairs. Inside the barn, his carpenter's tools, his broadax, and even his scythe was sold. In the studio, his palette and the pebbles he had picked up on the beach at Grand Manan were sold along with the paintings. In spite of the careful framing and listing of each painting, most paintings sold for only $20 to $40. The highest price was $180. All of it, the family homestead and hundreds of paintings, gone in the course of one hot August afternoon. In the end, the only one to profit was the auctioneer. Ina pursued the Conants through the courts, but she had little success.

William Preston Phelps had already been living at the Concord State Hospital for six months at the time of the auction, and it's virtually impossible to know what he knew, if anything, about the event. He lived for another five years before dying on January 6, 1923. His funeral was attended by a few family members and a scattering of old friends. It was noted in one of the newspapers that the burial in the Edson cemetery in Lowell took place during the biggest snowstorm of that winter.

Two days after the funeral, the administrator of the hospital wrote to Ina to say that they had found two dollars in Preston's pocket and that they were enclosing a check in that amount, along with his trousers.

The works for which William Preston Phelps was most famous are almost all among the missing. His *Evening*, his *Morning*. Most prominently missing is the great painting of the Grand Canyon, last known to have left the auction in the hands of the auctioneer, who knew well that Preston regarded it as his masterpiece.

In the years that followed, the Phelps homestead changed hands several times and has now been added onto and seriously renovated. The studio, which stood idle for many years, was burned by vandals in 1971 and has since been torn down and replaced by a house of modern design. The paintings of William Preston Phelps have been found here and there at auction and in antique shops. In the 1960s, a painting of his could be had for $100 or perhaps less, but interest in his work returned and the value climbed. Recently a painting of the mountain sold for $40,000, though most of his paintings can be had for between $5,000 and $10,000.

William Preston Phelps was not only the "painter of Monadnock"; he was a painter of place, this place. The scenes around the sugarhouse, in the farmyard, inside the barn, and in the woods, scenes that were so commonplace to him and his neighbors, exist now for us on the many canvases he left behind, which are there for us not only as works of art but, because of the honesty of his work, as a testament to our history. After that cold February day in 1917 when he was taken by force from his home, William Preston Phelps never again saw his beloved mountain. But since that time, countless collectors and admirers have seen the mountain as he saw it, in all kinds of weather. His work has not only given us pleasure but also an invaluable record of the mountain and of the region, just as it was.

The Poor Farm

JOHN R. HARRIS

The poor you always have with you.
—Matthew 26:11

The circle of support for those least able to care for themselves in the Monadnock region has expanded gradually over time. Before 1820 families were expected to care for their own least fortunate. New residents suspected of being paupers could be "warned out," or banished by selectmen, and those who were orphaned, abandoned, or incorrigible were "vendued," or auctioned off, to townspeople who agreed to provide for their care at a fixed price. In the mid-1800s town farms emerged as a method for consolidating the needs of the indigent. Many town farms were notorious for their squalor and lack of compassion.

A summary of the records in Westmoreland, where the county farm has been located for over a century, illustrates how individual and town responsibilities for the poor have evolved.

1783   Voted that a woman who resides at the house of Joshua Pierce who is warned out of town be carried out of town according to the directions of the law. Voted that it is the sense and opinion of this town that no shaking Quaker who is not an inhabitant of this town be allowed to stay in town any more than one night at one time.

1784   Voted to pay Reuben Dagget his 20 pounds for taking a poor child as good as money was when the bargain was made between him and the town.

1787   Voted that the Selectmen vendue the poor to them that will keep them cheapest. Voted to choose a committee to take into consideration and allow or relinquish any of the rates of the poor as they shall think proper.

1792   The poor bid off at vendue as follows: Black Dinah by Caleb Briggs for three shillings, ten pence per week; Lucy Witt's child to Ebenezer Harrington for one shilling, ten pence; Joshua Johnson by Joel Priest for five shilling, ten pence; and Moses Thompson's family also cared for by the town, by Elijah Temple.

1808   Voted to see if the town will build, buy, or hire a building suitable for a workhouse for the Town's poor and buy or hire a piece of land proper for the same.

1832   Voted to purchase the Daggett farm for $2,000 for the purpose of establishing a town farm for care of the poor.

After 1850 larger county facilities, often designed to combine the functions of charity, mental and physical health, and incarceration began to appear in New

The Alms House of Cheshire County served the poor, the insane, and criminals.

Hampshire. In 1867 Cheshire County delegates voted to purchase the Sabin farm along the Connecticut River in Westmoreland for thirteen thousand dollars to be used as the site for the County Farm and Alms House. However, at first many towns were reluctant to consign their poor to this new facility.

Beginning in 1872 the Cheshire County Commissioners published annual reports summarizing the operations of the farm, Alms House, and House of Correction:

Inmates at the Alms House and the House of Correction worked on the county farm to feed themselves.

1872	The number of inmates at the County Alms House this year was 37. The number of paupers assisted away from the Alms House was 160. The number of transient paupers assisted during the year was 226. Of the number assisted away from the Alms House, one is at the State Reform School, one at Vt. Asylum, two at N.H. Asylum. Several others are cases that cannot be removed to the Alms House, and a large number who receive a smaller amount of aid than would be required if moved to the farm.
1873	Those at the Alms House have been at all times supplied with a plenty of good and wholesome food, comfortable beds and clothing, and with such care as necessary to make them as comfortable and happy as possible under the circumstances of their condition, subject only to such restrictions as have been deemed necessary for their own good, and the proper management of the institution.
1875	An item of considerable magnitude in the expenses of the County is for the board of prisoners confined in the jail. By law the jailor is entitled to two dollars and fifty cents per week for their board, besides key fees to be paid by the County. The law also provides that such persons may be sentenced to hard labor at the House of Correction if there is one in the County. The Alms House could be arranged at a small expense so as to

be available for a House of Correction, as has been done in several other counties. [A house of correction was added during this year.]

1876–7   The increase of pauper expenses was incurred mainly for aid given to the employees of the Keene and Manchester Railroad, who were defrauded of pay and labor and left without means of subsistence upon the public for support. The pauper expenses for the past year would have been, in our opinion, more than two thousand dollars less than they were the year previous, had it not been for this class and those who came in search of labor upon said railroad, who were without means of support, and had to be aided. However, considering the general depression of business through the country, the tendency to disregard the law and commit crime, it is not surprising that our pauper and court expenses are large; and they will continue to be heavy so long as business everywhere continues to be depressed, and the tendency to do wrong unchecked. [See the expanded entry for this year, below.]

1878   "What shall be done with the Tramps," seems at present to be one of the most serious questions before the people. As will be seen by report, they are not only a disagreeable, and perhaps dangerous element in community, but very expensive.

1882   The citizens of the County are greatly indebted to the "Orphans Home" at Franklin, NH and to the "Home for Little Wanderers" at Boston, for taking from the Alms House and from all parts of the County many of the little waifs and orphan children, and after training a year or two, providing them with good homes in responsible families; thus relieving the County of the care and cost of their keeping, schooling and maintenance.

1883   The County has twice been indicted on account of the condition of the Jail. The House of Correction, at Westmoreland, and in connection with the Alms House, was temporarily located there in 1875, for the accommodation of the tramps that at the time were infesting the State, —as it was not thought advisable to admit them to the Alms House as paupers. But now a different class are sent there, and different provisions ought to be made for safely keeping and employing them. It should not be continued in connection with the home for the unfortunate poor. [A new county jail was constructed in Keene in 1885. Prisoners were housed at the facility until 1922, when the jail was closed and sold to the city of Keene. Prisoners were transported to Manchester between 1922 and 1926, after which time one wing of the County Alms House was remodeled to function as a jail and house of correction.]

1903   The electric lighting plant installed in the spring of 1902 has been in constant and successful operation, and while it is found to be somewhat expensive to maintain with gasoline at fifteen and one-half cents a gallon we should not wish to dispense with it and go back to such imperfect and dangerous means of lighting as when using kerosene lamps.

1905   According to the State Board of Charities and Corrections, for the year ending Oct. 1, 1904 there were committed to the county houses of correction in this state, 1575 prisoners, 1467 men and 108 women. Of this number 1,337 were sentenced for drunkenness. The total number of inmates (not including convicts) cared for at the ten different almshouses in the state was 1,675; of this number 971 are given as men, and 704 as women. Apparently men are more willing to accept quarters at an almshouse

Insane women were housed in a separate building beginning in 1910.

than women, and give up more easily the struggle for an independent existence. These figures will not apply to the Cheshire county farm as we now have, exclusive of convicts, 42 males and 49 females. The causes given for the support of these 1,675 inmates are as follows: 219 (adults) feeble minded, 373 insane, 62 epileptics, 661 feeble minded through old age or sickness, 3 as blind and deaf, 29 as intemperate, 16 as widowed or deserted, 94 infants, and 218 cause not given.

1915   "It seems to me that there should be a law enacted requiring that the annual county report should contain the name of each person assisted outside of the county farm, and to what extent each was assisted. . . . it does not seem right for the genteel poor to be screened from the eyes of the public by their identity being kept from the public, because if these people now supported in whole or in part by the county outside of the farm were to have their names appear in the county report the same as those who are obligated to go the farm, there would not be so many calls for assistance" [A. A. Whitman, Alms House superintendent].

1919   At a visit of the delegation on the 28th day of February there were thirty-nine head of cattle, some of which were infested with vermin and in poor flesh. The hospital building was in particularly bad condition. It was uncompleted, the floors were not level, daylight could be seen through the casing and joints, and there was not a door frame or window frame properly set. Taking it all in all, the hospital, in the minds of the committee who are familiar with such things, was one of the most poorly constructed buildings that they ever examined [Special Committee Appointed to Investigate the Condition of County Affairs].

1924   During the first part of the year an epidemic of the "Flu" prevailed at the County Farm and not withstanding the good care and medical attendance rendered, there were quite a number of deaths among the old people. [Twenty-three inmates died as opposed to nine deaths in 1919].

1936   Previously it has been our misfortune to record the damage done by the flood of 1927 and the fire of 1933 at the County Farm, but during the year of 1936 we experienced both. While we had to make extensive repairs after the flood of last March, the fact that the water began to come into the buildings that were occupied by human beings, and that the Farm was practically isolated and surrounded by water for a number of days, made a most distressing situation. Fortunately, no lives were lost and no sickness ensued, but one building was badly undermined and about four acres of tillage land belonging to the County was washed away.

1950   There has been a good deal of concern about our jail at the Farm. There is no way to segregate the prisoners in separate cells, and the trouble makers are continually with the others. We have had a number of undesirable families from bordering states come into the County to take up residence in camps or abandoned old homes, who have demanded aid about as soon as they got here. After thorough investigation it has been found where these families belonged and with the assistance of other agencies, they have been returned to their former locations.

1954   It has been a trying year for all who have the responsibility of maintenance and well-being of the Institution. State Officials have condemned two of the present buildings so far as medical patients are concerned, demanded more nursing care in the infirmary and many other changes in the building's structure. Women inmates in the Women's Building, so called, were transferred to the infirmary.

1957   Since there are no more institutional homes for foster children in NH it has meant much investigation of foster homes and the study of children before they are placed in the present homes. We have assisted 56 foster families this year.

1971   The last year in which inmates at the Almshouse were identified. The list includes two women, aged 57 and 44, and three men, aged 86, 71, and 60. [Thereafter, the facility began to accept applicants based on poor health rather than dire economic need.]

1974   A new jail was finally constructed at the County Farm for $800,000. [This facility was expanded by thirty-one beds in 1988, and a much larger expansion of the jail was being considered in 2004.]

1978   This was our first full year in the Maplewood nursing home [which replaced the older Alms House and hospital], and despite some continuing problems with the air handlers and a few other small problems, we feel that we have the finest facility for the aged in New Hampshire.

1988   After many years of debate between various county delegations and commissioners, a contract was finally let for demolition of the remaining six old nursing/jail administrative buildings at Westmoreland.

1876–77 Cheshire County Commissioners Report

INMATE POPULATION

No. of paupers at Alms House, May 1, 1876	50
No. of paupers admitted during the year	67
No. of paupers discharged during the year	56
No. of paupers died during the year	7
No. of paupers at Alms House, May 1, 1877	54

The Cheshire County Farm includes some of the most productive agricultural land in North America.

Alms House Inmate Selected Representation

Name	Age	Received from	Date admitted	Nationality	Remarks
Males					
Bryant, Kendall	19	Jaffrey	Jan. 14, 76	American	Escaped May 28, 1876
Buffum, Mijamin	79	Richmond	Aug. 6, 75	"	Died, May 1, 1876 cause gen. debility
Burpee, Asaph E.	40	Dublin	Dec. 13, 75	"	Town pauper
Driscoll, Denny	6	Keene	Sept. 16, 76	Irish	Discharged Oct. 10, 76
Driscoll, John	5	"	Sept. 16, 76	"	" " "
Driscoll, Hanney	3	"	Sept. 16, 76	"	" " "
Gassett, Walker	79	Marlow	Feb. 5. 74	American	
Grimes, Waldo	19	Marlow	July 6, 71	"	Escaped May 28, 1876
Grimes, Hosea	17	"	July 6, 71	"	
Gustarson, John		Harrisville	Oct. 27, 76	Swede	Discharged Oct. 28, 1876
Hinds, Charles	14	Walpole	Dec. 8, 76	American	Disc. Jan. 25, 1877
Hinds, William	12	"	Dec. 8, 78	"	
Hinds, Matthew		"	"		Born at Alms House Dec. 31, 1876
Jordan, Thomas	45	Keene	Dec. 2, 76	Irish	Died April 8, 1877 cause hydrophobia
Scott, Fredrick	2	Winchester	March 9, 76	Amer.	Sent to Home for Little Wanderers, 2/20/77
Smith, Luther	63	Swanzey	Oct. 19, 76	"	Readmitted, insane
Females					
Bishop, Prudence	86	Richmond	Jan. 9, 69	Amer.	
Calahan, Mary		Swanzey	June 6, 76	Irish	Disc. Aug. 31, 1876
Corlis, Lois	81	Jaffrey	May, 17, 76	Amer.	Disc. Aug. 8, 76
Dickerson, Sarah	50	Swanzey	Nov. 1, 70	"	Insane
Driscoll, Bridget	23	Keene	Sept. 16 76	Irish	Disc. Oct. 10, 1876
Gannett, Ada	3	Westmoreland	Aug 5, 76	Amer.	Sent to Home for Little Wanderers, 2/20/77
Hinds, Sarah	35	Walpole	Dec. 8, 76	"	
Hinds, Clara	10	"	"	"	

Hinds, Emma	4	"	"	"	Sent to Home for Little Wanderers, 2/20/77
Pratt, Cyrena	71	Alstead	March 1, 76	Amer.	Died, June 2, 76 congestion of lungs
Riley, Bridget	40	Keene	June 9, 70	Irish	Insane
Underwood, Esther	60	Swanzey	April 24, 68	Amer.	Died, June 11, 1876 scrofula
White, Mrs. Wm. R.		Marlboro	Aug. 15, 73	"	Town pauper, insane

ESTIMATES AMOUNT AND VALUE OF PRODUCTS OF FARM FOR 1876

Hay,	70 tons	$900 00
Corn	650 bushels	487 50
Oats	430 bushels	215 00
Oat straw	18 tons	180 00
Corn fodder	16 tons	160 00
Potatoes	525 bushels	395 75
Beans	2 bushels	6 00
Vegetables	100 bushels	60 00
Pork	2,486 pounds	198 88
Beef	11,423 pounds	799 61
Poultry		35 00
Dairy		450 00
Eggs		50 00
Pickles, canned & dried fruits		25 00
Palm leaf hats		14 00
Total		$3,974 74

EXPENDITURES

Arad Fletcher & wife, Supt. & matron,	1000 00
Eddie Fletcher, assist. Superintendent,	350 00
Emeline Livingston, assist. Matron,	106 43
Ruth Thomas, assist. Matron,	154 26
Charles Bridgman, salt fish & molasses	62 35
Charles Bridgman, sugar & flour	153 01
CA Wakefield, earth closets	54 00
Earth Closet Co., commodes	30 00
Dr. J A Loveland, medical attendance	52 00
C D Shedd, shoes for Alms House	14 70
Rev. Jos. Barker, attending funerals	12 00
James Starkey, wood	112 50
H P Muchmore, coal	82 81
Pollard & Holbrook, molasses & tobacco	75 60
Home for Little Wanderers, admission, Four children	100 00
NH Asylum for Insane, board & Incidental expenses, county paupers	1,333 40
NH State Reform School, support & Instruction, 6 inmates	459 14

TOTAL PAUPER EXPENSES

For support of paupers on the Farm	$4,612 66
For aid of those outside of the Farm	$11,423 17

The Green Army of Camp Annett
Jonathan Schach

In 1933 the newly inaugurated president Franklin D. Roosevelt, promising a New Deal for the faltering nation, pushed the Emergency Conservation Work Act through Congress. With this act, the Civilian Conservation Corps, or CCC, was born. Roosevelt sought to employ the ranks of idle young men in the work of mending the country's exploited natural resources. By the time the program was canceled in June 1942, over three million men had participated in conservation projects in all fifty states.

The Monadnock region was home to several CCC camps. Camp Annett, southeast of Jaffrey on the Annett State Forest Reserve, was one of the first in the country and housed 191 men when it opened in June 1933. The camp was closed in June 1937 but later reopened in October 1938 as a forest fire hazard reduction camp in the wake of the devastating 1938 hurricane.

Ralph Hoyt was a forester at Camp Annett when it opened in 1933. His son, Ralph Hoyt, Jr., recalls visits to the camp with his father. "My dad was lucky enough to get a job as a forester there. We was real happy about it, because the job paid 75 dollars a month, which was a lot of money in those days.

"Most of the boys were from Boston 18 to 25 [years of age.] I think they were happy to be there, because if they were in Boston they would just hang around the streets. Most of their fathers weren't even working. Most of the families didn't have any work, because it was real bad during the Depression. There wasn't hardly anyone working.

"They were paid 30 dollars a month and they sent 25 dollars of that home so they only had five dollars for themselves, but they did pretty well on that. They

Camp Annett, winter of 1936. The front entrance was constructed with paper birch logs.

Interior of one of six barracks that housed the CCC boys. Three wood stoves, stoked with cordwood the boys had cut and split the previous season, provided heat throughout the cold New Hampshire winter. A latrine was attached at the end of each barrack.

could buy cigarettes about ten cents a pack then, and the movies, they let 'em go, cheaper. They used to go for 20 cents to the movies.

"They had army officers and National Guard who were in charge of the men, and the foresters were more in charge of the work part of it. They'd get up in the morning, and they'd all go out and stand in reveille there. Then they'd go out for retreat when they put the flag up and down. It was more or less something like the army, only it wasn't. It got a lot of those guys used to it, so when the war came along they went in, and they knew how to live with other fellows.

"My dad's crew, he built roads and dug water holes mostly all over different towns; some of them still exist, some of them have been filled in. They planted a lot of trees. My father's crew wasn't involved with that much. And they thinned the forest out and they worked on blister rust, pulling up all the currant bushes. He built trails with the boys up Monadnock.

"They built the road up Highland Hill, which was a fire look out—still is. His crew had a side camp and I went up there when I had my November vacation from school, and stayed with them. It was pretty cold. The boys would get up in the morning, and break the ice in the stream to wash up in. They were in tents with a wooden floor, and they had a cook tent. Bathroom facilities weren't too much. They had a slit tent trench with two posts and a log across. They'd sit over that. I don't know, seemed all right. I remember one night, they took them all in the truck, and they went to a dance in Swanzey. I went with them but I sat mostly in the cab of the truck and ate hot dogs."

Earl Merrill joined the CCC after the camp had reopened following the hurricane. "When I went into the Cs" he recalls, "I was getting as much as the old man was getting or even more—at least when I got 36 dollars.

"Primarily at that time they were cleaning all the stuff from the hurricane that had gone over, and making trails. We worked quite a bit around this whole general area, especially in the summertime going around, and burning a fire line around the lumber piles so in case of a fire it wouldn't destroy all the lumber. A lot of the junk from the hurricane, a lot of the dead wood they would pile up in different open areas, and in wintertime we would go up and burn that and watch it, but you couldn't do it year round.

"Everything was done with a shovel. ... Things have changed. Now, nobody even knows what a shovel is anymore."

"You couldn't feed all the guys steak, there wasn't enough, so who got the steak?"

"When I went in, things were starting to get better and they were starting to close some of them down. . . . I was [there] in 1939. I was seventeen. I reenlisted for another six months, but didn't stay long, because I got a job back home in the mill."

"I know my dad when he'd get new boys in he'd ask them 'Do you know how to drive a Dodge pick-up?' and if any of them said yes, he'd give them a wheel barrow. He thought that was a big joke," said Ralph Hoyt, Jr. "Of course everything was done by hand, they didn't have any loading machines. Everything was done with a shovel. Even when they built the roads they shoveled it from the truck with a shovel. Things have changed. Now, nobody even knows what a shovel is anymore."

Camp menu for August 6, 1935. ("It was nothing fancy but it was all good, tasted good. In those days you didn't get much like that," said Ralph Hoyt, Jr.):

Breakfast	Dinner	Supper
oranges	ham	roasted lamb
wheat crispies	sandwich spread	potatoes
milk	jam	sweet corn
scrambled eggs	boloney	cole slaw
potatoes	cocoa	stewed tomatoes
bread and butter	peanut butter	bread and butter
coffee		gelatin
		coffee
		cucumbers

"One advantage of being a cook was when they'd get a hindquarter in, the cooks would chop it up, and you'd always have a little steak," said Earl Merrill, who was a cook in 1939. "Well you couldn't feed all the guys steak, there wasn't enough, so who got the steak? The cooks and the army guy. I remember he was kind of spoiled. He would come around in the evening after the kitchen was closed."

Lost Ski Areas
Mortimer Peebles

From the 1930s through the early 1980s, many people learned to ski close to home on small hills. They didn't drive to a big resort with chairlifts and condos clinging to the mountainside. These town and college runs usually had a rope tow powered by a car engine, a short vertical drop, and possibly a warming hut.

Jeremy Davis, the founder of New England Lost Ski Areas Project (www .nelsap.org), counts 162 closed ski areas in New Hampshire. In the Monadnock region there were small rope-tow operations in Antrim, Dublin, Fitzwilliam, Jaffrey, Hancock, Keene, Troy, Nelson, New Ipswich, Peterborough, Rindge, Temple, and Crotched Mountain in Bennington and Francestown, which has been revived. Both Jaffrey and Keene had three different runs.

Today's skiers might disdain these hills. The vertical drop at the Fitzwilliam ski area was 240 feet. The Ark Ski Tow in Jaffrey had a 150-foot vertical drop. Hancock's Sargent Camp Tow and the Elm Tree Slope in Keene each had a drop of about 100 feet.

The Bretwood Tow was typical. Ellis Barrett built the tow on his Keene farm in 1953 and ran it until 1960. He never charged anyone to use it. (The state took him to court saying he had to register the tow. Barrett said if that were true everyone with a tennis court or basketball court should have to register them. He won the case.) He groomed the hill after finishing his daily farming chores, and helped children up the hill. His rope pulled skiers up about 800 feet. (The vertical drop was about 100 to 150 feet.) It was powered by a John Deere tractor with a Studebaker transmission. People still come up to him and tell him that they learned to ski on his hill. His daughter grew up to teach skiing at Killington in Vermont. "The kids had a lot of fun," Barrett said.

The cost of insurance brought such informal arrangements to an end. Owen R. Houghton, dean of students at Franklin Pierce College from 1975 to 1990, remembers skiing on the college's three slopes, as well as "the trip downhill my two young sons took with several students in an old aluminum canoe." "We were forced to close the area after several warm and snowless years, and most specifically after the famous multimillion-dollar Stratton Mountain suit sent our insurance premiums from $200 to $4,000."

In a few places the motor house still stands, a small shed beside an overgrown hill; in other places gears, flywheels, axles, and pulleys are rusting in the woods.

The Fitzwilliam Inn built a novice/intermediate ski area in the late 1940s. The Inn expanded the ski area in the 1960s, adding several rope tows, a chairlift, a base lodge, and snowmaking. An all-day ski pass cost $4.50 in 1970 (children, $3.50). The slopes closed in the mid-1970s.

"What Ails New England?"

Twenty years or more of uneventful living have wrought some very eventful changes in the social and religious life of back towns of New England. Depopulated in part by the railroads and the West, and repopulated in part under the changed conditions, some of them have wandered wide of their Puritan traditions, broken up the old neighborhood associations, and locked up many of their churches. Here can be found dozens of places where the Christian faith, that took early and deep root and grew to fill every nook and corner of the community, is rapidly disappearing, and has little or no part in the present life. Other communities there are that never wandered, but have simply stood still and decayed. They lost their best blood to the cities and the West, and they live but in the most woeful depletion.

—"The Decay of the New England Churches," *Nation*, 1886

The "Decay of Rural New England," of which we hear so much in these days, has now become the subject of discussion as far away as London. The *Saturday Review*, in one of its late issues, devotes a special article to the subject, which we here reprint for American readers:

> The American press is deeply concerned for the fate of rural New England. It is being rapidly depopulated. Scarcely any part of the civilized world, not even the clays of East Essex and North Lincolnshire, has been so heavily hit by what with doubtful accuracy is termed the "depression of agriculture" as the wintry valleys and stony uplands that have been the cradle of so much that is vigorous in American life. What in England may be fairly called depression, since the whole country comes within the region depressed, should, in America, be spoken of simply as a shifting of the centres of production. Under this process the farmers of New

Backing into the twentieth century. Nathan Curtis house, Stoddard, 1901.

England and Old England have been about equal sufferers, with this difference, however—the Englishman, either in shape of owner or occupier, is almost compelled to face the difficulty. Emigration, as an alternative, could only be possible or desirable for a fraction of the strugglers. The New Englander, however, has had infinitely greater facilities and greater temptations for such a migration, and he has yielded to them so generally that the statistics of decline may well cause agitation in the minds of those who are left behind. If the State of Indiana were to develop some grave and unforeseen defect and half of its people were to deport themselves into Colorado, no one would very much care except the remnant who were compelled to cling to the sinking ship. But the desertion of the old homesteads of New England appeals most strongly to the sentiment of all Eastern Americans, and an American upon a topic of this kind is the most sentimental of living men.

—New England Magazine, 1891

The land prices I shall tell of will hardly have time to grow cool before their values undergo multiplication in changing hands. For modern, intensive farming will be applied to the depleted interior of New Hampshire. And the moment that it is clearly seen that a new type of farming is as mentally interesting as writing lyric poetry and as financially profitable as clerking it in a department store—then the young men will come back in a ruddy tide.

Farms for Sale

All the farms described below and many more were seen by the representative of *Country Life in America*, and all of them presented a fighting chance, and more.

No. 1—300 Acres for $2,700

One mile from Elmwood, Hancock township. House cottage-shaped, 6 rooms below, 4 above; good view. Barn, 36 × 60; lean-to. 13 × 30; 3 horse stalls, 20 tie-ups. Forty acres in tillage; 175 pasture; 85 woodland. Two hundred Baldwin apple trees yield 125 barrels; would yield 500 if rightly treated. Elevation 800 feet. A chance for milk, fruit and poultry.

No. 2—300 Acres for $3,500

About three miles from Peterboro, 1½ miles from Tarbells station. House strongly built, square, brick colonial. Barn, 36 × 70, with 75-ton silo. Cuts 35 tons hay. One hundred apple trees need pruning. Apples bring $1 a barrel; cost of barrels, picking, etc., 30 cents; net profit, 50 to 75 cents a barrel. Elevation, 925 feet. View admirable. Six superb elms in front of house.

*—"New Hampshire—A State for Sale at $10 an Acre,"
Country Life in America*, 1905

Possibly those critics who assert that political morality is at a lower ebb in New England than in many other states of the union, have not even heard of graft and political "decadence" in St. Louis, Minneapolis, Pittsburgh and other cities, of the conditions in Colorado, of the political murders in Kentucky, of the wholesale corruption in Delaware, of the viciousness of Tammany politics, nor of the issuance in the State of New York of one hundred thousand fraudulent naturalization papers.

—"Is New England Decadent?" *World Today*, 1905

New Hampshire is burdened with an army of superfluous tax-eating politicians. She is ruled by alien corporations, which use or devour her natural resources, employ her inhabitants at low wages, and take the profits out of the State. Her educational system is now, as always in the past, shaped more to facilitate the progress of a few through college and university than to help the children of the rank and file to get a sound school preparation for useful careers and good citizenship. Like Maine, she has lost and is still losing, because of these conditions, thousands of the ablest of her native sons and daughters of the old stock, who seek fairer fortunes in other States, and is replacing them with a poor grade of immigrants from other countries, who lower the average of political morality and general intelligence and who are rather a burden upon than a pillar of support for the State.

—"What's the Matter With New England? New Hampshire: A Study in
Industrial Vassalage, Political Medievalism, and the Aristocratic
Ideal in Public Education," *New England Magazine*, August 1907

Now, New England, once proud to be called the refuge for the oppressed of all nations, has at length proved a churlish hostess to her alien guests. She finds that they come without the wedding garment called for by her own somewhat strict conventions, and she begins to look upon those who have so freely accepted her hospitality hardly as friends and fellow citizens, almost as a hostile army of invasion. Taking this attitude, which has vastly increased the difficulty of making one with herself the strangers whom she finds provokingly wedded to their own ideals, she querulously blames upon them and theirs the ills that must befall "a house divided."

To these New Englanders, one people with more than two centuries of English Puritanism behind them, and with their racial, religious and temperamental characteristics intensified by training and tradition, have come the Irish Catholic, and the Portuguese Catholic, the French Canadian Catholic and recently the Italian Catholic. Now also are coming thousands from Central Europe, many of them also Catholic.

Before 1840 New England was as one people, and New Englanders, however much they might disagree among themselves, knew by instinct the minds of one another, were used to the habits and ideals of their fellows. To-day the native New Englander of the old stock begins to be almost a stranger in the land of his ancestors, and it is not surprising that he resents the change.

—"What Ails New England?" *Putnam's Magazine*, 1909

It almost seems as if old communities, like old people, lost their enjoyment of society, their social genius, you might say. . . . There was a spirit of life in the air that prevails at all times when "things are doing." You feel it in haying time even now, in the woods when we log in winter and in a saw mill. We felt it all the time then. The community [an unnamed town "in the middle of New Hampshire"] was advancing.

We were better off in my boyhood, not merely in comparison, but actually. We actually had more money. For instance, the railroad used to burn wood and paid $5.50 a cord, not best quality wood, either. It cost much less to get out your wood then and a dollar went farther. To-day, if we hire a man, he has to have $1.25 a cord for felling trees and cutting it into four-foot lengths and after we have hauled it to the village, we get $4 a cord for first quality wood, sometimes wait for our money and sometimes don't get it at all. Railroad used to buy all we could furnish. We sell only a limited amount now.

Some of the money I got for wood sold the railroad, I put into railroad shares. . . . It was a blow to us when the railroads began to burn coal. The potato bug got here then. The population of the town had begun to decrease. California, the Middle West, and our own manufacturing towns were taking away people. The more people went, the more other people wanted to go. In a way, it was sort of fashion, the thing to do, this going away. A young fellow going away, felt important, was important.

It makes a chap feel lonesome to drive to town these days. . . . It makes you feel bad; sort of takes the spirit out of a man to drive down past all those houses, big old houses and big old barns that used to be full of children and cattle once. The Yankee did something once. The Yankee storekeeper squeezed the Yankees out of the farms just as the Yankee mill owner by paying too small wages for a man who can read and write to marry on, has driven the Yankee breed out of the mills and out of existence. Sometimes they say the Yankees, the town laborers, have run down. What happened was that the strong, ambitious, and the prudent didn't marry and the sick, weak, and careless did and folks point to their children as examples of degenerated stock. The sturdy Yankee didn't degenerate—merely died out.

It's an old man's country, New England is, for men last a long time here. The farming districts are a long time dying, because the people are . . . a lot of us are right on the edge of having to quit. Grey-haired men are doing a lot of the farming that is done in these grey-walled fields.

—"A Prosperous New Hampshire Farmer," *The Independent*, 1911

By reputation a blue-stocking, an aristocrat, a saint, and withal a prude, New England sits alone, the national wallflower. She has ceased to belong. . . . A New-Englander looks like an American, dresses like an American, frequently acts like an American, and almost talks like one. . . . Strange, then, that a race that fought and bled to vanquish secession should have secession thrust upon them! It amounts to that. Outsiders they are, aliens in their own country. . . . To the West she represents the "effetest East." To the South she is occasionally a plague, the rest of the time, a myth. Only by courtesy, not to say chivalry, do we include her in "the United States of America and of New England." . . . For her own part, she is "nicely, thank you," unaware of her isolation, and, in the main, unaware of

America. . . . When she thinks of America, as happens now and then, she marvels at its extreme provincialism. One might imagine her a suburb of Europe, facing east, not west. She goes abroad because she believes in "seeing her own country first." . . . A Danish baron (of whom the less told the better) once remarked to me: "I understand your liking for New England. I, too, prefer to live in another country, near my own."

—"New England, the National Wallflower," Century, May 1916

The last decade of the nineteenth century was a despondent, dreary, drudging period for the New England farmer. According to economists, his profits in 1897 reached the lowest level that they had touched in half a century. I distinctly remember—for it was my peculiar privilege to be an experienced boy farmer at that time—I distinctly remember selling potatoes at twenty-five cents a bushel and milk at one and three-fourths cents a quart.

Conditions in our rural districts during those closing years of the nineteenth century became positively grim. If the exodus of the young had been serious before, it grew doubly so then, when poverty, celibacy, and stagnation were the only heritage at home. And on those who remained, held fast by age, by poverty, by sickness, by incompetence, or by dependent relatives, on those least fitted in the struggle for existence, fell its intolerable burden in the hour of an economic crisis. It fell on minds rendered restless and gloomy by Puritan theology, devitalized by an antiquated hygiene, dulled and crushed by a lonely isolation that increased around them daily. The scarcity of vigorous young men and the difficulty of getting even the barest living threw on the shoulders of the sickly and middle-aged a crushing load of overwork and incessant worry ideally conducive toward nervous break-downs. Is it any wonder that within a dozen years after 1897 the literary pictures of New England grew both numerous and tragic, that the pathologist and the social worker began ominously to shake their heads over her? Once the breeding-ground of authors, she has now become their feeding-ground, a source of plentiful copy for them to graze on. When that literary vogue is over—whether the future belongs to the immigrant or the beef trust—the curtain must fall forever on a social life that was once the brain center of a continent. Its peculiar virtues, vices and misfortunes alike have eaten into its being like deadly acids.

—"Nervous New England," North American Review, 1919

Some there are, of course, who declare that it is not cows we should milk, but city people. The latter come with full money bags, overflowing with profits that they have got Lord knows where. What more should we ask unless it were manna from Heaven? To accept this philosophy would eventually make peasants of all who lack the peculiar mixture of suavity and independence that characterizes the hotel landlord. The blunt truth is that our urban friends, in relation to the soil itself, are largely parasitic. . . .

In fact, there is some ground for thinking that the city person is, as the old playwrights usually had him, the villain of the piece. Often smooth, rich, and sophisticated, he comes to indulge himself. His clothes, his motor cars, his houses can hardly fail to arouse discontent. If his scale were only slightly above that of the rural people, such discontent might well be a wholesome spur. Too often, however, the newcomer moves, like a prince, upon unapproachable levels.

—"New England Brings Some Ghosts Back to Life," *World's Work*, 1928

New England has one industry nobody can take from it—the Summer resort industry; one that shares its troubles with all parts of the country—agriculture; and one which is highly potential for the future—timber growing. Only one New England State has made a survey of the resort industry, New Hampshire. There, it was discovered, resort property paid one-sixth of the town taxes. And this industry is constantly growing in every State. The geographical position of New England, as well as its natural features, makes it an inevitable playground, but the development of the motor and tourist highways has brought everywhere the threat of destruction of those charms which nature and three hundred years of neat living have given the land. Roadsides, vistas, whole villages are being made hideous by signs, filling stations, cheap camps and other abominations. The old New England of elms and gray barns and white homes and green fields is disappearing. Nobody has done so much to bring this about as the natives themselves in their Yankee greed to catch the pennies of the tourists.

—"New England in 1930," *Current History*, 1930

America is rachitic with the disease of bigness, but New England has built up immunity against the plague. It is impossible to imagine Concord tattooing its lowlands with white stakes, calling itself "Villa Superba: The Sunlight City of Happy Kiddies and Cheap Labor," and loosing a thousand rabid salesmen to barter lots on a Vista Paul Revere or a Boulevarde de Ye Olde Inne to its own inhabitants or suckers making the grand tour. There have been factories, of a kind, at Easthampton and Deerfield for a hundred years, but their Chambers of Commerce will never defile their approaches with billboards inviting the manufacturer of dinguses to "locate here and grow up with the livest community in God's country." Pomfret or Riverton or Pittsfield will never set itself a booster's ideal, "One Hundred Thousand by 1940." Bigness, growth, expansion, the doubling of last years' quota, the subdivision of this year's swamps, the running round in circles and yelling about Progress and the Future of Zenith—from these and from their catastrophic end, New England is delivered for all time.

Here, if you have a Buick income, you do not buy a Cadillac to keep your self-respect. You buy a Chevrolet and, uniquely in America, keep it year after year without hearing that thrift is a vice, a seditious, probably Soviet-inspired assault on the national hour. The superannuation of straight-eights and the shift from transparent velvet to suede lace are not imperatives. You paint the Bulfinch front; you do not tear it down. You have you shoes pegged while the uppers remain good. You patch the highway; you do not rip it out. . . . the town abides.

It [New England] is the first American section to be finished, to achieve stability in the conditions of its life. It is the first old civilization, the first permanent civilization in America. . . . It will be the elder glory of America, free of smoke and clamor, to which the tourist comes to restore his spirit by experiencing quiet, ease, white steeples, and the release that withdrawal from an empire brings. It will be the marble pillars rising above the nation's port.

—"New England, There She Stands," *Harper's*, 1932

Evidence from landscape history and agricultural censuses does not support the thesis of a region-wide nineteenth-century decline in farming for New England. On the basis of output per farm acre, New England has been one of the most productive agricultural regions in the United States. Urban and industrial growth and associated changes in rural culture are more important than comparative advantage in explaining the actual post-1900 decline in agriculture.

The decline of New England agriculture remains one of the best-known, generally accepted themes in American historical geography. Told and retold, the tale has become part of the region's identity. . . .

Writers in the traditional vein have often exaggerated the magnitude of the decline through selective and erroneous citing of census data. . . . The drama would have been much dulled if these writers had pointed out the contemporaneous decline in farmland elsewhere in the United States, but few did so. Although the decline in other areas was not as steep as that in New England, which, according to the census, lost 33.5 percent of its farmland between 1880 and 1930, the magnitude of decline elsewhere certainly lessens the significance of any agricultural problem specific to New England. New York and Pennsylvania lost 24.4 percent and 22.7 percent of their farmland during that period; smaller but still significant declines were recorded for several other states such as Maryland, which lost 15.4 percent, and Ohio, where the drop was 12.3 percent. These decreases occurred mainly in the rapidly industrializing regions during the late nineteenth and early twentieth centuries, a period of worldwide agricultural readjustment. While environment and comparative farm economics constrained New England agriculture, they cannot account for its decline.

This decline can best be understood primarily as the result of cultural change in rural New England. As the nineteenth century progressed, fewer and fewer rural New Englanders wanted to farm. An 1858 pamphlet entitled "Farm Life in New England" expressed concern about the trend and lamented "that the farmer's life and the farmer's home generally are unloved things." In 1853, Albert Comings told a meeting of the Connecticut Valley Agricultural Society that "farming is now unpopular with the young men. It is also with the young women. They have come to associate the name of farmer with ignorance, with stupidity, with clownishness."

For a region long infused with the ideal of the yeoman, the emerging image of the rube was a remarkable change.

—"Did New England Go Downhill?" Michael M. Bell,

Geographical Review, 1989

Part Four

RETURNING

MÓNADNOCK REGION
in Southern New Hampshire

• VISIT AND *live* IN THIS

Year 'round

VACATIONLAND!

Brochure advertising the Monadnock region, c. 1940. "You would be happy, contented, in a region like this. Amidst its high, health-giving altitude, ambition is nour- ished, —you feel more like working and can do more," promised the local boosters.

Introduction

In 1899 the governor of New Hampshire invented an unusual new holiday, one that did not celebrate a hero or a battle. The new holiday was an admission of economic failure dressed in the can-do optimism of a booster. The holiday, Old Home Day, was a plea to return to a poor state.

"I wish that in the ear of every son and daughter of New Hampshire, in summer days, might be heard whispered the persuasive words: Come back, come back!" wrote Governor Frank Rollins. "Do you not hear the call? What has become of the old home where you were born? . . . Do you not remember it—the old farm back among the hills, with its rambling buildings, its well-sweep casting its long shadows, the row of stiff poplar trees, the lilacs and the willows?"

Rural New Hampshire was fading away. The abandoned farms and towns were but a shadow of their former selves. The state government was in debt, as were three-quarters of the towns. New Hampshire, it was said, "was a good state to emigrate from." Rollins wanted the prosperous native sons to return and buy run-down farms for summer homes; he wanted them to contribute to fixing up their hometowns. And he wanted his state to welcome them back with newly painted inns serving fresh food, with good roads, and with a statewide network of bicycle paths. In his many speeches the governor offered specific housekeeping pointers.

Old Home Day was a success. "All doors were open, all hearts were glad. Hospitality was infectious," said Rollins. The homecomers were welcomed with "open arms and brass bands, decorations, street parades, public meetings and banquets." The visitors purchased abandoned farms, made donations to the schools, libraries, and churches, helped pay for historic markers, road repair, and trees. A banker in a western city sent his hometown one hundred cherry trees.

The country towns had renewed hope and courage, a broader outlook, and higher ideals, Rollins said. "We learn that we are not forgotten, that the pulse of all those who are scattered over the world still beats true to their native state." The holiday spread to other states, and is still celebrated by many towns in New Hampshire. In the century since the first Old Home Day, many generations have answered the call to come back. The good roads were built (without the bike paths). The state learned to cater to tourists. New Hampshire is poor no more. It's the sixth-wealthiest state in the nation (in terms of personal income), and it has the lowest percentage of poverty in the country.

Part four looks at several generations of those who have returned to, or discovered, New Hampshire.

The Folks of the Monadnock Region Want YOU for a Neighbor!

If you're tired of the city, with its noise, its rush and its dirt, the folks of the Monadnock Region invite you to be their neighbor . . . to share with them this land rich in traditional culture and Yankee genuineness, a land that Nature has generously endowed with her entire treasure of beauties.

You would be happy, contented, in a region like this. Amidst its high, health-giving altitude, ambition is nourished, —you feel more like working and can do more.

Enjoy "a home among the hills", —in the Monadnock Region, —with its long list of advantages. Here you find scenic splendour at every hand, backed up by modern needs. Wide-surfaced concrete roads speed you quickly back from Boston, while local firemen and state and local police have guarded your interests while you were away. Pure water, seasonal vegetables fresh from near-by gardens, modernly managed stores at your service, good schools, economical living costs and the convenience of electricity in all but three towns are other advantages of the region.

Many sites bordering mountain, lake or main street are available, with a choice of re-building a typical home or consummating those plans you have drawn; —and bear in mind that the low tax rate on Monadnock Region property is not the least of its benefits.

Whatever your pursuit, —industry, commerce, agriculture or rest, live in our region and be happy!

You'll find no noisy elevated trains in the Monadnock Region, no clanking subway or street cars, no conglomeration of shrill whistles or bells, no midnight motor horn serenading. If you like to live where traffic lights go off at 11 p.m., where eight or nine hours of unbroken sleep await you, —where you can be healthy and happy, move into a home "Among The Hills."

Would you like room for a garden? a rose bush? an apple tree? or even a handy garage? or just a place to sit and enjoy a mid-summer eve? Where in the metropolitan areas? —and if you found such a place, could you afford it?

No, the Monadnock Region is not one big farm, —but it is a spot where you can live happily, economically and healthfully . . . where you know your neighbor, —and call him a friend!

—John E. Coffin, *Inviting You to Visit and Live in the Monadnock Region: "Land of New Hampshire Charm,"* c. 1940

Perhaps you know what a vitamin is. If you remember your Latin, you may guess it has something to do with life. Anyways, its something you eat, and if you get enough of the right kinds then you may reasonably expect to enjoy good health.

Yet you may have found that it is hard to get acquainted with Mr. And Mrs. Vitamin and their numerous family, so I'd like to introduce you to another kind of vitamin that you don't eat—you just breathe them in. Of course this is not medical advice, though many have found it a good substitute, and perhaps your local medico would echo it. This new-old vitamin is not Vitamin A or Vitamin I or Vitamin R, but a combination of all three—Vitamin AIR, otherwise known as New Hampshire Air. Away from the smoke and dust of the big cities, New Hampshire air keeps the snow clean and allows the human lung to function at its best. It has a magnetic quality because it attracts the very best people. You will come to think of it as intoxicating—it tends to keep you always in good spirits. It is gently soporific when liberally used, and at the same time it is such a mental stimulant that its effect upon the mind can never be entirely eradicated after one returns to the ordinary business of life in the foreign parts from which you may come. The memories always fondly linger. So if you would really know your vitamins, try New Hampshire Vitamin AIR.

> —"New Hampshire Vitamin," *New Hampshire Troubadour*, c. 1930

New Hampshire is peace and beauty . . . freedom, stability, and contentment . . . the refreshment of clean air . . . the scenic charm of lake, forest, countryside, mountains, seashore, and laughing streams . . . a sturdy character built in three centuries of American traditions . . . outdoor sports . . . happy children . . . a satisfying way of life.

> —"New Hampshire Is Peace," *This Is New Hampshire*, State Planning
> and Development Commission, c. 1950

Abbott Thayer in the Spell of Monadnock

On the porch of Abbott Handerson Thayer's two-story, wood frame house, at the end of a dirt road up from the south side of Dublin Lake, his young acolyte, Richard Meryman, painted Mount Monadnock as it really was, its peak rising distantly beyond a screen of tall pines on a foreground field of white snow. When Abbott Thayer painted from the same spot, his Monadnock loomed immediately, a massive and towering totem—a portrait of his own spiritual, hyperbolic nature. The mountain's "wild grandeur" was to him a shrine, a "natural cloister," and in his daily life it was a personal cathedral spanning all Nature within reach of his curiosity.

At the turn of the century, Abbott Thayer was a leader in a movement labeled the American Renaissance and considered one of America's preeminent figure painters. His aspiration was no less than "the highest human soul beauty," a perfection he embodied in virginal, idealized young women, made eternal and exalted by angels' wings. He scorned the labeled religions, considering them narrow and hypocritical, disengaged from the boundless mysteries of existence. Art was his church—"a no-man's land of immortal beauty where every step leads to God." Describing his concept of painting, he wrote, "It is as though a man were shown a crystal, a perfect thing, gleaming below depths of water, far down beyond reach. He would dive and dive again, driven by his great desire to secure it, until finally, all dripping, he brought it up. But that in the end he could bring it, a perfect being, to us was possible solely because he . . . had been given this divine gift of seeing."

To Thayer, an Emersonian Transcendentalist, Nature itself was "a path leading to the Creator himself." An obsessed student of wildlife, he called his preoccupation a "second child" who "has hold of one of my hands and my painting has hold of the other." His curiosity had been in overdrive since the age of six when his father, a horse and buggy doctor, settled in Keene, New Hampshire, the hometown of Thayer's mother, Ellen Handerson. Abbott roamed the banks of the Ashuelot River, the meadows, and woods collecting eggs and birds and teaching himself taxidermy. Virtually his only childhood reading was Audubon's *Birds of America*. He kept pet squirrels, rabbits, and owls, and began painting the animals he trapped. When he was sixteen, the family moved to Dorchester, Massachusetts. There his formative mentor was a jeweler and amateur painter of animals, and young Thayer received paid commissions for dog portraits. In 1867, when he was eighteen, his family settled in Brooklyn. He studied at the National Academy of Design in New York City, and for the next eight years supported himself as an "animalier," painting dogs, cats, horses, cattle, birds, lions, tigers. When he was twenty-six, Thayer married Kate Bloed, a gentle, equally unworldly woman who

Abbott Thayer, *Mount Monadnock*, after 1911.

shared his spiritual bent. They immediately left for two years in Paris, where he studied at the Ecole des Beaux-Arts under the great Jean-Léon Gérôme, and was one of a generation of young American artists in Europe absorbing the anima of the Italian Renaissance. Back in America, Thayer was a successful portrait painter, living a nomadic existence, but often with a studio in New York City. In 1886 the family summered on the Stearns farm in West Keene and he painted his first "angel" portrait, his eleven-year-old daughter Mary.

Thayer began summering in Dublin two years later. A laureate of Monadnock, he prowled "that elemental thing which is the leaven of all intellectual lives; the virgin forest where Time alone has left his traces, where his mark is on every stage of growth, from moss-covered soil, through tiny saplings to the perfect tree, to the solemn skeleton that faces a few winters' storms before crashing down to lie still at last, and begin the gentle change through all the beautiful mossy stages back to mother earth." While collecting specimens—he and his son Gerald by 1905 had collected 1,500 bird skins; Thayer could skin a small bird in the dark—he spied on the mountain the pileated woodpecker with its "wonderful energy," the winter wrens, the hermit and olive-backed thrushes, the juncos and myrtle warblers in green golden spruce tops, flying squirrels and lynxes inhabiting that decomposing wood on the forest floor. To Thayer the mountain summit had "the mysterious exaltation of mere height, and with it the inexpressible experience of *silence* coupled with light and sight." Once at dusk Thayer stood on the summit and made a sucking sound with his mouth on the back of his hand. Great horned owls circled him and one landed on his nearly bald head.

The house was a gift from admiring, affluent Mary Amory Greene of Boston and Dublin, a direct descendant of the painter John Singleton Copley. In 1887 in West Keene she became his art student, helper, correspondence secretary, and writer of substantial checks. That winter she followed him to New York and performed the same offices. Mary Amory Greene's stepmother-in-law, Mary Abby Greene, had in 1882 bought virtually the entire south side of Dublin Lake on the Monadnock foothill called Lone Pine Hill. She then parceled out property to her family, including Mary Amory Greene. Boston intellectuals received house lots, and Loon Point was given to the parents of the artist Joseph Lindon Smith. In 1888 Mary Amory built Thayer's house to his specifications for summer use. He moved in year-round thirteen years later.

Mary Amory Greene was one of a small cluster of admiring women who made themselves the Master's support group, trying to mitigate the chaos of his life. Another was Emmeline "Emma" Beach—sprightly, selfless, efficient, moneyed (her father owned the *New York Sun*). In 1888 Kate Thayer slipped into a melancholia so severe she was committed permanently to a mental hospital. When disorganized Abbott Thayer found himself alone with three children, their practical friend Emma was a savior, keeping the family functioning during long visits. Kate died in 1891. He married Emma four months later. "When Abbott was about to fall," said his mother, "someone always shoved a mattress under him."

The Thayer household was home to a pair of prairie dogs christened Napoleon and Josephine, a macaw that died of a broken heart when Gerald married and moved away, a crow who returned each spring and ate out of the cats' food dish, and a spider monkey once discovered brushing its teeth with Emma's toothbrush. One evening at the dinner table, with a great flourish, Thayer lifted the hood from a platter, revealing a porcupine he had pulled from a tree. It then strolled the table, eating from the family's plates. "The serving and ornament of life," as the wife of the painter Thomas Dewing put it, held little interest for ascetic Thayer. The cottage itself, described by his daughter Gladys as "somewhat on the order of a camp," was merely sheathing over a wood frame. In the winter, the only heat was four fireplaces. The only water came from a hand pump in the kitchen, much later supplanted by a pipe from a crenellated tower. There was an outhouse. Lacking electricity, the lighting was oil lamps and candles.

Paranoid about the possibility of tuberculosis, certain that fresh air was the anti-dote, Thayer sometimes kept windows open in the winter. Each night the whole family, dressed in buffalo skins, trekked out to individual, three-sided lean-tos (a canvas hung across the fourth side), each with a bunk below a bookshelf. Though scrubbed and immaculate, Thayer habitually wore knickers, high Norwegian boots, and a paint-spattered Norfolk jacket formerly owned by the great philosopher William James, a present from James's sons. In winter he donned long underwear. As the weather warmed, he cut off sections, reducing it to shorts by summer.

Erratic, a thicket of eccentricities, Thayer described himself as "a jumper from extreme to extreme," and admitted that his brain only "takes care of itself for my main function, painting." Wholly impractical and blissfully improvident, he seemed everlastingly hard up. Though his paintings sold to wealthy patrons for as much as ten thousand dollars, he would plead for advances from his two wealthy patrons, John Gellatly and the railroad car magnate Charles Freer. Once he asked for a loan from a man who then noticed a thousand-dollar bill protruding from Thayer's vest pocket.

His soaring aspirations, hitched to a feverish sensitivity, blighted Thayer with the turbulence of a perfectionist alive in an imperfect world. Probably bipolar, he swung on what he called "the Abbott pendulum," rising to heights of tranquil inspiration and grace only to plummet down into "a sick disgust with myself." He admitted to "oceans of hypochondria," and his letters are a catalogue of exhaustion, sleeplessness, "overdrawn" eyes, minor illnesses, headaches, and "general morbid down-troddenness." He spent time in sanatoriums. He fled strangers, preferring the safety of acolytes drawn to him by the force field of his questing mind and the idealism, even nobility, of his character and vision. Whatever the subject, he raised it to a higher level of interest. One of the students he mentored was William James, Jr., son of the great philosopher. James described himself standing in Thayer's studio gazing at *Stevenson Memorial*, his great painting of a winged beauty, contemplative and Olympian upon a huge boulder. "I felt myself to be 'in the presence.' Here was an activity, an accomplishment which my own world had never touched. This *could* be done—was being done by this friendly

Abbott Thayer had a fervent belief in fresh air. The family slept outside, even in winter. Each night the whole family, dressed in buffalo skins, trekked out to individual, three-sided lean-tos. A canvas hung across the fourth side.

little man with the distant gaze. This was *his* world where he lived and moved, and it seemed to me perhaps the best world I had ever met."

These acolytes were the outgrowth of Thayer's impossible standards. Compulsively dissatisfied, repeatedly repainting and spoiling the "God given" passages, he hit on the scheme of assistants who copied each day's work. Ending up with two, three, and four versions of a picture, he worked on all of them and "finished" the most promising. But months later he might ask owners to ship pictures back for more work. Once he went at night to the Harrisville railroad station to open a crate and touch up a work by lamplight.

The first of a long series of assistants was Richard Meryman (1882–1963), who was hired in 1906 and became an honorary family member, returning year after year to Thayer's inspirational presence—and all his life kept a picture of the Master on his bureau. He became for seventeen years director of the art school of the Corcoran Gallery of Art in Washington, D.C., while painting portraits and landscapes. Another disciple was Alexander James (1890–1956), brother of William, Jr. He and Meryman eventually settled in Dublin and were part of the small artists' colony that formed around Thayer. When James's portraits and landscapes were prized by clients, he decided that because they were popular, they must not be good. Painting such portraits was "a pimp's profession," and he began specializing instead in portraits of New Hampshire characters, portraying the inner man.

One summer student in 1903 was Rockwell Kent (1882–1971), who believed that Thayer taught him to paint "as a human being, not an artist." His time with Thayer awakened a fascination with the Far North expressed in famous wood-engraving illustrations and oils of Monhegan Island in Maine and the frozen wildernesses of Greenland, Tierra del Fuego, and Alaska. Mingling mysticism and science, Kent was also a lecturer, architect, farmer, and radical pamphleteer who became a Communist Party member. He later married and divorced Thayer's niece, earning Thayer's permanent wrath.

Briefly part of the art colony was Frank Benson (1862–1951), a major American portraitist, a depicter of sun-dappled Victorian social life, and a painter of wildlife, especially birds and ducks in flight. Also there was the sculptor George Grey Barnard (1863–1938), described as "a short-legged Napoleon," whose medieval sculpture collection, unearthed by farmers in the French countryside, ultimately became the founding core of New York's medieval museum, the Cloisters.

Attracted by Thayer, George de Forest Brush (1855–1941) moved down to Dublin from Cornish, New Hampshire, in 1899. Their friendship dated back to art school in New York and was cemented during their two years together in Paris at the Ecole des Beaux-Arts. Both essentially spiritual, they were to a degree soul mates, sometimes inviting each other to give critiques of their latest works. Like Thayer, Brush kept his Dublin life elemental, his farmhouse free of such luxuries as electricity, running water, and heat beyond wood stoves. His joyous charm alternated with a stern and compelling intensity, and he, too, considered art a sacred enterprise, a medium for the exaltation of humanity. He repeatedly painted his wife, Mittie, as a Madonna with her little daughters and son. These

Abbott Thayer, *Monadnock Angel*, 1920–1921.

children were the primary playmates of the Thayer children, and both sets of parents educated their offspring at home, preserving their elevated innocence uncorrupted by vulgarizing public school and the outside world. After the summer residents had fled oncoming winter, the two families were sole companions, snowshoeing, ice-skating, visiting each other by sleigh on roads packed flat by a huge roller pulled by six horses. In the evenings, they shared the Thayers' absorption in music; Abbott played a violin given him by Brush and whistled Beethoven themes.

When Richard Meryman first arrived in Dublin he asked at a village store where Abbott Thayer could be found, and was directed to the town hall. On the second floor he found Thayer in front of a large box, waving a brush within its

Abbott Thayer, *Dublin Pond, New Hampshire*,
1894.

green interior. After greeting Meryman, he called out, "All right you can rest now."
A hitherto invisible man climbed out of the box, his coveralls and face green.
Thayer hoped to tour this stunt in a vaudeville show and make some money.
But primarily it was an offshoot of his theories detailed in his book *Concealing
Coloration in the Animal Kingdom*, the apogee of his wildlife studies. Published
in 1909, it was written by Gerald with, as Thayer put it, "I feeding all the silk into
his loom." He continued, "For four years this set of discoveries my poor brain has
been vexed with have kept me at work hours almost every night with pencil and
pad under my pillow, and this has kept me drawn off so that I never filled up to
the point of running over or out of the painting faucet." Emma suffered nervous
prostration after two years of managing the off-kilter household and daily cor-
recting the book's proofs. With his painting at a standstill, Thayer was desperate
for money, having spent many thousands of dollars of his own money achieving
the ultimate, sumptuous book with superb color illustrations painted by Thayer
himself, Gerald, Richard Meryman, and Rockwell Kent.

Thayer argued that birds, mammals, insects, reptiles are concealed from prey

Abbott Thayer, *Spring Hillside*, c. 1889.

and predators by eliminating all contrast with the background. This is done by blending—mimicking the background—and by disrupting the denizen's contours, thus erasing shape and identity. Thayer coined the word "countershading," and explained that "animals are painted by Nature darkest on those parts which tend to be most lighted by the sky's light, and vice versa." Wiping out the gradations of light and shade that give shape, Nature flattens an opaque animal and reduces it to a blank space. This can also be done by "dazzle," by strong, arbitrary colored markings that break up the image. Thayer believed that only an artist could have arrived at his understandings, since they depended on a knowledge of hue and chroma, values and intensities that enhance or obliterate when juxtaposed—the German and French color theory he had mastered in Paris.

Despite the respect of the ornithology community, Thayer found himself combating doubters. Typically, he had made extravagant claims—that shadows are blue in winter snows and conceal blue jays, that flamingos are pink so they can disappear in front of sunsets—and he insisted his convictions be accepted in toto, as holy writ. He especially aroused the outrage of the vociferous big-game

Abbott Thayer, *Monadnock No. 2,* 1912.

hunter Teddy Roosevelt, who labeled the entire proposition "literally nonsensical." TR refused to attend one of the demonstrations in New York's Central Park where Thayer made a hummingbird disappear in a bush and asked dignified scientists to lie on their stomachs and gaze at the rear end of a deer to witness the white patch blending with the sky. Only in 1940, nineteen years after his death, did Thayer's theories officially enter the natural history canon when a major British naturalist published a paper titled *Adaptive Coloration of Animals.*

During one of Thayer's immersions in Nature on Monadnock, at about 2,600 feet along the eastern ridge just off the Pumpelly Trail, he discovered a sign announcing "PRIVATE WAY. NO PASSING." It had been nailed on a tree by order of Louise Amory of Dublin and Braintree, Massachusetts, the wealthy widow of William Amory, former treasurer of the enormous Amoskeag Mills in Manchester, New Hampshire. Thayer immediately set off a tempest that blew up from the very origins of New Hampshire, beginning in 1610 when a grateful King James I bestowed on Captain John Mason land grants in the New England territory. Mason had led a flotilla invading the Hebrides and contributed various gifts of equipment. Though the captain never journeyed to the New World, he became in 1632 vice president of the Great Council of New England. In 1635 he received a grant from the Council, confirmed by King Charles I, awarding him a large share of the land "which henceforth shall be called by the name of New Hampshire." That year Captain Mason died and his heirs, blocked by the Puritans, spent a hundred years futilely fighting to establish ownership.

In 1746 the heirs submitted to a nifty land grab engineered by the Loyalist New Hampshire governor, Benning Wentworth, to benefit his son, one of a syndicate of twelve men known as the Masonian Proprietors. They bought Mason's grant and became the province's controlling elite, selling off the land in lots. Dublin in 1749 was "granted" as Monadnock #3 to forty individual owners. During the next 160 years farmers through squatters' rights and purchase took possession of some 500 acres of Monadnock. By 1911 this land, plus 400 more acres, had been purchased from farmers by Louis Amory, the Reverend George Weld (her son-in-law by a previous marriage), and the Hart Box Company, which planned to lumber its acreage. The farmers' deeds read "to the Jaffrey line," the first established boundary to the south. Since the steep, rocky terrain was untillable, nobody had taken this seriously—until Louise Amory deduced that she and Weld could lay claim to essentially the northeast face of Monadnock, including the summit.

For Thayer the sign, plus a road and two houses Amory had built high up the mountain, were a blasphemy to its "primeval, wild nature-purity." To him the mountain was "a thing that belongs to us all," and he feared that "now, electricity with motors etc., backed by money, has swept away the old comfortable guarantee [*sic*] of *impracticability* of occupying the high slopes of mountains, and villas, villas, villas will insidiously creep up along those roads that these people have already built." He vowed that "those spruces, after all the centuries of hermit and olive-backed thrush voices, shall not know the Victor talking machine if I can stop it."

With the help of Gerald, he contacted influential voices in New England, and appealed directly to Amory and Weld to preserve the mountain "untracked by man's follies." He argued that "in view of the general doom of the purely wild forms, any forest preserved in this way is destined to grow forever more precious." He admonished them that "as rightfully might you write your names across the face of the Birth of Venus or the Sistine Madonna, because you had bought it for $200,000, as write with your road across the upraised face of the until-now shrine of many pilgrims." He bewailed the possibility that Monadnock would suffer the same vulgarization as Dublin's lake, which was becoming a summer enclave for wealthy vacationers from St. Louis and Boston. He wrote: "It is the *beginnings* that doom or save. The usual luxury loving class has followed to Dublin the worshipers that first came, until all the place's attributes which attracted those first comers—the atmosphere of peasantry amidst primitive nature, etc.—one by one gave way, and now our mountain tarn gleams at night with a belt of city lights and roars by day with stinking motors. . . . Imagine the deathly heart-sink at discovering that the same doom had, as it were, passed your barriers, and smuggled itself into your respect, and made you its tools."

Louise Amory, once upon a time the personal secretary of the polymath Dr. Oliver Wendell Holmes, Sr.—medical doctor, biographer, poet (*The Wonderful One Hoss Shay*)—was an independent woman of intellect and steely whims who did not take kindly to such lecturing. When she and Weld were unmoved by those lofty rants, Abbott and Gerald Thayer mapped the lots in question, traced their history, and consulted legal authorities who concluded that those wild mountain ledges were still owned by the descendants of the original Masonian Proprietors. The Thayers enlisted the Society for the Protection of New Hampshire Forests, which located eighty-nine of the heirs scattered as far away as England and Mexico. A court hearing ruled in favor of the Society. The heirs deeded their acres to the Society, and, for the sum of one dollar, Amory and Weld voided their claims to 300 acres of contested land, which also went to the Society. The newly secure preserve placed the mountain's summit and nearly two miles of the Pumpelly Trail along the skyline beyond encroachment.

In 1928, the Hart Box Company sold its tract to the Society. At her death in 1944, Louise Amory's will left her remaining 625 acres to her daughter, Amory Glenn, and free of Thayer's hot breath, now stipulated that "the wild mountain forest . . . be kept in its present condition . . . and no buildings shall be constructed thereon which would mar the beauty of this singularly beautiful mountain." In a domino effect, the state of New Hampshire and the town of Jaffrey acquired the other mountain flanks, and Amory Glenn has given 300 acres into a conservation easement. So the pristine, safeguarded Monadnock of today is largely the legacy of Abbott Thayer's prodigious passion.

The same intensity toward Nature left a second and improbable legacy. Abbott Thayer was the father of military camouflage. When World War One began in 1916, he virtually stopped painting and poured his fanatical energy into a campaign to convince the Allies that his concealing coloration theory could be adapted for uniforms and hardware and airplanes and navy ships. The French used his book and the Americans formed a camouflage corps unit, sparked in part by Thayer's cousin, the muralist Barry Faulkner from Keene. But his ship camouflage schemes were ignored despite a continuing crusade that included a meeting with the assistant secretary of the navy, Franklin D. Roosevelt. Thayer's frenzy of frustration was so profound that he once contemplated suicide and immediately committed himself to a sanatorium. There were frequent attacks of nervous exhaustion. He began painting and finished *Monadnock Angel*—a facing angel with extended arms protecting the mountain. But in 1921, his health eviscerated, he suffered a series of heart attacks. He died on May 29, 1921, and was cremated.

Gerald Thayer, barefooted, carried the ashes to the heights of the Pumpelly Trail just before sunset. As he afterward wrote, "In this gay solemnness and translucent beauty were given forever back to wind and sun and stars the scanty mortal remains of our artist, father, friend. Of those dainty upland plants he loved so well . . . some two or three may feel at root a faint enrichment. The old gray stones know nothing; they are charged with no new secret. . . . [But] it will be proper and just for any of us so desiring to regard Monadnock, the mountain, as in a very real sense his monument."

A Dublin Summer
Mark Twain

October 9, 1905

Last January, when we were beginning to inquire about a home for this summer, I remembered that Abbott Thayer had said, three years before, that the New Hampshire highlands was a good place. He was right—it was a good place. Any place that is good for an artist in paint is good for an artist in morals and ink. Brush is here too. So is Col. T. W. Higginson. So is Raphael Pumpelly. So is Mr. Secretary Hitchcock. So is Henderson. So is Learned. So is Sumner. So is Franklin MacVeigh. So is Joseph L. Smith. So is Henry Copley Greene when I am not occupying his house, which I am doing this season.

Paint, literature, science, statesmanship, history, professorship, law, morals—these are all represented here, yet crime is substantially unknown.

The summer houses of these refugees are sprinkled a mile apart among the forest-clad hills, with access to each other by firm smooth country roads which are so embowered in dense foliage that it is always twilight in there and comfortable. The forests are spiderwebbed with these good roads, they go everywhere. But for the help of the guideboards, the stranger would not arrive anywhere.

The village—Dublin—is bunched together in its own place but a good telephone service makes its markets handy to all those outliars. I have spelt it that way to be witty. The village executes orders on the Boston plan—promptness and courtesy.

The summer homes are high perched, as a rule, and have contenting outlooks. The house we occupy has one. Monadnock, a soaring double hump, rises into the sky at its left elbow—that is to say, it is close at hand. From the base of the long slant of the mountain the valley spreads away to the circling frame of the hills, and beyond the frame the billowy sweep of remote great ranges rises to

Absolute Twain. During his second Dublin summer, in 1906, Mark Twain posed for a series of photographs on the front porch of the house he had rented from George Upton, off Upper Jaffrey Road.

view and flows, fold upon fold, wave upon wave, soft and blue and unworldly, to the horizon fifty miles away.

In these October days Monadnock and the valley and its framing hills make an inspiring picture to look at, for they are sumptuously splashed and mottled and betorched from skyline to skyline with the richest dyes the autumn can furnish. And when they lie flaming in the full drench of the midafternoon sun, the sight affects the spectator physically, it stirs his blood like military music.

These summer homes are commodious, well built and well furnished, facts which sufficiently indicate that the owners built them to live in themselves. They have furnaces and wood fireplaces and the rest of the comforts and conveniences of a city home and can be comfortably occupied all the year round.

We cannot have this house next season but I have secured Mrs. Upton's house, which is over in the law and science quarter two or three miles from here and about the same distance from the art, literary and scholastic groups. The science and law quarter has needed improving this good while.

The nearest railway station is distant something like an hour's drive. It is three hours from there to Boston over a branch line. You can go to New York in six hours per branch lines if you change cars every time you think of it, but it is better to go to Boston and stop over and take the trunk line next day. Then you do not get lost.

It is claimed that the atmosphere of the New Hampshire highlands is exceptionally bracing and stimulating, and a fine aid to hard and continuous work. It is a just claim, I think. I came in May and wrought 35 successive days without a break. It is possible that I could not have done it elsewhere. I do not know. I have not had any disposition to try it before. I think I got the disposition out of the atmosphere this time. I feel quite sure, in fact, that that is where it came from.

Confessions of a Part-Time Squire

NEWTON F. TOLMAN

A stranger from the city phoned to ask about a piece of land we planned to sell, and I arranged to meet him down at the crossroads. "You can't miss me," he said, as though we were meeting at Forty-second Street and Broadway. "I'll be in my station wagon. Just look for a white Country Squire." Without thinking I replied. "That's fine. We don't have any color bars up in this country, but as a matter of fact I'm a white country squire myself."

Technically this was not quite true. Up here the real English-style country squire requires a very substantial private income or a rich wife. I practice the art only in certain seasons: when skiing is good, during the spring trout season, and in the fall shooting months. The rest of the time, except for a little sailing, tennis or bird-watching in summer, I work.

But we do have quite a few neighbors who are full time country squires. This part of New Hampshire seems to attract them, though it is not easy to fathom why. Our native country gentlemen of leisure had become almost extinct a generation or two back, and the incumbents of this happy way of life have moved up here from everywhere. It may be that they sense something of tradition, for we once had country squires who could hold their own in any company.

Sometime around 1880, one Louis Cabot bought up large holdings in the townships of Dublin, Harrisville, Nelson, Antrim, and Hancock. Farms of one hundred to five hundred acres with buildings more or less intact could be bought for a pittance in those days. The railroads had isolated the hill country, and farming had moved westward. The Cabot estate, most of it never accurately surveyed, at a conservative guess may have run to more than a hundred thousand acres. For a time we were pretty well surrounded by Cabot land, my grandfather having been one of the few natives silly enough to refuse all offers of the estate agents.

One day Mr. Cabot was touring the back roads, as was his wont on summer days, behind a fast team driven by his coachman. He passed a large open slope growing up to poplar whips, a promising situation for woodcock. Cabot was an upland game enthusiast and bought land with an eye for bird cover. On coming to a farmhouse, he stopped to inquire of an old man who was outside splitting wood.

"Looks like good woodcock country along here. Are there many birds around?"

"Plenty of 'em," the man told him.

"Is that land across the road for sale, by chance?"

"Dunno."

"Don't you own it?"

"Nope."

"Well, then, who does?"

"Rich old cuss from Boston, name o' Cabot."

Most people like to think comfortably that in the last fifty years or so we have made great strides in tolerance and broad-mindedness. But when it comes to leading the kind of life you want to live, up here in the country, I wonder. I can readily think of a dozen men, roughly contemporary with our grandfathers, who followed the happy lot of the country squire. And they were highly respected men who led exemplary lives. My father would say, "That Harry So-and-so, lives out to West Keene, never worked. Always had money. . . ." This was not meant to imply that Harry was queer, or unintelligent or a second-class citizen. It was, rather, a tribute to Harry's good sense.

By way of contrast, consider the neighbor we called on the other day. Though it was early for cocktails, he was already so potted he fell off the wharf when he was showing us his boat, and we had to fish him out. Now he is obviously a fine chap and has no reason at all to drink too much. No reason, that is, except that being a genuine country squire these days has proved too much for him. His neighbors all insist he is hopelessly eccentric and a real misfit, and even that he is not quite right in the head—just because he tries to lead a sensible life freed from the bonds of some active conventional occupation. Persecution has caught up with him.

Most country squires of today, because of this attitude of intolerance, haven't the nerve to accept the title. And they go to the most elaborate lengths to deceive the public. Some pretend to farm or sell real estate or analyze something. We know a chap who has been "writing a book" for a half a lifetime. Another has an elaborately equipped small office building complete with secretary on the lawn of his extensive estate, so that he can "run his business" from the country. Then there is one poor fellow who for years has driven all the way to Boston each week. He spends a couple of days down there in a hotel and comes back full of wise talk about the financial world, a routine he fondly imagines we accept as proof he is really a working man.

In the very early 'thirties we had a wave, a real migration of young married couples moving to the country. These were the ones who still had a lot of money left after the Great Depression struck. There wasn't much doing then in the business world, so while their less fortunate fellows sold apples or went on WPA, these fledgling country squires and squiresses moved up here and showed us how to live.

At the time we must have known some twenty such couples, settled around here in elaborately rebuilt farm houses or summer places. In about five years hardly any of them were still with us. It was a soft generation, perhaps, reared as it was on bathtub gin, F. Scott Fitzgerald and the Moral Rearmaments movement. Somehow they all seemed to get the idea that being a country squire mainly involved throwing parties and swapping wives. Some became alcoholics,

The house staff of Dr. Herbert K. Faulkner, c. 1890s. Faulkner, a physician in Keene, summered in Dublin. In 1899, there were 237 servants in a town with a year-round population of 620. By World War I, the "Chauffeurs' Ball" had become a regular summer-ending ritual. "There is the most perfect harmony and good feeling between all classes in the community," reported the 1920 edition of the Dublin history.

some committed suicide, some smashed themselves up in cars or planes, and one or two survived and went back into business.

The fact is, being a country squire—successfully—makes medicine or law look easy. It is the only field that leaves a man with no excuses. No excuse for not voting in every primary, getting put on every committee, entertaining visitors or house guests whenever they decide to drop in, helping a neighbor fix his plumbing or pacify his wife when she gets in a temper.

Anybody else can be sure of a quiet evening just by pleading a tough day at the office, or can escape some obnoxious local gathering by taking a business trip. Anybody else can say, "Gosh, Henry, ordinarily I'd give a few bucks—nobody knows better than I how much this town needs a bird sanctuary—but things are awfully tight in my line just now. Maybe next year."

A country squire must also keep in constant training, like a fighter or a ballet dancer. Why? Because all his friends expect him to look ten to fifteen years younger than his age. Or at least theirs. He must be ready, every time some old friend drops by: "Say, old boy, you don't look a day older. Must be hard as nails, but of course it's the life you lead up here!" And being hard as nails, he must be careful to stay vigorous up to ninety or so. Who ever heard of a country squire dying young? And when he does eventually pop off, the proper method is by being tossed from a spirited horse, or perhaps strangling himself in a tangle of fish line while landing a salmon.

Even so, just give me the rich wife or the bundle of Tel. & Tel. Shares, and this will be the life for me. Some fellow who needs it can have my place in the work-a-day world. Let society look on me as it may, I will know how to spend every precious hour, so long as there are still fish in the waters, birds in the covers, and snow on the ski slopes.

The house known as Auf der Hohe (On the Heights) was built in 1884 and burned in 1919.

REPORT

How to Build a House
Raphael Pumpelly

We found the Newport climate too relaxing during summer for the children, and sought a place in the mountains. When in 1883 we visited at Dublin, N.H., my wife's sister, Mrs. Hill, we walked through long abandoned roads to a hill-top, and looked out over a tree-bordered lake to the far-away Green Mountains. We had found what we craved. Could we get it? We should need to buy two adjoining farms.

I authorized Mr. Gleason to pay for them up to a stated amount. He bought them for considerably less. When, a month later, I went to stake out the position for a house, I found the hill enveloped in a dense cloud—no mountain, no lake. Fortunately I was able to find where I had stood with my back against a stone wall, and noted the different features of the landscape. Walking forward from this point, I chose the spot for staking. An architect made a plan embodying my wife's ideas, and Mr. Gleason let the contract. We did not see Dublin again till we came there in the next June, and found the house furnished and dinner on the table.

Far from Nebraska's Prairies

LINDA DYER

Willa Cather stepped off the train in Jaffrey for the first time in late August of 1917, only a few months after the United States entered World War I. An earnest belief in the war that was supposed to end all wars pervaded the town. Jaffrey had already sent about thirty of its young men to the war. Its mills were working full tilt, supplying denim for army fatigue uniforms, hobnails for soldiers' boots, and wooden crates for the shipment of war materials. Rows of vegetables, planted in support of the slogan "Food Will Win the War," thrived in victory gardens all over town. More than twenty gardens, in fact, flourished behind the home of Wayland Goodnow, a local shopkeeper who offered his space to others who lacked proper growing conditions or had no land of their own. Nevertheless, Cather stepped onto a train platform that was bustling not with soldiers or war-related activity but with tourists coming to Jaffrey's resort hotels. Outside the small, gray, clapboard depot, Model T Fords, Cadillacs, and Reos competed with horses and buggies for parking space.

A robust, outdoorsy-looking woman, Willa Cather was almost forty-four years old when she discovered Jaffrey, but she still moved with a boyish energy, an enthusiasm for life. She had written professionally since her student days at the University of Nebraska, but it was not until the publication of *O Pioneers!* in 1913 and *The Song of the Lark* in 1915 that her work began to gain notice among the critics. She did not come to Jaffrey to write, though. She came to visit with her dearest friend, who was vacationing with her husband at the Shattuck Inn.

Though she had lived in cities for over twenty years, Cather was well acquainted with small, country towns like Jaffrey. With a population of 2,500, it was about the same size as Red Cloud, Nebraska, where she had grown up. The shops that lined Main Street, like those of her hometown, served townspeople and farm folk alike. Jaffrey's roads, like those of Red Cloud, were still unpaved. But Jaffrey was unmistakably a New England town. When the Shattuck's car left the depot and turned onto Main Street, it took her over the Contoocook River, which provided power for a host of small mills along its banks, including the White Brothers Mill on the corner of Main and North Street, with its arched windows and handsome brickwork, its mansard roof and Tuscan-style campanile tower. Large maple trees, planted in 1860 as part of a town beautification program, lined either side of Main Street. With her first glimpse of Mount Monadnock, framed by the roadside maples, Jaffrey would remind her far less of Red Cloud and much more of a still-earlier part of her life.

Although her novels will forever associate her with the landscapes of the West, she was born in the tiny town of Back Creek in Virginia's Shenandoah Valley, where her father was a sheep farmer. Her early childhood was spent at Willow

Willa Cather at her meadow study. She enjoyed her mornings writing in a tent, and spent the afternoons wandering.

Shade, a large, multiple-chimneyed brick home in the valley, looking up at North Mountain. The early settlers of both Back Creek and Jaffrey were Scotch-Irish who were scrappy enough to deal with the hardships of a remote, rugged land. Moreover, just as many Revolutionary War veterans came to Jaffrey to buy land and begin farming after the war, others, like Cather's great-great-grandfather, settled in Frederick County, Virginia, after serving in the war.

As the Shattuck's car made its way toward Jaffrey Center, the similarities continued to pile up. The houses were somewhat different in style but of similar vintage to those she had known in Virginia. She passed old farms, saw animals grazing, and caught sight from time to time of the mountain against the sky. Here was a place like her birthplace, a conservative society in which generation followed generation on rocky soil that was both hard-won and well loved.

Her family's move to Nebraska when she was nine had been traumatic for her. It created a dramatic tension that is at the heart of all her work—the East and the West, the old and the new, the cerebral and the sensory. She did not come to Jaffrey to work, but her first impressions were influenced by the novel she had begun to write the previous winter. *My Antonia* is the story of Jim Burden and his friendship with Antonia Shimerda, a Bohemian girl. It begins with Jim's arrival in Nebraska, where he moved at the age of ten to live with his grandparents, following the death of his parents in the Blue Ridge country of Virginia. In writing it Cather was recalling her feelings as an eastern child coming to the vast openness of Nebraska. Even before the car pulled up to the Shattuck Inn, the landscape of this place began to rub against *My Antonia*'s prairie images. She had put her writing aside when she came to Jaffrey, expecting only to enjoy a three-week visit with her friend. A novel-in-progress is not that easily separated from its creator, though. It usurps the writer's subconscious, even on holidays away from work.

The Shattuck Inn could accommodate two hundred guests and attracted a well-educated, cultured crowd, including many academics and professionals. The building was a massive, three-story frame structure, painted white with pine green shutters. Unpretentious despite its size, it presented a decidedly country appearance. Gambrel-roofed wings, like huge barn bookends, dominated the compact central block. Carefully tended flower gardens added bright touches of color against the dominant green of the fields and woods that surrounded the inn. Porches on every side were lined with high-backed wooden rockers, offering guests what they had come for—pine-scented serenity and spectacular scenery.

The inn had been in business since 1868, when Rachel Shattuck began taking in summer boarders in the family farmhouse. By the time Willa Cather came, the inn was under the management of Rachel's son, Edmund. He was a tall, dignified man with thinning hair, offset by heavy eyebrows and a walrus mustache. The inn had prospered and expanded under his direction. An astute businessman, he was solicitous and attentive to his guests and extremely particular about all the details of the inn's operations. He was a good cook, too. The Shattuck Inn became known not only for its exceptional location and fine service but for its

Cather returned regularly to Jaffrey, always staying at the Shattuck Inn in the same small corner room tucked up under the eaves with a view of Mount Monadnock.

"excellent table" as well. Good food was important to Cather and to her art. "My mind and my stomach are one," she once told an interviewer. "I think and work with whatever it is that digests."

Perhaps because the inn was crowded with guests when she arrived, she chose a dormer room on the third floor. She was taken up to it in a small, cagelike lift. Tucked up under the eaves on the northwest corner of the inn, the cozy room with floral-print wallpaper was among the inn's least expensive, but it was the perfect room for her. When she was eleven, her father had opened an insurance and farm loan business and moved the family from a farm on the Nebraska Divide to a cramped house in town. At first she shared a dormitory room in the attic with her brothers, Roscoe and Douglass, but when she reached adolescence, her parents felt she was too old to share a room with her brothers. They partitioned off an ell-shaped gable wing of the main attic to make a private room for her. She settled in like a nesting bird, working at a drugstore to earn money for rolls of flowered wallpaper for its walls and making cheesecloth curtains for its large window. The room became, in a sense, an extension of her uniqueness, set apart from outside expectations. In that small room, the young writer cherished her privacy, the chance to be alone to read and think and dream. She didn't know it then, but it was the beginning of her life as an artist.

She had written most of *O Pioneers!* and nearly all of *The Song of the Lark* in Pittsburgh in a room that reminded her of that girlhood room, a third-floor sewing room at the home of Isabelle McClung, the friend she had come to visit in Jaffrey. Shortly after the publication of *The Song of the Lark*, Isabelle's father died, the house was sold, and Isabelle married Jan Hambourg, a concert violinist. In that turn of events Cather lost her favorite place to write. Moreover, although her friendship with Isabelle would always be a devoted one, the marriage changed their relationship. She could no longer depend on Isabelle, as she had before, to be always available to protect and quicken her work. In the wake of these changes, she suffered many unproductive months in which she feared she had lost the ability to write at all. Now, with *My Antonia* underway, this snug dormer room on the third floor of the Shattuck Inn held hope of a new place to write as well.

The windows of her room looked out over Helen Shattuck's largest flower garden and a large vegetable garden to its west, bordered by Russian Mammoth sunflowers. Beyond the garden stretched an expanse of thick woods with the majesty of Mount Monadnock beyond that. She had always been passionate about landscape. Throughout her life she looked to the land for elemental truth, untainted by self-importance and false values. The mountain she saw from these windows stood alone, imposing but not intimidating, austere and yet accessible, steadfast and serene. Some say that Mount Monadnock has more lovers than any other single mountain in New England. Willa Cather was one of them. Years later she would tell one of her fellow guests at the inn that she had been in the Alps and she had been in the Rockies, but she always came back to Mount Monadnock. Somehow, she said, it "satisfied" her.

She enjoyed her visit with Isabelle, but the simple three-week holiday she had anticipated became instead two glorious months of writing. Her work routine involved two other friends from Pittsburgh who were renting a house called "High Mowing" on Thorndike Pond Road, not far from the Shattuck Inn. They suggested that she could pitch a tent in the meadow that sloped down from the house toward Stony Brook Farm. It is not clear how this invitation came about. Some conjecture that it was probably uncomfortably warm in Cather's small, third-floor room. Others suggest that because it was crowded at the inn, she needed a quieter, more secluded place to write. It may have been simply a matter of wanting to be outdoors instead of cooped up inside.

Her habit was to write in the morning, limiting herself to two or three hours in order to maintain a sense of play in her work, to make a game of creation. She began the day dressed in a middy blouse and cotton skirt, long her morning uniform whether she was writing in New York or visiting her family in Red Cloud. She wore a straw hat to shade her eyes from the sun and added a jacket or cardigan sweater if the weather happened to be cool. She carried a little portfolio with her papers and pens but kept her ink bottles in the tent, which had no floor and was furnished with nothing more than a table and camp chair. Her meadow workplace delighted her. She once remarked in a letter to Carrie Miner Sherwood that in order to work well she needed to feel as carefree as a thirteen-year-old at a picnic in Garber's Grove, a favorite spot when the two were growing up in Red Cloud. Her meadow study seemed to encourage just that effect. Each day she followed the same route to her tent, walking a half mile up a dirt lane across from the inn. At the end of the lane she slipped through a hedge and cut over to the meadow.

By the time she arrived in Jaffrey, she had written the introduction and book one of her novel and was ready to begin the next section, "The Hired Girls." She liked to write her first drafts in longhand with a fountain pen, letting her words spill onto the paper in a rush. She was aiming at raw material, relying on intuition and her own interest in the events she was depicting. Revision would come later. On her first run-through she was eager to bring the unbridled vitality of life to her writing rather than stifling it with self-consciousness. "Unless you have something in you so fierce that it simply pours itself out in a torrent, heedless of rules or bounds—then do not bother to write anything at all," she said. "Why should you? The time for revisions is after the thing is on paper—not before." After spending the morning writing in her tent, she clambered over a stone wall and walked back to the inn through the woods.

She kept the rest of her day uncluttered, with enough activity to keep herself amused, yet kept at a regular, unhurried pace. She spent most of the afternoon outdoors, sometimes climbing the mountain trails but often just wandering through the woods around the inn, usually with a copy of F. Schuler Matthew's *Field Book of American Wildflowers*. She once confided to her friend Elizabeth Sergeant that she needed almost to dissolve into nature daily in order to be reborn to her task.

In the evenings at the Shattuck Inn guests wrote letters or read in the inn's library, visited with one another in the parlors, played cards, or worked at handmade wooden jigsaw puzzles in the smoking room. She made a few friends among the guests, but for the most part she kept her distance. She attended musical entertainment when it was offered in the evening, but she always retired by ten o'clock. She would be up early the next day, heading off to her meadow tent. When she left Jaffrey in late October, she had finished her first draft of "The Hired Girls" and was in high spirits.

Against her family's wishes, Cather chose to stay in Jaffrey forever.

She would return regularly to Jaffrey in the years that followed, always staying at the Shattuck Inn in the same small corner room tucked up under the eaves with a view of Mount Monadnock. It became her favorite place to write. She had discovered it at just the right moment in her life. Jaffrey's woods and fields and mountain, so like her Virginia beginnings, offered her the same sense of security she had known in earliest childhood, while her snug dormer room reminded her of the girlhood room in Red Cloud she cherished. The ambiance of the Shattuck Inn bore out her belief that all art, including the art of living, is a matter of taking pains.

Love affairs, be they with people or with places, build on an initial attraction. In the years to come, that landscape would adapt itself in other ways to the novels she wrote there, whether she was writing about a professor's house on the shores of Lake Michigan, the archbishop's diocese in New Mexico, or seventeenth-century Quebec. Jaffrey became more than a working place. It provided her, as well, with solace in times of loss and a refuge in times of trouble. In the end she chose to stay forever. Today's visitors will find her in the southwest corner of the Old Burying Ground by the 1775 Meeting House. She is buried under the spread of a sugar maple along an old stone wall—the prairie novelist laid to rest in the most New England of settings.

Grandfather's Farm

More dead people than live ones inhabit my dirt road. The count is two hundred eleven dead, thirteen alive. When you move into a mixed neighborhood like that, it's wise to make changes cautiously, balancing personal preferences with local expectations.

When I moved here, thirty years ago, the challenge was even greater. I was moving into my grandparents' farm, and my grandfather was buried between his two wives in the adjoining cemetery. My father was buried one row to the east. The house was still fully furnished with all the things I'd known as a child: the tall chest with forty drawers where my grandfather hid candies, magnetic Scotties, and trading cards for me; the big kneehole desk where he sat each morning to write doggerel for the *New Yorker* and where he opened their rejection slips; and the high canopy bed where I'd join my grandparents for orange juice, graham crackers, and hot, lemon-scented washcloths to start the day.

The very first night I discovered how hard it would be to take ownership of this much-loved place. I put my children in their cribs, then tucked myself into the canopy bed. Immediately I rolled into the deep trough on the right-hand side of the bed, the trough my heavy grandfather had worn over many years. I thought of him lying there with my grandmother; I thought of him sick and tossing about. Too much! I fled into the guest room, not the one I'd used as a child but the one for grownups. There I could sleep.

The next day was Dump Day. I decided to perform a small exorcism ritual. My grandfather had installed a mechanical stair to haul him from the first floor to the second. I would get rid of it, get rid of this reminder of his sick days, rewrite the story with a better ending. It took a wrecker bar, bolt cutters, and several sweaty hours, but I demolished the rails, the motor, and the gray metal chair and hauled them off to the dump. Piece by piece I hurled them off the hill toward Mount Monadnock. They joined the piles of garbage, rusty appliances, and construction debris smoldering below.

Old Mr. Hunt, the dumpmaster, came over to chat. "Too bad," he opined. "I heard your grampa paid over two thousand dollars for that. I bet someone woulda paid you at least eight hunnert for it and took it apart as well."

Siggy was the commander in chief of domestic operations and of the dairy when my grandparents were alive. Her idea of breakfast was a spread on the side table of three kinds of cereal—oatmeal, Wheaties, and Cheerios—three kinds of freshly picked berries in special berry bowls, a dish of grated maple sugar and one of white, a pitcher of yesterday's milk, and another one of Jersey cream so heavy it had to be spooned onto the cereal. There was homemade sausage and bacon, fresh baked bread, and several jars of homemade preserves.

At first I struggled to re-create this effect for my family. It was "the way things were done at the farm." I even bought heavy cream and mixed it with sour cream to simulate the spoonable cream I remembered. One day I dropped one of the three berry bowls, and it shattered. I felt shame—and then liberation. From now on I would only have to pick two kinds of berries. Soon the cereal was offered in boxes, and the bread was store-bought.

"Too bad," my husband said, "but that thick cream always made me feel sick."

By then I was spending a lot of time washing dishes. One morning I finally noticed that the view from the kitchen sink was of a solid wall with shelves holding boxes of SOS pads, cans of Bon Ami and Ajax the foaming cleanser, bottle brushes, and worn sponges. Clearly Siggy's aesthetic needs had never been considered. But mine were going to be, and "Yes, Mr. LaRoche could come in a week and put in a window and move the clothes washer and make a counter. And yes,

Alma Allen, from Harrisville, painted this scene of the farm. Alma was a close friend of Siggy, who "was the backbone of the farm when I was a 'Grandchild Visiting' in the summer," recalls Nancy Hayden. "She was cook and CEO; every meal had multiple, yummy options. Siggy was designated commander in chief when my grandparents returned to New York for the winter. And that is how her artist friend came to the farm to paint. I hope Siggy and Alma had lovely days together, each working on her 'projects' and sharing the delicious Finnish treats Siggy baked so well. I can smell the cardamom."

Grandmother in the garden. Madeline Borland Pell cultivated colossal delphiniums.

he would be happy to use old wood from the shop barn. And maybe he'd even left it there himself when he did some work for my grandmother in '33."

So it was done and was a vast improvement, except that the window looked out on a bramble and burdock patch.

That meant that we dug it all up, saw how rich the soil was, and moved the vegetable garden. Soon it looked like Findhorn, with cabbages the size of wheelbarrows.

Which in turn meant that the kitchen grew so appealing that people wanted to hang out there, but there was no place for them to sit. So we demolished the wall behind the sink with its nearly new window and extended the kitchen.

Now people stay in the kitchen when I cook. I'm sure Siggy would be horrified at first, but then she'd glance out the window and spot a goldfinch bending down a thistle head or a hummingbird hovering in ecstasy in a jewelweed, and perhaps she'd give grudging approval. Probably not, though; more likely she'd have Tony or Eugene get those weeds out. So would I, if I had Tony and Eugene to command.

The plants around the farm have changed gradually and moved around. I discuss changes mentally with my long-dead grandmother, and occasionally sense approval.

Descendants of her hollyhocks still seed themselves in the front border, but, without the manure from the cows, I couldn't keep the soil rich enough for her colossal delphiniums.

My creamy daylilies, though, are prettier than her common orange ones or her gold ones with the brown smudge on each petal. And the peonies I brought from my childhood home are thriving. They were old even before we moved into that house in 1950. Festiva Maxima, they are called. I translate that as Huge Party, but my Latin is frail.

Mam—my grandmother—used to sit in the back garden and appliqué delicate chintz flowers on quilt squares. There was monkshood in that garden then and huge bushes of mountain laurel. The laurel kept the walls too shaded, though; moisture was trapped and the sills rotted out.

So now there's myrtle with little white fritillaries and a wonderfully scented, salmon pink azalea, planted farther from the wall. There is also a very Zen rock with polypody ferns struggling to establish themselves on top. Usually when I sit there, it is to sip a glass of iced tea before weeding some more. My grandmother's gauzy dress has given way to my jeans. It is startling to realize that her pink rose and her Siberian iris bloomed this June, and that she has been dead for fifty years.

Somewhere along the way I noticed that the farm was still known as the old Mason place, the name of the owners preceding my grandparents. At that pace it wouldn't be mine for one hundred years. So we all proposed names and finally chose "Too Bad Farm"—too bad about all the mistakes we'd already made and all the ones we were still doomed to make through ignorance or hubris. Too bad also in the superstitious way of not wanting to attract the gods' attention and letting them notice how lucky we were.

Lately I've realized that the farm is finally mine. Two trees fell in recent storms: a willow and a maple. In a crotch in the willow, ten or twelve feet up, a croquet ball with a red stripe was embedded and had been almost completely surrounded by new wood. One of my children had really sent another's ball to Kalamazoo in some hard-fought game that no one can remember. And in the center of a core of crumbly decayed wood in the maple rested our old tetherball, looking like an improbable dinosaur egg waiting for global warming to restore its habitat.

In my turn, I've grown crotchety about new people in the neighborhood, people who move too fast, people who've cleared so many trees that their house is visible from mine. Theirs is the only visible house, the only reminder that it is no longer the eighteenth century and that the farm has survived its first two hundred years. "Don't choke on the small bones," I remind myself, and "remember that New Hampshire grows great trees; just wait sixty years or so."

Since I've lived here, the contents of four households and accumulations from many auctions have been added. Almost nothing has been removed. I could never face the task of packing it all up, so I imagine I'll just stay here, first at the farm, then at the cemetery. Actually I'll have to rest just outside the cemetery; the family plot is full, and the rest of the cemetery is spoken for. But I measured, and I could be less than two rods from the rest of my family. And I've learned how to establish my own place without disrupting what's already there. It's mainly a question of time . . . and listening carefully to the neighbors.

Back to the Land

I can remember the day that I became a vegetarian. It was hot even before the sun came up. Usually, even the hottest days were pleasant on the mountain, where we had lived for one long year of ecstasy. There was often a breeze that came up the river valley. But that day, there wasn't a breath of air. We were renting an old farm, a farm that had been previously rented to a group of free spirits who enjoyed living in the nude. Word had gone round the town and tradesmen had gotten into the habit of dropping by there to ask directions. Their feigned disorientation was rewarded by the sight of the various young residents greeting them au naturel. However, it took longer for word to get around that the nudists had left and we had moved in. And so the stillness of our first months there was periodically interrupted by knocks at the door and disappointed faces when we opened the door fully clothed.

We were there for a more serious kind of freedom. We hoped that by living in such a place, we could provide for ourselves. It was the time of the nation's first and, to date, most serious oil crisis. We had moved there from Philadelphia. It was 1974. We were in our early twenties. My husband, Michael, and I had both worked in publishing before quitting, packing up our cats, houseplants, and camping gear, and heading for New Hampshire.

We just wanted to live where we didn't have to think about escalating rents and parking spaces. But once we arrived we realized that these small freedoms could lead to others. In the dense earth beside the stream that ran past the back door of the first apartment we rented, we planted our first garden, which rewarded us

The perfect little wood wagon, an old VW with the right front seat removed.

with an abundance of carrots and tomatoes and beets and lettuce, grown from seeds we had bought from a revolving rack at the hardware store. Though my father had taught me a great deal about gardening when I was growing up in New Jersey, he had not taught me anything about living self-sufficiently. I wanted to know more, so I bought and read books of all kinds about gardening and homesteading. We bought Helen and Scott Nearing's *Living the Good Life* and were inspired by their story of leaving New York in the 1940s and moving to Vermont, living on the vegetables that they raised and building their own house.

Scott Nearing preached one guiding principle: *pay as you go*. We took it to heart. We saved, hoping to be able to purchase a piece of land for cash and then build a small house, working in the way that the Nearings advised, one segment at a time and never going into debt. When that farm in Winchester came up, we leapt at the chance to rent it. The rent was reasonable for an old Cape (the perfect shape for wood heat), a barn that was sound, and 250 acres for privacy with room for the animals we hoped to have. The farm was in an obscure section of Winchester known as Ashuelot, on the top of Gunn Mountain, and looked out onto what seemed like the entire Connecticut River Valley. To the west, we could see a portion of Vermont. Looking south, down the hill, we could look straight down the main street of Northfield, Massachusetts, and in the distance Mount Tom and a glimpse of Connecticut. No one else lived on the hill at that time and we loved the silence and the wild feeling that living there gave us. We saw deer and fox far more often than people.

Celebrating an illicit crop on the old homestead.

The first thing we did when we moved in was to go down into the basement, disconnect the furnace, and throw the main switch to the electrical box. We had collected oil lamps at flea markets and bought two woodstoves, one for the living room and one for the kitchen ell. In the beginning of the summer, we started to cut wood for the following fall. We had never even used a woodstove before, much less depended on one for our heat, and we certainly did not have a chain saw. Or a truck. We cut the trees with a bow saw and brought the logs back to the woodshed in my old Volkswagen, from which we had removed the right front seat. As such, it was the perfect little wood wagon and we hauled many loads throughout the summer, accumulating the ten cords we thought we would burn that first winter.

The area seemed full of the Nearings' disciples at that time. There were communes here and there, and many of the members worked at the health-food store in Brattleboro, appropriately named the Good Life. I remember clearly the day that one of the clerks there was arrested by a swarm of state policemen who brought her out from the store into the sunlight in shackles and chains. She was suspected of being a member of the underground, radical Weathermen and was later put on trial in New York City. She was acquitted and returned to Brattleboro, where she changed her name and ran for selectman. Such was the nature of that community.

The bookstore prominently displayed books that, like the Nearings', explored other aspects of living off the grid: books on gardening, solar energy, composting, building your own house, heating with wood. There was even a wonderful book on how to grow marijuana, which we added to our little library. Since none of the aspects of country living came to us as second nature, books were an important part of the education we needed in order to go back to the land. Books did not provide us with everything. We also learned a lot from friends. Several other couples were homesteading near our farm. One couple, Jamie and Bob, lived on a hundred acres of landlocked land, three-quarters of a mile into the woods. We could walk cross-lots and get to them quicker but mostly we walked in on the rutted road that led to their cabin. They used a horse—a big brown workhorse named Dan—for transportation and, in the winter, they had the hood of an old car, which they turned upside down and hitched to the horse. This provided a kind of surfboard sleigh, which made such things as bringing lumber and groceries in to the cabin an easy task. Or at least an *easier* task.

They knew about as much about living off the land as we did. We were all having our baptisms by fire, literally. Our first woodstove was not really a woodstove but a coal stove, but we didn't know the difference. Neither did we know enough to install it a good distance from the living room wall. To save space, we backed it right up against the wall and lit it up. Pretty quickly, we figured out it needed some distance from the walls. Fortunately that lesson came without incident. Bob made a woodstove out of an old oil barrel and installed it in their little cabin. The heat filled the room and for a while it seemed like the greatest thing since sliced bread. The stove itself was brilliant, but they didn't realize that dry wood literally doesn't grow on trees and by February they were wandering about at night, on snowshoes, pointing their flashlight up into the treetops in hopes of finding a standing dead tree—good dry wood for their stove. They had never heard of a widow maker (and neither had we) and they were fortunate that Jamie was not made a widow when Bob cut those trees down.

But they got through the winter, somehow. And we did too, though we eventually bought a chain saw, which was another item that required on-the-job training. Michael learned quickly, though there was one tree I remember vividly, a great big "wolf" tree at the edge of the forest. It was oak and big around as five men. Michael notched it and then cut it, dropping it the wrong way and hanging it up in the taller tree beside it. It hung by a thick hinge of sinew and bark, so perilously that Michael decided not to get too close. He solved the problem by shooting his rifle at the remaining hinge that was holding the tree from falling. Many shots rang out before the big oak thudded to the ground with a shudder. We all shared our experiences and learned from each other. And laughed at our mistakes. Like orphaned children of the forest, we brought each other up into the lawless world of self-sufficiency.

There were other ways to learn, too. I worked for a time at a printing company in Brattleboro and befriended an older woman named Marge who worked packing books in the bindery. She lived in Chesterfield with her bachelor son Skip. Her husband had died but she and Skip still lived the lives of the old Yankee farmer—bread baked in the oven, crocks of coleslaw fermented in the root cellar, hens pecked in the yard. And the pigpen was rarely without a little porker fattening for the smoker. The garden was a work of generations of cultivation.

Since Marge lived right on my route, I often gave her a ride home when we got off the seven o'clock shift. And sometimes I went in for a chat. Skip liked to talk and they were generous with what they knew.

Marge and Skip gave us our first rooster—he was old and they no longer wanted to feed him. They said we could kill him for meat. With their guidance, we did. The meat was tough and the experience was unpleasant but the rooster was going to die anyway and the economy of this act appealed to our newfound sense of country logic. Marge and Skip sometimes came to visit and when they did, they usually brought a dozen double yolkers—I had never even heard of a double yolker much less imagined you could gather a dozen into a carton at one time—and a slab of home-smoked bacon. They encouraged us to get a pig and we thought about that but we wanted chickens first. With their counsel, we bought our first flock of laying hens, Golden Comets, still the prettiest hens I've ever seen.

It seems I could reach back and pull up an entire encyclopedia of things that Marge and Skip taught us. So much of what motivated us to become self-sufficient was fueled by our outrage at the proliferation of nuclear power plants, one of which was nearby in Vernon, Vermont. What was serendipitous was that their way of life, which was simply sensible, gave us many tools toward our goal of self-sufficiency. Marge and Skip and the thousands like them in the hills all around here had no particular opinion about nuclear power and understood little about it. They were still grateful for the conveniences electricity had brought them and seemed confused when we talked about living without electricity: why be connected to the grid that was feeding off of foreign oil and posing a serious health threat to those who lived near it? We were coming to believe there was a simpler way to live one's life. Ironically, Marge and Skip showed us part of the way.

And so on that hot summer morning, we had been up before the sun, getting ready for the big day. Michael was sharpening the axe and I was splitting wood

The first and last mass beheading on a hot August day.

next to the fire pit beside the barn. We needed a good hot fire, big enough to boil water in the cauldron, so, with our other axe, I was splitting pine logs into splinters. In the stall above us, I could hear the ladies moving about in their coop. Six weeks before, we had ordered one hundred chicks, which had come to us through the mail, in boxes. We had all the equipment for the slaughter. Expanding our thinking from the experience of that one rooster that Marge and Skip had given us, we reasoned: if we were going to eat meat, we should provide it for ourselves, take responsibility for the whole of the matter. Purchasing the meat in the grocery store seemed to sidestep what it really meant to eat meat. Not just the act of eating it, but participating in all of what resulted in having a piece of chicken on the dinner plate.

The little chicks grew quickly into little three-pounders and before we knew it, it was time for the day of the kill. We wanted to finish the task in a single day's work. We had divvied up the work, imagining a kind of assembly line of two: I would catch the birds and bring them to the block and hold them, my hands covering their folded wings, while Michael beheaded them. (We discovered the true meaning of the expression, "Like a chicken with its head cut off.") I would hang them to bleed and then pluck them. Michael, who was a hunter and a fisherman, would gut them and cut them into parts, which I would wrap and stash into the big coolers.

The day began early and our energy was determined. However, by noon, we were at the point of stunned exhaustion, never having imagined what we had gotten ourselves into. We were spattered with blood as if we had been involved in some kind of mass murder. I was finding the sight of the naked chickens, their bony hips protruding in an almost human-like manner, the stuff of future nightmares. But the smell was worse. It was a hot, muggy day. Whereas we often had a good breeze up on that hill, that day was still and the big maples on the front lawn only faintly stirred from time to time. Mostly, everything was still and soundless. We had set up barrels with plastic bags, one for the chicken heads, one for the legs, one for the guts, and one for the feathers. Some people say that the worst part of killing chickens is the smell of the wet feathers and I agree with that but there was something more. Perhaps it was just blood, which I had never smelled before. The smell lingered around me for days afterward, no matter how many times I showered, washed my hands, and changed my clothes. If there is such a thing as olfactory memory, I had it, and have it, as I believe I can still, almost thirty years later, summon the smell of that August day into reality.

(Smells seem to represent at least some of our experimental failures. Our homesteading neighbors tried a different method of raising protein: they stocked their little pond with hundreds of trout fingerlings. They didn't realize the pond was not big enough and before those fish reached maturity, the pond ran out of oxygen and all the fish died, leaving a stench of dead fish that traveled half a mile up the road to our offended noses.)

I'm sure you can see where I am going with this. Although we carefully wrapped each chicken into foil and plastic and stashed it all in our neighbor's freezer (we swapped freezer space for meat), that was the day I gave up meat.

For many years, in fact. I never tasted those chickens and am not even sure, at this point, what ever did happen to them. Michael joined me in my vegetarianism. We read *Diet for a Small Planet* and agreed with the logic of that book: instead of growing grain to feed the animals to feed us, eat the grain and let the animals live.

Living on that farm, we were able to save up the cash for the house that we built on seven acres of land we had bought down the road. Heeding Scott Nearing, we paid as we went and built the house, which we designed and built piecemeal—we laid the cement-block foundation, dug the well, raised the rafters, and built the four-flue brick chimney almost entirely by ourselves or with the occasional help of our compassionate friends. The standard-size Cape had solar hot water, a wood cookstove, a composting toilet, oil lanterns, and, eventually, a slate roof. One woodstove in the center of the house comfortably heated the entire house. There was no backup heating system. We pumped water by hand into a pressurized tank that allowed us to draw water from the tap—a design that provided me with the material for the first magazine article I ever published. We were especially proud that the house was energy-efficient and had no dependency on anything but what we could provide for ourselves, including the fuel to heat ourselves through the long New Hampshire winters. Many of our friends lived in teepees and one-room cabins built from slab wood and scrap plywood. They hauled their water in buckets from a stream and hot water was strictly from a kettle on a woodstove. Ours felt like a real house, one that had its own sense of beauty and one that demonstrated that self-sufficiency meant neither deprivation nor substandard living.

But there are no two ways about it: living close to the land, growing and preserving all our food, harvesting all our heating fuel, pumping all our own water, and finishing the last details of the house—tiling the kitchen floor, putting slate on the roof, trim around the windows in the bedrooms—was a lot of work. And no matter how well we provided for ourselves, life still required money—to pay taxes, to buy cars (which were always on their last legs), to fill them with gas, to buy clothing and certain food items such as flour and sugar and dog food that we could not grow. What we found was that we still needed jobs, which meant time away for our already labor-intensive lives.

We lived like that for about seven years. Some people say that the strain of a life like that caused a lot of couples to split up. Surely no one kept records on that particular sociological phenomenon. It was certainly harder to live the way we did than it was to live the ordinary American life of our parents and of, not so surprisingly, most of our high school and college friends. I remember once a woman called us out of the blue and told us she was writing a book about people who had moved from the city to the country. She had heard about the house we had built and wondered if she could come to interview us. We agreed and she came and we told her the story of how we had moved to New Hampshire from Philadelphia, and of how we had come to build the house. We showed her all the clever aspects of the house, including the beautiful copper hatch Michael had designed into the roof so that he could clean the chimney (or extinguish a chimney fire) without ever having to go up onto the roof. And then, at the end of the interview, we told her we had decided to divorce. I remember how her mouth dropped, ever so slightly, and how her speech faltered as if we had suddenly died in front of her. Now that I look back on that afternoon, I suppose her reaction was not dissimilar to that of a lot of people. When your lifestyle makes a statement, whether you intend it or not, people take an interest in how it's going. Your life almost becomes a spectator sport. People perhaps invest a bit of themselves in your way of life, either damning it or egging it on, hoping it will triumph or fail. Many more people knew who we were than we knew. We had gone out on a limb and people wanted to see if it would break or hold.

So it broke. At least to some degree. We divorced, as did Jamie and Bob and others of our land-loving friends. Unceremoniously and without explanation or analysis, a subculture came to an end. Whether we were hippies or back-to-the-landers or homesteaders or the counterculture—we're all gone, even though we're still here. There aren't any free spirits living in teepees or one-room cabins around here anymore. It's unlikely you could knock on the door of an old farmhouse now and have it opened by a naked young lady. I have heard of few young pioneers who are building their self-sufficient dream house in the woods, though there may be one or two out there. (I hope so.) Virtually all our homesteading friends are divorced now, leading relatively conventional lives. Maybe this region was like Paris in the twenties or New York in the fifties, where artists could live cheaply and pursue their dreams. It was like that here once, too, our lifestyle being our art.

We sold the house in 1981, for ninety thousand dollars cash, split the money, and went our separate ways. That house, built for cash and sold for cash, laid the ground for every house I have owned since. It would be fair to say that living the way we did gave us the best economic advantage we ever could have had or will have. The little self-sufficient Cape evolved away from its clever beginnings into an ordinary house on a nice plot of land. The solar panels are long gone and I understand that the composting toilet, which worked beautifully for us, was immediately removed and a flush toilet and septic system installed—as was an oil furnace and a regular water pump. Michael and I both remarried and moderated our lives. In a way, we followed the path of that idealistic house. We both still use woodstoves, but just provisionally. I still grow a lot of food and sometimes I bake bread and occasionally put up pickles or sauce. But it's just something I know how to do, nothing I have to depend on. Lately, though, I've been thinking about getting a little flock of laying hens—just for the eggs.

Getting Out of the Hole in Nelson

JIM COLLINS

The Nelson town hall is a mecca for contra dancing.

On a warm summer night in Nelson the contra dancers arrive, "spilling"—as Dudley Laufman would write in a poem—"into the hall like a tipped over basket of many colored balls of yarn." In the small, white-clapboarded building, Dudley plays accordion and calls the figures. A slew of skilled musicians crowd around him on the low stage. They're playing fine tonight, spirited, the kind of night that made piano player Bob McQuillen "ring" with the music. Everybody's getting along. The dances heat up; skirts fly as couples twirl, as partners promenade down the lines. Couples bunch up in a far corner, a quirk of the old hall's sloping floor. The windows drip with moisture, the air smells of sweat and hair and dust. "Chorus Jig" ends, and a few dancers sashay over and throw open the hall's tall windows.

The year could be any in the past several decades, but let's place it in 1972. The country dance revival sweeping across New England is in full flower in the hill towns circling Mount Monadnock. In the tiny village of Nelson, in a town of barely more than three hundred people, at the epicenter of the revival, history and cultures and countercultures converge in an old town hall that has held dances nearly continuously since it was built in 1797. Barefoot, long-haired dancers fill the lines. They are the latest wave of immigrants here: educated, idealistic, transplanted from Cambridge and Connecticut, New York and New Jersey. They live in fixed-up old farmhouses and cabins without running water. A few of the dancers, their T-shirts dark with perspiration, walk over to benches pushed tight against the walls and gulp water from glass jars. Couples exchange glances, exchange partners.

Dudley pauses for a breather, then pulls a favorite stunt. Instead of telling the band what comes next, he arranges the dancers and explains the new figures to them. The musicians look at each other and shift uncomfortably. Dudley pauses, then turns and says, "Go ahead, boys—let's have 'Ross's Reel Number Four' in F!" The boys hit it without missing a beat, the surge of anxiety passes, and nobody seems to mind. Dudley beams. A hall full of dancers balance and swing, high on the movement and the feeling of being part of a community.

At the center of the swirl stands Dudley Laufman, a young, charismatic accordion and fiddle player who insists on using the fine old dance music that has all but disappeared from New England kitchens and grange halls—not old square-dance standards like "Pop Goes the Weasel," but really old tunes from the British Isles and French Canada like "Money Musk" and "Coleraine." He found old players tucked away in the hills who could teach them. He backed himself with any musicians who cared enough about that music to learn it right. He took the torch of a dying oral tradition from the hands of a few old-timers and fired up an entire generation of young people. Some nights, now, twelve or fifteen instruments play behind him, and everyone can feel it: the energy is kinetic, intoxicating. People have seen square dancing before, but this is *different*.

Nowhere—then, or now—is the scene stronger than in Cheshire County in southwest New Hampshire. Country dancing has a richer heritage here than anywhere in the entire country. It has shown a remarkable resilience going back to the days before the Revolution. Yeoman stock of Scottish, English, and Irish families brought the music and dance forms with them from the old countries. Dance masters from Boston helped spread waltzes and quadrilles around the highlands, and especially contras: line dances in which partners made simple moves, joining hands in a circle, crossing forward and back, swinging, dos-á-dos. But the long winters and rugged isolation of the region kept most outside influences at bay. The dancing generally took place in kitchens and barns, and passed down through generations in families. After the Civil War, when minstrel shows and military bands made contras out of date and out of fashion elsewhere, the old dances hung on around Monadnock and in remote pockets of Vermont and western Massachusetts. The jigs and reels were kept alive—sometimes single-handedly, it seems—by passionate itinerant musicians such as John Putnam of Greenfield, Massachusetts, and John Langdon Britton of Cheshire County. With the Industrial Revolution and jazz eras came new assaults on the old ways, but also a new group of immigrants from French Canada to work the mills in Keene and Swanzey and Harrisville, immigrants who infused their own flavor of old-time fiddle tunes and dance steps.

In the roar of the 1920s, with old-fashioned contra and square dancing fading fast or already gone from much of the country, a number of factors conspired to save it—and then revive it—in the Monadnock region. The natural beauty of the mountain and the area's pristine lakes had, for some years, been attracting summer people. Following the stock market crash of 1929, many of those summer folks, along with other city dwellers, moved here permanently and became fascinated with the "country" customs they discovered. A few years later New Hampshire's nascent ski industry began attracting weekend visitors. All these outside visitors and residents did something remarkable to the region:

Dudley Laufman, the pied piper of the revival, made contra dancing seem historic and quaint and hip at the same time. The contra dancers were not quite a cult but had the same feverish energy as a religious revival.

they helped create its unusual "Chautauqua" atmosphere, that confluence of a rural, working landscape and an intellectual, curious, cultured populace. They did something more: they created a demand for a form of entertainment that popular culture had left behind and that the local population could provide but couldn't, alone, sustain.

The newcomers sought out people who could play and teach them to dance. Old natives who hadn't danced in years suddenly found themselves back in town halls and walking beginners through steps at family gatherings. In Nelson, the Tolman family regularly played for summer guests, and their reputation for playing authentic dance music attracted lapsed and aspiring musicians from miles around. Fiddler Dick Richardson of Marlborough started up a band, with Nelson's Ralph Page calling the dances. Richardson's band played all over. During the summer it played two dances a week at the Peterborough town hall. Jimmy Ross called weekly dances in Francestown and Swanzey, Shorty Durant in Stoddard, Larry Pickett and Larry Gautier in Keene. In 1946, back home in New Boston after a stint in the navy, Bob McQuillen attended his first dance in Francestown and was smitten. For a year after, he went to dances and learned to play tunes on his accordion; then he joined Richardson's band. A decade later, another key link in the chain: Dudley Laufman, a young musician who had grown up around kitchen junkets on a dairy farm in Fremont, arrived late to a dance in Peterborough. It was dark. He remembers the sound of a waterfall in the Contoocook River fading as pulsing, lilting music seeped through the barn's windows. "McQuillen was playing the accordion and John Tromblay was on piano; Russ Allen and Dick Richardson on fiddle, Junior was playing the bass, and Ralph was calling . . . and I'm telling you that was just beautiful, the way the sound came out, and the thump of the dancers' feet—the floor was moving up and down. The whole effect was just perfect, and I thought, 'It can't stop. It's got to continue.'" And Dudley Laufman decided to learn to run dances in the same vein.

By the mid-1960s Ralph Page had slowly lost much of his following to television, the big bands, and cheek-to-cheek dance clubs. His crowd of die-hard farmers, laborers, and housewives had dwindled as it aged. The younger crowd, in love with the automobile, found his square dances less and less novel. Nobody else around was still calling squares.

Page's formality and insistence on playing the same handful of songs—"Turkey in the Straw," "Darling Nellie Gray," "Redwing"—didn't cut it with a younger generation. One night in Peterborough, Page threw a dancer out of the hall for clapping and stomping with the music. A few weeks later in Marlborough, his dance attracted just eight people. The music came from a Victrola.

Meanwhile, Dudley Laufman was hitting the scene at exactly the right moment.

Like Page, he was gruff and headstrong, but Dudley wore his hair long, wore caps and capes and turtlenecks, and wrote poetry. He lived self-sufficiently, ate no meat. He made contra dancing seem historic and quaint and hip at the same time. At the 1965 Newport Folk Festival, sixteen thousand fans went wild for

By the mid-1960s, old-school caller Ralph Page had slowly lost much of his following to television and cheek-to-cheek dance clubs.

229

Dudley and his thrown-together band of minstrels called the Canterbury Country Orchestra, the same night they booed Bob Dylan for playing electric guitar.

Dudley's dancers weren't the local communities of rural folk who had sustained the old dances in good times and bad. These new dancers, disenchanted with an increasingly fast, artificial culture, in search of an idyllic rural lifestyle, looked to the dances to provide a sense of community, a sense of place. Dudley and his old-time music gave them something they yearned for, something real, something authentic.

In the early years of the revival, Dudley put a thousand miles a week on his Volkswagen, and dancers followed him with fanatical devotion. Many of them knew one another only from dances: in Nelson and Dublin and Harrisville, in Fitzwilliam and Peterborough, Brattleboro and New Boston. Knew one another not by name but by style and the way they'd swing or smile. They were part of a movement, not quite a cult, but with the same feverish energy as a religious revival. They measured their time, as local dancer Jack Perron put it, in the days between dances, space in the distance between dance halls. Some of them happily drove two hours or more to a dance hall, danced all night, and drove right back, and did it again the next week and the next and the next. Perron himself had once walked twenty-six miles to get to a dance up in Acworth. They felt a joy in dancing with strangers—there was something solid and intimate about that close contact, the firm press of a hand against your back as you let yourself get spun around a dusty room, the heft of another person's weight leaning back against your grip, the promenade's hand cupping a fleshy or bony hip, the smell of another person's sweat and hair. There was something comforting in the familiarity of the moves, the recognition of the other dancers up and down the lines, the potluck suppers beforehand, the infants and toddlers asleep in the corner. There was sexual energy, the flirtatious gaze in a move called the "gypsy," young women without bras, all those bare feet and legs. There was the high of the group in complex motion—the intricate "country corners" and diagonal castoffs that, seen from above, maybe from the high balcony in the Peterborough town hall, looked like a kaleidoscope, all color and motion and geometry. And there was the music—old, maybe, but full of toe-tapping beat and fast fiddle licks and high harmonies. For many it was a pleasure just listening.

Dudley Laufman was their pied piper. He was the organizer, the caller, the leader of the band. He worked the floor teaching the moves. He read the mood of the crowd, adjusted the pacing, knew when to talk and when to play. His was hard work, though it was lost on most in the music and the swirl. He preferred the traditional old patterns, which were simple enough for the kids and old folks to join in, with plenty of standing-around time for watching the relatives, as if he were still playing for folks on the farm.

But the new generation that longed for the rural idyll also liked rock and roll, and, in time—over eight, ten years—this younger crowd included fewer and fewer neighbors, more engineers and college professors who commuted to dances, drove hours to hear hot bands, hit three or four dances a week. They wanted more challenging moves. They spiced the sedate figures with fancy twirls and flourishes. The dances became as important as the dancers, because the dancers were interchangeable. A dancing community evolved, one based on shared values and interests, one that had a rhythm to its gatherings and an understood protocol, but it wasn't the kind of community Dudley originally had in mind. To Dudley, dances were still for relaxing after the work was done. Now he heard people demanding harder aerobic dances, more *exercise*.

For a while, Dudley allowed himself to change with the scene. He allowed "radical" foot stomping and hand clapping. He encouraged the new dancers to show their free spirits. But some old-school callers, Ralph Page among them, criticized him for compromising tradition in return for more calling jobs and more money.

Dudley told them he didn't have much use for tradition. (Though he spent a lot of his time raising money to ensure the recording of the old-time fiddle music of Dick Richardson. And he was involved in creating the annual Ralph Page Legacy Weekend at the University of New Hampshire.) In a poem, he'd written, "Well sonny, when you can learn to dance like a Bulgarian, maybe we will learn to play like one. In the meantime, it's all in fun. Why waste time being authentic in this shiny-floored gymnasium in the city? Let's be unauthentic together and work for improvement, you with your feet, us with our strings, it's fun we're after."

Increasingly, though, Dudley's dances weren't fun for the regulars. Many of them tired of his insistence on the same simple dances, and of his intolerance. Rifts grew between him and his musicians, who wanted to expand and experiment. Some nights he even growled at Newt Tolman, who'd exposed Dudley to many of the old tunes in the first place.

By the late 1970s, cliquish alliances had spread through the dance world, factions in a big club. Musicians who had played behind Dudley now struck off and called their own dances. They patiently taught dancers more challenging

Harvey Tolman holds his fiddle and bow high in his signature Cape Breton style.

and complex figures, while Dudley insisted that less talking and more dancing meant more fun. More and more local dances sprang up—in the Pioneer Valley, on New Hampshire's seacoast, in central Vermont, in the Boston suburbs—further diluting Dudley's following, but spreading his passion, and the movement broadened, deepened, built a foundation. Many dancers who had been obsessed with the intensity of the scene realized they simply liked dancing—maybe not three or four times a week, but perhaps a couple of times a month—and in the Monadnock region a fad quietly evolved into a way of life. As Dudley gradually turned his teaching to schools and summer camps and small family junkets, Newt Tolman passed the music on to his nephew Harvey in Nelson. Rodney and Randy Miller, extraordinary fiddlers, moved in. Jack Perron, Mary DesRosiers, and Steve Zakon took over calling, and soon were running the big dances. McQuillen played with them all, and plays still.

He's here in Nelson tonight, playing piano on a raw March Monday in 2004. The old town hall has been renovated recently, but the workers have taken care to preserve the funky slope of the hardwood floor. McQuillen, who has written hundreds of dance tunes, wrote a dance in the sloping floor's honor called "Getting Out of the Hole in Nelson," which is exactly what he's helping people do on this grim night. Outside, the rain has changed over to wet snow, the slush freezing along the roadsides, the region's climate as contrary as ever. The Monday night dances in Nelson, by now, have been going on for years—barely advertised, the bands consisting of whatever musicians happen to show up. The regulars include fifty-somethings who have been dancing here for thirty years, the back-to-the-landers who stayed, still in the granola chic of flowing skirts and Birkenstocks, beards and braids and ponytails now gone gray. A few high school students have driven over from Keene, curious, new to the dances. And a couple of older folks, too: a grizzled man in a flannel shirt and suspenders, a white-haired woman in a cardigan sweater, knee-length skirt, and high socks. By 8:30 there are enough to fill a second line. By 9:00 p.m. the windows are dripping with moisture, and a few dancers walk over and throw them open wide.

Don Primrose, a caller from Sullivan, sets up for "Lady Walpole's Reel," one of the old ones. The Nelson dance has a reputation for being hard-core, for attracting dancers who know the steps without prompting. Primrose walks them through the figures once, says, "Now ladies chain, forward and back," perhaps only dimly aware of the part of the chain that all of them now occupy. Harvey Tolman holds his fiddle and bow high in that signature Cape Breton style of his, and hits the beat with McQuillen's first note. On another night it might be Mary DesRosiers's boy, Conor, on piano, an electric-guitar-playing, dreadlocked teenager whom McQuillen has taken on as an apprentice with a grant from the National Endowment for the Arts. "He sounds exactly like Johnny Tromblay," says McQuillen. Halfway through, Primrose puts down the mike and steps off the low stage, grabs a partner, and joins in the dance. The musicians play away, their pounding, lilting notes rising out through the opened windows into the darkness, and it's Peterborough in 1955, Acworth in 1973. The dancers do their thing, balance and swing, slap the wall in ritual where the downhill slope of the floor has bunched them up again. No need for prompting now.

Eminent Domain: Evicted to Create Pisgah Park

ELIZABETH GETCHELL

The spring day Forrest Doolittle opened the letter from the state he began to lose his will to live. This is what his son, Fred, told me. He showed me the original letter, in perfect condition, dated May 17, 1968, mailed to his father from a Mr. Russell B. Tobey, Director, Division of Parks in the State of New Hampshire, Department of Resources and Economic Development, Division of Resources Development. The kind of big, important title you are given when you have to tell a family they must allow government crews on their land, implying they must soon sell their home to the state, and that the state has the right to take it—the right of eminent domain. The letter clearly informed Forrest that "under the laws of 1967, Chapter 394:18, the Division of Parks [was] investigating areas of development of a new state park in the southwestern part of the state."

"Eminent domain," a phrase that exudes power just by the sound of it. The first documented use of the term was in 1738. It expressed the idea of the sovereign power having the right to control private property for public use. Haven't land and property always been taken by those with more power?

As outlined and explained at a public hearing held in Concord on December 22, 1967, the "Pisgah Wilderness" area in Hinsdale, Chesterfield and Winchester has been selected as the site of this new park. . . . Areas under consideration require on-the-ground investigation . . . necessitating the cutting of survey lines through wooded areas. . . . As an owner of property located within the area of interest for this particular park, your understanding and cooperation are being enlisted to

Flora, Edwin, and Forrest pose in front of the family farm. After leasing the farm for 64 years, the Doolittles finally managed to buy their home in 1948. In the 1970s the state demolished this farm, and others, to make way for the new park.

assist the State in this effort. . . . Unless we hear from you to the contrary within one week of the date of this letter, we will assume that you have no objections and will proceed with the work.

One week. One week does not give a man much time to think on the matter.

The Doolittle farm lies on the Old Chesterfield Road just north of what is now Pisgah State Park's visitors' center in Winchester. Benjamin Doolittle was the original owner from around 1805 until the mid-1850s. Then the Reverend Elias Marble purchased the two-story house. He "farmed six days a week and preached the seventh." In 1856 the property was sold to Erastus Dickinson, who, with his brother Ansel and later his sons, bought and owned most of the land that would become Pisgah State Park. The Dickinsons started much of the logging in the area and owned a number of mills in Winchester and Ashuelot. In 1884, Erastus first leased the farm to Abigail and Edwin C. Doolittle, Forrest's parents. It was Ansel's son LaFell who thought of the idea to establish the park. The logging in Pisgah had stopped, most of the Winchester and Ashuelot mills were no longer viable, and much of the land was no longer inhabited.

Forrest was born on the farm and had lived there all his life. In 1948, after his second-oldest son, Fred, graduated from high school, when both father and son were working in the paper mill in Ashuelot, Forrest earned enough money to buy the farm from the Dickinsons. After sixty-four years of Doolittles paying Dickinsons a regular lease fee, the farm became their own.

Nowadays few people would argue that New Hampshire's purchase of the land in the park was a bad decision. In the far southwest corner of the state, 13,421 acres of land are protected forever. Pisgah is the largest state park in New Hampshire. Its mountains, woods, reservoir, ponds, roads, and trails make Pisgah an undeniable boon to the Monadnock region. In our age of wide support for wise management of forests and parks, we can only thank the state planners who had the vision to protect this wild and diverse landscape.

To the naïve eye the landscape of Pisgah State Park now shows little evidence of human influence and industry. Nature is in charge of nearly all of Pisgah's acres. Fields evolve to forests. Forests mature and change in composition. Insect and animal populations may surge and shrink. Beavers build dams, flood land, change the course of water, then move on to different streams. Natural processes sort themselves out. Two park rangers at Pisgah manage the people who use the land, but they go home at night.

But to the trained eye, there is much evidence of a history rich with human occupation. Pisgah was far from empty in 1972, when the state bought ninety parcels of land. (Most of the land was owned by three lumber companies.) Park visitors now can read signs planted next to cellar holes to learn about some of the former residents—about the farmers, loggers, and preachers, and about the houses, cider and logging mills, sugarhouses, and one-room schools whose foundations they might stumble over in what is now forest. But no one will ever again make a home on this land. No one is even allowed to spend the night. Camping is forbidden.

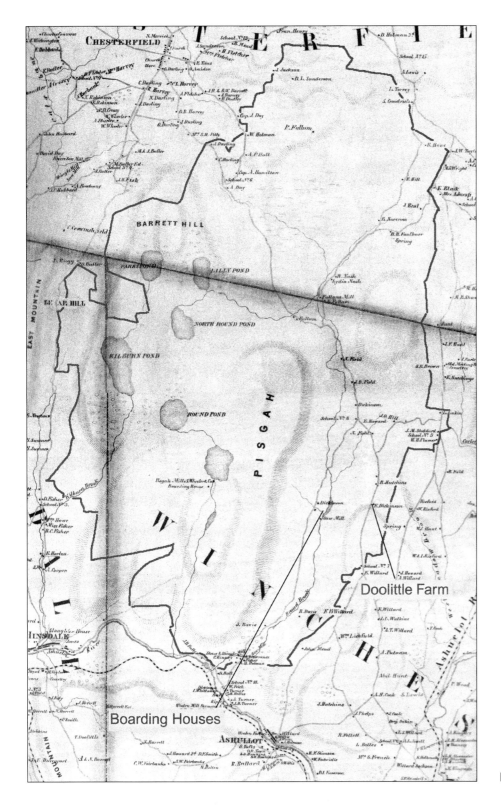

Pisgah State Park outlined on an 1858 map.

When Fred Doolittle was young, his family tended seven hundred apple trees on their farm and sold apples and cider locally. They had a cider mill across the road, and a sugarhouse on property they owned up the Old Chesterfield Road. Everyone—seven sisters and brothers, wife alongside husband—pitched in with the work on the place. The family harvested a hundred or more bushels of potatoes a year. They milked ten or twelve cows and raised a few pigs, had horses and oxen. Most of the time Forrest had additional work at the Dickinson logging mill in Broad Brook Village, down what's now called the "Doolittle Trail" from their farm. Later he was employed at the box company in Winchester or the paper mill in Ashuelot.

Fred knew well the vast forested landscape of Pisgah. He was a quiet, adventurous boy. "'Course, naturally, being brought up in the woods I always liked huntin' and fishin' all the time. I'd go deer huntin', and walk all the way from the house up into the Pisgee Range. I never shot any deer up there; I just liked to walk the woods. I liked the woods. I'd die if I shot a deer up there. I could never bring it home; it's so far. 'Course I wasn't very big either. Only weighed a hundred pounds or so," he laughs.

"Dad used to take us down to Broad Brook and all through the whole area explaining everything. He's the one who taught me about Broad Brook Village, the different things down there, the houses, and who owned 'em. And Fullam Pond and all the ponds around there. He used to walk around the woods showin' me different things. 'Course most of the time to get to most of these places we'd have to take a horse and wagon.

"We used to take some of our cattle up on land we rented or leased or somethin' on the Old Spofford Road. We used to drive them all the way from home, all the way up through the back roads and pasture 'em up there for the summer. And there used to be a tremendous blueberry field up there, and we'd check on them at least once a week, on the weekend usually. Sundays my father never used to do any work around the farm. It was a day of rest. We didn't have no car or anything. We'd pack a picnic lunch and load all of us kids into the wagon, and away we'd go," he laughs again, remembering the scene. "We used to pick great big water pails full of blueberries. Mother used to take and can 'em all. 'Course we had no freezer or anything. And all the meats, we had to can everything. We'd butcher our two big pigs. She'd have to stay up day and night almost to cure the meat. She salt-cured it and put it in these great big crocks down the cellar with all the potatoes. There was a full-size cellar that went the whole length and the whole width of the house."

"His mother was a great, great cook. Oh, was she a good cook!" adds Fred's wife, Janet.

As we talk, Fred nervously shuffles the photographs he has brought out to show me, pictures of his family, of the Dickinson logging operation in Pisgah, and one print of a field with trees in the background, the kind taken with a disposable panoramic camera. This long rectangular picture is not very clear, and I can't see much of interest in it. But the way he keeps holding it and looking at it shows how important it is to Fred. He took the shot in 1999 after the park cleared some of the old Doolittle farmland to enhance the growth of browse for wildlife. As a result, the area including the few apple trees left had been opened up some, allowing more light. Once again the place looked more like a farm than forest land, and more like his home than it had in many years. He doesn't say so, but I get the feeling it means a lot to Fred that he can again see this land for what it had been—the ground that grew the simple food that carried his large family through the winters.

Fred and Janet Doolittle were forced to sell to the state, and surrender their dream of returning to the family farm.

Forrest Doolittle had no intention of leaving his farm there at the end, after the letter of May 1968 that told him the state would soon own it. Forrest's wife, Elsie, had been dead from cancer for nine months. The state took awhile in its on-the-ground investigations, surveying, planning, negotiating, buying, hiring—whatever it takes to establish a new park. But Forrest wasn't taking good care of himself; he knew what was coming and he intended to hold his ground, no matter if his body gave out first.

"'Course we was goin' up there every single day cuz he wouldn't come live with any of us kids," says Fred.

"I'd go up there to make him his supper," adds Janet.

"We'd take care of him and do some of the chores around there. 'Course at the last he didn't have no cattle. Just had the dog, Rusty, up there with him. But he said he was gonna die there and he did, basically."

I ask them what ailment took him.

"I think he was just plain brokenhearted. That's what I think, don't you, Fred? Just plain brokenhearted."

At the very end he was coaxed to the hospital, but he refused medication. Forrest Doolittle was buried on December 19, 1968, on his eightieth birthday, his will to live long since faded, agree his son and daughter-in-law.

All this came soon after Fred and Janet decided to move out of a trailer they'd been living in. One day Janet heard chain saws on their property. She called Fred at the mill and he rushed home and stormed over to the sawyers. The electric company had decided to string power lines directly over their trailer. They had no say in the matter. So they moved to the house on Elm Street in Winchester where they still live. Fred and Janet had hoped to buy the Doolittle farm from his father. Fred's sister Shirley was also interested in it. Before the state took it over, Fred tried to buy even 25 or 30 acres of his family's 148-acre farm.

"I had quite a few arguments with the first park manager up there. What was his name? . . . Cecil Parker. I didn't have no interest up there to do anything at all [with the new park], see, the way I thought I was being treated. I never got along too good with him. Automatically I was shot down cuz, 'course, I wanted to buy it. 'Course, I realized I couldn't. But I thought there was some way I could finagle it around. 'You can buy it, but we're going to take it by eminent domain if we have to,'" Fred says, mimicking the state employee whose words had burned him.

The problem with the Doolittle farm was that it lay in the Broad Brook watershed. The state had decided to subsume the entire watershed inside Pisgah State Park bounds. As his father's executor, Fred had to sell, and he and Janet had to surrender their dream of returning to the family farm. "That's the way the water runs down off the hills. We got wiped out."

Fred says that after his father died, after the auction of everything the family didn't want, he kept a night-light on in the house to discourage vandals. That light in the window reached out to all that was known and loved by the Doolittle family—house, barn and outbuildings, kitchen garden, orchard, cider mill, potato fields, sugarhouse down the road, and maple woods. Keep safe. You will not be forgotten.

The state bulldozed and then burned all their buildings. What's left is the farmhouse foundation, which was mostly filled in, for safety. Fred and Janet stayed away from the park for two to three years. But time can heal and land draws you back. They live only about four miles down Old Chesterfield Road from the park. Both retired now, they chat with park staff when they see them and keep their family's farmhouse cellar hole clear of trees and shrubs.

"A lot of times when we get bored at home we go up there, walk around, trim brush, pick up trash. It's nice and peaceful and quiet up there. You hear the birds," says Janet.

"Yeah, we feed the mosquitoes and blackflies," chuckles Fred. "I still like it up there."

Can the trump card of eminent domain ever be excused by those who lose their home? When a home is taken away and destroyed by a more powerful authority for a public purpose—so that everyone can enjoy a beautiful, wild landscape—can the common good ever make good to those who paid the most to clinch the deal? It seems that Fred and Janet have forgiven the state. As long as they can, they will continue to maintain the Doolittle cellar hole and pick up the cans and bottles tossed from car windows or stashed by people partying on the land his family once farmed. They care for their family place as they care for the aging members of their families who need them, with regular, loving attention. They also pick and enjoy apples from what's left of the orchard—a few trees, all old and tall and misshapen, most hidden in among other trees now.

"This year there was no apples to speak of. 'Course we had that freeze. There was a few apples, but not like there was other years. The Northern Spy apples are very good for pies," says Fred with a smile that tells me he's enjoyed many such pies in his life.

"But not this year."

The afternoon after I met with Fred and Janet at their home, I walked around the old Doolittle farm. I saw the cellar hole, stone walls, a few apple trees. I tried to imagine the land as the productive farm it had once been. On my way down the Doolittle Trail to Broad Book—the trail Forrest used to walk to his work at the Dickinson logging mill—I spotted a park sign explaining that the park had cleared land to restore some once-common "old fields" that are essential for many wild animals.

The return of a clearing on the old Doolittle property is an invitation to the birds, deer, and moose who now find more to eat there. Fred said moose never used to be found in Pisgah, but he has seen droppings by the apple trees, and their big tracks crossing the road by the farm. Sure signs they are there now. I hope he gets to see one soon.

Pisgah, a Place Apart

Jonathan Schach

*And there stood the trees such as one does not expect to see this side of the Rockies.
Pine trees with stems twelve feet around at the butt, rising 100 feet clear without
branches, their tops so far away that there was a strange, distant sound to the wind
that blew through them. Trees so huge that the ridges in the bark were as deep as
the fingers of your hand. A forest without underbrush, save for the long, graceful branches of moosewood that grew now and then between the great trunks.*
—New York Times Magazine, 1926

Pisgah has always been a place apart in the Monadnock region. As the rest of the
region was cleared and settled, what is now Pisgah State Park remained a rugged and inaccessible wilderness. As late as 1926 it was estimated that the "Pisgee
tract," as it was called, contained 600 to 700 acres of old-growth forest. Although
small, relative to the 700,000 acres of old growth in New Hampshire's North
Country around the same period, this tract was quite remarkable. Most of the
old growth in Winchester and the surrounding towns had been cut soon after
European settlement.

Researchers from Harvard's forestry school have studied Pisgah old growth
extensively since 1907. In the 1920s the college purchased 20 acres of prime old-
growth forest to serve as a long-term study site preserved from logging. Most of
the Harvard Lot, as it was called, was leveled in the hurricane of 1938.

Despite its large reserves of timber, Pisgah was considered to be of little value
for many years because it could not support agriculture. Titles to land often

Oxen hauling logs on a scoot in "Pisgah City."

lapsed because owners were unable or unwilling to pay property taxes. Erastus Dickinson and his younger brother Ansel bought these lots piecemeal at bargain prices. In time they acquired over 5,000 acres within Pisgah. Ansel Dickinson formed the Dickinson Real Estate and Lumbering Company, and logged extensively in Pisgah between 1850 and 1870.

About this time, a prodigious supply of white pine was maturing on thousands of acres of abandoned pastures across central New England, fueling a boxboard boom that would climax in 1907. Ecologically speaking, central New England is a W-shape region centered on the Connecticut River Valley from Woodsville, New Hampshire, to Deerfield, Massachusetts. The ends of the W extend from Vermont's Champlain Valley to northwestern Connecticut and from Rockland, Maine, south to Worcester, Massachusetts. The forest of this region is a transitional type, a mix of the boreal coniferous forest to the north and the temperate deciduous forest to the south. As early as 1885, eight mills and four box shops in the Winchester area were using an annual harvest of six million board feet of timber.

In 1889, Ansel Dickinson's four sons, who had taken over the business and extensive landholdings upon their father's death, merged their company with two others to form the New England Box Company based in Greenfield, Massachusetts. Before long, New England Box was the leading wooden box manufacturer in the United States. The family retained their private landholdings, including Pisgah, under the Dickinson and Sons Real Estate and Lumber Company. The Dickinsons viewed Pisgah as a timber reserve to be used sparingly when other sources of wood were not available or too costly. Still, logging reduced Pisgah's old growth considerably.

Logging at that time was conducted in the winter when the logs could be transported over the snow. Russell Herman recalled driving a team of horses over the ice in Pisgah. Herman was a teamster for the paper mill. He was born in Nova Scotia in 1895 and moved to the United States when he was twenty-eight. A year later he settled in the town of Ashuelot and got a job working for the Dickinsons as a woodchopper and a driver.

New England Box Company in Ashuelot (below left).

Old-growth white pine and hemlock forest in Pisgah before the 1938 hurricane.

Loggers in Pisgah.

"Well, people has got an idea that a horse has got to be awful scared of ya to draw. They got the wrong idea there," Herman recalled. "Ed [Squire], he drove a team, yes, up there for a number of years. He had this team—he always wanted to get a new team all the time. This was just a green team. And he was going up across the reservoir that morning. So the horses stopped. Well, Squire had his horses and sang out 'Jump!' And they'd make a lunge and go ahead. Well, what made them stop was, the ice was thin. They knowed it. And when they lunged he just made a jump and that was it. Both went in. He lost both of them, down went both of them. Well, they cut the ice and dragged them over across and drawed them up out of the pond and in the spring, when they laid there all winter, Ed and I went up and buried them. And that's what they figure, that the horse, he's got to be scared of ya in order to draw, but no, no . . . no, no, I'd seen that done and I told him, I said, 'You're crazy when you think that.'"

Although a number of cellar holes provide evidence of families who attempted living off the land in Pisgah, most residents earned their keep working for the Dickinsons and a couple of other local businesses, cutting, hauling, and sawing trees for lumber, tanning bark, and fuel wood. The workers, often with their families, lived in camps near small steam- and later electric-powered sawmills. Some of these temporary settlements were known by grandiose names like Pisgah City and Nash City. The logging camps of Pisgah had the roughness and the transience of other boomtowns, Herman recalled: "I lived in one tent the first winter we was up there. Fred Turndrick lived in the big tent. His whole family was up there. And Squire and his wife lived in a tent. Theirs was twelve feet by twenty-four feet, and I think that Turndrick's was bigger than that one. Some of the other teamsters, they boarded in the boardinghouse."

One scandalous story people still tell is the murder that happened up at the boardinghouse. "Bella Collins and Bill Murphy ran the boardinghouse," Herman said. "They seemed like they weren't getting along too good for the last few years. An old fella from Winchester there got running around with [Bella] and old Murphy didn't like that. This old fella had a car, and they was out one Sunday.

Sawdust pile generated by the mill in Broad Brook Village. Note the two people standing on the pile.

They drove back and she was huggin' him up in the car and she says to Bill, she says, 'How do you like that Bill? How's it look Bill?' So, Bill didn't like that. They went to bed and there was fighting back and forth. They kept going through it and [Bella] got up to go out to call up old Casey Jones, that's the fella she was hanging around with. We called him Casey Jones. By God, when she come out her bedroom door, he shot her with a shotgun. She died not too long after he shot her. Old Bill tried to cut his throat, but he had a razor with some awful nicks in it and he didn't do a very good job. His neck was bleeding, and he was laying in the sawdust pile and he had sawdust in it and oh my, so Bolton took him to Keene up to the hospital and he didn't live too long up there. He died."

Pisgah is a quiet place today. With the logging camps gone, the essential place can be seen. As far back as 1903, a *Keene Sentinel* article served to remind readers of the wilderness in their midst: "Cheshire County possesses within her borders a specimen of nature's handiwork which is extremely rare and which, if once destroyed, can never be duplicated. That more has never been heard, and written about this tract seems strange. One would suppose that every person in this country who is interested in the study of nature would be familiar with so rare an acquisition, and that the children in the schools would have been told the story of the trees that looked down on the first explorers who came up the Connecticut and Ashuelot valley."

Since the 1970s, when Pisgah became New Hampshire's largest state park, with more than 13,000 acres, the people have held that reserve in common as well as the responsibility of stewardship. But the preservation of its wild character and its healing silence are not necessarily held in perpetuity. As all-terrain vehicle users push for greater access and cutbacks in state-park funding necessitate a return of logging in Pisgah, silence and natural heritage are in jeopardy. If there is a place in the Monadnock region where old forests can be left to the weathering fates and regenerating forces of nature, a place where visitors and pilgrims seeking inspiration can listen beneath cathedrals of tall pines and hemlocks for the "strange, distant sound to the wind that blew through them," let it be Pisgah, a place apart.

The Return of the Wild

SY MONTGOMERY

Selinda Chiquoine was cleaning house in Hancock one autumn Saturday morning when, over the roar of the vacuum, she heard a frantic knocking. She opened the door to find a tall, breathless stranger at her threshold.

"There's a m-m-m!" he stammered. "A m-m-m-m-m!—

A middle-aged guy she'd never seen before was trying to tell her something he obviously considered of great importance.

"It's a m-m-m-m! . . . A m-m-m-m-m!"

"What on earth is this guy so excited about?" Chiquoine wondered. Finally, he made himself understood: he held his thumbs to his temples, palms out, fingers spread. Chiquoine glanced at the pasture across the way to see a moose in full Bullwinkle rack amble off toward the trees. At the other end of the pasture, two resident horses were pacing nervously in a circle—as excited by the moose as were the people.

No wonder: with its massive head, rubbery, sensitive muzzle, and stunning size (it can weigh 1,800 pounds and tower seven feet at the shoulder, while its antlers can weigh 70 pounds) a moose is a staggering sight. *The History of the Town of*

A young beaver glides through a West Peterborough marsh. Trapped nearly to oblivion, one last colony of beaver remained in the state in 1901. Their revival began in the 1950s.

Gilsum, N.H. from 1752 to 1879 records a hunter who had a similar reaction three hundred years ago: "He was so excited he forgot to shoot, but cried out, 'I see the moose! I see the moose!' who of course speedily got out of the way."

It was the moose's unlikely majesty, more than its rarity, that struck the hunter. "Many pioneers would have starved but for its abundance," Helenet Silvers says in *A History of New Hampshire Game and Furbearers*. Up north, moose were so plentiful that, in Warren, a 1754 report had it that a certain Joseph Patch often had as many as twenty-five barrels of preserved moose meat in his cellar; near Lancaster, the town history records that a Nathan Caswell killed ninety-nine moose one winter.

"Although they were less abundant than in the north," Silvers writes, "there is evidence from the frequent records for the southern New Hampshire towns that moose were not uncommon in the south, until they had been killed off or driven out by settlement." Moose need dense woods for cover, twigs and leaves for browse, water lilies for summer sustenance; this they found throughout the state—before the forests were destroyed.

The clear-cuts not only ruined their habitat but also made easier work for the gun. Within sight of Monadnock, the last moose was killed in Peterborough in 1760. In nearby Antrim, the last moose was shot in 1790. The ungainly giants persisted farther north into the mid-1800s, but by the time legislation was passed to protect them, in 1875, the only moose left in the state were in Coos County, on the border with Canada. And even then, they were not really protected. In July and August of 1885, three moose were shot illegally by a visiting New Yorker—who then came back in September and killed two more. The Fish and Game commissioner who complained about the poacher was reprimanded by his boss for his action, "lest the visiting sport become displeased with the hospitality of New Hampshire and fail to return to spend his money here."

But after a century's absence, these North Country giants are making a comeback—along with many of the other impressive wild animals who disappeared as New Hampshire's forests fell: black bear, wild turkey, beaver, fisher, otter. Now, as the state recovers from a hundred years of clear-cutting, unsustainable farming, unregulated hunting, and a murderous bounty system, "You've got a greater chance of seeing any of these animals than your great-grandmother did," says Eric Orff, fur-bearing biologist with the New Hampshire Fish and Game Department. Today, he proclaims, "It's the golden age for wildlife in New Hampshire."

For the land surrounding Monadnock, the comeback is perhaps even more amazing than it is in the rest of the state. New Hampshire's south was settled early and farmed hard. Its animals—particularly wolves, bears, and mountain lions—were persecuted with ferocious zeal. Today, the region's perilous proximity to Boston (you can see the city from Mount Monadnock) renders the regenerating forest especially vulnerable to development. Still, the animals are returning—and here, they are welcomed back more warmly than in any other part of the state.

Now is an exciting time to be watching animals in the shadow of Monadnock, and a moment of rare opportunity: Today, thanks to a lucky confluence of history, geography, and demographics, we have a second chance to save what we nearly destroyed.

"WILD ANIMALS. These were numerous one hundred and twenty five years ago in portions of New Hampshire, and especially in the towns around the base of Mount Monadnock," reports *The History of Fitzwilliam, N. H. from 1752–1887.*

This was a situation that the white "settlers" felt should be remedied. Wild animals were bad. Though some were good to kill for food or fur, in general it was thought wild animals should be slain just to get rid of them. In the town histories they are often described as "monsters," their ways "greedy," their appetites "rapacious," and even their voices "hideous."

Early town histories abound with accounts of wild animals terrorizing people. A story reported in the Fitzwilliam history, collected by Dr. Silas Cummings, tells how Mrs. Withington was out picking blueberries when she saw a bear peacefully doing the same—"a sight that sent her home with such rapidity that she had no time or courage to look behind her." The *Historical Sketch of the Town of Troy . . . 1764–1897* reports another terrifying sight: a bear in someone's yard, who, the account goes on to mention, retreated at the moment a woman brandished a broom. A Fitzwilliam bear of the same era was scared off by a housewife shaking her checkered apron. Gilsum's town history tells us that children often ran into bears—and scared them away by shouting. One twelve-year-old boy brushed against a bear in the dark, and returned home without harm. A 1770s incident, related in the Troy town history, is particularly telling: One of the early settlers was returning from a neighbor's house with a sack of potatoes on his shoulder, when "he saw in the path just before him what he took to be an enormous bear, just in the attitude of making upon him a fatal spring. . . . He moved a step, then paused—took another step, paused again—the poor man clearly saw his doom in the monster's teeth and the fire of his eye. . . . But be not alarmed," the account tells us, "for the man escaped, his antagonist was only a *stump.*"

Though black bears were often seen, unless they had been injured by a gun or trap and were cornered they never attacked people. Wolves, too, left people alone, though they sometimes took sheep and calves. The catamount, or mountain lion, though a powerful predator and greatly feared, seldom ventured near human settlement and, even when persecuted with teams of hunters searching its native woods, was almost never sighted; nor were its smaller cousins, the bobcat and lynx.

Though the actual dangers posed by these "monsters" were often imaginary, settlers' retaliation was gruesome and thorough. The murder of Monadnock's last wolf, a crippled female with three legs, is celebrated in several town histories. Pursued by bloodhounds and men from Jaffrey, Winchester, Fitzwilliam, Rindge, and Winchendon, Massachusetts, she was wounded by gunfire, bludgeoned, and finally shot to death in a hunt in the winter of 1820. The catamount, never numerous, was believed extinct in the state by 1850. Even ravens, poisoned and shot because people believed they killed sheep (falsely) and lambs (seldom, and then only sickly ones), were gone from the state before the century's end.

A skulk of fox (pelts). Foxes, like wolves, bears, and mountain lions, were persecuted with ferocious zeal. "When I grew up, everyone had a gun behind the door," biologist Eric Orff remembers. "If you wanted it, you shot it."

Bears had disappeared from the region by then, too, although a bounty remained until 1957. Bobcats were nearly gone as well, though bounties persisted on them until 1972.

Many animals not killed out of fear were exterminated by greed. Once "sheep fever" hit in 1810, virtually all but the steepest mountains were converted to pasture. Hardly a scrap of land remained for wildlife cover; animals without wool were shot for food, trapped for fur, or exterminated as varmints. Wild turkeys were extinct in New England by 1850. Deer were scarce. New Hampshire's moose were gone from everywhere but the far north by 1875—by which time the southern region's fishers and otters had been trapped nearly to oblivion. One last colony of beaver remained in the state in 1901. New Hampshire's white settlers had found, here, a wildlife paradise, and left it an Armageddon: almost all the forest denuded, the animals shot, poisoned, and trapped, and even the rivers, harnessed for processing wool, dammed and polluted.

And then something wonderful happened: the collapse of New England's economy.

The bottom fell out of the wool market. The people moved away. The land and the waters began to recover. And the animals, slowly, began to venture back.

The beaver returned in the 1950s. As the industrious rodents expanded wetlands with their dams, their skillfully engineered waterways created habitat for many other animals: from moose to great blue heron, from mink to ducks. (Otters even give birth inside abandoned beaver lodges.) Fishers came back in the 1960s, after a thirty-one-year hiatus from trapping. Today the crazy quilt of their five-toed footprints in the snow are among the commonest tracks in the woods. In 1975, the state released twenty-seven wild turkeys from the Allegheny Mountains of western New York in Walpole, and since then, birds from their lineage have been transplanted all over the state. Sometimes you can see flocks of a hundred in a single cornfield, and Fish and Game estimates there are now twenty-five thousand in the state. There are now almost certainly more wild turkeys in New Hampshire than when the white settlers invaded the Indians' territories.

As for catamounts, there aren't supposed to be any. But people keep seeing them. There have been many sightings, but none, perhaps, more vivid than the catamount Leandre Poisson saw on his Harrisville property in an open field in full daylight. Low-slung and tawny, it walked gracefully across the pasture, remaining visible for such a long time that Poisson had time to go into the house and get the field glasses for a better look. There was no doubt about it: with the head of a maneless lion and a long, thick tail, the catamount looks like nothing else.

New Hampshire is now home even to animals who never lived here before. In the 1950s, folks began seeing critters they thought looked like coyotes—western animals who had never before been reported in New England. The spread of these supremely adaptable canines through the state has been astonishingly swift. They swept from Colebrook to Seabrook in eight years—a territory it took bears half a century to recolonize. Genetic studies show these wild dogs' mixed heritage: they are part western coyote—and part eastern timber wolf. In a sense, the wolves, too, have come home.

They've returned to a world vastly changed. The forests are back, covering nearly 80 percent of the state once again, making New Hampshire the second most tree-covered state in the nation. But the forests are different. For instance, gone are the majestic, spreading chestnuts, once one of the dominant species. They were wiped out by chestnut blight, contracted from Japanese chestnut trees imported by a Long Island nursery in the late 1800s.

The people are now back, now, too—but, importantly, *we* have changed. "When I grew up, everyone had a gun behind the door," biologist Eric Orff remembers. "If you wanted it, you shot it. People have grown away from that culture, and the worry about where the next meal is coming from." Now, so many people put out food for wildlife—from backyard bird feeders to deer pellets—that their efforts constitute a major new food resource for everyone from bears to wild turkeys, offsetting, perhaps, the demise of the chestnut.

Today, few of us are farmers. Only 5 percent of New Hampshire residents live on farms. Fewer than a hundred dairy farms are left in the state—seven times fewer than in neighboring Vermont—a situation Ted Walski, Turkey Project

Turkeys in winter. Extinct in New England by 1850, today's wild turkeys are descended from a small flock released in Walpole in 1975.

biologist for New Hampshire Fish and Game, laments; more open fields means more habitat for wild turkeys and other species like cottontails. We don't use the land to grow food or sheep or cows. We use the land to grow houses—where we find wild animals that our ancestors feared literally at our doorsteps.

Yet sometimes we don't even recognize them. In Peterborough, at the home of Steve and Elizabeth Marshall Thomas, one of the women Elizabeth had hired to help care for her aging mother reported seeing something alarming in the dark. Out the window, the helper reported, she saw a man in a fur coat, eating blueberries off the bushes with his lips. (It was, of course, a black bear.)

To some, it seems, "There's a moose on every highway, a bear in every dumpster, a deer in every garden, a beaver in every ditch," says Eric Orff. And when people consider this a problem, though they don't get out their .22 anymore, they call Fish and Game: "Come get *your* bear out of *my* yard."

Biologists agree there's room enough for more wild animals in New Hampshire—but their population is limited by what Fish and Game calls "cultural carrying capacity"—the number of wild animals their human neighbors will tolerate. That's the reason the state instituted, in 1988, the first season on moose in eighty-seven years.

In 1985, the state commissioned a survey of residents' opinions toward moose, bear, and deer, as of this writing the most recent such poll. Conducted by Mark Duda and Kira Young of Responsible Management of Harrisonburg, Virginia, the survey broke the state into five regions—North, White Mountains, Central, Southeast, and Southwest—and interviewed about one hundred residents in each. Consistently throughout all regions, the majority of respondents were happy with the numbers of these animals as they stood. But Monadnock-region residents were far more enthusiastic than others in the state in their support of *increasing* the populations of these returning animals, particularly bear and moose.

One-fifth of southwestern residents wanted to see more bear—twice as many as the state average, and more than twice the 6.1 percent of southeastern residents who said so. An even higher percentage wanted to see more moose near Monadnock: 26.9 percent of southwestern respondents wanted more moose, as opposed to 16 percent statewide. (Importantly, among *all* those who supported increasing populations of these animals, support remained strong even if the increase meant more car collisions with deer and moose, more damage to gardens or landscaping, more bears destroying bird feeders and trashing garbage bins.)

For deer, the picture was slightly different, and for a different reason: the North, with its thicker forests, which deer tend to shun, scored highest, wishing for a larger deer herd. About a third of northern respondents were hunters, the highest percentage in the survey, and they were hungry for venison. Southwestern respondents came in third in their enthusiasm for more deer—but only six of them were hunters. More typical was the same sentiment that prompted the wish for more moose and more bear: "I would like to see them out in the backyard."

Why do returning animals find a warmer welcome in the southwestern corner of the state? People in this region "may not have to deal with the destruction from bears of their beehives or cornfields, the moose collisions, the deer chewing up their whole garden," says biologist Ted Walski. Because of highlands and poor soils, the few farmers who returned to New Hampshire avoided the southwest. (Instead, there are estates: "I've seen what the deer do to the estates in Dublin," Walski says—"but they can have the gardener replace those expensive shrubs.") Collisions with wildlife are less feared around Monandock, because there are fewer highways on which to collide. And because there are fewer highways, there are fewer people.

These facts arise from a revealing history. "Land protection goes way back in this area," says artist and conservationist Rosemary Conroy, "and Monadnock is at the heart of it." She's a former spokesperson for the Society for the Protection of New Hampshire Forests (SPNHF), and a board member at the Harris Center for Conservation Education in Hancock, which has protected 8,700 acres in Hancock, Peterborough, Harrisville, Antrim, Stoddard, Nelson, and Keene since 1982. For land conservation, "Monadnock," Conroy says, "is almost like a power source."

At a crucial point in history—shortly after the turn of the nineteenth century—Monadnock's scenic beauty attracted writers, artists, and vacationers. The works of the artists in colonies in Walpole, Dublin, and Peterbough "were glorifying the land, the beauty of the land," explains Brian Hotz, land protection specialist for SPNHF. "Writers' words inspired people to recognize this landscape was unique. Paintings inspired people. Vacationers went home to Boston and New York, and started to talk about it and do land protection." In 1904, when a sawmill on Monandock's south slope planned to cut five hundred acres of timber, Dublin and Jaffrey residents rallied to save the forest, and when the threat of more logging spread, the painter Abbott Thayer put a halt to it.

To this day, even though the organization is headquartered in Concord, SPNHF's highest membership rates come from Cheshire County, the heart of the Monadnock region. The conservation ethic has stayed strong: in the 1970s and 1980s, when the state proposed to reroute traffic from Route 101 in Dublin by creating a major bypass through Harrisville, a consortium of citizen conservation groups worked tirelessly for twelve years to defeat the plan—and deflect the explosion of unwanted development.

One of the main arguments that ultimately defeated the Dublin bypass was that it would disrupt the native wildlife that had begun to return to the area. During the heat of the battle, "we walked every single wildlife corridor on snowshoes," Harris Center director Meade Cadot remembers. "We recorded all the deeryards and fisher sign and otter sign, all the trout ponds." Wildlife, they found, was thriving. "There was one wetland, Brush Brook, where the Highway Department said there was no trout left there," Cadot recalls. "One day, Fred Murphy, a big burly Irishman and the so-called Highway environmentalist supporting the bypass, was with us. His snowshoe broke through the ice—and when he lifted it up, he kicked a trout out of the water!"

With the return of Mondanock's wild animals has come an unexpected blessing—a restoration of the human soul. "When there's nothing dangerous in the

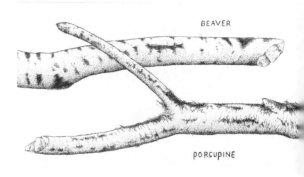

Gnaw marks left by beaver and porcupine. The animals are returning—and in the Monadnock region, they are welcomed back more warmly than in any other part of the state.

woods, we stop paying attention to what's around us," says Dr. Richard Estes. (Though he spends half the year studying wildebeest in Africa, he lives in Peterborough—where, one recent afternoon, his wife, Runi, opened the back door to the garage to find a moose stepping gingerly between a parked bicycle and the car. It trotted out onto Granite Street and into the woods.) "Big wild animals make us more alert, alive, much more in tune with our surroundings," Estes continues. "Having them back brings us closer to what our ancestors had—but with an appreciation that our forebears did not."

As the animals restore us, they inspire us to further restore the land. "People are thrilled to see the larger animals coming back," says SPNHF's Brian Hotz. "That's what people want to protect land for." Cadot agrees: "There are a lot of reasons for conservation—water quality, air quality, recreation, et cetera. But what really turns people on is wildlife." The animals have proved powerful ambassadors for conservation.

Today, the Monadnock region's wildlife faces the same pressures as those chewing away at the rest of the world. The population of the state is slated to grow 21 percent by 2020, with four million more acres projected for development by 2050. "Places nobody ever thought they would build on, they're building on now," says Cadot. "We've got to keep the land protection going."

Now, with computer programs, aerial surveys, and detailed species inventories, "we have the technology to protect the habitat that should be protected for the next two hundred years," says biologist Orff. "The only thing we need is the will."

Part Five

HERE AND NOW IN THE GLOBAL MARKET

Big-box shopping comes to Rindge.

Introduction

Every culture has its ritual theater, stories that are told over and over in a pre-scribed fashion. The *Wall Street Journal* tapped into one of those set stories when it looked in on how the Japanese were getting along in "Our Town," Peterborough, New Hampshire. Minebea Company of Tokyo had bought New Hampshire Ball Bearings in 1985, a hometown company founded in 1946 and looked after by a generous man, Arthur "Bud" Daniels.

Everyone performed to the script for the *Journal*'s reporters: the Japanese were efficient and deaf to local concerns; the locals were insular country mice, hicks in the sticks, as the 1990 story played it. "This is the town you may know as Our Town, the model of the New England village romanticized in Thornton Wilder's famous play. But, the way some local folk see it, Peterborough may be turning into Their Town." This is one of the oldest stories: us and them. A stranger comes to town. Here come the Japanese, cast as Godzilla.

"The company used to be a family where you felt good about working hard and where they cared for you," said one laid-off worker. "Now they want us to work like animals." The four Japanese managers had removed all stools and desks from the factory floor; production timers rooted out slow workers. "We're not teach-ing them new ways, we're teaching the basics," said the plant's efficiency expert. Twenty years ago American manufacturing led the world, but no more, he said. This company was "like a frog in a small pond. They couldn't see the wider ocean." None of the four young managers lived in Peterborough. One drove through town, but only rarely got out. Another manager said that he was "sometimes harassed by residents," but was working on his English and hoped to "improve his contacts with Americans."

Over on Grove and Main streets, the Americans felt invaded. At the Peter-borough Shoe Store, the store's owner, "in a lather over the Japanese," was "angrily recounting where he was when Japan bombed Pearl Harbor." He was interrupted by the manager of Roy's Market, who poked his head in to ask: "If we have 30 Knights and 20 Masons, how many lobsters do we need?" The two huddled, "coming to terms with the great issues of the upcoming Second Annual Masonic-Knight Cookout." Next door at Nonie's Bakery and Luncheon-ette, a laid-off supervisor said, "Well, the Japanese might just own this town. But, no, they'll never own our souls."

The town historian was succinct: "The biggest thing we've lost in Peter-borough is a sense of control," she said. This was echoed by a conversation between two veteran workers on the factory floor: "The world's gotten smaller, more competitive, and we've got to respond. That doesn't mean we've given

In sight of Monadnock. After years of fight-ing, a Connecticut developer plants big-box stores in a former Keene cornfield.

up. I'd say Our Town is still ours." The second worker replied: "But we don't know what 'ours' means anymore."

The American-born president of the ball bearing company had no patience for any of this talk. "Look, I don't really care about the townspeople—I have a business to run." And, no, he had not read *Our Town*, though his wife had given him a copy two years earlier. "If the Japanese had read *Our Town* they might not have come here," he said. People in town "want to know everything about everybody. They're busybodies."

All around, it was the kind of press coverage that both the company and the town wanted to forget. No one was ordering reprints of the article. The company immediately made some timely donations to the proper cultural interests and many photos were taken of men in suits handing off checks to other men in suits. Grip and grin. Another ritual. Welcome to globalization, Peterborough; now get in line.

Part five looks at the mix of small-town and global changes.

Taxi

ERNEST HEBERT

I was twenty-four when I entered Keene State College in 1964. With the help of the GI Bill and a variety of jobs I graduated debt-free five years later. These were the days when you could buy a house on Glen Road in Keene for under twenty thousand, and a house and five acres in Gilsum (or most other nearby towns) for four figures. I worked at Markem Machine Company, West Street Texaco, the laundry of the former Elliot Community Hospital on Main Street, and during a seven-month hiatus in New Orleans I was an attendant at DePaul psychiatric hospital. But the job I held the longest and the one that had the most effect on me was as a driver in Keene for Ideal Taxi.

Driving cab in a small northern town was not the same as driving in a big city, where the passengers were mainly local people of means or visitors from out of town. In Keene most of the passengers were people without access to cars—welfare mothers, old folks, drunks, guys busted for DUI, the mentally retarded, the handicapped, the crazy, and regular folks down on their luck.

When the bartender at the Coney Island Lunch on Church Street wanted to get rid of a drunk he'd call Gus our dispatcher, shout "Coney Island," and slam the phone down. You'd drive over to get the drunk. Sometimes he (it was always a he) would make it to the car on his own power; sometimes you had to stuff him physically into the back seat.

Most of my customers liked to talk, mainly about their troubles—bad health, bad luck, bad habits, bad companions, old age, and the age-old human problems of the heart and the pocketbook. My few customers of means rarely spoke. The contrast provided me with an insight into our class structure. The down-and-out reveal themselves. The more successful people are, the more guarded they are, and the less you can know them from the inside out.

Occasionally a homosexual, usually drunk, would proposition me. I used to fantasize that an attractive woman passenger would come on to me, but it never happened. Once a fellow I'd gone to St. Joseph's School with challenged me to a fistfight.

"Buzzy, I'm not mad at you," I said. "Why would I want to fight you?"

"I'm not mad at you either, Ernie, I just want to fight."

I brought Buzzy to his mother's house. He was twenty-six years old. Some years later I was a reporter for the *Keene Sentinel* when Buzzy was jailed, a member of the infamous Troy Boys gang that killed a family in a robbery in Tewksbury, Massachusetts, and a man in Athol.

Downtown Keene was small, and you saw the same people day after day on Main Street (the widest paved main street in the world, or so the story went). You got to know their faces, walks, wardrobes, and demeanors. Most were strangers to me and would remain so, but they were part of the downtown and I was always happy to see them. One was a forty-something woman, tall, stately, plain face, good body, and she dressed very well, dark brown hair always in place. What I liked about her was the way she held her head—high, aloof, the message: always alone, but proud. She never made eye contact, never smiled. I'd think: she's got nobody—me neither. I dubbed her the Sexy Spinster.

I made a lot of deliveries in my taxi, brought groceries to senior citizens, medicine to the sick, six-packs to gambling parties in the North End. One day Gus told me to bring beer and a bottle of Canadian Club to an apartment downtown, the customer not a regular. I walked up a couple of flights of stairs, wondering whether I'd get a tip, hard to come by in the late 1960s in Keene. I was met at the door by a big, confident-looking man wearing suit-trousers, no shoes, black socks, and an undershirt. He looked me over with an amused smirk. Sitting on the couch watching or pretending to watch TV was the Sexy Spinster. She seemed surprised I was at the door, and she immediately got up and went into another room. "It's okay, it's the cab," the big fellow called out. His voice was soothing but also full of command. The Sexy Spinster came back into view, standing in the doorway, looking off somewhere as if out the window at the Congregational Church at the head of the square. The big fellow reached into her handbag on the coffee table. She winced. He took out some money, paid me, and added a dollar tip.

Another customer that sticks in my mind was a man I called Sartre because he bore a faint resemblance to the existential philosopher Jean-Paul Sartre. He lived in the Ellis Hotel, which was on the west side of Main Street south of the Colonial Theater, and which by the 1960s was on the skids. Periodically, I'd bring Sartre a bottle of good whiskey (can't remember the brand) and a carton of Camel cigarettes, which was what I smoked in those days.

Sartre talked in a raspy whisper. He obviously suffered from a respiratory dis-

Taxi wrangler at work: Joan Copely, owner of Ideal Taxi. Joannie was kind of a mother figure to her customers.

ease, probably emphysema. I never saw him outside his room. He was a small, finely made man who always wore a rumpled white shirt and shined shoes. His room was messy, but comfortable, with books everywhere, appealing to a college student just starting to find his way in the world. I also saw papers and manila folders. I imagined that Sartre was writing a great philosophical tract. On the walls were paintings and artsy photographs that reminded me of Cartier-Bresson, one of my heroes. However, I saw no family pictures or evidence that Sartre had loved ones. At night, outside on Main Street, I would see the glow from his room on the third floor. The light was never off. Sartre was a man waiting to die alone. By any objective standards Sartre's situation was appalling and sad, but I found it romantic. I imagined that Sartre had something to tell me about the world.

My neighborhood was right up Church Street from the Coney Island Lunch. I lived in a run-down apartment house with four other students—Jeff Parsons, Jack Brouse, Dwight Conant, and Larry Howard. We were a compatible bunch, and remain friends to this day. The Keene State campus was an exciting and vital place. We students argued the merits of our involvement in Vietnam; we protested policies of the college administration; we believed we could make America a better place. My creative writing class with Professor Malcom Keddy produced at least three writers who would go on to write books—Marilyn Treat, who published a chapbook of poems, Joseph Citro, author of many books of the macabre, and me.

I liked the campus environment. The world I saw in my taxi was starkly different from campus life. Once a little kid swore at me, and his mother smacked him in the face and said, "That kid has the worst fucking mouth on him." An elderly woman I took to church every Sunday warned me: "Young man, don't get old." She never called again, and I never knew what happened to her. I was watching Sartre prepare for the white light, and the Sexy Spinster falling apart. No doubt the fellow she'd taken up was abusive, but he had a hypnotic hold on her. At first when I brought booze to the apartment she would stand aside, embarrassed. I wondered why she would be there to begin with, since she could have ducked out of the room when I knocked. Once I saw her in her slip slumped over on the couch, inert from too much drinking. All the time her lover would stand aside, letting me get an eyeful. I finally figured out that he wanted me to see her; she was in plain sight at his insistence. Humiliating her was part of the kick for him. I wanted to help the Sexy Spinster, but I had no clue how to proceed. So I did nothing, said nothing, tried to pretend I didn't care.

One day Jeff Parsons and I decided to paint our apartment. We called the landlord, who said he would provide the brushes and paint if we came by to pick them up. The landlord was George Miller, a name out of my childhood, but until he answered our knock on the door of his middle-class home and I laid eyes on him I never put together the man I knew with my landlord. George Miller had been the manager of the Latchis Theater when I was a kid.

In the days when I grew up male authority figures were referred to as mister,

257

as in Mister Miller, the theater manager. But in fact us kids did not call George Miller mister; we called him George. George Miller was the only black person I saw regularly. Racism among white working-class youngsters in Keene in the 1950s was subtle, often unconscious (as in George instead of Mister Miller), and sometimes kind of funny. I heard more than one adult insist that Negroes (accepted terminology) could not be found in Keene because "they can't stand the cold."

These were the days when two players dominated the news in major league baseball, Mickey Mantle and Willie Mays. I rooted for Mays without ever really noticing his skin color. One day one my friends informed me that Willie was a "niggah." I switched my loyalties to Mantle without ever really knowing what a "niggah" was, since there were no discussions about race, just sideways street talk. It was the tone in his voice that I was responding to.

It wasn't until I was in my teens that I began to be conscious of racial issues. In the middle of a class discussion about the civil rights movement, a teacher opined that the Negro race was "different" from the Caucasian race. (In the 1950s in Keene to refer to people as "different" was to brand them with the mark of Cain.) When a student questioned his theory, the teacher said, "You ever smell one?" Suddenly, I began to understand what racism was all about, how it worked. The teacher's offhand remark made a liberal out of me.

Though I was naive about race during my youth, I was aware that skin color was social currency. Light skin was good, dark skin was suspect. One of my brothers stayed out of the sun in the summer because he was afraid it would darken his skin. I even had a little personal brush with segregation in the South. When I was in the army at Fort Bragg in North Carolina in 1962, I and some other white guys would go to Myrtle Beach. I tanned up real dark. One afternoon halfway back to base we stopped at a joint for a beer. The bartender eyed me suspiciously. I thought he was going to ask me for my ID (I was barely twenty-one). Instead, he said, "Boy, unless you show me your ass is white, I'm not going to serve you." I was in uniform when I was challenged.

I received a more hands-on education in racial matters in New Orleans, where I lived for seven months. I worked the eleven to seven shift in the mental hospital with a woman partner. Her name was Joan Cotton. With a lot of time on our hands, we often talked for hours. She and another black attendant, a moonlighting schoolteacher named Alphonse Pierre, were my tutors in race relations.

By the time I started college and began to rent from George Miller, he was an old man and quite frail. Miller had come to Keene as a youth to work in the former Cheshire House hotel and restaurant on Main Street. He stayed in town after the hotel closed, invested in real estate, and by all appearances became quite well off. For us college students it seemed only just and kind of cool that a black man should become a slumlord in a small northern town.

Often at night driving in downtown Keene, I'd look up at Sartre's room. Seeing the light on was always a comfort to me. I made a few inquiries to learn about

Sartre and hit a dead end, though I didn't try very hard. He'd become a figure in the world of my imagination, and I didn't really want to know the real person. I didn't realize it at the time but I was preparing for a life as a fiction writer. What I wanted from Sartre was wisdom, secrets, arcane knowledge. I had it in my head that a cultivated man, obviously sick and alone, would have some clues about life and meaning. I would bring him his whiskey and cigarettes and linger some. I'd make comments on his books, or about some current event, trying to get a conversation going. At first Sartre became annoyed. He probably thought I was hanging around in hopes of a bigger tip. And then I think it dawned on him that this young taxi driver was looking for mentors. One day he asked me if I was a college student. After that he would let me stay a few minutes before hustling me out with the simple words, "Excuse me, young man, but I'm tired."

Over the course of time I told him about myself, my background, growing up in Keene, speaking only French until I started kindergarten, almost flunking out of high school, my secret lonely walks on the trails behind Robin Hood Park, my time in the army, my desire to be a writer and find the right girl. I thought we were having intense if brief conversations. It wasn't until years later that I realized I was doing all the talking. Sartre told me nothing about himself.

My class at Keene State graduated in 1968. Because I'd taken some time off to go to New Orleans a few years earlier, I had another semester to go. My love life was still in a shambles and, with no idea what I was going to do when I got out of college, I was a little scared, adrift. I lost interest in my taxi customers, and in Keene. I figured if I could get out of town I could clear my head, so after three years I quit my job as a driver with Ideal Taxi and hit the road with one of my roommates, Jack Brouse. It all worked out. Somehow getting away allowed us to come back with clearer heads.

Soon I was engaged to be married. A week or so before my wife and I set out for California in the fall of 1969, where I was enrolled in graduate school at Stanford University, I saw the Sexy Spinster walking down Main Street. She must have dumped the big fellow, because she'd regained her regal and lonely bearing. I was driving my Chevy down Main Street one night when I looked up at the Ellis Hotel. No light on in Sartre's room. I went over to see the guys in the taxi office. They told me they hadn't heard from him in months. I went over to the hotel where a clerk, who was new on the job, didn't know who I was talking about when I described Sartre, his habits, his room, his books, his dignity. For reasons I still don't understand, I have vivid memories of this man I never knew, and I feel his loss to this day.

I went back to Ideal Taxi recently and the current owner, Joan Copely, let me drive a 4:00 p.m. to 8:00 p.m. shift. As it turned out our agreed-upon date was February 1, 2003, the day the *Columbia* shuttle went down.

In the late sixties, the taxi stand was downtown on Gilbo Avenue. In 2003 it was in a run-down industrial building on the corner of Washington and Burdett streets. Before Joannie moved in with her dispatcher's desk, fridge, bulletin board, TV, and a lounging couch, the place had been a Harley motorcycle shop. (When I was growing up, the building housed a manufacturer of explosives.) In the sixties, five cabs stayed busy through all the shifts. In 2003 Ideal Taxi, the only taxi company in town, had three cabs, two of them out of commission. The lone working cab was a 1993 Ford Taurus with 160,000 miles.

My first customer was a young black woman from a housing project. She was going to Wal-Mart; second customer, white woman, different project, same destination. Later I returned to Wal-Mart and drove them to their tiny apartments. I brought their packages in, snooping to see what they had purchased—bare essentials: toilet paper, paper towels, laundry soap, canned soup, canned meat, bread. The black woman was quiet, nervous, dour, new in town, she said. The white woman never stopped talking, complaining about a man who had attempted to assault her fourteen-year-old daughter. My customer handled that problem by threatening to dismember the man.

My next customers were "regulars," brothers in their thirties, one with long greasy hair and a scraggly beard, the other with a mustache that covered his lips. They were making a beer run to a local market. The fellow with the mustache had a truck but no driver's license. Busted for DUI. His brother had health problems. "I'm not supposed to drink, but . . ." He let the words hang there and laughed.

Then Joannie and I drove out to a Tanglewood mobile home park because a friend had called Joannie saying that another friend, an old woman, wasn't answering her phone. Joannie and I went to check on the old woman. We didn't run the meter. The old woman was okay. Wouldn't say why she wouldn't answer her phone. Her dog barked all the time we were there.

It was dark now, and Joannie sent me to a Keene institution, the Eagle Club on Church Street, only a couple blocks away from where I had lived thirty-five years before. I pressed the buzzer and the bartender let me in. The pool tables were busy, the bar was bumper-to-bumper with patrons. Everybody stopped what they were doing and stared at me as if to say who the hell is this guy. "Taxi?" I yelled, looking for my fare. "That's me," said a guy in his fifties. Then a young woman came over and put a five-dollar bill in my hand. "Give this to Joannie. I owe her for last week."

My fare was a good-natured fellow. We talked about the old days in Keene. I brought him home to a sad little apartment in the North End. He tipped me a dollar because, "Hey, it's your first night on the job." He said I was lucky to work for Joannie.

As I was learning, Joannie was kind of a mother figure to her customers. Joannie started as a driver in 1986, when a repetitive stress in her hands prevented her from continuing in her factory job in Swanzey. She took over the taxi company in 1994. Now, at an age when most people are retired, she worked a day job at Wal-Mart and came in to dispatch from 4:00 to 10:00 p.m. on weeknights, and worked all day on Sunday driving as well as dispatching, handling calls from a cell phone in the car.

My next customer was a man in a red and black outdoorsman shirt, long hair, beard, unsmiling and tense. For no apparent reason, he blurted out that he hated drunks.

Another customer was "a charge," a sullen young woman I picked up at a video store and drove home. Joannie told me that her tab was paid by her father. My last call came in about 7:45 p.m. I drove several miles out to a local motel. Four people in their twenties smelling of booze and cigarettes piled into the car, three men and a woman. The apparent leader of this crew was a fellow with long blond hair who had to have a window open because "I'm claustraphobic as hell." He told a story of the last time he was in Keene, when a woman friend "swatted" the taxi driver. Everybody in the car laughed hysterically but me. I left them at a bar in downtown Keene. They tipped me a dollar. By the time I returned to the dispatching office they had called for a taxi again for a return to the motel.

"I just dropped them off at the bar," I said.

"They got kicked out," Joannie said.

In four hours of taxi driving I took in thirty-seven dollars and fifty cents in fares, plus two dollars in tips. None of my customers mentioned the *Columbia* disaster. In the course of conversation I raised the issue with two different customers, and they both dismissed the subject in the same way, letting me know they had enough troubles of their own to deal with.

PAUL B. HERTNEKY

Il Sentimento della Casa
(A Sense of Home)

Every time I asked someone about the Italian neighborhood in Keene, they answered with a question: the Italian what? Granted, most of those I asked grew up elsewhere. But even natives, on the whole, couldn't tell me much. They had heard of the Italian Club, but they couldn't say exactly where it might be. And Keene is a small city.

At one of its busiest intersections stands a clue, a two-story house with "Antonio Carbone 1925" neatly lettered over the front door. When I first saw that doorway, and the Carbone Window and Awning Company in the next building, I felt a surge of familiarity. Something about the lettering, the tidy working-class houses, the ethnicity, reminded me of the immigrant families I grew up with.

Soon after, I heard that McDonald's was built on the land formerly occupied by Pete's, a neighborhood spaghetti joint. Too many geographic coincidences, I thought. So I wasn't surprised when I detoured into the streets behind Carbone's and saw front yard shrines to the Virgin, neat squadrons of tomato stakes, number ten cans on doorsteps with seedlings emerging, dozens of plastic chairs around tables on porches and decks. It suddenly all made sense; and it was a sense of home.

The neighborhood has always been home to Dennis DiTullio and nobody loves it more. He grew up on Speaker Street in the house his mother, Helen, still lives in. It's just around the corner from his house on Cobb. But, on one Sunday afternoon, like every Sunday afternoon, we reached Mrs. DiTullio's by cutting through the backyard next door, where Dennis and Laura's daughter Angela lives.

The first day I visited the neighborhood, Dennis and I walked a couple of

The DiTullio family and friends making cement in the old neighborhood, c. 1930s. *Standing from left to right:* John Di Lorenzo, Fiore DiTullio, John Properzio, Antonette DiTullio (passing the wine), Amadeo DiTullio, John DiGiulio, Dominic DiTullio. *Seated in front:* an unknown boy and Pat DiLuzio.

blocks, up Cady Street over to Hooper, to see his cousin, Victor Dintino. Kids flew in and out of the screen door, down the steps from the deck, out to the swings in the backyard like a swarm of mosquitoes. Vic and Nancy Dintino, grandparents to most of the kids, have "always!"—Dennis said as he cut the air at chest height—"always, had an open door. You never have any idea who you're going to find at that house."

When Dennis, his son, Anthony, and I entered the house, the crowd of family squeezed around the table tried to make room for us, to no avail. Besides, Vic was already on his feet, pouring us wine and ushering us out to the table on the deck. A party ensued when the Dintinos heard that I had come to make wine with them. Vic and his son, David, brought out bottle after bottle of their own vintages to sample. I didn't know how much I could take until a son-in-law fixed me a plateful of linguine.

I've been eating homemade marinara sauce my whole life. I am grateful for every meal laid before me, but, like most people, I suffer inferior red sauce badly. Well, to compare most sauces to Vic's is to compare Sanka to Starbucks. Later, I would learn that Vic Dintino could serve spaghetti and meatballs to three hundred with about two hours' notice. I think he may have done the pasta course that preceded Christ's miracle with the loaves and fishes. A son of Abruzzi and Calabria, red sauce and wine run through his veins. So with my first mouthful of his linguine, I thought *strangolopreti*, a weird Italian term reserved only for dishes succulent enough to "strangle a priest."

Let me push away from the table for a minute to end any emerging deception. I am not Italian. Never have been. But maybe my Hungarian gypsy instinct helps me decode host cultures, learn their customs, and grant them respect in turn for a seat at their tables, or, in my youth, maybe a date with their daughters. My grandparents came to this country and settled among other immigrants, mostly Italians, so I fall in with them easily.

Before Vic could say good-bye, he disappeared into the high jungle of tomato plants in his garden, then popped out minutes later with about thirty pounds of gnarly looking tomatoes. (The perfectly shaped ones I had been buying from a local organic farm all summer tasted like balls of yarn compared to these.) Lugging my tomatoes, we skipped over to say goodbye to Dennis's mom. She handed me a big dish covered with foil and filled with gnocchi that her eighty-four-year-old hands had crafted early that morning. Dennis helped me carry the goods to my car in his driveway. Then he ran into the house and came out with a bottle of wine and a bag full of pears from his tree.

My god, I thought, driving home. I hadn't been treated like this for twenty years. No, wait, it's the same when I visit my hometown. Italians never grow out of their largess. The intensity and hospitality increases when they're together, and this neighborhood keeps them together.

I mentioned the names of the streets because they're names of players on the 1912 world champion Red Sox (apart from Cobb)—Heine Wagner, Hick Cady, Harry Hooper, Tris Speaker, and Smoky Joe Wood. The flat, fertile patch of land, bounded on two sides by an elbow in the Ashuelot River, accommodated the Keene Baseball Grounds until the 1920s. Then a couple of Irish speculators bought the parcel and called it Homestead Villa, a name that promised immigrants a sense of comfort, ownership, and upward mobility. The two hunting and fishing cabins squatting on the property commended it as a place where the new settlers could live off the land.

The next time I swung my car into the DiTullios' driveway, the headlights swept over Anthony, bent by the curb, spraying a grape crusher with a garden hose. I hustled over to help him hold it, picking stems out of its studded steel rollers. On that starlit October night, the icy water stung. And the crusher's oak frame and long crank handle made it a heavy, awkward piece of equipment. But it had made the trip from Abruzzi nearly a hundred years ago and the wine wouldn't be the same without it.

When Anthony's great-grandfather, Domenic Coppola, first got off the train in Keene, he was working on the railroad that connected to Boston. He had come to cut stone, but the railroad needed men and he needed money. So he drove spikes and laid ties and shoveled rocks. But every year at this time, he did what we were doing—picked up his grapes from a railroad siding, fresh from California, and headed for the cellar.

When the neighborhood took root, Italian families also clustered on Butler Court, Foundry Street, and on streets across the river. But, as the first homesteaders died off and nearby Keene State College snapped up their properties, the houses in Homestead Villa became a sanctuary, the core of the community. Today, twenty-eight modest dwellings, most with tiny yards and intensive gardens, cover the neighborhood's seventeen acres. Coppola's was one of the first houses to be built, hard by the banks of the Ashuelot.

His son, Joe, is now eighty-eight and lives within a few blocks of where he was raised. He is the eldest of five siblings, and was the only boy. Three of his four sisters still playfully tease Joe about the sleeping arrangements in their three-bedroom house. The parents had one room, Joe had another, and the four girls crammed into the remaining room.

"He was the king!" Helen says. "We shined his shoes and cleaned his room." Her granddaughter groans at the patriarchy. Dennis laughs. And his uncle Joe sheepishly looks up from his plate and whispers "I was appreciated." One stipulation, though: Joe shared his room with dozens of sausages hanging above his bed.

Adjacent to the river, the Coppolas found rich soil for the gardens. And all the families found fish in the river and streams, rabbits and deer in the woods, ducks and geese flying overhead. "We didn't have any money and we didn't really do anything with money," John Grossi told me. "We ate the stuff we grew and shot." They walked to the Catholic church, the rail yard, the quarries, and to the mills. They foraged for mushrooms and dandelion greens and berries and God knows what else. The mortar in Dennis and Laura's chimney is mixed with silt from the river.

That masonry was the work of Clemente "Mindy" DiBernardo, who built the house in 1922, next to his parents' homestead. He and his neighbors also poured

The Italian neighborhood is marked by front yard shrines to the Virgin, neat squadrons of tomato stakes, number ten cans on doorsteps with seedlings emerging, and large gardens.

the blocks for the cellar. They took turns helping each other and the original houses can still be identified by their distinctive foundation blocks.

Now Anthony and I were descending the bulkhead stairs, shouldering crates of grapes. I felt the sticky sides of the crate, heard neighbors laughing below, and smacked my head against the low overhang, temporarily blinding myself, but I shook off the pain like a tough *paisan* from eighty years ago.

I didn't want to whine in the presence of Timmy Carbone, a former football star, then coach, who was tipping grapes into a crusher while his son turned the crank. The low ceiling forced me to crouch, but I found a space for my head between the rafters while taking my turn at the crusher. The grapes, zinfandel, merlot, some carignane and petit syrah, looked good going in. They were plump but with enough desiccated bunches—raisins, essentially—to give the juice character.

We worked elbow to elbow in the tiny room, which is part bottling storage, part shrine to nearly a century of wine making. There's just enough space for two standing barrels, two barrels on their sides, a hundred or so bottles, some empty and some filled with previous years' wines. Those bottles wear labels made of rough strips of masking tape marked with ballpoint pen—merlot 02, zin 01, muscat 02—that kind of thing. The pipes overhead are patriotically wrapped in red, white, and green crepe paper. And hanging from nails on the rafters, as if this place isn't hazardous enough for my noggin, are hundreds of corkscrews, from novelty pulls to picnic tools to menacing pigtailed gadgets. The more wine I sipped, the more I needed a hard hat.

But I kept my head in my work, only occasionally distracted by the robust women depicted on the crate labels, dazzling illustrations that Dennis had used to panel part of the wall I faced while cranking the crusher.

Last year, Anthony's wine took second place in a regional competition. That fact was noted among the records of pressing dates, rankings, and comments that had been scrawled on the shelving supports, again in ballpoint, over the last twenty years. Anthony's prize has been the family's best showing. He poured me a glass and one mouthful sucked me back to the cellars of my youth. It had a low-tannin, smooth, drink-me-till-dawn appeal. No crappy additives. Pure juice, the essence of homemade wine.

The Carbone and DiTullio boys and I finished our work, took up our glasses, and toasted, *a salute*. Anthony added, "Well, good job guys. Now it's up to the grapes . . . and whatever else." After a few days, we would press the fermenting mash and transfer the juice to the mother barrels, where it would spend the rest of its working life.

During the first week in the mothers, fermentation reminds us of the living culture within. Bubbles rise and a lavender foam slides down the girth of the barrels. And then it falls asleep. That's when we cork it and, as tradition demands, Dennis drapes a rosary over the top of the barrel. Into the steel collar he sticks a holy card depicting Saint Rita, patroness of the neediest, a favorite among steerage Italians. She will protect the transformation of fruit to spirits . . . she and the grape-picking pinups on the wall.

Toasting an occasion. Five generations of change have done little to alter community traditions.

Cooling off under the stars in Dennis's backyard, the river only a few yards away, it's easy to see how the river and the railroad tracks once set the borders of this enclave. And it's also hard to forget that this house arrived by rail, from Sears Roebuck in Chicago. Mindy DiBernardo took a crew to the siding to pick up the shipments, piece by piece. Maybe the wine sets loose my imagination, but the recent past comes alive here. I can almost hear the trains. When I cut across Angela's yard toward Helen's house, from what was center field to left, I'm tracking down a line drive off the bat of Red Sox slugger Hick Cady. Like the wine in the barrels, much happens out of sight.

In another subterranean haven, the first generation of immigrants built the Marconi Society, officially the Guglielmo Marconi Societa Italiana Di Mutuo Soccorso (William Marconi Italian Society of Mutual Help), a men's club. The windowless basement serves as the historical and structural foundation for the Keene Italian Club, a private bar and function room upstairs. For the women, the basement of the building on Wood Street also houses the Societa Italiana Femminile Santa Francesca Romana (Women's Italian Society of Saint Francesca Romana), named for a Roman aristocrat legendary for her charity.

Although the Italian Club welcomes all nationalities, the Marconi Society requires Italian heritage. With 120 members, the society is now growing by the month, reflecting a boom in the local population and an increasing number of Italian men who like each other's company and want to preserve their traditions. At their meetings, they wear tricolored sashes and plan community support events. They award scholarships, buy health insurance, and help families who fall on hard times. After they meet, they eat, and Vic Dintino is usually in the kitchen. The night I visited, the chatter at my table surrounded the upcoming Pumpkin Festival and preparations to raise money by selling meatball sandwiches. The Social Committee would make enough for six hundred sandwiches, and Timmy Carbone would brew sixty-four gallons of minestrone, just like last year.

Should it be any surprise that the kitchen takes up almost half of the society's square footage? On the night of meatball making, vats of sauce bubbled on the stove. Meatballs roasted in a multitiered oven that had been salvaged from a defunct hotel. By nine o'clock, the temperature in the kitchen had risen to eighty-five degrees. Around the center butcher block worked six helpers, surrounded by another twenty tasters and happy hangers-on. Kids played red rover in the empty meeting room while the adults crammed into the hottest space, snacking, sweating, drinking, howling, and loving each other at the top of their lungs.

To survey the scene, I stepped away, into the meeting room. Plaques, banners, and photos line the walls. One plaque lists the founders' names—many of the same names belonging to the kids locking arms and issuing dares. Over in the corner, two of the founders' progeny, Michael and Dori Carbone, who are now in their eighties and married sixty-two years, sample the meatballs with their granddaughter, a doctor up from Boston.

I suddenly feel like I'm standing inside a throbbing heart, one that pumps blood, wine, sauce, heritage, and pride into gardens and basements and veins. Over five generations this community has changed, yet nothing has died.

The wine barrels and crushers, the recipes, the children carrying the same names, the memories, the very handiwork, the trodden shortcuts—all evoke the daily lives of those who had gone before and bring them, front and center, into the midst of the living. They brush the skin and raise gooseflesh through accounts and appearances, like the time Mindy and Sabat DiBernardo materialized at the foot of the newly married DiTullios' bed. Laura woke Dennis and described them—a couple she had never seen—to a tee, welcoming her to the house they had built.

Twenty-six years after his father's death, Dennis still can't even speak of him without choking up. He quietly wept throughout our visit to the family graves in the cemetery. Their presence, the bubbling in their kitchens, the kick of their wine, the assurance of their embrace and affection, cling to him. He knows that his people, corralled by the river and the rails, will always be together. Here, he feels their company.

On Halloween night, the neighborhood glows with jack-o'-lanterns and porch lights, chirps with toddlers and laughing parents. Dennis and Laura hand out candy at the bottom of their steps, around an inlaid stone map of Italy. Through the shadows pass railroad men and resilient women. In the cellars crouch brothers of the grape and sisters of mercy. The wind rattles through the dry leaves, applauding the boys in flannel and spikes.

And the Ashuelot cradles the neighborhood in the crook of its elbow. With the millponds gone, the river runs freely through this intimate quarter. Abruzzese and Calabrese ancestors marvel at a scene they could only imagine—the abiding gardens, the sheltering trees, the whispering river, and the giggles of enduring love. In all of this, nature often takes a turn for the better, and here it takes a turn for home.

"This Is a Great Country, and Don't Forget It"

Dayton Duncan chronicled the 1988 New Hampshire presidential primary in his book *Grass Roots*. In one chapter he contrasted the tightly scripted visit of Vice President George Bush with Republican Pete du Pont's long-shot candidacy:

"Good morning, I'm Pete du Pont, and you're on *Open Mike*. What's your question?" The voice came across any radio tuned in to radio station WKBK early in the morning. Du Pont, the former congressman and governor of Delaware, scion of the fabulously wealthy chemical company family, candidate for the Republican nomination for president, was sitting in a small booth in the station's studio in downtown Keene, announcing his visit by being the guest on the daily talk show.

Du Pont had no organization at all in Cheshire County. Early as it was in the campaign cycle, virtually every other campaign in the state could name at least four to twenty people in the region already committed to their candidate and probably doing some sort of preliminary organizational work. Du Pont's—and Al Haig's—had no one. (Du Pont had been to the outskirts of the Monadnock Region in January. Ending a day devoted to agricultural issues, he had attended a reception in Temple, in neighboring Hillsborough County. The campaign had promoted the reception site as a local farm. It turned out, in fact, to be a private hunting reserve. The thirty-five guests included a few Democrats and some federal employees—prohibited by law from doing any real campaign work—who had shown up as a favor to the host, a family friend of du Pont's whose principal concern was turning out a decent-size crowd.) Lacking any local contacts, du Pont's campaign brought him to Keene without much planning and apparently without any clear objective other than to move him randomly round the city, get some "free" media, and attempt to reach voters directly, even though in April the voters were more focused on the first balmy spring day than on politics.

After the radio show—during which du Pont fielded questions about the war in Central America (he supported the Reagan policy), Social Security (he wanted to make some radical changes in it), and the price of tomatoes (he couldn't explain to the angry caller why they were so expensive)—he went to Keene High School, where he told a hundred students and five teachers during study hall that his presidential platform was "a little different." He proposed forcing anyone on welfare to work for local governments, eliminating all farm subsidies, and testing and searching teenagers for drugs and punishing offenders by taking away their driver's licenses until age eighteen. The general consensus of the group, 95 percent of whom were old enough to drive but too young to vote, was that du Pont was indeed "different," but perhaps even a little weird. Their questions were uniformly hostile.

Du Pont's next stop was Yankee Lanes, a bowling alley not far from the high school. Sixty women were startled when a tall, patrician-looking man in a business suit, trailed by two aides, disrupted their morning bowling league to introduce himself, press some brochures into their hands, and leave. After lunch at Lindy's Diner, where he spent most of his time talking with Will Fay, a reporter from *The Keene Sentinel* and the only person in Keene whose face he recognized, du Pont headed out the door for a stroll up Main Street.

For an hour du Pont searched in vain for anyone to talk with for more than a few seconds. People he encountered on the street were polite, some a little bemused, when he would stop them, give them a brochure, and start to recount the reception at the high school to his drug proposal. "I don't think those kids liked it," he told them. (Which of course was the point; he wanted the *adults* to like it.) At the City Hall the mayor and most of the top officials were gone. His chat with the dispatcher at police headquarters was interrupted by radio calls. Outside the district courtroom, three people were sitting. "Pete du Pont, running for president," he exclaimed cheerfully. "How're you all doing today?"

"Just terrific," one answered sarcastically—he was waiting to be arraigned.

The candidate spied the local Social Security office across the street and marched in, figuring to engage them in debate over his own proposals. "I'm sorry, sir, but I really would appreciate it if you didn't disrupt things," said the women at the reception desk. "We're trying to get some work done here."

"Can't I just go back to the desks and say hello?" du Pont asked.

"No. I really would rather that you just left." (Had du Pont gone on to win the White House, regardless of whether Congress would have gone along with his Social Security reforms, Keene would undoubtedly have had its office closed.)

At the fire station around the corner, he figured he'd finally found some people with time on their hands. But the fire chief was on his way to a meeting with the Secret Service for Bush's visit, and after du Pont sat down with five firemen and had just enough time to explain his driver's license drug program, the alarm went off. Someone had overdosed and needed help. "There you go," a fireman said as they climbed into the ambulance. "That guy just lost his driver's license."

Wandering into the local senior center, du Pont discovered twenty people getting ready for a talent show. He listened to a ninety-two-year-old woman do an impersonation of George Burns. He ordered an aide to find three cue balls for him, and after summoning a drumroll from the band ("What for?" asked the drummer. "To introduce me properly," he said), he amused them with a demonstration of his juggling abilities.

Back down Main Street, he entered Timoleon's, another restaurant, and went to the kitchen to meet Lindy Chakalos, the cook-owner.

"How ya' doin? I'm Pete du Pont, running for president. Here's some literature for you."

"President of what?"

"The United States."

"What party?"

"Republican."

"Who against?"

Du Pont named his opponents.

"Let me tell you something," the cook told him. "My father came to this country and went through Ellis Island. But my son is at *Dartmouth*. This is a great country, and don't forget it."

(Du Pont didn't. The story became a standard refrain in his stump speeches for the rest of his short-lived campaign, offered as proof that even though it was far from his own personal history of privileged upbringing, he understood the promise of America.)

At the Keene Chamber of Commerce offices in the city's bus station, du Pont borrowed a telephone for an hour to make fundraising calls. He made more calls from a pay phone at Peter Christian's, yet another restaurant, had a glass of iced tea, and then shaved in their restroom. His final stop of the day was at Keene State College, where, after an interview on the college radio station, a political science class verbally tore apart his positions on Central America, the Strategic Defense Initiative, and drug testing. The weather, at least, had been sunny and warm.

The day had proceeded as if du Pont and his campaign had studied the campaign of Jimmy Carter in 1976 but only understood part of it. Du Pont had just spent more consecutive time in Keene than any of the other candidates before him (or after, with the exception of Gary Hart, who in late January 1988 would also devote an entire day—and evening—campaigning within the city limits). Like Carter, he had taken his campaign to the streets. He had managed to appear on two radio shows, and the *Sentinel* devoted two stories to his visit. Missing, however, was any attempt to make real connection with someone who might carry on his campaign locally in his absence, the kind of meticulous organizational work that was another hallmark of Carter's model. Du Pont was observing some of New Hampshire's primary rituals, but without comprehending their purpose.

His encounters left more of an impression on him—he was still retelling the Ellis Island story next February—than he left on the city. To a great extent the primary campaign at this juncture was confined to the small universe of activists, and at least in Cheshire County du Pont wasn't participating in that campaign. The twenty people at the senior center might remember that someone running for president had juggled for them, but on the whole his trip to Keene in April would be forgotten by the month's end, let alone by primary day ten months later. He came and went without leaving much of a trace.

The Last Mill in Town

PAUL B. HERTNEKY

By all historical standards, Bennington, on the eastern edge of the Monadnock region, should stand at the brink of ruin. Its powder mill and cutlery mill and cotton mill have all been closed. Its company-owned houses, built more than a century ago, strain the budgets of their blue-collar owners. No more trains run through it. No tourist industry has grown around it. And the last remaining mill in this town of 1,440 is locked in a battle with global competitors.

Yet Bennington breathes, and draws life the way it has for eons—from its rock and water. Here, a seventy-five-foot plunge in the Contoocook River has attracted seekers of sustenance for roughly six thousand years, when it was exploited by Abenaki hunter-gatherers in an era archeologists call Archaic. Colonial settlers also rushed to Great Falls, as they called it, and quickly harnessed its power for mills. Crotched Mountain, an impediment to early travelers, now finds its north face blasted with snow guns and strung with ski lifts. Though small, the mountain is closer to Boston than most and easy recreation for locals.

The natural features that attracted early man still dominate. When viewed from the disused railroad bridge, above a menacing stretch of falls, the allure of this spot makes itself as plain as the open valley and the promising fishing holes swirling below. The Abenaki heard these falls for miles. So, although farms and

The longest continuously running paper mill in America. Since 1819, paper has been made on the spot where the Monadnock Paper Mill stands today.

Mill owners have harnessed the falls on the Contoocook River in Bennington since they replaced Abenaki fishermen.

industry have come and gone, the very word archaic remains an apt description of Bennington. The town is characteristic of an earlier period.

How else to explain the only single-mill town remaining in the Monadnock region? Long after millers and industrialists from Antrim to Hinsdale shut the gates, released the rivers, and left their workers with grim prospects, how could Bennington's survival seem anything but archaic? Here stands the longest continuously running mill in America.

Since 1819, paper has been squeezed, first from flax, then from pulp on the spot where the Monadnock Paper Mill stands today. Thundering locomotives, clattering machinery, roaring white water and air whistles stitched together the days and decades of swing-shifting workers filing into the sprawling factory. Its crimson expanse of brick stands in contrast to lush lawns. Its red neon sign in stout Lubalin type glows without a burnt-out inch, shimmering in the river, refracted in the steam that billows from a towering brick smokestack. Like a relic, the scene from Route 202 is that of a vintage postcard or a model train display.

But none of its charm can protect the mill from gigantic competitors at home and in the Far East. Nor can it slow the mobility of workers. Less than fity years ago, the mill's paper bore the fingerprints mostly of Bennington residents. Today, many of the town's manufacturing workers often drive away for other opportunities. And the mill has created a leaner, more efficient operation. It struggles for new markets and its highly skilled workers produce more specialty paper—for filters and backings and sensitive packaging—every year. Diminishing markets, an aging workforce, and a local populace that's more diverse, mobile, and opportunistic have combined to change the mill's role in town. The fortunes of Bennington no longer fall to the mill's owners.

Richard Verney, who has been running the Monadnock Paper Mill since his father died in 1978, acknowledges Bennington's evolution with some relief. "It seems like this mill has meant everything to the town for a long time. It probably means less now," he says.

And he's right. The mill's landholdings, roughly 450 acres, an estate and the mill, account for a decreasing percentage of the property tax base—down 5 percent in the past decade. The mill's workforce has dropped from a peak of 254 in 1988 to just under 183 today, with only one-sixth living in Bennington.

But he recognizes the importance of the mill to his employees and his customers. And he's proud to spare them the vagaries of dealing with a huge corporation. "Because I get my salary from this place, I feel differently than if I were living in New York and had somebody running it. I do think people know I'm committed."

In an archaic switcheroo, the black horses and coal cart that once signaled the arrival of a rail shipment have been replaced by Verney's German luxury sedan that signals the boss is on duty. For better or worse, that symbol of prosperity and pride, or diligence, or authority, or downright elitism, hits any visitor right between the eyes. It is, however, characteristic of an earlier period.

Contrary to local assumptions, the Verney family are newcomers when compared to the land barons who owned other mill towns. Richard's father, Gilbert,

Monadnock Paper Mills 1887.

Investing in tradition. Some Bennington workers have had family working in the mill going back five generations.

was an English merchant marine who reportedly jumped ship in Rhode Island in 1923. He found work in a textile mill and, at night, studied textile designing at the Rhode Island School of Design. In 1940, he opened his own mill in Manchester, and bought seven more mills in the subsequent decade.

One of those mills was in Peterborough. And in 1948, when Arthur J. Pierce, the former owner of Monadnock Paper Mill, died, Gilbert Verney scooped up the estate. "Rumor is, he bought the mill because he wanted the house" (an 1820s mansion overlooking the valley), Richard says. "He essentially bought the whole town, then decided to get out of the real estate business."

Pierce owned many of the workers' houses, and, according to local lore, he also owned the general store. Reflecting an affectation that harks back to an earlier period of swashbuckling industrialists, Mr. Pierce liked to be called "colonel" although he had never served in the military. He also bestowed his largess by building a school and a power plant, named after the colonel himself. His management style and ownership of houses and stores assured that the paper mill came under the protection of a strong union. "He had quite a reputation," Richard says. "If he fired you, a half hour later he had a truck at your door and he'd say, 'I don't know where you're going but get out of my house.'"

Vastly different stories are told about Gilbert Verney. Sam Zachos, a former union president, says, "Mr. Verney was generous and kind, easy to talk to. He liked coming through the mill. And he believed in people." In testimony, Zachos spent fifty-two years with the company.

Jimmy Cleary, a relative greenhorn, with only fifteen years in the mill but a lifetime in Bennington, remembers the elder Verney's sense of fun. "Everybody came to the company picnics . . . right there outside the mill. I was a kid and we chased greased pigs and had the greased pole contest, all kinds of games. The old-timers played cards on the hill. All the families were there. And the Verneys too."

Most of the workers who have grown up in town or worked several decades at the mill are wistful about the elder Verney's leadership. Millwright Mike Beauchamp recalls how Gilbert Verney walked to his office through the mill every Saturday morning. "He came in looking great in his pin-striped suits that he always wore. And he just took his time, shaking hands with the guys and asking how their families were, was everything okay in the mill, was there anything he could take care of for us? He really was interested in us and what was going on down there."

Verney invested heavily in the mill, doubled its capacity, and drove it toward technical development and specialization. That kind of reinvestment and innovation have continued, but today's American paper industry is suffering from worldwide overcapacity and cheap imports. State-subsidized mills in China and Korea enjoy tariff-free exportation to the United States. "But if we try to go into their markets, we get whacked [with tariffs]," Richard Verney says.

So, instead of running seven days a week, the mill runs six or five. That means the manufacturing employees work swing shifts. A bleary-eyed Cleary sipped his coffee after finishing an 11:00 p.m. to 7:00 a.m. shift while describing life on the swings. They run first shift (11:00 p.m. to 7:00 a.m.), second shift (7:00 a.m. to 3:00 p.m.) and third, considered the worst (3:00 p.m. to 11:00 p.m.).

I've worked these shifts in a steel mill and they play hell with sleep patterns. Jimmy Cleary had been responsible for the entire sloshing, howling, and whirring mill all night long. Five generations of his family have worked in the mill. And he felt grateful, if tired.

He recalled passing a thirty-year veteran "dragging himself out as I was walking into the mill, and I thought, I don't want to be here doing this for as long as he has."

Recently, Cleary accepted a management job, a rare move among the rank and file. "For one thing, it's really hard to fire a union employee, and management has no protection. Guys thought I was crazy to give up working outside and move inside. But you know what? I can easily keep my job; all I have to do is do it well. My father encouraged me to move inside. And it's the best decision I've made." Jimmy has now taken a management job and he says, "it would be perfect without the shifts. But nothing's perfect. Utopia's right around the corner . . . and it stays there."

The end of the process, the sheeting operation in 1950 (above) and today—the winder on the Number One paper machine rolls up to 10,000 pounds of paper (below).

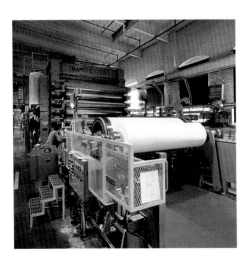

After fifty-two satisfying years at the mill, leisure finally came to Sam Zachos. He and his wife, Linny, live hard by the highway that once bisected the Factory Village, Bennington's humble name when it was part of Hancock and a few other neighboring towns, before it won incorporation in 1842. Without much of a backyard, the couple park their thirty-five-foot motor home on the front lawn, where it's ready to go.

Zachos graduated from high school one Friday in 1950, took the weekend off, then went to work at the mill on Monday. He stayed until 2002. He harbors no romance for his first job as a trimmer helper or his promotion to trimmer operator, lifting and shoving all day long. "Nothing moved on that machine unless you moved it. I wouldn't wish that job on my worst enemy." Yet he did it for "eighteen and a half years." After that, he moved into shipping and steady daytime work. He served as president of the union for "fourteen and a half years." (His accounts reveal distinct reverence toward accuracy when it comes to tenure.) Zachos says, as a union leader, "I knew I could handle the company, but it's a different story handling some of those guys I worked with."

His parents migrated from northern Greece and his father went to work at the mill. Sam and Linny found comfort in Bennington, where more than thirty Greek families once lived, mostly on a dirt road known as Greek Alley that runs directly behind the mill's smokestack.

The town always seems to brandish markers of an earlier era. At a time when his fellow paper magnates grow more distant from their mills' communities, Richard Verney slaps the table and says, "I think participating in civic matters is a good thing to do. Here's a difference between this company and many others: I live here. And I don't want to live in a dump. I don't think anybody does. Besides, I've been entrusted with this company."

He leans back and pushes up his sleeves. "It's like this: when we were kids, we were taught to wear a coat and tie on airplanes." He stops there to see if he's made his point, then explains, "Not everybody gets to go on airplanes."

"It was a *privilege*?" I ask.

"Yeah. Subliminally, we were given a kind of work ethic."

He and his family might have sold the mill for a good price years ago, but they balked, afraid that the massive conglomerates might abandon the mill and the town. Now, suitors are fewer and farther between. But the work ethic at the mill pays off as long as it can continue to turn out paper that's known by every true graphic designer and printer. Monadnock makes beautiful, bright paper that begs to be touched. The adhesive and technical papers meet precise specifications.

An industrial work of art like the Monadnock Paper Mill would be hard to walk away from. But, a lack of interest from the upcoming generation of heirs leaves Verney's options open. For now, he intends to find new markets and customers, increasing the value of the operation and its products, while remaining committed to his community.

"It scares me that U.S. manufacturing is hurting. We can't all be doctors and lawyers," says Verney, who knows that rural towns need volunteers who don't mind getting their hands dirty. A perfect example is Mike Beauchamp, a mill worker for forty-seven years, the chief of a volunteer fire department, and the cofounder of an EMT unit. When someone is injured at the mill but not so severely as to need an ambulance, Beauchamp will get out of bed and take the worker to the hospital. He's paid for these responses, but he does them as a favor. Likewise, when the alarm goes off at the fire station, Beauchamp can leave his job and answer the call without hesitation. His wife, Joy, says, "It's a relationship. Gosh, yes. And that's the way things have always been."

Bennington cannot escape the way things have always been. And yet, some modern adaptations, though seemingly minute, can be impressive. The roaring mill, with its enormous machinery, still beats fibers into submission and cooks them in hundreds of gallons of water. But instead of drawing water from the river, the machinery pumps it from a well and, instead of discharging the waste into the river, the mill recovers and reprocesses 98 percent of the unused water and fiber. On the manufacturing floor itself, few workers can be seen. One or two technicians sit in glass booths, monitoring and controlling the operation with sophisticated computer programs.

Although the Monadnock Paper Mill is the last mill in Bennington, it distinguishes the town as a place where a tangible and valuable product continues to be made from raw materials. The men and women who enter its gates, like those who came before them, diverge from the modern trend toward mere assembly, servicing, interpreting, analyzing, or placing one cog in an unseen corporate machine. Out of water and trees they make paper, a product for which world demand is writ large.

Boys and girls still fish from the bridge above the power station. The volunteers who run the town today are a mill foreman, a restaurateur, and an investment banker. They all grew up in town and carry vestiges of another era. One of the town's two restaurants, Alberto's, oddly called "Bat's" by locals whose accent probably flattens the owner's name from Bert to Bat, sits alongside the Great Falls within sight of the paper mill. The loyal customers have enjoyed the same steak pizzaola and chicken parmesan for decades. Bat's son wonders whether he should introduce something trendier. But for now, he'll keep things just the way they've always been.

The Working Life

I. Marlborough Mill

Rita Grace, a lifelong resident of Marlborough, talks about working in Marlborough's Cheney-Cote label mill in the late 1960s:

"I was on second shift. Cheney's daughter [Bonnie] and I were the only ones working. That was before OSHA came around. Sometimes Bonnie didn't come to work and I was there all by myself, from five in the afternoon until one in the morning running four looms and when you stop and think about that, today that's against the law!

"But I remember down Cheney's, they weren't modern like Minnewawa [mill], because it was a small family that took it over and the looms weren't the best shape at all. I don't know how they even lasted as they did.

"I remember in the summertime it used to be so hot in that place the wax [to repair shuttles] used to melt in your hand and Bonnie would say to me, 'You think it's gonna be hot tonight?' And, I threw that wax against the wall and it stuck and I said, 'You bet it's gonna be hot tonight!' That's how we used to gauge on how hot we were gonna be. And, then in the wintertime we used to have to get humidifiers running to get all the moisture in. I think the looms ran best at 62 percent humidity. Then they used to have a smash where all the threads would break; the shuttles would go flying. You could get an awful nest there if you didn't watch it.

"But they were good to me. Paul Cheney or Albert Cote, they would come back probably seven to nine and work on the looms or the cards and Veronica [the owner's wife] always sent me dessert. When Albert would come down, she'd send dessert with him and that was kind of a nice treat. And then, they taught me how to repair the cards so if there was a mistake in the label I used to take the ladder out, climb all the way up to the top and fix the hole in the card that was torn, come all the way down. I'd lock up the shop at night when I left, shut the lights off, and I don't remember if it was the landing—when they put the man on the moon, but Paul Cheney told me, he said, 'You quit work at ten and you go home and don't miss any of it.' And I got paid to do that.

"And then when the high school, up in the attic, started [on] fire—the bell tower was burning. Well, Albert Cote came down and he says, 'Rita,' he says, 'Have you had supper yet?' And I says, 'No, not yet.' He says, 'Take your lunch, go up on Cemetery Hill, the school is burning down.' He says, 'Don't come back until the fire is out.' [Laughs] And I got paid but I was only up there probably for an hour or so and they pretty well had it out and I came back and Albert says, 'Is it burnt down?' I says, 'No.' He says, 'Well, why didn't you stay there?' And I said, 'Because they got the fire out.' He says, 'Well, you spent a good many years in school, I didn't want you to miss that.' [Laughs] But they were very good to work with.

"It was a family affair and we did a lot of Lord & Taylor labels. We didn't do any trim. I remember coming home with a whole roll of Lord & Taylor labels

Woman at a loom in the Minnewawa mill, which was one of several label mills in downtown Marlborough.

The Jacquard loom was programmed with a deck of punched cards, which determined the weaving patterns. "If there was a mistake...I used to take the ladder out, climb all the way up to the top and fix the hole in the card that was torn, come all the way down," recalled Rita Grace.

and I think I cut all the labels off my blouses and sewed in Lord & Taylor and so didn't my sisters! [Laughs] And I think a few other people got a shot at those Lord & Taylor labels. But then the label business was pretty well . . . it was on its way out when I left there.

"And I went to Minnewawa. Theirs was built in, their system where they had steam come out in the wintertime and the dehumidifiers were built into the system and the eight looms I had was right over that steam pipe in the middle of the winter, my clothes . . . my back was wet from that steam blowing on me and I got one hell of a cold and I told my boss, 'This is the last week I'm here!' and I left. I think I was there about a year but that wasn't so personal. That was a business and there was a lot of out-of-towners on the second shift. It wasn't the Marlborough people. The first shift were the town people because they had the seniority. They had the day work. So I wasn't quite as comfortable working there as I was with working with the Cheney-Cote family."

The Working Life

II. Lawrence Tannery

Geoffrey Douglas

The A. C. Lawrence Tannery was massive in every sense. Between its size—fifteen buildings, more than 200,000 square feet, splayed over twenty-one acres on the west bank of the Ashuelot—its history, and the number of lives it had touched, it cast a shadow over Winchester, New Hampshire, like nothing before or since.

When Stephen Johnson began work there, as a young chemist just out of college in the spring of 1941, the company (depending on how you dated its beginnings) was somewhere around a hundred years old. Its output was tanned shearling skins—treated sheepskin with the wool still on it—which would then be shipped to garment workers, usually in New York, for assembly into gloves, slippers, jackets, or coats. It was a complex process that Stephen delights in explaining. At the time, he says, it involved the leaching of tree bark—originally oak and hemlock, later quebracho, a South American hardwood—to remove the tannins used to treat the skins. But the skins themselves had first to be prepared: hot-washed to cleanse them of maggots, then pickled in pits to preserve them, then finally tanned. "Depending on where you worked, in the cellars or the drying rooms, it could be a dirty job."

Chet Bomba of Winchester worked "pulling pits" at the Lawrence Tannery during one summer while he was a college student. He remembers the work vividly. "The sheepskins came into the tannery stacked up on railroad cars. Some still had feet attached and occasionally even the head. Although I liked being

The sprawling A. C. Lawrence Tannery dominated Winchester like nothing before or since.

outdoors, the skins had maggots and so on and so forth, and it was one hell of a poor job on a hot day.

"Inside the tannery, my job was pulling pits. That is one messy, messy job. The pit is filled with brine, and the sheepskins are thrown into this brine solution. . . . Then, when the chemist determines the hide is cured properly, you pull the pit so that the hide can go to the next stage. Pulling these things, it's a gut-wrenching job, because, you know, a sheepskin is heavy soaked with water, and pulling it over the side of the vat and flopping them over the side is exhausting.

"First time I went in there, I was a young man and I was gung ho, and I think I pulled nineteen pits. Then you went to shower. When I got out of the shower, there was a man waiting there, and he asked me. He said, 'What, are you crazy? You can't turn all those in. We never pull more than eight or nine pits a day. You're going to ruin it for all of us.'

"I had to give up a lot of those pits. No, I'm serious. Then after that I knew how much to turn in."

These jobs supported generations of Winchester natives, as well as many from Keene, Richmond, Hinsdale, Swanzey, and across the river in Brattleboro, Vermont. At the high point, in the late war years, with half the bomber jackets of the Allied forces being prepped at the Winchester plant, the tannery was operating around the clock—seven hundred employees on three shifts, processing eighty-four thousand skins a week—with buses arriving and departing three times daily from Keene.

"It was a good-paying job for the time," John Gomarlo, who worked there only two and a half years and not as long ago as Stephen, told a local reporter not long ago. "A lot of the residents in town—this was their first job, and they retired from it."

Making leather in the nineteenth century. The skins were washed to remove maggots, pickled in pits, then tanned using the bark of hemlock or oak. "Depending on where you worked, in the cellars or the drying rooms, it could be a dirty job," said Stephen Johnson.

The war, of course, was the zenith. Not long after it ended, a workers' strike froze the factory for two weeks—management had tried to add a thirty-minute unpaid lunch break to the 7:00 a.m. to 3:00 p.m. shift. By the early 1950s, A. C. Lawrence was back to its prewar levels of two hundred and fifty or so employees processing around twenty-four thousand skins a week; slippers and women's powder puffs were the big items by now. Stephen Johnson won't say so—he is relentlessly upbeat in every personal view he expresses—but it must have been at least a little sad.

"The leather industry went to pieces," is the most he will concede, citing the twin effects of synthetic leathers and the growth of foreign competition—both of which were being felt by the early 1960s. "The company began to cut back. I'm not sure when we dropped under two hundred [workers], but it must have been somewhere around then."

Twenty years passed, with the company in a jerky but inexorable decline. Stephen over the course of these years was put in charge of coloring and dyeing, then made foreman of soaking and washing. In 1970, his thirtieth year with the plant, he was made employment manager. He retired in 1984, after forty-three years of service. There were roughly one hundred employees still on payroll at the time.

It's difficult to get him to say much about what happened at the end. "Mistakes were made. Rules got broken. I wasn't too involved with all that." His voice drops; his eyes lower to the heavy-bound pamphlet he has been cradling all this time in his lap: *Lawrence Leathers: A Short History of the A. C. Lawrence Leather Company, Inc.* Half an inch thick, with a century's worth of black-and-white photos of working men in period clothes, it is dated 1982.

That was the same year, as it happened, that the EPA began its investigation. By the end of it, A. C. Lawrence and several of its officers had been convicted of discharging contaminants into the Ashuelot, filing bogus readings to avert detection, and violating federal hazardous-waste laws stemming from the storage of a degreasing solvent—three hundred drums of which were found buried on company land. In 1987 the tannery closed its doors. It sat abandoned—collapsing slowly—for fourteen more years, drawing arsonists, juveniles, and at least the rumor of rats ("A. C. Lawrence was once an economic mainstay of Winchester," an EPA administrator wrote four years ago. "Its old buildings are now dilapidated and a hazard to area kids, who appear to have set up a clubhouse there.") In 1994, the town took possession of the tract for unpaid taxes. In April 2001, on a Sunday morning walking tour organized by a local preservationist the week before the tannery was to be razed ("one last bittersweet tour," the local paper called it), Stephen Johnson and six others showed up.

There is nothing there today. Acres of baked dirt, what's left of some concrete foundations with weeds poking up through the cracks, a few dozen rotted barrels, some discarded wood pilings, a giant hulk of rusted machinery that looks as though it might once have housed a rotor or some gears—all of it behind a chain-link fence topped with barbed wire, just west of a narrow bridge that crosses the Ashuelot. Two unmovable boulders, the size of small trucks, block the road that leads to the bridge from Route 10. Under it, the river, steeply banked on both sides, is pale green and swirled with eddies; overhung with elm and hemlock, it flows south toward whiter water, then toward town.

MARTHA WEINMAN LEAR   "How Did It Go Today?"

Up here at the MacDowell Colony in Peterborough, New Hampshire, home of the true blue ice, we skidded one recent evening from our studios in the woods to the lounge in Colony Hall. By the great stone hearth, beneath the high-beamed ceiling, between the stout clapboard walls, within the encircling calm of towering pines, beyond which stretch meadows, hillocks, more towering pines, we raised a glass on the eightieth anniversary of his death to Edward MacDowell: composer, benefactor, granddaddy of all we survey.

Then we went in to dinner. We sat at three tables, the nineteen of us currently in residence—*colonists*, as we say: eight writers, five composers, six visual artists. We had beef stew. The vegetarians had bean-curd stew. (I have observed in repeated visits to MacDowell that most of the vegetarians are writers; I do not have, and do not think I want to have, an explanation.) We drank from half-gallon bottles of wine, amusing red or hilarious white, $4.29 at the local A&P. We talked:

How did it go today? we asked. Not bad, we said. And we did not mean the world. The world is elsewhere. I am not sure where it is, but it certainly isn't here. In recent weeks the presidential hopefuls, that foal-footed lot, were wimping and booting each other up and down these glassy hills, causing, I suppose, many a boo-boo, and they weren't here either. We did not know, we did not care, we would

Lunch, in wicker baskets, each with the studio name painted on the lid, is delivered silently to each artist's doorstep.

not have crossed the street to see. Even those of us normally addicted to a daily fix of toxic substance, news, don't know what's happening and do not give a damn.

How did it go today? Well, of course. It is the ski lodge question after the long hard day on the slopes, precisely that kind of obsession with performance, replayings of the weather, the conditions, the number of runs, the speed, the light, the nuances of style, the minute and crucial changes of technique, the rackings-up on moguls and the rare sweet high of a schuss. We are still grading ourselves on today and already planning—it is just 7:00 p.m.; we've not yet even begun our nightly revels of Ping-Pong—our strategies for tomorrow. We are stunned by our own capacities for obsession.

I have been in residence here four times in a ten-year period and each time worked like blazes. Most colonists do, most of the time. Once I stayed for two weeks and went home with forty new pages in my pocket, such a roll as I had never dreamed to get on. No one knows how we get on it, or how it gets on *us*, this rampant productivity, and everyone has a theory. There is talk of the goodness of country air. I do not buy this theory. I'll bet the countryside is littered with writers who are breathing well and working asthmatically. Another theory has to do with our distance, in all dimensions, from the dailiness of life. This one is much, much better. Imagine it:

You and your typewriter, your easel, your piano are in one of thirty-one studios scattered amid 450 acres of fields and woods, almost no studio remotely visible from any other, each in remarkably different style (the question of what all the *others* are like is a small, exquisite preoccupation at MacDowell and someone is forever trying to organize a house and garden tour, but there are resistances): a log cabin here, a fieldstone cottage there, a clapboard with a porch, a gingerbread house, a bit of snitched Tudor, a wee villa with Italianate arches of stone.

No one is going to drop by here for a cup of sugar. There are protocols here. You never visit any studio without an invitation. Lunch, in wicker baskets, each with a studio name hand painted on the lid—Phi Beta, Monday Music, Veltin, New Jersey, Star, Schelling, Mixter (I do not know from what or from whom these names derive; part of the charm is the mystery, the wood-shaded genealogy)—is delivered to each doorstep by gnomes who do not knock, do not whistle, just leave the basket and occasional replenishments of firewood and kindling and go off in pickup trucks that are utterly, miraculously silent, as though their tires wore booties. Fresh linens come once a week. Cleaning, so as not to disturb you, will be done only upon request, though not *unreasonable* request. "Once every two weeks," a discreetly posted note advises, "is not unreasonable." But few of us request it, preferring to pan our own dust for glintlets of gold. No telephone. (In Colony Hall, yes, but you are summoned only for emergencies.) No neighborhood errands, no business meetings, no benefit or community or protest meetings, Con Edison on hold, friends and family on hold, household on hold, all of that other endlessly demanding, infinitely distracting life on hold.

And I am sure that all of this cosseting opens us wide to our productivity. But there is something else at the core. It is the formalization of the commitment to produce. It is the basic efficaciousness of Weight Watchers, Smoke Enders, Alcoholics Anonymous, the Berlitz course, the exercise class, the subscription series, even, on occasion, the marriage license. Formalization of commitments.

A writer does not come here to have a writer's block. Not to deny or be respectful of the muse (muse, I swear, I'll respect you *plenty* afterward), it simply isn't done. In this New England climate, not parsimonious but spare, commendable frugal, a writer's block, which in New York is something to dine out on and bemoan in a boastful way, like New York itself, would be a frivolous shame and a waste. Work is what you come here to do. Work is what the others are doing, or at least trying to do; you don't see them, but *you know they are there*. You would feel out of place, out of synch, out of style not doing it. So you do it. There are exceptions, but no frivolous ones. They still speak here in funereal tones of the composer whose studio burned down, and a year's worth of work with it, and he went and sat in Colony Hall, just sat, catatonic, for days. It is the worst work story any of us could imagine. Yesterday the lights blew. It happens often here, with the ice weighing down the power lines, and always before it had engendered a certain festivity—Whee, school's out!—as the electric typewriter would suddenly die, and I would go for a walk or dream by the fire and once simply drove to Boston and spent a splendid afternoon in Filene's Basement. But now I have a computer. When a computer dies, it is different. My heart nearly died too. How much work—for I am a fool about backup files, saving, all that business—had been lost? Would I too be sitting, catatonic, in Colony Hall? Then the power came back, the scribbles came back on the screen intact, and I felt like closing shop for the day to celebrate. But that would have been, in that circumstance, a frivolous shame and a waste.

My studio is Watson, the most improbable of the lot. Uppity airs, pearl gray façade, white pillars all about, pilasters, flutings, portico, the works. It dates back to 1915, seven years after Edward MacDowell's death, eight years after he and his wife, Marian, a musician too, had established a country retreat for artists. God knows what epiphanic architectural moment dictated the creation of this little number, Greek temple out of Tara, beneath the New Hampshire pines. I know only that it was built in tribute to Regina Watson, a composer (1845–1913), whose friends footed the bill, and so (it is said) Marian MacDowell accepted in silence and in grace, although she found the design all wrong, far too grand, for this setting. She was absolutely right. I love it.

It is huge by MacDowell standards, a room roughly twenty by thirty feet, done in Impoverished Nobility: gilt chandelier, scratched but splendid concert grand, immense rococo worktable, sofa by the fireplace, reclining chair (torn, grungy, wonderful, sagging with the weight of a thousand ruminations), and in a corner, as in some corner of every studio, the tombstones.

The tombstones. Thick wooden plaques some twenty inches long and shaped just like that, they bear the names and dates of residence of all colonists. There are ten such plaques in Watson, going back to the 1920s. To read them is to smile bittersweet. Peering at the signatures, some as faint as old sepia in family albums and with the sense that they *are* family albums, I see that Elinore Wylie lived here in 1922; Louis Untermeyer in 1925; Padraic Colum and Mrs. H. H. A. Beach, a composer who never let go of her initials, visited often through the 1930s; the composer Margaret Starr McLain signed, "D-day, 1944!"; Nancy Hale and Mary Lee Settle came in the 1950s; Louise Varèse, James Baldwin, and Leonard Bernstein in the 1960s. In the 1970s they begin, as though wood is growing scarce, to sign both sides of the tombstones: Leonard Bernstein again, Michael Tilson Thomas ("musician-songplugger," he inscribes), the screenwriter Walter Bernstein, the poet Isabella Gardner, the writers Nora Sayre and Judith Thurman; and in the 1980s, Barbara Grizzuti Harrison, Meg Wolitzer, Romulus Linney, Tillie Olson, who writes: "Writer (?)." Hundreds of names.

I feel the pleasure of their communal presence when we gather for performances. We do this in the library, a fine stone building whose shelves are crammed with books written by colonists and typically inscribed: "For the MacDowell Colony, where this work was finally done, with affection and deepest gratitude." (No one has to attend the performances and everyone does. In these compactions of time and space and energy, we are one big shipboard romance. We support each other, applaud each other, make vows of lifelong devotion and even believe them. And some of these bonds, in fact, do endure; I have several that I cherish.)

One recent week Galway Kinnell read his poems and George Tsontakis played tapes of his music. The next week the poet Jean Valentine read, and the novelist Carole Maso. Then I read, and composers James Primosch and Mr. Tsontakis played, keyboard and strings, Mozart, Cole Porter, compositions of their own. We quit early, as usual, and went back to our digs to check out the inner-weather reports for tomorrow, but the melodies lingered on. *All* the melodies linger on. Sometimes here in Watson at night, I think I hear Bernstein humming. Lovely, Lenny, I say. How did it go today? Not bad, he says, not *bad*.

And Not So Well for Others
Dawn Powell

The MacDowell Colony isn't the right setting for every artist. Dawn Powell (1896–1965) was a brilliant comic novelist who was often overlooked in her day. Her novels of her Ohio birthplace and her adopted New York City have been rediscovered and republished in the Library of America.

Powell was at the Colony in June 1949 after a serious operation. She was struggling with a novel. She wrote to her husband:

I do not think—now that I am really well, as I seem to be—that I could endure this weird setup of rubbing your nose in whatever you're doing day and night with no change of scene or pace or face. It is a definite strain for so lax a person as myself to keep rigid 6 p.m. dinner hours—7:30–8:30 breakfast—and the politely veiled law of appearing at whatever reading or concert some egotistical colonist announces for the evening.

I was told one did exactly as one pleased about these matters and God knows how any normal person could stand the pace. Rap on tumbler at dinner and composer says, "I wish to announce *I* will play my concerto in the library tonight or my chorale for mixed bar and grill and all are welcome." At this point, Charles Norman inevitably springs to his feet, writhing with wounded ego, and says, "The following night *I* will read my poetry in the Watson Studio and all are welcome." "Welcome" simply means By God any colonist not showing is in the doghouse. Last night I discovered this when George Milburne and I innocently skipped the second rendering of an operetta about nymphs and shepherds by Lydia Pinkham's grandson and were found in Gatto's Italian Restaurant drinking beer and playing the jukebox. You would have thought we had defiled the reservoir—not for beer-drinking for they were all there doing that, but *they* had attended the concert. Now I see why they asked me three times if there was a mistake in my name's not being on list for going to see the Peterborough Players play *Blithe Spirit* Wednesday. By God, the colonists *always* attend that summer theater opening. No compulsion, naturally, but in case you change your mind, Miss Powell—

Also I talked to town people. No fraternizing, please.

Did you know MacDowell was off his rocker up here the last few years? I know why. There is a bird all over the place supposed to have inspired "To a Wild Rose" as it sings [its] first four notes. (I *would* say it was "From the Halls of Montezuma"—until frowned on and told it was the Wild Rose bird.) Well, this bird shrieks this from every tree and bush and after MacDowell had written the song (and very likely taught the bird to plug it) he wanted to do more profound work but the damn bird kept dinging away at his old popular hit till the poor man cracked. My theory is that Mrs. MacDowell started this place after his death to see how many other artists would be driven nuts by it, too.

Drawing Our Desires: The Endless Keene Bypass Controversy

WILLIAM CRAIG

Most maps lie about everything but roads.

As a picture of the world, your average map is abstract to the point of mendacity. The Ashuelot River, for example, with its pools and islands, side swamps and falls, is anything but a smooth blue line. Mount Monadnock, wrapped around in pleated ridges and valleys, is everything but a cross and an elevation number. And even the furthest fraction of a city such as Keene—even a hamlet such as Surry—can't be described by a dot.

But the black line of a road is an honest approximation.

Roads are that much an imposition of our will upon the landscape. A road—particularly a modern, asphalt highway—is a line drawn on the earth. Technology

Paving the "widest street in the world." Main Street Keene catches up with the automobile age, summer 1921.

enables that line to flow over, under, around, or through almost any geographic feature imaginable, from the Everglades to the English Channel. Ordinary obstacles, from hills to brooks to neighborhoods, are, practically speaking, no obstacles at all. Where the line is drawn—or where it is erased and drawn again, a few hundred or a few thousand feet this way or that, preserving or destroying this or that home, field, or farm—is not really a matter of geography or engineering. It is a question of desire.

In 1956, at a midday meeting in the gymnasium of what was then Keene Teachers College, engineers from New Hampshire's highway department told Governor Lane Dwinnell, members of the state Executive Council, and more than 350 locals why the city and its citizens should desire a network of new, big, better roads.

Keene is a city on the way to nowhere but itself. Its location at the bottom of a bowl of hills in the state's southwest corner is inconvenient to all the region's great, transforming interstate highways: I-93, I-89, I-91, I-90. But even in the early 1950s, New Hampshire's traffic engineers could foresee a time when Keene's can't-get-there-from-here isolation might create its own kind of chaos.

On any map, Keene's historic place at the heart of Cheshire County is as obvious as "X marks the spot." Like crossbones and skull, Routes 9, 10, 12, and 101 transpierce the city. Those routes are descendants of colonial-era turnpikes that snarled to form a settlement. In horse-drawn times, there was no drawback to having every important county road tie up in front of the courthouse; two early, outlying meetinghouses were even ox-pulled in to add to the crossroads' busyness. But by 1956, Keene's quaint centrality was causing trouble.

Automobile drivers could easily depart Cheshire County in any direction, but getting into or across it meant facing the delaying fact that all roads led through Keene. And once they got there, those roads didn't feed into an orderly grid of city blocks: the main routes still insisted on angling in to meet at (or just shy of) Central Square.

The postage-stamp-size park that had attracted a century and a half's bound-for-town, horse-and-buggy traffic was an absurdly inadequate axis for high-volume, pass-through auto traffic. Citizens attending that first informational meeting were already familiar with rush-hour traffic jams backing up West, Court, Washington, Main, and Winchester streets as commuters jockeyed around the square like Indy drivers banished to a midget track.

And because Keene's side streets meander, there was no hope of simply diverting traffic to the next numbered avenue, or declaring every other line on the grid one-way. From its signature square to its straggling back streets, the city's historic layout was inimical to automotive traffic. The situation was already bad, and much worse congestion was to come, the engineers warned, unless a "bypass" was built to swing just-passing-through cars around and away.

Of course, that wasn't the first these citizens had heard of such a plan. Years of site surveys and research had preceded the engineers' presentation. In 1955, a group of worried business owners called the Keene Service Associates had polled the 225 shops then operating in downtown Keene and found that 200 proprietors were opposed to the bypass. That year's city council passed a resolution against it.

Most of those who attended the meeting in the Teachers College gym on July 19, 1956, had probably already made up their minds.

Then, as now, those in favor of the bypass project were most impressed by the engineers' essential argument: a numerology of need, in which every new car in Cheshire County would emphasize the inadequacy of Keene's road net. Crowded streets and unsafe intersections were already causing delays for shoppers and school buses, commuters and fire trucks. How could Keene grow and prosper if the map of the city itself obstructed progress?

In 1956, progress was the promise of several supporting arguments. The Keene Regional Industrial Foundation spoke for those who foresaw that a bypass route would germinate manufacturing plants on the outskirts. Employees at these new businesses would get to work more easily. One Foundation member told the meeting that a bypass would bring back "the quiet streets of the past."

But that was just what worried the downtown merchants. They weren't comforted by some proponents' belief that a quieter, less congested city center would attract more shoppers. Citing the effects of bypasses on downtowns across the country, some feared they would lose 25 or even 50 percent of their trade. Tourists, impulse buyers, and hungry-on-the-way-home commuters were crucial customers: those shoppers needed to see the storefront to discover their desires. Bypassers, the merchants insisted, were not the same as passersby.

Other critics wondered whether the inevitable development of industries and shopping malls along the new out-of-town roads wasn't the real point of the whole bypass business. One Keene attorney called the project nothing more than that archetypal American enterprise, "a land-development scheme." And those opposed included some who couldn't imagine what all the fuss was about. Anyone who wanted to know the true meaning of traffic troubles ought to try driving in New York or Boston.

Nevertheless, the first round of New Hampshire's epic infrastructural fracas went to the engineers. The 1956 city council contradicted its predecessor and voted approval. Mayor J. Alfred Dennis, the planning board, and the Chamber of Commerce joined industries including American Optical, Markem, and Miniature Precision Bearings in endorsing the plan's first phase, which laid down more than ten miles of asphalt to braid and extend Routes 10, 9, and 12, creating a new, wide way to swing below the city and link up with Route 101.

The six-million-dollar, 2.4-mile project did much to streamline traffic to the west and south. If you look at a map of the southwest corner of the city, it's easy to see how the first phase—and many subsequent elaborations—drew a good deal of traffic out of the downtown. Travelers from Westmoreland and Winchester no longer needed to putter down Keene's Main Street on their way to Peterborough or Jaffrey. Workers from a host of outlying hamlets could skip town on their way to jobs in the new industrial parks.

Perhaps it was a coincidence or a direct result, but the city suffered the same

Construction on the Route 9 bypass of Granite Lake in Nelson. Many routes converge in Keene. The city, designed in colonial times to draw all visitors inward, scribbles bypasses and detours around its horse-and-buggy heart.

death-of-downtown syndrome that afflicted highway-hooked Manchester, Lebanon, and Berlin—not to mention Boston, Detroit, and Los Angeles.

Many other factors, from postwar affluence and the baby boom (both factors impelling a rush toward suburban home ownership) to television's shut-in gestalt have been blamed for that plague-like emptying of inner cities, from which many have yet to fully recover.

Whatever the cause, it can't be denied that, for Keene's shopkeepers, the years after the initial bypass completion were far worse than the most dire fears articulated at the 1956 meeting. Score upon score of the old businesses gave up, and at times the empty storefronts and upstairs offices seemed to outnumber the occupied. Yet the traffic that still needed to move through town could sometimes clog Main, Winchester, Washington, and other key streets at rush hour.

Meanwhile, out of town, the new routes attracted enough industry and sprouted enough strip development to generate traffic problems of their own. As the region's population grew, and its road net still steered all cross-county traffic toward (though no longer always through) Keene, travel along the bypass gradually became tedious and frustrating in its own right.

Back through decades of the *Keene Sentinel*, there's not a year since the mid-1950s in which traffic, construction, and some iteration of "the bypass controversy" don't make headlines.

In each decade, the highway department and later its successor, the Department of Transportation, returned with a plan for the next phase of the fix. At each presentation, engineers maintained that their latest plan—the map with black lines drawn just precisely here, just this straight and just this wide—was the best possible solution. Traffic studies, geographic facts, and engineering experience made each ink stroke inevitable and immovable.

But with each presentation, an increasingly well-organized opposition demanded more information and more sway. To their original concern for downtown business, opponents added consideration of noise and safety factors, the unity of neighborhoods, and the integrity of the ecosystems the engineers proposed to disrupt. And sometimes, when the opposition hollered loud enough, the engineers moved the lines.

Such responsiveness, such sensitivity to local concerns, was of course commendable in a state agency. But it also suggested that each new plan, presented as a unique and optimal response to Keene's particular problems, was in fact just bureaucratic boilerplate: lines drawn in the obvious places, in the usual way.

Over the decades, many of these theoretical lines were moved, or even erased, because some people desired changes more than the Department of Transportation cared to fight them. Significant amendments were made to the eight-million-dollar, mid-1970s project that tidied up Route 9's progress through the city's northern neighborhoods. And a 1980s proposal to expand Route 10 was defeated because conservationists objected to its route through wetlands.

Opposition groups amplified the implication: if the plans could be changed by desire, how inevitable were the engineers' readings of the landscape, their interpretations of statistics, and their theories of traffic management? How valid their assumption that the way to cope with more cars was to keep building more roads? Who could say with certainty that the DOT engineers weren't causing as much trouble as they claimed to cure?

According to Anne Faulkner, a past president of the Concerned Cheshire Citizens—at century's end, the most important civic group opposing the Department of Transportation—the state's definition of progress has always been "bigger, faster and wider. Is that really progress, or do we have other measures, like safety, lower fuel emissions, aesthetics and the pace of life? Is there a way to improve traffic that doesn't involve the 'bigger, wider, faster' model?"

The Concerned Cheshire Citizens, working in alliance with the Conservation Law Foundation, mounted a tenacious and partly effective defense against the "final" and most tremendous phase of the DOT's plan for relieving Keene's worse-than-ever congestion. Budgeted at more than $75 million, this project took a classic interstate-era, biggest-is-best approach to the problems of the overwhelmed original bypass. A tangle of cloverleafs and loops looking, on paper, like Celtic macramé, the plan featured twenty-six lane-miles of pavement, three thirty-foot-high overpasses, the asphalting of twenty-nine acres along Route 101, and the destruction of at least thirty acres of wetlands.

These swampy acres gave the CLF firm enough footing to wrestle the DOT all the way to New Hampshire's Supreme Court. The lawsuit stopped the project dead from 2001 to 2004, giving the Concerned Cheshire Citizens time to raise public awareness of the plan's gigantism. They touted the greater safety and lesser economic and environmental impacts associated with more modest "roundabout" interchanges, and championed the wetlands' vernal pools, habitat crucial to numerous wildlife species. Meanwhile, the implications of a possible courtroom defeat held up DOT projects around the state.

Though the judges eventually sided with the engineers, transportation policymakers had gotten the message: bigger isn't better when it's politically impossible to build. In a compromise plan announced in March 2004, the state gave up—for a few years, at least—on freeway-style interchanges, including the sprawling "trumpet" configuration at the meetings of Routes 9, 10, 12, and 101. Lane widening and a possible roundabout would ease traffic until about 2012, engineers projected, when gridlock would again demand megasolutions—and the "trumpet" and other currently unacceptable proposals might win approval. In the meantime, however, the state promised to give thorough consideration to environmental impacts and alternative engineering concepts.

The Keene bypass controversy has already been around longer than many major elements of New Hampshire's civic scene. It has lasted longer than William Loeb's ownership of the *Manchester Union-Leader*, and much longer than the no-broad-based-taxes "Pledge." It is only four years younger than the "beauty contest" format that made the first-in-the-nation primary a truly national event. There has been a Keene bypass controversy longer than there have been fifty states, and since before there was a Cuban embargo. The bypass fight has lasted longer than the Cold War, longer than all America's shooting wars laid end to end. The country's first railroad was built at Quincy, Massachusetts, in 1826, and the golden spike linking East and West coasts was pounded down in 1869 at Promontory Summit, Utah—a span of forty-three years, five less than the bypass dilemma has lasted so far.

Even alternative engineering concepts aren't likely to resolve what is, essentially, a confrontation between the sprawling imperatives of the automobile age and the community focus of Keene's original design—the in-drawing, X-marks-the-gathering-spot map of traditional communities everywhere.

Keene's version was especially strong and beautiful, and is still lovely enough to have been named, in 2003, one of "America's Dozen Distinctive Destinations" by the National Trust for Historic Preservation. Ironically, the Trust cited "the city's well-managed growth . . . and walkability for residents and visitors," suggesting that its judges ignored the outside strip's wild growth, and never noticed downtown traffic so bad that residents fear fire trucks can't reach their homes during rush hours. The city's old-fashioned, narrow-streeted, axial layout started causing trouble as soon as the last Cheshire County household sold its horse, and will do so until four-lane roads cut across the arms of the antique "X" in every direction, scratching out the city the Trust praised as "a truly distinctive slice of America."

But even that sacrifice won't solve the traffic problem. The miles of asphalt already laid around Keene have only lured more manufacturers, more jobs, more stores, more shoppers, more residents, more cars. With half-million-dollar starter-home prices down in flatland pushing ever more quality-of-life refugees into Cheshire County, it may never be possible to build bypass roads big enough, quickly enough to handle the traffic they attract.

Could there be hope in the antithesis? If the DOT stopped building bigger bypass roads, and no more megastores were built, would traffic statistics in Keene's strip zone eventually stabilize? Being willing to live with only as many megastores as existing roads can handle—even being willing to buy up and tear down some stores in order to bring traffic levels down—might give Keene (and the state) control over an otherwise self-perpetuating problem.

And it might cost a great deal less than $75 million.

As for downtown Keene, the antithesis to more automobile-accommodating destruction could be to make no more concessions to horseless carriages. In Europe, keeping cars out of historic city cores obviously unsuitable for auto traffic is common practice. Pedestrian zones in cities such as Boston, Burlington, Montreal, and San Antonio have become must-see destinations. Valuing preservation above "progress" might even be a lucrative investment.

Which brings us back to maps, to recognizing roads' black lines as the tracery of cultural desires. After half a century of crosshatching the map with vain attempts to appease the automobile, perhaps Keene's citizens should be expressing their wants with the other end of the pencil: limiting and, where possible, even erasing acres of asphalt. But if its leaders and voters don't desire to question essential premises of our automotive culture, the city designed in colonial times to draw all visitors inward will just have to go on scribbling bypass barriers, scrawling detours around its horse-and-buggy heart.

The Last Train Out of Town
John R. Harris

Railroad travel, reaching its heyday about 1920, had seemed so permanent a
part of our economy and way of life for so long that now its passing away makes
us wonder if indeed anything is permanent, or what the future may hold.
—Heman Chase, 1967

Barry Faulkner mural.

Muralist Barry Faulkner captured the carnival-like atmosphere of shooting cannons and marching bands to celebrate the arrival of the first train in Keene on May 16, 1848. The Cheshire Railroad Company spent four years and an estimated $2,500,000 to complete the line between Fitchburg, Massachusetts, and Bellows Falls, Vermont. The arrival of the "iron horse" from Boston twice a day solidified Keene's reputation as the industrial hub of the Monadnock region.

The railroad transformed the landscape of the Monadnock region as well as the imaginations of those who lived there. Trestles, tunnels, overpasses, and culverts were constructed to minimize steep grades and connect centers of commerce. Time and progress was measured by the sound of the locomotive.

The arrival of the railroad created winners and losers, as industries and municipalities competed for connections to the existing rail lines. Cities like Keene struggled to accommodate a maze of tracks and sidings for loading and unloading freight, while towns that were bypassed, like Stoddard and Roxbury, quickly began to wither.

The railroad magnified disasters as well as successes. On July 17, 1897, J. A.

The wreck at Pemberton crossing.

French photographed the wreck of freight train number 216 at Pemberton crossing in West Keene. According to the *Keene Sentinel*, "no gala day or celebration ever drew more people to West Keene than the railroad wreck on Saturday." An estimated five thousand people visited the site where engineer Milan Curtis was killed and where more than five hundred pigs escaped from their overturned cars into the nearby woods.

Throngs of spectators greeted the arrival of the streamlined Flying Yankee in April 1935. Powered by a six-hundred-horsepower diesel-electric engine, and capable of speeds in excess of sixty miles an hour, the Flying Yankee became a regular feature of the region, and was later renamed the Cheshire in 1944.

The long demise of the railroad in the Monadnock region took place in two stages: first, beginning in 1958, passenger trains were taken out of service; and then, in the 1970s, freight trains began to disappear. Harold Larro, one of the last men to operate the local trains in 1980, recalls what the last days of railroading in the region were like.

"The Boston and Main came up through Brattleboro and Hinsdale at the time, and they dropped off and picked up cars in downtown Keene on Tuesday and Saturday. Just two of us were responsible for all the freight work. Switching the load off the main track, pulling individual cars into sidings . . . replacing ties, clearing ice, checking the condition of the goods, and cutting brush. There were only six crossings left open when I worked: Island Avenue, Winchester Street, School Street—there was two crossings there, Main Street, and Water Street. And there were no lights at most of these crossings, so the conductor would get out and flag the crossing to halt automobile traffic. The train moved slowly—maybe ten or five miles an hour.

"You could surmise that the end was near. . . . Convenience was the main advantage of trucking. Your truck could deliver right to the manufacturer's or customer's door, where with a train you would have to switch it out, or wait for a car to come in, and they'd get lost or mixed up in the yard somewhere, and be late. Except for a couple of old trainmen, most people in Keene didn't seem to care much about the loss of the railroad in 1980."

The Flying Yankee.

GERALD BURNS

Quiet Boomtown

When Roland Goddard, longtime resident and former municipal official of Rindge, celebrated his one hundredth birthday recently, he was asked his opinion on the state of the town now. "Rindge is looking pretty good," Rollie replied, and immediately added: "It's changing. I don't know anybody anymore. The town has got so many more people." Many more people it has, certainly than Mr. Goddard could have expected when he began his service to the town. Since 1950, Rindge has grown far more rapidly than any community in the Monadnock region, and recent projections indicate it will continue to grow over the next twenty years faster than every town of any size in the area.

If it has been largely unexpected, this growth has also been not all that obvious. Rindge has hidden its population bulges from eyes less knowing than Rollie Goddard's.

In the late 1980s, at the peak of the increase, with residential construction taking place at a "phenomenal" rate, the manager of the first major grocery store scheduled to locate in Rindge is said to have stood at the town's principal intersection and called out, "Where are all the people?" Yet when the grand opening of the store took place in 1990, those people materialized in numbers that overwhelmed management's preparations. Within a year or two the Rindge Market Basket had become the second-highest profit earner in the company's New England chain.

The story of Rindge becoming the region's quiet boomtown begins in 1945. As of that date, there was little reason to expect growth in the community: none had occurred for 120 years. Population had declined more or less steadily from

Houses are selling faster than they're being built, and "before the last nail is pounded in, people are waiting out front in their cars, with their suitcases, ready to move in," said one resident.

a high of nearly 1,300 in 1820 to just a little above 600. The caption on a photograph of an old homestead, in a Rindge Board of Trade brochure produced a few years earlier, must have captured the feeling many had about the town itself: "Sweet but Abandoned. Monadnock Still Stands By." A study undertaken by the State Planning and Development Commission in 1945 delivered the bad news bluntly. Rindge was in decline, and the prospects for industry and agriculture, the two mainstays of local economic activity in the past, were bleak. The only hope for "advantageous development," the study advised, lay with residential development. The community needed to capitalize on its scenic beauty, strategic location, and abundance of available homes and home sites in order to regain vitality.

Whether this report provided a practical blueprint or merely proved prophetic, residential growth did come to Rindge. The takeoff did not happen immediately. Peter Eleftheriou, whose family has run a restaurant in town for many years, remembers that in 1962 new home construction was such a rare event that local kids would rally with the cry, "Come on, let's go watch them build a house!" But eventually momentum began to build. Between 1950 and 2000 the population of Rindge rose from 707 to 5,451, an increase of 670 percent, by far the highest rate of expansion anywhere in the Monadnock region (the nearest contender is Sharon, at 437 percent). Granted, part of this increase came from the founding of Franklin Pierce College, whose students are counted as part of the town's total in the census. But the lion's share of population growth in Rindge came between 1970 and 1990, when the college students had been absorbed into the town's base. During that period, the rate of increase continued to lead the region. In the 1980s alone, while that doubting-Thomas manager wondered where the people were, the housing stock in town nearly doubled, and the Planning Board was forced to meet as often as twice a week to consider building permit and subdivision requests.

An abandoned homestead in a shrinking town. Population in Rindge had declined from a high of nearly 1,300 in 1820 to about 600 in 1945.

Over the early 1990s this residential activity slowed dramatically—"You couldn't give a piece of land away," recalls a realtor—but commercial development picked up the slack. The Market Basket Plaza, Wal-Mart, and Hannaford's all opened along Route 202 during this period. What's more, beginning in the late 1990s and continuing into the new century, residential growth has accelerated again. Office of State Planning projections now show Rindge with a population of 7,030 in the year 2020, an increase of 24 percent since 2000, a rate exceeding that of New Ipswich and all other area towns but one (a smaller community, somewhat difficult to compare).

This remarkable expansion, which fits an emerging national pattern of "low-density growth in outlying places," has brought many benefits to Rindge. Recall the first words in Rollie Goddard's appraisal: "[The town] is looking pretty good." The influx of new residents has fulfilled the hope of the 1945 report, reversing the historic trend of depopulation and injecting new money, skills, and vitality into the community. Few now would be likely to describe Rindge as "abandoned." From a backwater, the town has moved into the mainstream of American economic and social development. It had been there before only during the early, waterpower phase of the Industrial Revolution and, prior to that, during the period of agricultural settlement that founded the town.

Recent developments appear to recapture something of the spirit of the first population boom here, which brought over a thousand settlers in the span of several decades following the Revolution. John Herbers, a leading prophet of today's trend, speaks of the rush to outlying places as the latest manifestation of a frontier psychology, characterized by the desire for "independence and space," and by a deep-seated American yearning for a "new life in a new place." By this token, the most recent arrivals in Rindge may be seen to be following in the footsteps of the first settler, Abel Platts, and the other pioneers who pushed into the wilderness of "Monadnock Number One" (the settlement's original name) in the eighteenth century.

At the same time, the new growth is also deeply problematic. What some call "low-density" development looks suspiciously like "sprawl" to others. Under either name, it poses serious issues for Rindge. True, this type of settlement proceeds with much less visible disruption of the landscape than suburban development (and this is why Rindge has been able to hide much of its recent growth from casual observation). But it tends to take place in relatively unspoiled—and therefore relatively easily spoiled—natural areas. Offering "scenic beauty" to attract new residents may turn out to be a devil's bargain. The impetus behind low-density development is "people putting space between themselves," Herbers observes. The result has been what he calls the "big new spread-out small town," a pattern of settlement "diffused, fragmented, without a center." How then do people come together, and how do they focus their efforts for common purposes?

What is at stake in this locally flooding tide of low-density growth is nothing less than the character of Rindge, as a place and a community. Can it accommodate these many private visions of a good life lived on a broad margin, close to nature, without sacrificing the integrity of its natural resources, without losing

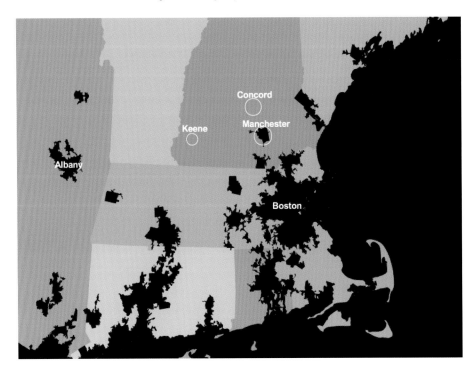

Ruralburbia. As people push north with the old frontier hunger for new places, southwest New Hampshire is becoming a suburb sprawling in the woods. The new pattern of settlement is "diffused, fragmented, without a center." Population in 1990 is at left; population in 2000 is at right. Note the spread of the densely populated areas.

its small-town feel? This is not just a question of policy but one for individuals who have been caught up in the changes facing the town.

Audrey and David Tetreault left a congested area of Connecticut for the seemingly wide-open spaces of Rindge in the early 1970s, becoming part of the first wave of "low-density" migrants to arrive in town. They quit their jobs, liquidated their assets, and built a one-room cabin, where they lived without electricity for ten years. They came for privacy and solitude—"anonymity, really," David says—and for a time their forty-three acres of woods and cow path of a road succeeded in putting plenty of space between themselves and others.

Some time in the early 1980s, things began to change. An old farm on the road went up for sale, making room for ten houses. Some of the new neighbors displayed an inclination to treat the forty-three acres as their own, ripping around the property in a snowmobile, among other trespasses. The Tetreaults were twice robbed during this time. There have not been, to their way of thinking, any improvements lately. Another, even larger subdivision is opening at the far end of their road. The units are selling faster than they're being built, and "before the last nail is pounded in, people are waiting out front in their cars, with their suitcases, ready to move in."

Asked if they have met any of the new people, Audrey and David answer no, not recently. And in the past, meetings tended to occur only in the case of an encroachment—that is, unless the interlopers met the Tetreaults' 110-pound German shepherd first. In any case, the "people who are coming in don't want the same things we do," says Audrey. Asked if they have ever attempted action to stop or slow the growth, they indicate they've appeared before the Planning Board, but have found that in the end it does no good. "Special interests rule . . . the population has drastically increased . . . the town of Rindge will literally choke itself."

The Rindge meetinghouse, built in 1796, marks the old center of town. It is one of the few in the state that is still divided between church and public use.

And they have had enough. Their home and property are up for sale. They plan to move to Washington, New Hampshire, where their daughter owns land at the top of a mountain, and where, according to David, no one is likely to locate a Wal-Mart. "What we came for is gone," Audrey says, with a catch in her voice. "We'll look for new horizons." (In December 2004 Audrey passed away in their new home in Washington.)

In the big new subdivision at the other end of the road from the Tetreaults, one of the first units to be completed is the new home of Ed and Susan Valcourt. While they haven't mentioned anything about waiting out in the road with suitcases, they did move into their sizable modern Colonial as soon as it was habitable. And it is clear that they, and their five-year-old, Elizabeth, are thrilled to be here.

Ed and Susan had been living in Pepperell, Massachusetts, and working in Nashua, New Hampshire, which both found depressingly overdeveloped. They find Rindge a refreshing change. Ed, in particular, likes the "whole layout" here, the "scenery, the woods, the mountain views." He enjoys being in the woods— could live off the land, he says—and relishes the opportunity for hiking, fishing, and bow hunting straight out from his front door. A pair of high-powered ATVs, stored behind one of the doors of their three-car garage, will add another dimension of outdoor recreation, come good weather. Susan's explanation for why the family ended up here has a slightly different emphasis. She likes it rural, "but not too rural"; she's glad for the supermarkets nearby. She also mentions the factors of more affordable housing prices and quality schools. Both husband and wife concur on the importance of Elizabeth's education in their decisions, and both express regret that local voters turned down a recent proposal for a new high school.

Does the couple plan to get involved in town affairs? Ed looks a bit pressed: he's busy all week, commutes an hour each way to Nashua, and has many weekends blocked out to work on the house. For her part, Susan has taken a break from working while the family gets settled. Although this might seem a recipe for social isolation, she has already enrolled Elizabeth in a playgroup sponsored by the town's Recreation Department, and is meeting other moms through that.

Susan worries, though: has the population here been increasing as fast as some have said? In fact, she has already answered her own question, by mentioning that all eight of the mothers she's met through the playgroup have moved in from Massachusetts within the past three years. But the discussion leads on to a consideration of how much development might be too much for the Valcourts, cause them to flee Rindge as they've just fled the Nashua area. Susan has seen her once-rural hometown of Acton, Massachusetts, completely transformed, where among other things a high-quality school system served as a magnet for new families. She makes it clear she does not want that experience repeated. Ed is concerned by the commercial development along Route 202; he's seen busy strips come into existence in the bat of an eye in Nashua. He also casts a wary glance at the hundreds of acres held by a wealthy property owner near the subdivision. If these were to sell, "there would be a

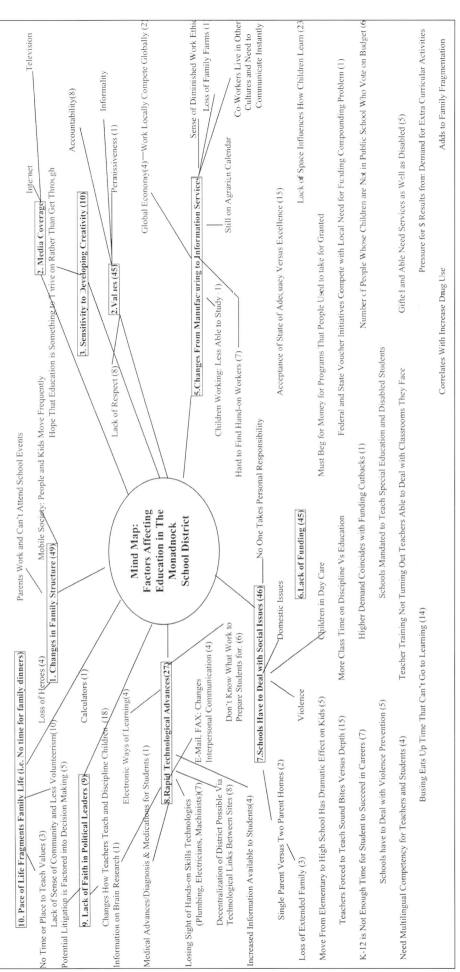

The Mind of the Monadnock School District, 1999. A modern maze. In April 1999, the Monadnock Regional School District took on the twenty-first century. One hundred and sixty people met to plan the district's future. At one point, they were asked to identify the issues that affect schooling. These were written on a large sheet of paper, leaving us with a time capsule of the worries of one school district at the end of the last century.

lot of new houses going up"; and if that were to happen, "I would move on, just like that."

Unless a certain ATV and a certain German shepherd have a run-in somewhere in the woods linking their properties, the Tetreaults and the Valcourts may well never meet each other. But what they want is not so different, after all. They share the frontier psychology that pushes Americans to start over in new places. In this way they are like the town's first settlers.

But if the frontier spirit has proved invaluable in creating and more recently reenergizing the community, it also carries certain liabilities. For one thing, the arriving "pioneers" tend to bring with them, like seeds clinging to their clothes from the more settled territory they've departed, habits and expectations that go to reproduce the very conditions they are seeking to escape. For another, the famed frontier impulse "to move . . . to occupy unoccupied places" typically becomes an inclination to "move *on*," as Ed Valcourt puts it, when the once-unoccupied place begins to fill up. A cycle gets established that is hard to break. Thus both couples, fleeing congestion where they lived, became part of the boom that has made Rindge the fastest-growing community in its area. The Tetreaults' "new horizon," the now-small hamlet of Washington, turns out to be the one town in the Monadnock region projected to grow more rapidly than Rindge over the next two decades. The view from the top of their daughter's mountain may yet include a Wal-Mart.

One way of counteracting this cycle, an antidote to the excesses of the frontier spirit, is to be found in Scott Russell Sanders's ground-breaking book *Staying Put*. Sanders makes a case for the environmental, social, and spiritual benefits of remaining in a place, even as it comes to be fully "occupied." One Rindge resident who embodies this stance is Debbie Sawyer.

Debbie predates the low-density boom, having come with her parents to live in a cabin on the shore of Lake Monomonac in the 1950s. She and her husband, Kevin, also a local product, did jump onto the bandwagon in the late 1980s when they built a roomy Cape on six acres for themselves and their two sons. Rollie Goddard laments that he doesn't know anyone in Rindge anymore, but Deb Sawyer, whose neighborly instincts were also formed in an earlier era, and who remains active in practically everything that goes on in town (outside of politics, which she tries to stay clear of), knows lots of her fellow residents, and their stories, too.

Deb takes her interviewer on a driving tour of Rindge's back roads. "That's new!" she exclaims, time and again, as a big new home in the $300,000 range looms into view from its clearing in the woods. "Haven't seen this before," as she wheels into a freshly cut subdivision access road. While Deb's general response to the new is to greet it with a welcoming wave, her comments do strike more pensive notes. "Kevin and I canoed in that brook down there once. The hill on the other side used to be solid green before those houses went in. My friend Mary and I sometimes walked this road [which happens to be the Tetreaults' road], but not anymore; the traffic goes too fast for it to be safe."

Changes coming closer to home are especially unsettling. Stopping for coffee at her house, she gestures to the area out back. It has always offered an uninterrupted woodland view, but somewhere out there a logging operation is going on; a makeshift road has been put in; building lots will likely be made available. Deb jokes about starting a whispering campaign, exaggerating the smells from a restaurant not far from the lots, in order to discourage potential buyers.

The moment seems right for a stock question about leaving Rindge. But first a setup, which should be cut-and-dried, given all the evidence of transformation she herself has pointed to: Do you think Rindge will be able to stay the small, beautiful town that you grew up and raised your family in? The answer, though, doesn't follow the script: "Yes, I think it will." The words are measured, come in a tone of gentle conviction. They have been preceded by a call from a friend, wanting to know where the two will walk that afternoon; it seems there are still roads in town safe and pleasant to stroll down. Apparently, Debbie Sawyer's acceptance of the new is anchored in her faith in the essential endurance of the old. Somehow the question about leaving never gets asked.

Unquestionably sincere, is the faith of this longtime resident in the unchanging character of her town well placed? It's worth noting that no less a local partisan than the Cape Cod writer Robert Finch once held a similar belief about his home community. But the ravages of "human change" have left him disillusioned. "There is a point," Finch writes in his essay "The Once and Future Cape," "a very definite and noticeable point in our relationship with a place, when . . . we begin to be convinced, against our very wills, that our neighborhood, our town, or the land as a whole is already lost, that what is left is not some viable and salvageable entity, but merely a collection of remnants no longer worth saving."

Will Rindge reach such a point of no return? For the Tetreaults, of course, it already has. For the Valcourts and Debbie Sawyer, it has not, and they are counting, each in their own way, that it will not. Yet it appears that neither of their fundamental instincts, for moving on or staying put, is in itself sufficient to avoid this fate for the town. Perhaps another approach is needed in Rindge, one that somehow owns the strength and even the necessity of these opposing orientations, yet goes beyond them in actively reckoning with the challenges of growth.

Enter Maryann Harper. Like the Tetreaults and the Valcourts, Maryann came to Rindge in 1981 seeking a "new life in a new place." She and her husband, Bill, were members of a group associated with the philanthropist John Hunt, who had selected the community as the site of an experiment in "green" living. "We were hippies," Maryann cheerfully concedes.

Culturally distinct from the ordinary run of Rindge residents, and physically set apart in the group's reserve atop "Hunt Hill," Maryann did not have her first dealings with the town did until 1983 or 1984. This was about the time the Tetreaults noticed big changes occurring and the Planning Board was proposing to limit the number of building permits issued. She and Bill, who was getting his start in the construction business, were about ready to build their own home, and they objected to the proposed restriction. As a countermove, Maryann ran for, and won, election to the Board.

The "Growth Management Ordinance" was a dead letter by the time she assumed her seat. But her experience changed her outlook in two key respects. First, she had moved from the periphery to the center of town affairs, and the experience led her to identify strongly with the larger community—to feel herself a citizen of Rindge for the first time. She won a position on the Select Board in 1988. Second, in the course of processing the mounting volume of development-related applications, Maryann became convinced, after all, of the need for some kind of growth management. She helped craft the town's "Phased Development Ordinance" and a moratorium on requests for new subdivisions.

She began to get increasingly out front on the issue, especially from her seat on the Select Board. She found herself resisting what she regarded as excessive pressure from the development interests in town. Push came to shove with the proposal for the first new major retail enterprise along Route 202, Market Basket Plaza. Strongly opposed to certain aspects of the plan, but finding herself increasingly without support from other officials and the public, Maryann "finally half gave in," and construction went forward. With this episode, she also burned out, pulling back from public office and public life for much of the 1990s.

Asked whether she could imagine leaving Rindge someday, Maryann pauses before answering: yes, she could. She's worried about the current pace of residential building and concerned that an attempt to offset its tax implications by encouraging business development might lead to chain-reaction growth such as towns in other regions have experienced. In addition, Rindge is no longer the same small town she quickly made her way to the heart of twenty years ago; it seems to her that people are finding it increasingly difficult to connect with each other. To top it off, she's getting a little tired of waiting up to five minutes for traffic that scarcely existed before, in order to cross Route 202 from Hunt Hill Road.

To date, however, these misgivings have prompted Maryann not to flee but to reenter the fray. She has recently become active in town affairs once again, most notably playing a leading role in "Rindge 2020," a joint effort with Franklin Pierce College to plan for the community's future. In addition, she's begun to voice her impatience with certain town policies, such as the absence of any significant impact fees for new construction, that may be aiding the recent resurgence in residential development. Her renewed activism has led to new strains, as longtime friends in government react to what they perceive as personal criticism. The strains leave her wondering, once more, whether the town can keep growing and yet still be a place she loves.

New Hampshire by the Numbers (2003)

POPULATION: New Hampshire is the fastest-growing state in New England and among the ten fastest in the United States with an average 1 percent growth per year. Eighty-five percent of the growth is concentrated in the southeastern part of the state—only one-third of the total land area. The state's population has doubled since 1950, and may triple by 2020. New Hampshire ranks fourth in the nation in attracting new residents from other states.

LAND USE AND SPRAWL: Each New Hampshire resident effectively occupies one-third more land area for housing, schools, shopping, roads, and other uses than twenty years ago, resulting in major losses of natural areas and widespread sprawl development. Over 150,000 acres were converted to developed uses between 1982 and 1997, a 37 percent increase in total developed land area in just fifteen years.

FORESTS: Forest cover has been declining steadily in New Hampshire for the past two decades. Between 1983 and 1997, development consumed almost 3 percent of the forest area, which is currently shrinking by 9,600 acres (0.2 percent) each year. Floodplain forests have almost been eliminated, and pine barrens are dramatically reduced.

WATER: Water use has increased much more rapidly than the state's population. All of the state's surface water is currently considered contaminated by mercury and is covered by fish-consumption advisories.

BIODIVERSITY AND WILDLIFE: Historically, twenty-four species of plants and animals have been eliminated from New Hampshire. The most recent was the Karner blue butterfly in 2001, from habitat loss. Over one-third of New Hampshire's wildlife habitat is at risk from global warming, and several species, including the purple finch (New Hampshire's state bird), are threatened by climate change.

FISHERIES: Mercury pollution and acid rain have contaminated most inland freshwater fisheries in New Hampshire, while habitat loss and overfishing have severely depleted coastal fisheries.

AGRICULTURE: In the fifteen years prior to 1997, New Hampshire lost 15 percent of its cropland.

ENERGY: New Hampshire is more reliant on oil (the burning of which creates greenhouse gas emissions) and nuclear power (with issues of long-term safety and potential health risk) than the national average. Transportation is the largest energy-consumption sector, and the state's sprawling development is increasing vehicle dependence.

CLIMATE CHANGE: Global warming scenarios project that New Hampshire's average annual temperature could increase by six to ten degrees Fahrenheit before 2100. New Hampshire could become as warm as Allentown, Pennsylvania, or Asheville, North Carolina, are now. Global warming threatens the state's economic activities, including ski tourism, fall foliage viewing, and maple sugaring.

ACID RAIN: New Hampshire, like the rest of New England and eastern Canada, receives some of the highest amounts of acid deposition in North America.

SOLID WASTE: The state has the highest per capita rate of solid waste disposal in the Northeast. In 1999, New Hampshire generated over 1.3 million tons of solid waste, an average of almost six pounds per person per day.

—*Sources*: Center for Environment and Population,
National Wildlife Foundation

RICHARD OBER

Is There a Monadnock Land Ethic?

In the Monadnock region, the grand mountain is ubiquitous. Drive around a corner or crest a hill and there it is, etched against the sky. No other landmark in the state, with the exception of the fragile and now-fallen Old Man, is so recognizable or emblematic. It defines our sense of place. It says "home."

But think twice about this. The landscape that shapes our lives is not the view of the mountain; it is the view from the mountain. Isn't what we see from the summit a more honest reflection of our ever-changing relationship with the land? Hasn't this always been the case?

Imagine, for instance, what a Jaffrey farmer of 1830 would have seen if he could have spared the time to climb to the top. Corrugated hills flowing west to the Connecticut River, and north, ever steeper, to the White Mountains. To the east and south a gentler plain, lowering to the Merrimack River and the sea. All but the wettest and steepest places cleared of forest, civilized by crop and

hoof, checkered with stone walls. Two-track dirt roads, muddy and furrowed by wagon wheels, connecting villages. No railroad tracks, no pavement, few smokestacks.

Although the region had effectively been settled by Europeans only a half century earlier, the pastoral landscape of 1830 was predominantly a human artifact, shaped out of necessity by a favorite New England archetype: Thomas Jefferson's resourceful, reverent yeoman farmer striving for self-sufficiency. With ax and oxen and flame he had tamed the wilderness. Life was the daily and seasonal cycle of cutting trees, burning stumps, milling wood, picking stones, building walls, plowing ground, planting seeds, harvesting crops, birthing and slaughtering livestock. When he was too old, his sons literally took up the yoke. From the wild they had created a garden, and there was no reason to think this one wouldn't last. "Buildings and fences they constructed as if to last forever," write the historians Ron and Grace Jager, "as if every farm established would be a farm forever, as if they had no inkling at all that the land was perverse and resilient enough to retrieve these fields from their grandchildren and restore them to forests again."

Resilient the land was, and how it would pain our farmer of the 1830s to see the view from the mountain today. The walls are still there, as are the streams and rivers, but they are obscured by an overstory of forest. Fields stand out as

By the time Alfred started the Sawyer Farm in the mid–nineteenth century, the world was closing in. The age of self-sufficiency was passing, and the brief sheep craze that transformed much of the region to pasture had crested and crashed.

random ornaments in the fabric, rather than as the fabric itself. He would question what had happened to the land ethic of his time—stewarding the earth to procure shelter and food, and in so doing commending oneself to Heaven. For as Jefferson said, "Those who labor in the earth are the chosen people of God." To allow the forest to return, replete with its wild animals and connotations of darkness and sloth, would have been unimaginable. Where was the pride? Who could have allowed this to happen?

The lapse would seem, in a word, unethical.

Yet don't we feel a surge of pride when we look out from the summit today and behold the mix of land uses? Ours is a partly wild landscape that harbors more bear and bobcat than there were in 1830. A picture-postcard landscape sprinkled with villages that define New England, white steepled and green framed. A working landscape where manure still wrinkles noses and log trucks slow traffic. A protected landscape where great chunks of forest that so bedeviled the farmers have been "saved" through conservation. A recreational landscape where people work on their physical and spiritual health. An aesthetic landscape that serves as a muse for painters and poets.

It is a landscape, in short, that still reflects and benefits from a strong land ethic—albeit a much more complex one that would be no more understandable to our nineteenth-century farmer than the landscape itself.

That raises a question: can something as weighty as a land ethic be so fungible? I think it can, based on a definition adapted from *The Random House Dictionary*. From the land comes everything necessary for life, human and otherwise. A land ethic, then, is the body of principles and values that respect this fundamental truth, and the conduct that demonstrates those principles and values by maintaining connections to the land. As Aldo Leopold taught us, "All ethics so far evolved rest upon a single premise: that the individual is a member of a community of interdependent parts. . . . The land ethic simply enlarges the boundary of the community to include soils, waters, plants, or animals, or collectively—the land."

This may be demonstrated in many ways, from subsistence farming because there were no other choices in the early eighteenth century, to gardening and environmental activism even though there are other choices in the twenty-first. On one end of the spectrum is our farmer trying to make ends meet on his two-hundred-acre section in Jaffrey in 1830. On the other is the contemporary professional who spends her weekends tending a community garden, and her evenings advocating zoning changes to conserve open space. Both are driven by the same impulse.

When the silo fell at the Sawyer Farm in 1983, it split the barn neatly in two and crushed to death thirty-two cows and calves.

Stunned by the loss, Peter and Ann Sawyer couldn't ask for help; nor did they have to. The response from their Jaffrey neighbors was immediate. Family, friends, and strangers converged on the farm and got to work. The surviving heifers were milked seven hours after the disaster. Town employees hauled

When the silo fell at the Sawyer Farm in
1983, it split the barn neatly in two and
crushed to death 32 cows and calves. The
response from Jaffrey neighbors was immediate.

away the dead animals and volunteers cleared tons of shattered concrete and
fresh silage. The Sawyers had recently bought insurance that would cover livestock killed by building collapse, but it wouldn't be in effect for two months. The
silo itself was uninsurable, and its builder was bankrupt. Facing $200,000 in
damages with no promise of compensation, Peter had no idea where the money
would come from.

Then the donations started to trickle in—from bake sales, art shows, concerts,
a young man in Massachusetts who had gone door-to-door. The Sawyers never
met him. A local contractor donated labor and neighbors piled sawhorse tables
high with food. Two veterinarians got the surviving cows to swallow a hundred
free "cattle magnets" so metal debris in the silage wouldn't shred their intestines.
Mechanics repaired a smashed truck and refused Peter's offer of payment. "This
is not charity," one woman said. "This is just people helping people." She might
have added, "this is our ethic." In all, $40,000 in cash and hundreds of hours of
labor were donated. Six weeks later the barn was raised and the Sawyer Farm—
then in its fifth generation and one of only three still operating in a town that had
forty-nine when Peter was born—was back in business.

Thomas Jefferson would have loved Alfred Sawyer, Peter's great-grandfather.
Born in Sliptown (now Sharon) in 1831, Alfred moved with his family to Jaffrey
as a boy, dodged a dysentery outbreak that killed three siblings, and worked as a
laborer on his father's farm until he came of age. In 1858 he and his father bought
the Haywood/Prescott Farm next door and he married Lucy Parker. Alfred and
his hired men cleared more land with oxen and wooden plow, picked stones, and
built walls. For their own needs, they grew and ate corn and barley and potatoes,
beef cattle, hogs, and sheep. They milked a few cows. Cash crops likely included
wool for the growing textile industry, cider, cheese, and an occasional load of
timber from the back forty. Over the next few decades, Alfred and his son Clifton bought several neighboring farms and expanded. They opened a commercial

Sawyer Census

1860 Agricultural Census Records
Alfred Sawyer
  Land: 160 acres improved, 40 acres
    unimproved
  Animals: 1 horse, 6 milch cows, 2 oxen, 7
    other cows, 3 swine
  Crops: 20 bushels corn, 30 bushels oats,
    1 bushel peas, 100 pounds potatoes
  Products: 20 tons of hay, 700 pounds
    of butter, 360 pounds of cheese, 25
    pounds of maple sugar, and 4 gallons
    of molasses

1880 Agricultural Census Records
Alfred Sawyer
  Land: 48 acres tilled, 160 acres meadow,
    25 acres woods
  Animals: 6 milch cows, 2 oxen, 14 other
    cows, 2 swine
  Crops: barley 1 acre-40 bushels, oats ½
    acre—12 bushels, potatoes ¾ acre—
    100 pounds, 175 apple trees—200
    bushels
  Products: 30 tons hay, 800 pounds
    butter, 300 pounds cheese, 100
    pounds maple sugar, and 6 pounds of
    molasses

dairy with high-grade Jersey cows. "As an example of wholesome country living and of New England character at its best, Jaffrey can offer no finer than Alfred Sawyer, a farmer and citizen of the highest type," reported the 1934 *History of Jaffrey*. The same book credited Clifton with developing the ancestral home farm to a "high state of cultivation."

The thing is, this was all very much going against the grain.

By the time Alfred started the Sawyer Farm in the mid–nineteenth century, the world was closing in. The age of self-sufficiency was passing, and the brief sheep craze that transformed much of the Monadnock region to pasture had crested and crashed. In the second half of the century, three forces—the railroad, the Industrial Revolution, and the Civil War—conspired against the upland farmers. Railroads carved straight lines through the region's natural dips and folds, choosing which towns thrived or languished. Trains carried produce to market, but they took away a more precious cargo: young people. To many farm sons and daughters, ten hours in a textile mill in Keene looked and paid a lot better than twelve in the fields.

Meanwhile many young men never returned from the Civil War, either lured to better soil south and west or buried under it. Land in Illinois in the 1850s, with its rich black topsoil free of rocks, cost one-thirtieth of what it did in New England, and a bushel of corn was four times as profitable. Many hill farms in the Monadnock region shrank, specialized, or were abandoned altogether. The forest, which had been reduced from 96 percent of the state's land cover in 1600 to a low point of 48 percent in 1861, started to grow back. From 1850 to 1900, the percentage of the labor force engaged in agriculture in New Hampshire would drop from 67 to 36 percent. The agrarian age was over, although many didn't want to accept the change. "Politicians and commentators continued for most of the nineteenth century to believe that the state's economy could rest on a backbone of diligent yeoman labor," write Nancy Coffey Heffernan and Ann Page Stecker. "The traditionally conservative farmer was probably too busy promoting and guaranteeing his self-sufficiency to offer public contradiction. Self-sufficiency was a demanding goal and one which, having for all practical purposes the weight of an article of faith, would die hard."

It is clear that Alfred and his son Clifton believed in this article of faith, and in the ethic of legacy. As other farms in Monadnock's shadow blinked out, they adapted and pressed on. The torch was passed to Clifton's son Jason, who took over the farm in 1921. Once again defying the odds, he built a large new barn and expanded the commercial dairy operation—the only hope for a stony upland farm in a society where attitudes toward land were changing fast.

In Jason's youth, even as the rural economy was in full decline, nostalgia for a rural ideal was taking hold in the hectic and polluted cities. Urbanites wanted to escape back to the countryside—not to live, mind you, but to tarry awhile. This phenomenon was especially prominent in southwestern New Hampshire, which was easily accessible by rail from Boston, New York, and Philadelphia. Many farmers who had not moved west or into the mill cities took in summer boarders to augment their meager incomes, and commercial hotels and retreats opened.

"My father brought us up to believe that the farm was the next thing to God," said Peter Sawyer. "And that's just the way it's always been."

Both catered to visitors who wanted to eat farm-fresh food, climb mountains, paddle canoes, clear their lungs with fresh air, learn about nature. Because these early tourists were often drawn by idyllic images from art and literature, the vibrant art colonies in Dublin, Walpole, and Peterborough served as de facto marketing agencies.

A natural alliance took hold among visitors, artists, and a new social movement—the early conservationists. It had been only a few decades since the state of New Hampshire had finally sold the last of its public land for settlement and commerce; now there was pressure to start buying it back for conservation. At center stage in this drama were the White Mountains, where an epic clash between timber interests and tourists gave birth to the Society for the Protection of New Hampshire Forests (SPNHF) and the establishment of the White Mountain National Forest. But it also played itself out in the lakes region, the Upper Valley, and, notably, the Monadnock region. In 1891, Pack Monadnock had been set aside as the state's first reservation, and in 1912 the painter Abbott Thayer helped SPNHF purchase much of Mount Monadnock from timber companies, and dispirited hill farmers.

State leaders capitalized on the sentiment. Under the leadership of Progressives like Frank West Rollins and Peterborough's Robert P. Bass, the state promoted tourism, supported the protection of mountains, established public parks, and invented the "tradition" of Old Home Day. The idea was to draw successful emigrants back to New Hampshire's small towns in the hope they might buy up abandoned farms for summer homes. An ethic was evolving that was born not of necessity and godliness as it had been for the yeoman farmer, but of aesthetic affection for the land and personal fulfillment.

Peter Sawyer was born in 1938 on the farm that had come down from Alfred to Clifton to Peter's father, Jason. At over three hundred acres, the Sawyer Farm was the largest of forty-nine farms in Jaffrey. Jason milked twenty-nine Jersey cows and sold wholesale to a large creamery. He also managed a home delivery milk route, raised hogs, grew hay and corn for silage. Peter was nine when he first drove the farm tractor. "That was the end of my playing days," he says.

Although he had four older brothers, it was Peter who, in his words, "was doomed to the farm." He took over in 1958 after two years studying agriculture at Cornell. It was a tough time for dairy farming. Cumberland Farms had recently introduced the one-gallon milk container, a convenience that marked the beginning of the end of the home delivery market, which was the most stable income for farmers like Peter. Excerpts from a 1961 diary kept by another Jaffrey farmer, David van Blackum, paint a bleak picture: "Don't think we were ever so poor. . . . I never worked so hard for nothing at all. . . . Business is terrible and getting worse. . . . Frank quit today and this time for good. I guess I will be back to 17-hour days. Some life."

A mile down the road from Peter's place, another branch of the Sawyer family was on a different course. Jason's brother, Roscoe, also had received a significant piece of land from Clifton, and had expanded it by buying a neighboring farm in 1915. He also ran a dairy business, making home deliveries and selling wholesale to large processors. But Roscoe and his sons Alfred and David diversified. Recognizing the growing interest in tourism, they ran riding stables, took in summer boarders, established Jaffrey's first airport, and opened a popular ice-cream stand and tourism cabins. The place was called "Silver Ranch," after the main house was painted with supposedly impervious aluminum paint. Over time, ice cream, airplanes, and horseback riding replaced farming.

Meanwhile Peter and Ann decided not only to stick with farming but to expand once again. By 1967 their 140 head comprised the biggest herd in Jaffrey, and in 1972 they added more than a hundred feet to the barn. By then, there were only 35 other cows in the entire town. "Most of the tillers of the soil and keepers of cattle and sheep are gone," wrote Jaffrey historian Alice Lehtinen in 1971. "The hillside pastures where cattle were grazing in 1933 have given way to brush, and little pines growing taller year by year began peeking over the stonewalls as the bucolic sound of cowbells was fading away." Those trees "growing taller" did not escape the notice of those who depended on the land for their livelihood, nor those looking for a way to connect with the land. Peter's cousin Harvey recalls cutting firewood at Silver Ranch and selling it for eighteen dollars a cord.

Logging has always been part of the economy in the Monadnock region. The massive chestnut and pine and spruce trees were gone by 1800, cleared for farming and milled into beams and floorboards for houses and barns. The early farmers all kept small woodlots for fuel and lumber and profit. As the farms were abandoned and downsized in the second half of the nineteenth century, second-growth forests helped fuel the Industrial Revolution. For each successive species, new industries would swell up, often to collapse when the trees were gone. Thus came and went the long-log mills, the tanneries, the clapboard mills, the turning mills, the boxboard factories. Woodlots were bought, cut, and resold again and again. With the farms largely gone by World War II, state policy increasingly recognized forests as New Hampshire's most valuable renewable resource, and used any manner of persuasion to promote their wise use. A poster from the 1940s declares, "Good Citizen or Visitor, Help us Prevent Forest Fires and save the Town, the State and Woodland Owners GREAT DAMAGE AND EXPENSE FROM FIRES. Good forests are one of our chief assets."

For Monadnock-region residents who wanted to work their land, forestry offered an opportunity to practice a form of stewardship that was often compared to farming. Although New England's naturally regenerating woodlands required little planting, landowners were urged to cultivate their woodlots, to thin or "weed" less desirable trees, to treat the forest as a crop to be harvested regularly. The tree farm program caught many landowners' imagination, and during the 1960s and 1970s the familiar green and white signs were cropping up all over the region. Treatment of the forest was coming full circle: from a vaguely malevolent force that had to be tamed by the early farmers, to a natural resource that could be mined for short-term gain, to an ethic of stewardship that demanded human care or even legal protection.

That ethic of stewardship found expression in the statehouse and voting booth through the campaign for current-use taxation in 1968. At that time, after decades of relatively low population growth, southern and central New Hampshire started experiencing the pinch of being so close to Boston. Land was becoming more profitable for development than for growing trees and crops, and sharply rising property taxes were making it harder for landowners to hang on to family properties.

Alarmed by the specter of conservation-minded owners being forced to sell productive open land just to pay their taxes, a coalition of conservation groups called SPACE (Statewide Program of Action to Conserve our Environment) hit on a sensible plan: undeveloped land should be taxed not at its potential value—as house lots or shopping malls, say—but at the value of its "current use"—growing trees and corn, for example. That would dramatically lower the assessment and the tax bills. Problem was, it was unconstitutional to have two fundamentally different taxing structures. Not to be deterred, SPACE convinced the legislature and then the voters to amend the state constitution allowing for differential taxation—no mean feat given how infrequently the document had been changed since 1784. By 2001, more than half the land in New Hampshire would be enrolled; it has been said that no single public policy has had such an impact on New Hampshire's landscape. Families like the Sawyers simply could not have survived without it.

Laws enabling current use and other related legislation in the 1960s and 1970s coincided with two other impulses of the time: environmental activism and "back to the land" homesteading. Americans of the middle and upper classes once again turned to the countryside, this time not just to visit but to live an intentionally "simpler" life close to the land. They cut and burned wood, planted gardens, and canned food—not because they had to, but because they wanted to. Related social traditions of potluck suppers, contra dancing, and sugaring parties followed.

To the earlier ethics of self-sufficiency, legacy, aesthetic enjoyment, and spiritual fulfillment was added yet another layer: respect and concern for the earth expressed in personal and political action.

Stunningly, an even larger disaster than the toppled silo struck the Sawyer Farm in 1999 when a terrific barn fire killed 130 cows, more than half the herd. Once again the town rallied and helped the Sawyers rebuild, but they never regained their footing. For the next few years they kept only a dozen cows for a few raw milk customers, and relied on hay as their cash crop. To pay the $15,000 property tax load, they sold gravel—literally carving the ground out from under them. Anything to keep from selling out. "My father brought us up to believe that the farm was the next thing to God," Peter said. "And that's just the way it's always been." In fall 2003 Peter contracted pneumonia and a staph infection and was hospitalized for ten weeks. They moved the animals to his brother Sheldon's farm in Walpole, unsure if they would ever return. (Peter and Ann's only child, Jennifer, was embarked on a career helping the disabled and not interested in farming.) Unable to imagine a life without farm chores, Ann began raising chickens and continued to milk one remaining cow. Her name was Mercy.

"This family is at a crossroads," said Peter's cousin Harvey, who with his four siblings still owned Silver Ranch and more than two hundred acres of land. "There are family issues, there are financial issues, there are 'who wants to work seven days a week?' issues. I don't know how much longer it will last. It gets more and more difficult as it goes through another generation."

Squeezing a living from the land is tough in the Monadnock region of the twenty-first century. Families like the Sawyers have kept at it against agonizingly long odds—out of legacy, stubbornness, and habit, yes, but more fundamentally because of their land ethic. Without that, the decision would be easy and the Sawyers could retire wealthy—their land would be worth millions to a developer. For now, they are taking it a year at a time. As Peter recovered at home in

Haying with horse and later with tractor. "As an example of wholesome country living and of New England character at its best, Jaffrey can offer no finer than Alfred Sawyer, a farmer and citizen of the highest type," reported the 1934 *History of Jaffrey*.

spring 2004, he was starting to think about haying his fields again and opening another gravel pit. But it looked like the dairy farm was done. "I don't know if we will be getting back into it," he said. "I kind of doubt it." He declined to speculate beyond that.

Since the mid-1980s, land values in the Monadnock region have spiraled steadily upward. Development pressure has swelled west from Nashua, north from Fitchburg and Worcester. Overall the region has grown at the same rate as New Hampshire as a whole—which is to say, faster than any neighboring states. By 2000, development was gobbling up an estimated 1,400 acres of open land in the region each year, with population projected to grow by another 21 percent by 2020. Some towns will far outstrip that average.

The unprecedented growth has driven land use issues to the top of our civic agendas. Through zoning changes, growth moratoriums, stricter subdivision regulations, and outright preservation, we have struggled to preserve something often referred to as "rural character." That's tough to define, but I think it comes back to our definition of a land ethic: respect for and connection with the land. Sometimes the struggle has played out in high-profile battles such as the proposed nuclear waste dump in Hillsborough in 1986. When our mutual sense of place is clearly threatened by powerful and distant foes, these skirmishes have united residents in common cause. At the nuke dump hearings, dreadlocked college students followed old guys in feed caps to the microphone. They sounded strangely alike.

Far more common and complex, however, are the everyday squabbles over land use. These arise from the reality that, as we have seen, our connections to the land comprise a complex and hearty stew. The simple stock is made of the activities that were required for self-sufficient farming in the wilderness and that still survive in pockets today: taking from the earth the basic necessities of life, food and shelter. To that stock have been added—because of population growth, cultural shifts, and economic forces—connections that are more aesthetic, spiritual, personal, and political. Individual flavors can still be distinguished, but the overall richness cannot be teased apart. And thus, unintentionally, we find ourselves at odds with one another: The cash-poor landowner who needs to sell timber so he can hang on to his woodlot is criticized by the ecologist worried about the impact of logging on habitat. The hikers blame hunters, who share their passion for the outdoors, for scaring them out of the woods in the fall. The new home owner makes romantic photographs of the farm across the road, but complains to the selectmen when ripe manure is spread to green up the fields.

Reconciling these differing values and connections is difficult, but the Monadnock region is as well positioned as any to make it work. There are encouraging signs. Neighbors still coalesce in the wake of tragedies like those that befell the Sawyers. We still have that mosaic of lands that unfolds from the summit of the mountain—wild, working, lived in. While large-scale farming is restricted to the rich soils of the Connecticut River Valley, community-supported agriculture, niche farming, and farmers' markets are making a go of it. The Monadnock region contains the state's highest concentration of conservation land outside of the White Mountains, and much of the protected land is still available for forestry and agriculture. The regional planning commission is engaged and active, and many towns are embracing innovative new ways to mix land uses. People tend to sink their roots deep, whether they have been here for several generations or several years. Our sense of place is strong.

But still the pressure bears down—economic, demographic, commercial, political. The key to sustaining a livable balance, I believe, is to recognize that our neighbors' connection to the land—their land ethic—may be unfathomable, strange, even threatening. But it is no less valid than our own.

Many writers from Henry David Thoreau to Aldo Leopold to Annie Dillard have explored the question of what it means to embrace and exercise a land ethic in different times and places. None of their work, however, better sums up the infinite complexity of why land matters than Ernie Hebert's homage to Howard Elman of Darby, New Hampshire, the fictional junk man in his novel *The Dogs of March*.

"Howard wanted land for religious reasons. He would hold the land like a Bible to be studied, interpreted, and mulled over on Sunday mornings, he a priest with priestly duties toward it. The land would have a house, a field, and thick wood. There would be boulders. Some of the land would have steepness. There would be giant moths, giant spiders, and flowers as delicate as a child's tear. . . . Even as the years passed he kept his dream of the land. . . . Indeed, the thought of the land was stronger the farther he was from it. . . . The black design of apple trees in winter, their lordships the boulders, queenly ferns—how was one to explain these things?"

The Last Hurrah for New England Thrift;
or, Use It Once, Toss It Out, Buy More

From the 1998 Town Report of Chesterfield, New Hampshire (population 3,500):

1998 saw a drop in market prices mid-year, but not in our efforts to recycle as much as possible.

Some changes we implemented this year were: composting of leaves and organic matter, and the collection of paints and household batteries and fluorescent lights. We also began accepting antifreeze.

Approximately 1,216 gallons of used motor oil was collected from residents, saving the town around $730 if we were to have purchased heating oil.

We shipped out 17.18 tons of used tires at a cost of $1,803.90.

Total tons (minus the above-mentioned 17.18 tons) of recycled materials sent out was 284.17. At a cost of $50 disposal fee per ton, a total of $14,208.50 was saved in hauling fees. The following is a breakdown of tons recycled in 1998:

Aluminum cans, 2.51 tons; car batteries, 0.61; books, 1.70; brown bags, 2.20; chipboard, 7.26; copper, 0.03; corrugated cardboard, 32.23; glass, 46.34; magazines, mixed paper, 58.71; bulk metal, 56.82; newspaper, 51.01; plastic, 11.41; rags, 1.72; tin cans, 11.61.

Total revenue from recycling was $22,987.96.

Total tons of solid waste (trash) hauled from this facility was 636.36.

Total amount paid for disposal at $50 per ton was $34,318. With that cost added to shipping and rental fees, the total cost for solid was $43,108.66.

With the upcoming closure of the Keene landfill, solid waste disposal fees are sure to go up. So let's all make a conscious effort to do our best to reduce, reuse and recycle.

Mr. Roy's Market

On the late-autumn day I tried to visit Mr. Roy, I drove to Peterborough through hills awash with unbelievable color. The foliage was on fire, golds and scarlets and yellows almost blindingly bright. This was my first fall in New England. I was newly arrived from Georgia, with my husband.

For two months I had been in utter awe at the landscape. Driving through the countryside, I couldn't believe its rural character—small villages, general stores, old cemeteries, farm stands with rows of pumpkins, grassy commons and white-steepled churches, hillsides of trees. And now the northern deciduous forests were throwing a wild and extravagant party.

The charm of the region made me ache with a strange mixture of gratitude and sadness—gratefulness for an emphasis on quality of life, and grief that so much of my homeland, the South, looks very different. The South has more or less chopped down its forests, and chain stores replicate themselves town to town, so each begins to look and operate the same. The South, as a region, is losing its history, its singular character, its small businesses; my homeland's subservience to corporations has been fatal to our small communities.

Because I have witnessed with my own eyes the disastrous effects that corporate hegemony has on human and civic life, I was intrigued when a friend told me about Roy's Market, a grocery in beautiful downtown Peterborough, "A Good Town to Live In," through which runs the Contoocook River. It began in 1956 when Mr. Albert Roy and his wife, Rolande, purchased Wyman's Market, then expanded it. Today, almost fifty years later, the market still pulses and prospers. Mr. Roy sold the store to his nephew Peter Robinson in 2005 and stayed on for one year to oversee the transition. I decided one day to go see Roy's and do a little shopping.

The store is located at the intersection of Main and Depot, with its curved corner entrance topped by the letters ROY'S MARKET. A week before Halloween, one storefront has been painted with ghosts and goblins by Brownie Troop 49, below which petunias and thrift and verbena blossom in wooden planters. Along the other storefront, fliers advertise barn tours and folk music concerts.

Inside, a single checkout lane is positioned two paces beyond the front door, the *Peterborough Transcript* stacked atop it. A mature woman with shoulder-length hair runs the register. "You're a day early," she's saying to an older gentleman who has placed a few items on the checkout belt.

"Yes, we needed a few things," he replies, leaning shakily into the counter. The cashier pushes a can of what must be soup and a box of crackers down the small belt.

"Will I see you tomorrow?" she asks.

"Probably," the man replies. "Thursday is the day my wife gets her hair done."

I am a seasoned eavesdropper. My husband complains that I find other people's conversations more interesting than my own. But this kind of dialogue, albeit banal, is sometimes the only proof we have of community and the only glimpses we get into other lives. I walk a few steps down Aisle 1, hidden from the checkout lane, and stare into the dairy cooler as I listen unabashedly to their conversation.

"She gets her hair done every Thursday, Mr. Simon?"

"She tries to, Denise," he says.

"That'll be $17.07, Mr. Simon." A crinkling of thin plastic follows and I see the gentleman, in his fedora, exit.

In the cooler, Roy's Market is selling soy milk alongside cow milk. There are cheeses and yogurts and eggs and even little logs of cookie dough.

"Hi Mr. Kelly," I hear Denise say. When the man asks how she's doing, she says, "I'm well for a Monday and the Red Sox won." Everybody's talking Red Sox. The team has whipped the New York Yankees and they have a chance to win the World Series for the first time since 1918. In a minute Denise tells Mr. Kelly his bill is $4.23. "And it's no bag for you," she says.

A townsman steps inside the door long enough to pick up a paper and hand the cashier a few coins.

A landmark in Peterborough—the red-shirted bag boys will carry groceries to your car. Mr. Roy has perfected the art of the little-box store. "We keep things small, pure and simple. We keep it very friendly," said Noel LaFortune, Mr. Roy's nephew and employee of 42 years.

I wander around. The store has four long shelves, about twenty-four feet long, with aisles so narrow that the metal shopping carts, parked immediately to the right of the front door, are miniature, about sixteen inches wide and maybe two and a half feet long. They'll hold about a third of what the supersized supermarket cart holds.

Roy's Market appears to sell anything one would need—fresh breads, wines and beers, spices, staples, canned goods, frozen foods, meats, cleaning supplies. Before a small specialty section, I stand and gaze at liver pâté, mint sauce made from Egyptian mint leaves, mango chutney, capers, anchovy paste, little tins of sliced conch, and black lumpfish caviar. I hear Denise ask the customer when he and his wife are heading to Florida for the winter. "It's going to snow pretty soon and we'll all be sledding," I hear her say.

Peterborough has about six thousand year-round residents. It's small enough that newcomers to the hamlet wonder, What do you do here? The townspeople have a saying to explain it: *In summer we watch the grass grow. In winter we watch the snow fall.*

I am waiting in line to talk to Denise when a tall, white-haired woman ahead of me drops her purchases onto the checkout belt. She turns away and moves quickly to the dairy aisle. She has forgotten sour cream, she says. She comes back with the cream. We're waiting.

"And the other thing," she says. "Oh dear. It's gone."

Denise sounds matter-of-fact. "What is it that you need, Mrs. Hames?" Does she know everybody by name?

"Frozen lemon juice." The woman remembers triumphantly and heads back to the frozen foods cooler that is full of pot pies and layer cakes.

When her bill is tallied and paid, a retirement-age man with no visible purchases takes his turn at the register. "I hear my wife ran up a bill down here," he says.

"Yes, Mr. Mills, she did." Denise reaches below the counter and pulls out an index box, full of alphabetized cards. "Sixty ninety-three," she says, and the man writes out a check.

"You still charge?" I ask.

"Oh sure," she says. "If Mr. Roy knows you. We've never had a problem with it." She is replacing the box. "Part of my job is to add up the charges every day."

Denise tells me that Mr. Roy isn't in the store and that's he's shy. He wouldn't want to talk much about himself and how he has managed to do a thriving business, despite the big stores. "You should talk to the meat cutters," she says. "Noel has been here forty years. He's Mr. Roy's nephew."

At the end of the dairy aisle is the butcher shop. Roy's is famous for its meats. On holidays the line is out the door and down the block, I've been told, for people purchasing Thanksgiving turkeys, Christmas roasts, and Easter lamb. If you have company coming, people have said to me, Mr. Roy will tell you what to prepare. He'll help you with the menu. He'll tell you how to cook the meat.

Mr. Roy's nephew, Noel LaFortune, has just turned sixty, with still-dark hair and a merry look on his face. He was christened Noel by being born at Christmas. He drew his first paycheck from his uncle when he was eighteen, in 1962, and has been an employee ever since. He's not shy and doesn't mind talking. How *does* Roy's Market stay in business?

"We wait on people," Noel says. "We decided long ago that the only way we could survive was if we rendered a service. The big chain stores are all self-service."

"What do you mean by service?" I ask.

"We specially cut meats," he says. "Whatever people want. Here, meats don't come prepackaged. If the customer wants one pork chop or a half pound of ground beef, it's not a problem. We give people what they want." He has just come from break and is tying on a white apron. "And we help them. If they come in and say, 'I don't quite know about this recipe' or 'How do I grill this?' we tell them."

A middle-aged woman approaches the glassed meat-counter. Noel's coworker, who is also Mr. Roy's nephew, takes her order and begins to wrap steaks. When another man strolls up, without buggy or basket, Noel pauses and greets the customer.

"Can I have that piece of haddock?" the customer says.

"I've been saving that for you," Noel replies. "I was wondering when you'd come." We all know this isn't true but it's a jolly kind thing to say. He wraps the fish and thanks the man.

"This is the best-selling part of the store," Noel tells me. "In fact, the meat counter is where Mr. Roy tries out new products." Marinades and hot sauces and flacons of black truffle olive oil line the top of the counter; fresh-baked whole-grain bread, wrapped in paper, is nearby.

"Besides good meat, what's Roy's secret?" I ask. Noel wonders why I'm so interested and I tell him that I study community and local economics, and that I'm curious about how small businesses thrive in the wake of corporate takeover. I tell him that I write about it.

"We keep things small, pure and simple," Noel says. "We keep it very friendly. We don't make a big deal out of the famous people. Like James Whitmore. When he comes in here, we treat him like he's an average guy."

Peterborough is a theater town. It is the subject of Thornton Wilder's play *Our Town*, and home to a host of community theaters and the famous Peterborough Players, a summer professional theater company, which often attracts well-known actors and actresses. A few weeks ago, townspeople staged a play of local-color stories called *Peterborough Verbatim*. The musical featured songs with lines like, "Why do we love our town?" The song asked, *Can it be the culture, the rivers, the hills?* The answer was, "Above all these things, it's we all have each other."

In one scene of the play, a town meeting's moderator listens to a proposal for a superstore—"Tweak a zoning reg or two," the character proposes.

A Mrs. Smith stands up: "No Big Box in our town," she says. "It just wouldn't fit. Drive-up windows, fast-food joints, possibilities won't quit. We want our Roy's, Steele's, the diner, and Nonie's too. It's off to Keene for the rest of you."

When the make-believe town votes, the zoning article fails, overwhelming in the negative.

Verbatim may have been theater, but it is also real life. One-stop chain stores in booming Keene and Rindge are luring business away from Roy's Market. Yet the store thrives, partly because the people of the town have chosen to stand loyal to each other.

The enamel top of the meat counter is shoulder high, so all I can see is Noel's face. He is working with his hands at something, always busy. I ask how the store is different from when he first started working.

"We've added to the shelves to make them taller," he says. "And we've responded to people's requests. They want organic now, health foods. If we don't have something in stock, we have a great distributor who can get us anything, quick."

A customer has been listening. She asks Noel if he can get venison. He pauses a few seconds, thinking, then says that he can. It will be farm raised. Just let him know when.

"The distributor lets you order in smaller quantities?" I ask. I know a country store in rural Georgia being slowly forced out of business because the stock demand does not satisfy the distributors.

"Oh yes, they break boxes for us," Noel says. He tells me that big stores give many items six facings, meaning the position at the front edge of a shelf. Most items at Roy's have one facing. The store is sixty by sixty feet, total. Open eight to six, it employs a dozen people, including a few high school boys who come in after school to bag and haul groceries, open doors for customers, and stock shelves. Roy's takes telephone orders and cashes checks and allows people use the phone.

If Roy's Market is quaint and polite and, no matter how you look at it, a little old-fashioned, Little Roy's, the companion convenience store located exactly behind the grocery, is lively and almost raucous. Late afternoon, people flow in and out even faster than at the big store next door, buying chips, snacks, stick ice creams, candy, sodas. Bill, who's worked for Mr. Roy for thirty-three years, greets many of the patrons by name. After I have stood around awhile, watching the flow, and after I have told him that I'm a writer, he tells me that he started working for Mr. Roy in 1971 at what he thought would be a temporary job, but on that salary he has reared three children. He meant to be a biologist. "This is still temporary," he jokes. "Until I find out what I want to do." He sobers. "Believe me, if nothing else, you get to see people. You get to see generations."

A man walks up to the little counter, on which are piled candies and a bowl of fruit and a lottery machine. "Hey Jim."

"Hey Bill. Two packs, please." Bill hands him his brand. Another guy, Mack, comes in and buys a six-pack.

"For a little store, it's beer and cigarettes or perish," Bill tells me.

An older woman is looking at the newspapers. "We attract men because of the beer," says Bill. "We attract the ladies because there's something to read." He laughs, pleasant and relaxed, glancing to see if the woman has heard. She hasn't. She gets in line at the counter and buys two gossip magazines. After she leaves, Bill confides that she's very wealthy. And reads trash.

Bill's coworker, John, arrives from the stockroom. "This is the pulse of Peterborough," he says. "This is the crossroads. The hub."

"If you want to know something, you come here," Bill says.

"Then you get your cold beer," John adds. Together, the two operate like Click and Clack, NPR's Car Guys, playing their good humor off each other.

"Some people are like clockwork," Bill says. "They come in every day at the same time and buy the same paper. We have the same conversations."

"We could tape it all and run a tape recorder instead," jokes John.

I ask them about their boss. "Mr. Roy's about as private a man as there is," one says. They're quiet. (No one uses Mr. Roy's first name.)

"How old is he?"

"Older than the Old Man of the Mountains," one says.

"He's seventy-nine," says the other.

Coming to live in New England is like reversing myself thirty years, to a time when towns across America weren't all trying to look the same and to a time when people mattered. Here I feel sometimes like the girl I was who could walk the mile to Baxley's, an old supermarket in my hometown of Baxley, Georgia. It had unfinished pine floors and shelves that even I, at ten or twelve, could see over. Baxley's had a meat counter with a real butcher behind it and usually only one checkout. But even then, although none of us knew it yet, that store had entered into decline, the last of an era, and the age of the corporate chain was upon us.

As I write this, a Wal-Mart (now the nineteenth-largest economy in the world and the largest employer in the United States) is being built in my hometown of 3,500 people, bringing its own supermarket, pharmacy, and gas station. All over the country, big business is clubbing small business to death and when Americans talk about entrepreneurship, I scoff—of what use now is that most American of traits? We are siding with corporate desires, not human needs.

I walk back up the street to do my shopping, making sure I stay on the sidewalk. When I was in Little Roy's, the guys laughed about a couple of people outside. "How can you tell a tourist?" one had asked. "They're walking in the streets!" A welder dashing in after work for beer had been listening. "And the town of Peterborough spent a million dollars on sidewalks."

I am midway along the block when a stranger pauses to address me. "There's Mr. Roy," she says. She gestures briefly upward. "I heard you were looking for him." I look up. A gray-haired man in glasses is standing at the upstairs window, cloth in one hand and spray bottle in the other, wiping at the pane. "He lives up there?"

"Yes," the woman says.

Mr. Roy was named Peterborough's Citizen of the Year in 1996, I learned later from Karen Bannister, executive assistant of the Chamber of Commerce. She said that he was asked to attend a dinner in his honor, which did not please him. He doesn't like attention, she said. But the dinner was a sellout, with a waiting list. She showed me a picture of Mr. and Mrs. Roy in the paper, sitting at the banquet, all smiles.

In her tribute to celebrate his award, Spud Fleck said: "Since I arrived here in 1970, I have felt at home at Mr. Roy's. They care about me. I walk in and I am greeted as a dear friend—nothing is too much trouble. The whole place has an atmosphere of friendliness. I feel as though it is a part of my extended family and I love going there."

In Roy's Market I take a basket and get out my list. I want to bake a fancy carrot cake from a recipe my friend clipped out of *Southern Living*. As I am choosing cage-free eggs from the dairy cooler, I hear the cashier asking a customer, "Did you mean to get regular eggs?"

"Inorganic eggs are fine," the man says. "I've lived this long eating them."

I find walnuts in the baking aisle and look a long time, all over the store, in fact, for flaked coconut, until I am directed by a stock boy back to the baking aisle. They don't have the can that the recipe calls for, so I take a bag. The sugar is not in the baking aisle. It's in the last aisle, near cans of condensed milk. Cranberry sauce is with the cans of fruit, which makes some sense. Locally grown organic carrots are in the small produce cooler.

I am amazed by the choices in mustard. I assumed a store this small would have a minimal selection. I count them. There are thirteen mustard brands, national and local—Gulden's, Inglehoffer, Butternut Mountain Farm, Annie's, Jack Daniel's, Nance's, French's . . . and a few of the brands have more than one flavor. I choose and head to the meat counter.

"What is bluefish?" I ask Noel's assistant, eyeing the hand-lettered sign above pink fillets.

He tells me and suddenly I remember fishing for blues off the coast of North Carolina. They travel in schools, feeding voraciously, striking fearsomely at whatever bait is thrown to them.

"Are these fresh?"

He says yes, they're still in season. For cooking, he recommends the grill. A woman beside me says she makes bluefish cakes by sautéing and flaking the fish, then mixing in eggs and bread crumbs and onions. She recommends them.

"Give me enough for a three-person family," I say. "We're all people with big appetites."

He hands me a package wrapped in butcher paper, its price written with a wax marker. "Anything else?"

Out of curiosity, I visit the Stop & Shop on my way out of Peterborough and back to my New England home, where my husband will season the bluefish and where I will cream butter and sugar and grate carrots for a cake. The supermarket is about 24,000 square feet, twenty times the size of Roy's; sells nonfood items like T-shirts, greeting cards, and plasticware; and employs, a manager tells me, seventy-four people for all its shifts. The supermarket's open until midnight; Roy's will soon be closing. The aisles are wide, the shelves tall. I pace off the produce aisle and measure about 140 feet of cooler space. Roy's had 10 or 12 feet.

I find the mustard—nineteen brands, most with multiple flavors. There's nothing I need here. I've already made my choice.

Here we go again. It is first rehearsal of the fifth production of Thornton Wilder's *Our Town* by the Peterborough Players. We're sitting in a circle of chairs on the plank floor of the two-hundred-year-old barn that became a theater in 1933, five years before Wilder's play about life in Grover's Corners, New Hampshire—written while he was a guest at the MacDowell Colony, two miles down the road—won the Pulitzer Prize.

There's a couple of hundred years' worth of stage experience in this circle. Rosanna Cox played a schoolgirl in the first Peterborough production in 1940. Bob Alvin and Colin Craig were in the 1960 show. Bob and Rosie were back in 1976 and again in 1983.

The veterans trade anecdotes—Rosie can remember Thornton Wilder coming to rehearsals in 1940 and rearranging the chairs for the graveyard scene, and Colin knew Fletcher Dole, the Peterborough milkman who was the model for Howie Newsome. He can remember Dole sitting in the front row at the first production.

Director Chuck Morey calls us to attention and starts to talk about what a privilege it is to do this play in this place. He played the Stage Manager in 1976, he directed it in 1983, and this year he's doing both. "It's a play about generations," he says, a fact underlined by the presence of his wife, Joyce Cohen, who played Emily ten years ago. She will play Emily's mother now, and their nine-year-old son is also in the cast.

We begin to read. We could almost recite it from memory—it's the most frequently performed play in America. But no one is tired of it. You have to admire the craftsmanship of the soda fountain scene, the theatrical boldness—even half a century later—of the third act, the dead of Grover's Corners sitting in straight-backed chairs, waiting patiently for what's eternal in them to come out clear. That's when the first stifled sobs are heard. By the time we're into Emily's farewell to earth, and clean clothes, and coffee, we are all weeping. Chuck reads the last lines and closes the script.

"Well," someone says after a moment. "It still works."

Appendix

YOU CAN GET THERE FROM HERE

My Favorite Views of the Mountain

Judson D. Hale, Sr.

"I'm from New Hampshire," I say when traveling outside the state, and then almost always I add, "the Monadnock region." If someone looks puzzled, I explain that's about twenty towns surrounding the most climbed mountain in the world, Mount Monadnock. (Yes, we were second to Mount Fuji, but recently, I understand, we've become number one.)

"Can you see the mountain from your place?" is not an unusual question in the Monadnock region, and although someone could be referring to Temple Mountain or Pack Mountain, they're not. In the Monadnock region, "the mountain" means Mount Monadnock.

Last fall, just for the fun of it, my wife, Sally, and I decided to revisit our eight favorite views of the mountain. It would, as always, require us driving through a large portion of the Monadnock region, beginning in the towns north of the mountain, heading west, then around to the south, and finally ending back at our house on the east side. With many stops and a meandering pace, it's about a four-hour tour.

Then, we got really ambitious. Why not take an extra day to see the best view of them all? The one from the summit!

Over the years, we've climbed Mount Monadnock from the long gradual trails on the Dublin side many times. But we hadn't ascended from the steeper Jaffrey side since two weeks after we were married in 1958. It would be interesting to see if we could still do it.

The White Dot Trail from Monadnock State Park in Jaffrey turned out to be a lot steeper and rockier than we remembered it being. A lot. (Would that have something to do with our age?) But, oh, how grand it was that morning to view the entire Monadnock region (and miles beyond) from up there on those same gray summit boulders on which have stood the likes of Henry David Thoreau, Rudyard Kipling, Ralph Waldo Emerson, John Greenleaf Whittier, and yes, Sally and me as newlyweds.

As always, we could see the sun reflecting off countless picture windows that face "the mountain" throughout the Monadnock region. So many of these homes are hidden away in the woods, seldom seen by anyone. But from the summit of our mountain, their whereabouts are revealed.

The next day, another gorgeous one, although feeling a bit stiff and sore, we packed a picnic and set out to circumnavigate that 3,165-foot mound of forests and rocks we'd struggled up twenty-four hours earlier. There were countless views of it along the way, each different, almost as though Monadnock is many mountains. The following eight have always been our favorites.

1. Of course, the quintessential postcard view of Monadnock is from where Route 101 curves around the Dublin cemetery, with Dublin Lake in the foreground. But the first of our favorites is halfway back into the cemetery, at my mother's grave. From here Dublin Lake is to our right and the mountain, just the summit and top of the north ridge, is visible through the branches of two giant oak trees. Someday, that will be our forever view.

2. In Harrisville, one of the most spectacular views of the gentler north side of the mountain is from Mason Road (formally Old Harrisville Road) running along above Dublin Lake and Route 101. From up here, it's a massive dominating mountain, living up to the dictionary meaning of the geological term, monadnock—"a hill of resistant rock standing in the midst of a peneplain."

3. When we got to Childs Bog on the way from Harrisville to Nelson, we remembered to turn off onto Breed Road. There's Monadnock, with no spurs or surrounding slopes, too far for its rocks to be visible, rising up dramatically over the waters of the bog, almost like a distant Matterhorn.

4. The view from the intersection of Thatcher Hill Road and Ogilvie Road in Marlborough, just off Route 124, is made even more dramatic by the huge open field in the foreground. Strange how, from here, the summit seems to come to a point, leaning south.

5. The mountain looks comparatively small—and very rocky—as seen from behind the post office in downtown Troy. Yet particularly rugged and beautiful . . . and the summit no longer comes to a point.

6. Still in Troy, on Monadnock Street, probably the most spectacular view of the rugged, rocky south side of Monadnock, with Perkins Pond just below, is from the back lawn of the Inn at East Hill Farm. It's a "wow!" It's equally wonderful from Route 124 as it bisects Perkins Pond, but the problem is that there's very little room to pull off the road along there.

7. We used to love the view from the 1755 Meeting House in Jaffrey Center but—guess what?—it's pretty well grown up now. So we took Blackberry Lane behind the Meeting House over to Thorndike Pond Road and were then able to see what the Meeting House view was like years ago. Trouble is, back then the Meeting House was part of that view.

8. We completed our circle of the mountain by taking Nashua Road off Route 124 to Temple and, from there, scooting out to Route 101, heading west. After cresting Temple Mountain and beginning our descent into Peterborough, we were treated to what we always have called our "coming home" view. Here, from the east, Monadnock appears to have three peaks. Although each seems to be about the same height, we well remember our previous day's tiring half-hour climb from somewhere near the middle "peak" to the real summit, the one on the far left.

Our "coming home" view of the mountain is also the view from our house off Goldmine Road in Dublin. Our spot is just a little closer. During clear, sunny afternoons, our picture windows glint and sparkle up there on the summit, too.

Directions to Some of the Places in This Book

Sokoki Homeland (pp. 15–27)

Carved Bow and Arrow, Surry

DIRECTIONS: From the intersection of Routes 12 and 12A in Keene, travel north on Route 12 for 5 miles. The trailhead is on the right, marked only by a gate set back in the woods. Just beyond the gate along the road is a Society for the Protection of New Hampshire Forests sign that reads "Indian Arrowhead Forest Preserve." There isn't an established parking area at the trailhead. There is a pull-off area 0.3 mile beyond the trailhead. There are two approaches to the site. The trail to the right is easier and well maintained. Follow the yellow blazes and signs. It is less than 1 mile to the rock.

Phineas Stevens (pp. 28–32)

The Fort at No. 4 Living History Museum

FOR DIRECTIONS: Springfield Rd.–Route 11, P.O. Box 336, Charlestown, NH 03603
INFORMATION: (603) 826-5700, toll-free (888) 367-8284, fax (603) 826-3368, http://www.stepintohistory.com/states/NH/Fort_Atno4.htm, email: info@fortat4.org

Parables of Place (pp. 65–72)

Pisgah Old Growth

The largest and most impressive tract of old growth in Pisgah State Park is a forty-acre section off of the northeast shore of North Round Pond. From the Horseshoe Rd. trailhead (the northern entrance to the park) the round trip is roughly 6 miles of moderate difficulty.

DIRECTIONS: From the intersection of Routes 9 and 63 in Chesterfield, head south on 63 for 3 miles. Turn left on Old Chesterfield Rd. At 0.3 mile turn right on Horseshoe Rd. The trailhead is at 2.5 miles. Trail maps are available at the trailhead kiosk. As with all backcountry travel, come prepared and do not travel alone.

Gap Mountain Reservation

DIRECTIONS: From the village of Troy, travel 1.5 miles south on Route 12. Turn left on Gap Mountain Rd. Trailhead parking is 1 mile on left. The hiking trail to the summit is easy except for the last stretch, which is of moderate difficulty. Round trip approximately 2 miles.

FOR MORE INFORMATION: http://www.beqbooks.com/gap/gap.htm

Stonewall Farm

DIRECTIONS: From intersection of Route 10/12/9 and Route 9W, follow Route 9 west 3.2 miles. Turn right on Chesterfield Rd. Stonewall Farm is less than 0.1 mile on right.

LEARNING CENTER HOURS: Monday–Friday 8:30 a.m. to 4:30 p.m., Saturday & Sunday 10:00 a.m. to 4:00 p.m.

THE GROUNDS: Open year-round during daylight hours for picnicking, hiking, visiting the farm animals, or to observe afternoon milking (4:30 p.m. each day). Admission is free.

FOR MORE INFORMATION: (603) 357-7278, http://www.stonewallfarm.org/index.shtml

Thoreau on Monadnock (pp. 73–89)

Monadnock State Park, N.H. Division of Parks and Recreation

FOR DIRECTIONS: http://www.nhstateparks.org/ParksPages/Monadnock/Monadnock
.html, (603) 532-8862

A Mill Girl's Offering (pp. 92–101)

Sarah Shedd Library, Washington, N.H.

DIRECTIONS: Travel north on Route 31 through the town of Washington; the library is
on the right just beyond the square. Parking is on the left.

HOURS: Tuesday 10–5, Wednesday 10–1, Thursday 1–7, Saturday 10–1

FOR MORE INFORMATION: (603) 495-3593, Librarian: Jo Ellen Wright

"Plant Your Apples on the Hills" (pp. 113–120)

Alyson's Orchard

DIRECTIONS: From the intersection of Routes 12 and 63 in Westmoreland, travel north
on Route 12 for 1.5 miles. Turn right onto Blackjack Crossing. At 1 mile turn left on Wentworth Road. The main orchard entrance is 0.6 mile on the left.

FOR MORE INFORMATION: http://www.alysonsorchard.com/alysonswood.htm, (800)
856-0549 (603) 756-9800

The Last 113 People (pp. 128–135)

Pitcher Mountain

DIRECTIONS: From the intersection of Routes 9 and 123 in Stoddard, travel north on
123. Trailhead parking is 5 miles on the right. The summit and fire tower are less than a
mile from the trailhead, and the hike is of moderate difficulty.

Land of Stone (pp. 138–151)

Wilder's Utopia (now occupied by Hampshire Country School)

DIRECTIONS: From the intersection of Routes 202 and 119 in Rindge, N.H., take 202E
for 5.3 miles. Turn left on Beaver Dam Rd. At 0.3 mile turn right on Hampshire Rd. The
Hampshire School is 0.2 mile on left.

FOR MORE INFORMATION: http://www.hampshirecountryschool.com/

Westmoreland Culvert

DIRECTIONS: From the intersection of Routes 12 and 9 in Keene, take 12 north 6.6 miles
to East Westmoreland. Turn right on Mt. Gilboa Rd. and travel 0.4 mile to the railbed
marked with an orange gate. Park on the right side and walk 775 feet back toward Keene
along the railbed. Hike down the steep slope beneath the railbed: the culvert face on
the left side is undamaged and on the right is partially collapsed. The final 50-foot drop
below the railbed is of moderate difficulty.

Hillsborough Bridge Tour

FOR DIRECTIONS: http://hillsboroughnhchamber.com/bridges.html

The Poor Farm (pp. 171–177)

The Cheshire County Farm

DIRECTIONS: From the intersection of Routes 12 and 63 in Westmoreland, travel on
63 south for 2.3 miles. Turn right on River Rd. and go 0.8 mile to the complex. Follow
signs.

The Green Army of Camp Annett (pp. 178–180)

Annett State Park

The site of CCC camp SP-55 is now a day-use recreation area.

DIRECTIONS: From the intersection of Routes 119 and 202 in Rindge, follow 119 east for 1.5 miles. Turn left onto Payson Hill Rd. directly beyond gas station. The camp is 2.6 miles on right.

Far from Nebraska's Prairies (pp. 211–215)

Willa Cather's Grave

DIRECTIONS: From the intersection of Routes 202 and 124 in Jaffrey, follow 124 west for 2 miles. In Jaffrey Center turn right on Laban Ainsworth Way, then left into the Jaffrey Meeting House parking lot. The cemetery is beyond the Meeting House entrance from the parking lot. Walk through cemetery gate and follow fence to the left. The grave is down the slope in the southwest corner of the cemetery.

Shattuck Inn Site

DIRECTIONS: From the intersection of Routes 202 and 124 in Jaffrey, follow 124 west for 2.2 miles. Turn right onto Dublin Rd. After 0.3 mile turn left into parking lot of Shattuck Golf Club. Straight back, to the left of the main building, is a stone platform/monument marking the site of the Shattuck Inn.

Il Sentimento della Casa (pp. 262–267)

Keene's Italian Neighborhood

DIRECTIONS: From the intersection of Routes 12/101 and Winchester St. follow Winchester St. for 0.3 mile. Turn left onto Island St. Immediately on the left is a small park that is framed by the Italian neighborhood.

"How Did It Go Today?" (pp. 282–286)

The MacDowell Colony

The Colony is open to the public only one day a year, on a Sunday in August: MacDowell Medal Day.

DIRECTIONS: From the intersection of Routes 101 and 202, cross 101 onto Grove St. Travel to the center of Peterborough. Take a left onto Main St. Go uphill and take a sharp right onto High St. The MacDowell Colony is located at 100 High St., past the Monadnock Country Club. The office is located in the large white building.

FOR MORE INFORMATION: (603) 924-3886, http://www.macdowellcolony.org

Quiet Boomtown (pp. 296–304)

Rindge Town Center

DIRECTIONS: From the intersection of Routes 202 and 119 in Rindge, take 202 east for 1 mile. Turn right on Main St. at the flashing yellow light and go 0.8 mile to Rindge Center.

BIBLIOGRAPHY AND SOURCES

General Bibliography

Anderson, Ross. *Abbott Handerson Thayer*. Everson Museum, 1982.

An Anthology of New Hampshire Poetry. New Hampshire Federation of Women's Clubs, 1938.

Baldwin, Henry I. *Monadnock Guide*. Society for the Protection of New Hampshire Forests, 1987,

Bean, Margaret C., ed. *Hearing by the Grand Jury on the Death of William K. Dean: April 11–22, 1919, Court House, Keene, New Hampshire*. Margaret C. Bean, 1989.

———. *Willa Cather in Jaffrey*. Jaffrey Historical Society, 2005.

Brown, Rosellen. "Paranoia on Main Street." *New York Times*, August 2, 1995.

"Celebrating 200 Years, 1799–1999." *Keene Sentinel*, July 26–27, 1999.

Chamberlain, Allen. *The Annals of the Grand Monadnock*. 1936. Reprinted: Society for the Protection of New Hampshire Forests, 1975.

Chase, Heman. *More Than Land*. William L. Bauhan, Publisher, 1975.

A Circle of Friends: Art Colonies of Cornish and Dublin. University Art Galleries, University of New Hampshire, 1985.

Clark, Charles E. *The Meetinghouse Tragedy*. University of New Hampshire, 1998.

Clark, Francelia, Dave Robinson, and Alison Rossiter. *Lake Nubanusit (Long Pond/Great Pond): Its History and Its People*. Nubanusit Lake Association, Inc., 2000.

Coffin, John E. *Inviting You to Visit and to Live in the Monadnock Region: "Land of New Hampshire Charm."* Monadnock Region Associates, c. 1940.

Coll, Helen. *Cultivating Life*. First Books Library, 2001.

Duncan, Dayton. *Grassroots: One Year in the Life of the New Hampshire Presidential Primary*. Viking, 1991.

The Grand Monadnock: An Exhibition at the Louise E. Thorne Art Gallery, Keene State College, June 23 to August 3, 1974. Society for the Protection of New Hampshire Forests, 1974.

Jager, Ronald. *The Fate of Family Farming*. University Press of New England, 2004.

———. *Last House on the Road*. Beacon Press, 1994.

Hawthorne, Nathaniel. *The American Notebooks*. Ohio State University Press, 1972.

Hebert, Ernest. *The Dogs of March*. Viking, 1979.

———. *The Kinship*. University Press of New England, 1993.

———. *Live Free or Die*. Viking, 1990.

———. *The Old American*. University Press of New England, 2000.

———. *Whisper My Name*. Viking, 1984.

Hodgkins, Georgina. *Prominent Citizen: Prime Suspect: A Personal Account of the Dean Murder Mystery, a Tragedy in Which the Author Was Involved*. Jaffrey Historical Society, 1996.

Hyman, Tom. *Village on a Hill: A History of Dublin, New Hampshire, 1752–2000*. Peter E. Randall Publisher, 2002.

Lord, Caroline M. *Diary of a Village Library*. New Hampshire Publishing Co., 1971.

Martin, Richard A. *The Only Mill in Town: The Story of the Pail-Making Industry in Richmond, New Hampshire*. Friends of Historic Richmond, 1995.

Mansfield, Howard. *The Bones of the Earth*. Shoemaker & Hoard, 2004.

———. *In the Memory House*. Fulcrum Publishing, 1993.

———. *The Same Ax, Twice: Restoration and Renewal in a Throwaway Age*. University Press of New England, 2000.

Menger, Marianne. *Monadnock*. Fitchburg Art Museum, September 26, 1999–January 9, 2000. Fitchburg Art Museum, 1999.

Meryman, Richard. *Dublin Lake Club: A Centennial History*. Dublin Lake Club, 2001.

Monadnock Institute of Nature, Place and Culture and New England Center for Civic Life. *Rindge 2020: Mapping Our Future*. Franklin Pierce College, 2001.

———. *Rindge 2020 Survey Report*. Franklin Pierce College, 2001.

Monadnock Perspectives: Commentary on Rural and Urban Design. 1979–1997.

Morris, Taylor. *The Walk of the Conscious Ants*. Alfred A. Knopf, 1972.

Neider, Charles, ed. *Selected Letters of Mark Twain*. Harper & Row, 1982.

Nevell, Richard. *A Time to Dance*. St. Martin's Press, 1977.

Nutting, Helen Cushing, ed. *To Monadnock: The Records of a Mountain in New Hampshire through Three Centuries*. Stratford Press, c. 1925.

Ober, Richard. *At What Cost? Shaping the Land We Call New Hampshire*. New Hampshire Historical Society & Society for the Protection of New Hampshire Forests, 1992.

Older, Julia, and Steve Sherman. *Grand Monadnock*. Appledore Books, 1990.

Olmstead, Robert. *Stay Here with Me*. Henry Holt and Company, Inc., 1996.

O'Rourke, P. J. *Republican Party Reptile*. Publishers Group West, 1987.

Pearson, Haydn S. *That Darned Minister's Son*. Doubleday, 1950.

Pool, Elizabeth. *Pen, Brush, Chisel and Clef: Dublin's Halcyon Days*. Amos Fortune Forum and the Dublin Historical Society, 1992.

Pumpelly, Raphael. *My Reminiscences*. H. Holt and Co., 1918.

Rumrill, Alan F. *J. A. French's Cheshire County*. Arcadia Publishing, 1998.

Sarton, May. *Plant Dreaming Deep*. W. W. Norton, 1968.

Sherman, Steve. *Basic Yankee*. Arco Pub., 1984.

Shire Town by Foot: Keene, New Hampshire. A Walking Tour. Historical Society of Cheshire County, 1996.

Suskind, Ron. "Peterborough, N.H., Site of 'Our Town,' Still Resists Change." *Wall Street Journal*, July 30, 1990.

Thoreau, Henry David. *The Writings of Henry David Thoreau*. Houghton Mifflin, 1906.

Tolman, F. B. *More Spit Than Polish at Tolman Pond*. Yankee Books, 1987.

Tolman, Newton F. *North of Monadnock*. Little, Brown, 1961.

———. *Our Loons Are Always Laughing*. I. Washburn, 1963.

White, Nelson C. *Abbott H. Thayer, Painter and Naturalist*. Connecticut Printers, 1951.

Whittemore, Suzanne Bergeron. *In the Shadow of Monadnock: Historic Tours of Cheshire County*. Historical Society of Cheshire County, 1993.

Whynott, Douglas. *A Country Practice: Scenes from the Veterinary Life*. North Point Press, 2005.

Sources

Part One: Introduction (pp. 9–10)

"Affidavit of Joseph Blanchard: Running the Masonian Patent Line." *Benchmark*, Summer/Fall 1985.

Batchellor, Albert Stillman, ed. *Documents Relating to the Masonian Patent, 1630–1846. Provincial and State Papers, Vol. 29.* Edward N. Pearson, Public Printer, 1896.

Belknap, Jeremy. *The History of New-Hampshire.* Vol. 1., 1831. Reprinted: Johnson Reprint Corp., 1970.

———. *The History of New-Hampshire.* Vol. 3, 1812. Reprinted: Johnson Reprint Corp., 1970.

Breckenridge, John A., ed. "The First Work on Surveying Mason's Curve." *Benchmark,* April 1976.

———. "The First Work on Surveying Mason's Curve, Part II." *Benchmark,* July 1976.

Clark, Charles E. *The Eastern Frontier: The Settlement of Northern New England, 1610–1763.* Alfred A. Knopf, 1970.

Dean, John Ward, ed. *Capt. John Mason, the Founder of New Hampshire.* 1887. Reprinted: Burt Franklin, 1967.

Fry, William H. *New Hampshire as a Royal Province.* 1908. Reprinted: AMS Press, Inc., 1970.

Hammond, Otis Grant. "The Masonian Title and Its Relations to New Hampshire and Massachusetts." American Antiquarian Society, *Proceedings,* new series, 27, 1916.

Johnson, Richard R. "Robert Mason and the Coming of Royal Government to New England." *Historical New Hampshire,* Winter 1980.

Lord, G. T., ed. *Belknap's New Hampshire: An Account of the State in 1792.* Vol. 3, 1812. Reprinted: Peter E. Randall, Publisher, 1973.

Page, Elwin L. "The Case of Samuel Alien of London Esq. Governor of New Hampshire." *Historical New Hampshire,* Winter 1970.

———. *Judicial Beginnings in New Hampshire, 1640–1700.* New Hampshire Historical Society, 1959.

Proceedings of the Seminar on the History of New Hampshire Relating to Land Surveying. Manchester, N.H., February 24, 1979. N.H. Land Surveryors Assoc., 1980.

Proceedings of History Seminar II: New Prospective on History of New Hampshire Pertaining to Land Surveying. Manchester, N.H., January 31, 1981. N.H. Land Surveyors Assoc., 1982.

Upham, George Baxter. "New Hampshire Town Boundaries Determined by Mason's Curve." *Granite Monthly,* January 1920.

Wadsworth, Samuel. "The Masonian Patent Line." *Benchmark,* Winter/Spring 1985.

Sokoki Homeland from Monadnock: K'namitobena Sokwaki (pp. 15–27)

This kind of research, synthesizing archival records, oral traditions, and family stories to bring hidden histories into the open, owes a great debt to many Abenaki people and scholars who have crossed my path. I am grateful to Howard Mansfield and John Harris for asking questions that require such long-winded answers. For the inspirations in this essay, I would like to thank, by name, the Sadoques family for their generosity and friendship, elders Don and Beverly Newell, Jeanne Brink and Charlie True for trying to hold Abenaki people together, Donna and John Moody for protecting the old ones and sacred places, Gordon Day for shining light on hidden corners of Abenaki history, Peter Thomas for sharing his transcriptions of and insights into archival records, and, not least of all, Lisa Brooks for all her work on the akwikhigans—the talking leaves that preserved some of our stories.

Aldrich, George. "History of Walpole." In *History of Cheshire County, New Hampshire,* D. H. Hurd, ed. J. Lewis & Co., 1886.

———. *Walpole as It Was and as It Is, Containing the Complete Civil History of the Town from 1749 to 1879.* Claremont Manufacturing Co., 1880.

Annett, Albert, and Alice E. E. Lehtinen. *History of Jaffrey (Middle Monadnock), New Hampshire: An Average Country Town in the Heart of New England.* Town of Jaffrey, N.H., 1937.

Belknap, Jeremy. "Monuments and Relics of the Indians." In *The History of New Hampshire (1791).* Sources of Science, 1970.

Brooks, Lisa Tanya. "The Common Pot: Indigenous Writing and the Reconstruction of Native Space in the Northeast." Unpublished dissertation, Cornell University 2004.

Browne, George Waldo. *The History of Hillsborough, New Hampshire, 1735–1921.* John B. Clarke Company, 1921.

Calloway, Colin G. *Dawnland Encounters: Indians and Europeans in Northern New England.* University Press of New England, 1991.

———. *The Western Abenaki of Vermont, 1600–1800—War, Migration, and the Survival of an Indian People.* University of Oklahoma Press, 1990.

Day, Gordon M. *The Identity of the Saint Francis Indians.* National Museum of Man, Mercury Series, Canadian Ethnology Service, Paper No. 71. National Museums of Canada, 1981.

———. *In Search of New England's Native Past: Essays by Gordon M. Day.* Michael K. Foster and William Cowan, eds. University of Massachusetts Press, 1998.

———. "Western Abenaki." In *Handbook of North American Indians, Volume 15: Northeast,* Bruce G. Trigger, ed. Smithsonian Institution, 1978.

Frink, Helen H. *These Acworth Hills: A History of Acworth, New Hampshire, 1767–1988.* Town of Acworth, N.H., 1989.

Frizzell, Martha McDanolds. *A History of Walpole, New Hampshire.* Walpole Historical Society, 1963.

Hayward, John A. *Gazetteer of New Hampshire Containing Descriptions of all the Counties, Towns and Districts in the State.* John P. Jewett, 1849.

Huden, John C. *Indian Place Names of New England.* Museum of the American Indian, Heye Foundation, 1962.

Keating, Mali. "North American Passage: The 19th Century Odyssey of an Abenaki Family." In *Visit'n: Conversations with Vermonters.* Vermont Folklife Center, November 2001.

Laurent, Joseph. *New Familiar Abenakis & English Dialogues.* Leger Brousseau, 1884.

Nutting, Helen Cushing. *To Monadnock: The Records of a Mountain in New Hampshire through Three Centuries.* Stratford Press, 1925.

Proper, David R. "A Narrative of Keene, New Hampshire, 1732–1967." In *Upper Ashuelot: A History of Keene, New Hampshire.* Keene History Committee, 1968.

Randall, Oran E. *History of Chesterfield, Cheshire County, N.H.* D. Leonard, Printer, 1882.

Seward, Rev. Josiah Lafayette. *A History of the Town of Sullivan, New Hampshire, 1777–1917.* J. L. Seward Est., 1921.

Stearns, Ezra S. *History of the Town of Rindge, New Hampshire, from the date of the Rowley Canada or Massachusetts Charter to the Present Time, 1736–1874.* George H. Ellis, 1875.

Stewart-Smith, David. "The Pennacook Indians and the New England Frontier, circa 1604–1733." Unpublished dissertation, Union Institute, 1998.

Temple, Josiah H., and George Sheldon. *History of Northfield, Massachusetts, for 150 years, with an account of the prior occupation of the territory by the Squakheags: and with family genealogies.* J. Munsell, 1875.

Thomas, Peter Allen. "The Sokokis in the Connecticut River Valley: Two Perspectives on the Past," from a paper given on November 6, 1999, for the conference "Reflections on Remembering and Forgetting: Revisiting 'The Original Vermonters:' Exploring New Research and New Directions for Collaboration in Abenaki Studies." University of Vermont, 2004.

Thoreau, Henry David. *Walking with Thoreau: A Literary Guide to the Mountains of New England*. William Howarth, ed. Beacon Press, 1982.

Wadsworth, Samuel. *Historical Notes of Keene and Roxbury, New Hampshire*. Sentinel Printing, 1932.

Wright, Harry Andrew. *Indian Deeds of Hampden County*. Harry A. Wright, 1905.

11,000 Years on the Ashuelot (pp. 33–43)

The research that inspired this paper was supported by the Monadnock Institute of Nature, Place and Culture at Franklin Pierce College with a grant provided by the Institute for Museum and Library Services, and by a grant from the Franklin Pierce College Faculty Research Fund. Particular thanks go to John Harris, Director of the Monadnock Institute, and Amy McIntyre, Administrative Manager. Field research was completed by FPC students Jeremy Beach, Adam Bonaparte, Angel Bottomley, Launa Eddy, Catie Galdauskas, Ryan Murphy, Shawn Patterson, Greg Peterson, Stacy Rizoli, Emily Saurette, Brooke Shunning, April Sprague, Michael Stilphen, Matt St.Pierre, and Virgil Wetmore. Mark Greenly, Dennis Howe, and Martha Pinello served as field assistants. Art Whipple generously shared his time and knowledge; the project could not have happened without his assistance. Tracy L. Botting provided lots of encouragement and editorial advice. Finally, I thank my Abenaki friends for their inspiration and generosity.

A Mill Girl's Offering (pp. 92–101)

Dublin, Thomas, ed. *Farm to Factory: Women's Letters, 1830–1860*. Columbia University Press, 1993.

———. "Lowell: The Story of an Industrial City." In *A Guide to Lowell National Historic Park*. 1992.

———. *Transforming Women's Work: New England Lives in the Industrial Revolution*. Cornell University Press, 1994.

———. *Women at Work: The Transformation of Work and Community*, 2nd ed. Columbia University Press, 1993.

Eisler, Benita, ed. *The Lowell Offering: Writings by New England Mill Women*. Lippincott, 1977.

History of Washington, NH. 1886. Reprinted with a new foreword, 1998.

Howe, A. P., ed. *Poems of Sarah Shedd*. 1883.

Jager, Ronald, and Grace Jager. *Portrait of a Hill Town: A History of Washington, N.H., 1876–1976*. Washington History Committee, 1977.

Jager, Ronald, and Sally Krone. *A Sacred Deposit: The Meeting House in Washington, New Hampshire*. Gwen Gaskell, 1989.

Larcom, Lucy. *A New England Girlhood*. 1889. Reprinted: Corner House Publishers, 1985.

Minutes of the Washington Circle, 1854–1860. Washington Town Archives.

Robinson, Harriet H. *Loom and Spindle; or, Life Among the Early Mill Girls*. 1898. Reprinted: Press Pacifica, 1976.

Weisman, JoAnne B., ed. "The Lowell Mill Girls." Mount Holyoke College Web page.

The Family History of Water (pp. 102–112)

Armstrong, John Borden. *Factory under the Elms: A History of Harrisville, N.H., 1774–1969*. Merrimack Valley Textile Museum/MIT Press, 1969.

Cantor, Norman F. *Imagining the Law: Common Law and the Foundations of the American Legal System*. HarperCollins Publishers, 1999.

Dunwell, Steve. *The Run of the Mill*. David R. Godine, Publisher, Inc., 1978.

Horwitz, Morton J. *The Transformation of American Law, 1780–1860*. Harvard University Press, 1977.

Humphrey, John. *Water Power of Nubanusit Lake and River, as used by Cheshire Mills, Harrisville, N.H.* 1903.

Hunter, Louis C. *A History of Industrial Power in the United States, 1780–1930. Vol. One: Waterpower in the Century of the Steam Engine*. The University Press of Virginia, 1979.

Josephson, Hannah. *The Golden Threads*. 1949. Reprinted: Russell & Russell, 1967.

McGouldrick, Paul F. *New England Textiles in the 19th Century: Profits and Investment*. Harvard University Press, 1968.

Steinberg, Theodore. *Nature Incorporated: Industrialization and the Waters of New England*. Cambridge University Press, 1991.

Temin, Peter, ed. *Engines of Enterprise: An Economic History of New England*. Harvard University Press, 2000.

Plant Your Apples on the Hills (pp. 113–120)

Apples in New Hampshire: An Industry of Remarkable Promise. Boston & Maine Railroad Information Bureau, n.d.

FEDCO Trees Catalog, 2004. Waterville, Maine, private printing.

Gates, Paul W. "Two Hundred Years of Farming in Gilsum." *Historical New Hampshire*, Vol. 33, no. 1, Spring 1978.

The Milford Cabinet, May 17, 1951.

Morison, George Abbot. *History of Peterborough New Hampshire, Book One—Narrative*. Richard R. Smith Publisher, Inc., 1954.

New Hampshire Invites You. State Department of Agriculture, 1926.

Pearson, Haydn S. *That Darn Minister's Son*. Doubleday, 1950.

———. *The New England Year*. W. W. Norton, 1966.

Rollins, Frank West. "The Abandoned farm in New Hampshire: Why it will soon be a thing of the past—the opportunity that yet lies ready to the hand of any enterprising business farmer." *Country Life in America*, September 1910.

Thoreau, Henry David. "Wild Apples," in *The Natural History Essays of Henry David Thoreau*. Gibbs Smith, 1980.

Transactions of the New Hampshire State Agricultural Society for 1850, 1851, and 1852. Butterfield and Hill, 1853.

Recollections: Marion Davis, Cattle Drover (pp. 120–121)

Friends of the Wapack Trail archives, Peterborough Town Library, Historical Room.
Constance A. Hall transcription of Marion Davis interviews.
Patty Hoffman, New Ipswich Historical Society.

The Last 113 People (pp. 128–135)

Department of Commerce, Bureau of the Census. *Fifteenth Census of the United States: 1930. Population Schedule*. 1930.

Farmer, John, and Jacob B. Moore. *A Gazetteer of the State of New Hampshire.* Jacob B. Moore, 1823.

History Committee of the Stoddard Historical Society. *A History of the Town of Stoddard, New Hampshire.* Stoddard Historical Society, 1974.

Town of Stoddard. *Annual Tax Assessment Records.* 1897–1930.

Wilson, Edgar V. *Memorial, Frederic Almon Wilson, 1822–1897, Cordelia Rebecca (Mack) Wilson, 1827–1913.* 1913.

All photographs are from the collections of the Stoddard Historical Society, Historical Society of Cheshire County, and the collection of the author.

Land of Stone (pp. 138–151)

Childs, John W. "Hillsborough's Old Landmark Retained by Bridge Repairs." *Monthly Bulletin.* N.H. State Highway Department, November 1925.

Cramb, Ian. *The Art of the Stonemason.* Betterway Books, 1992.

Grover, Nathan C. *The Floods of March 1936: Part 1. New England Rivers.* Department of the Interior, U.S. Government Printing Office, 1937.

"A Picture of Strength and Beauty." *Historical Society of Cheshire County Newsletter*, June 2003.

Prevett, Jeanne. "Timbertop: Relic from a Boomtown." *New Hampshire Seasons*, Fall 2001.

Steele, Allison. "Bridges Named National Landmarks." *Concord Monitor*, October 10, 2003.

Woodward, Christopher. *In Ruins.* Pantheon Books, 2001.

Additional research and field guidance were provided by John Harris and Howard Mansfield, whose assistance, and forbearance, are gratefully acknowledged.

The Tragic Life of William Preston Phelps (pp. 160–170)

"Catalog for the sale of the property of William Preston Phelps," prepared by J. E. Conant & Co. Auctioneers, Lowell, Mass., 1917.

A Circle of Friends: Art Colonies of Cornish and Dublin. Catalog for an exhibition prepared jointly by University of New Hampshire and the Thorne-Sagendorph Art Gallery of Keene State College, 1985.

Conversations and correspondence between myself and John Edward Phelps.

Hurd, Charles E. "A Painter of Monadnock." *New England Magazine*, February 1898.

Information on file about Phelps at the Whistler House Museum of Art, Lowell, Mass.

Keene Evening Sentinel, January through September 1917.

Kristiansen, Rolf H., and John Leahy. *Rediscovering Some New England Artists, 1875–1900.* Gardner-O'Brien Associates, 1987.

One Branch of the Edward Phelps Descendants, Stories and Genealogy Compiled by John Edward Phelps, 1957–1999. Privately published by John Edward Phelps, nephew of William Preston Phelps.

William Preston Phelps Papers, 1849 to 1950. Smithsonian Archives of American Art.

Recollections: The Green Army of Camp Annett (pp. 178–180)

Cline, A. C., and S. H. Spurr. "The Virgin Upland Forest of Central New England: A Study of Old Growth Stands in the Pisgah Mountain Section of New Hampshire." *Harvard Forest Bulletin No. 21.* Harvard Forest, 1942.

Harvard Forest archives. Petersham, Mass.

National Association of CCC Alumni. St. Louis, Mo.

Peterborough Transcript. June 8, 1933.

Wessels, Tom. *Reading the Forested Landscape: A Natural History of New England.* Countryman Press, 1997.

Recollections: Pisgah, a Place Apart (pp. 239–242)

Cline, A. C. "The Marketing of Lumber in N.H." *Harvard Forest Bulletin No. 10.* Harvard Forest, 1925.

Fisher, R. T., Director of Harvard Forest. Personal correspondence. Pisgah File, Harvard Forest Archives, 1926.

Herman, Russell. Interview conducted by Rodney Doolittle in the 1970s. Tape held by Friends of Pisgah, Winchester, N.H.

Lee, Mary. "New England's Virgin Forest in Danger." *New York Times Magazine*, July 4, 1926.

Shapiro, H. "Stories from the Dickinson Family and Others." In *Yankee Lands: A Land Use Curriculum Project.* Antioch New England Graduate School, Keene, N.H., 1980.

State of New Hampshire. *Biennial Report of the Forestry Commission, 1923–24.* Concord, N.H.

Wessels, Tom. *Reading the Forested Landscape: A Natural History of New England.* Countryman Press, 1997.

"A Wonderful Forest: Whose Seeds Were Sown Before Columbus Sailed." *Keene Sentinel*, August 5, 1903.

Quiet Boomtown (pp. 296–304)

Finch, Robert. *Death of a Hornet and Other Cape Cod Essays.* Counterpoint Press, 2001.

Herbers, John. *The New Heartland: America's Flight beyond the Suburbs and How It Is Changing Our Future.* Times Books, 1986.

Moe, Richard, and Carter Wilkie. *Changing Places: Rebuilding Community in an Age of Sprawl.* Henry Holt, 1997.

New Hampshire Association of Regional Planning Commissions: Data Center. http://www.nharpc.org/datacenter.php.

New Hampshire Office of State Planning: Municipal Population Projections 2005 to 2025. March 2003. http://nh.gov/oep/programs/DataCenter/Population/document/MuniProjections00.pdf

New Hampshire State Planning and Development Commission. "A Suggested Plan of Development for Rindge, New Hampshire." 1945.

Rindge History Committee. *Town on the Border: Rindge, New Hampshire, 1874–1988.* Phoenix Publishing, 1989.

Sanders, Scott Russell. *Staying Put: Making a Home in a Restless World.* Beacon Press, 1993.

The author thanks the following for taking the time to be interviewed: Maryann Harper, Sharon O'Keefe, Deborah Sawyer, Candice Starrett, David Tower, Audrey and David Tetreault, Ed and Susan Valcourt.

Is There a Monadnock Land Ethic? (pp. 306–316)

Annett, Albert, and Alice E. E. Lehtinen. *History of Jaffrey (Middle Monadnock) New Hampshire: An Average Country Town in the Heart of New England.* Four volumes. Town of Jaffrey, 1934–2000.

Cronon, William. *Changes in the Land*. Hill & Wang, 1983.

Heffernan, Nancy Coffey, and Ann Page Stecker. *New Hampshire: Crosscurrents in its Development*. University Press of New England, 1996.

Jager, Ronald, and Grace Jager. *New Hampshire: An Illustrated History of the Granite State*. Windsor Publications, 1983.

Nash, Roderick. *Wilderness and the American Mind*. Yale University Press, 1967.

Ober, Richard, ed. *At What Cost? Shaping the Land We Call New Hampshire*. New Hampshire Historical Society and the Society for the Protection of New Hampshire Forests, 1992.

CONTRIBUTORS

Jane Brox ("Plant Your Apples on the Hills") is the author of *Here and Nowhere Else* (Beacon Press, 1995), *Five Thousand Days Like This One* (Beacon Press, 1999), and *Clearing Land* (North Point Press, 2004).

Marge Bruchac ("Sokoki Homeland from Monadnock") is an Abenaki and a historical consultant and exhibit adviser for Historic Deerfield, the Pocumtuck Valley Memorial Association, Old Sturbridge Village, and Plimoth Plantation. She has won two awards from the Wordcraft Circle of Native Writers and Storytellers: Storyteller of the Year (2000) and Historical Writer of the Year (2002) for *1621: A New Look at Thanksgiving* (National Geographic Society, 2001).

Gerald Burns ("Quiet Boomtown") is a Professor of English and American Studies at Franklin Pierce College. He was in charge of the Monadnock Institute's study of Rindge, N.H. A Fulbright Scholar, he is the author of *Presenting America: Encountering the Philippines* (University of the Philippines Press, 1993).

Edie Clark ("William Preston Phelps" and "Back to the Land") has written extensively about New England for *Yankee* magazine, where she served as senior editor and senior writer for almost 25 years. She is the author of the memoir *The Place He Made* (Villard Books, 1995); *Monadnock Tales*, a long narrative poem about the mountain that was written in collaboration with the composer Larry Siegel to create a fusion of symphonic music and poetry; and *The View from Mary's Farm,* a collection of her essays (Powerbridge Press, 2005). She is currently teaching in the MFA program at Emerson College. She has lived in the Monadnock region almost her entire adult life.

Tim Clark ("Our Town") teaches English at Conval High School in Peterborough. He is a former managing editor of *Yankee* magazine.

Jim Collins ("Getting Out of the Hole in Nelson") is a former editor of *Yankee* magazine. He is the author of *The Last Best League* (Da Capo Press, 2004) about the Cape Cod Summer Collegiate Baseball League.

William Craig ("Drawing Our Desires") has written fiction, criticism, and poetry for print and online journals including the *Spectator, Art New England*, the *New Boston Review, StoryQuarterly, Creative Loafing, The Anthology of New England Writers*, and *Global AIDSLink*. He has received a fiction fellowship from the New Hampshire State Council for the Arts and is the founder of the annual Meetinghouse Readings in Canaan, N.H. He lives in Thetford Center, Vt.

Geoffrey Douglas ("Lawrence Tannery") is the author of three nonfiction books and many magazine articles written during the last 30 years. He teaches writing at the University of Massachusetts, Lowell.

Contributors

Dayton Duncan ("This Is a Great Country, and Don't Forget It") is a documentary filmmaker and the author of nine books about American history, among them *Grass Roots: One Year in the Life of the New Hampshire Presidential Primary* (Viking, Penguin, 1991). He lives in Walpole.

Linda Dyer ("Far from Nebraska's Prairies") has written for the *New York Times*, the *Christian Science Monitor*, and many other newspapers as well as in *Blueline, Small Pond Magazine, Ad Hoc Monadnock*, and other literary publications.

Kevin Gardner ("Land of Stone") has built and restored stone walls for more than 25 years with Owen Associates, a small family business. He is an equity actor, drama teacher, and theater festival judge. He reports on the arts for public radio. He is the author of *The Granite Kiss: Traditions and Techniques of Building New England Stone Walls* (Countryman Press, 2001).

Elizabeth Getchell ("Eminent Domain") has taught courses on nature and place-based writing since 1998 at the University of Vermont, where she is the student services coordinator in the Environmental Program.

Robert Goodby ("11,000 Years on the Ashuelot") is an Assistant Professor of Anthropology at Franklin Pierce College and a member of the Executive Committee of the Monadnock Institute of Nature, Place and Culture. He received his Ph.D. in Anthropology from Brown University in 1994.

Judson D. Hale, Sr. ("My Favorite Views") is the chairman of the board of Yankee Publishing, Inc., the editor of a half-dozen books, and the author of *Inside New England* (HarperCollins, 1982) and *The Education of a Yankee* (HarperCollins, 1987).

John R. Harris ("Borders," "Marlborough's Granite Quarry," "The Poor Farm," and "Last Train") is the executive director of the Monadnock Institute of Nature, Place and Culture at Franklin Pierce College and editorial assistant for the anthology. He received his Ph.D. from the University of North Carolina and lives with his family in Westmoreland.

Nancy Hayden ("Grandfather's Farm") lives at Too Bad Farm in Marlborough.

Ernest Hebert ("Taxi") is a Keene native, the author of seven novels, and professor of English at Dartmouth College. *The Dogs of March* (Viking Press, 1979) was cited for excellence by the Hemingway Foundation in 1980, and *The Old American* (University Press of New England, 2000) was named "outstanding work of fiction for 2001" by the New Hampshire Writers Project. Hebert was named the Sarah Josepha Hale Award winner for 2002.

Paul B. Hertneky ("Il Sentimento della Casa" and "The Last Mill in Town") writes mostly about food and cultural issues for magazines, newspapers, and radio. He teaches at Antioch New England Graduate School and lives in Hancock.

J. Parker Huber ("Following Thoreau") is the author of *Wildest Country: A Guide to Thoreau's Maine* (Appalachian Mountain Club, 1981), *A Wanderer All My Days: John Muir In New England* (2005) and the editor of *Elevating Ourselves: Thoreau on Mountains* (Houghton Mifflin, 1999).

Ronald Jager ("A Mill Girl's Offering") received his Ph.D. from Harvard University, and taught and wrote philosophy at Yale University until 1977. Since then he and his wife have lived in Washington, N.H., where they have jointly authored three books on New Hampshire history. He has also been a humanities consultant to the New Hampshire legislature and, as a freelance writer, he is the author of *Eighty Acres: Elegy for a Family Farm* (Beacon Press, 1990) and a New Hampshire memoir, *Last House on the Road: Excursions into a Rural Past* (Beacon Press, 1994).

Martha Weinman Lear ("How Did It Go Today?") is the author of the memoir *Heartsounds* (Simon & Schuster, 1980). She is a former articles editor of the *New York Times Magazine* and has written for most of the national publications.

Howard Mansfield ("Introduction" and "The Family History of Water") is the anthology's editor. He is author of several books about preservation and cultural memory, including *In the Memory House* (Fulcrum, 1993), *The Same Ax, Twice: Restoration and Renewal in a Throwaway Age* (University Press of New England, 2000), and most recently *The Bones of the Earth* (Shoemaker & Hoard, 2004).

Richard Meryman ("Abbott Thayer") grew up in Dublin across the lake from Monadnock. After 23 years with *Life* magazine, he has been a freelance writer of magazine articles and books. His latest is a biography of Andrew Wyeth (HarperCollins, 1996).

Sy Montgomery ("The Return of the Wild") is the author of a dozen books, including *Walking with the Great Apes* (Houghton Mifflin, 1991), *Spell of the Tiger* (Houghton Mifflin, 1995), *Search for the Golden Moon Bear* (Simon & Schuster, 2002), and *Journey of the Pink Dolphins* (Simon & Schuster, 2000) which was a *Booklist* Top 10 Sci-Tech book for 2000 as well as a finalist for England's Thomas Cook Travel Book Award. She is a commentator for National Public Radio's *Living on Earth*.

Guillermo Nuñez (artist) has illustrated book covers, political cartoons, and the *The Granite Kiss* by Kevin Gardner (Countryman Press, 2001). Originally from Havana, Cuba, Nuñez and his wife and two children divide their time between Andover, Mass., and Cape Cod.

Richard Ober ("Is There a Monadnock Land Ethic?") is executive director of the Monadnock Conservancy and an independent writer whose work explores the relationship between people and place. He is a coauthor of *The Northern Forest* (Chelsea Green Publishing Co., 1996) and the editor of *At What Cost? Shaping the Land We Call New Hampshire* (New Hampshire Historical Society/Society for the Protection of New Hampshire Forests, 1992) and other books. His family has been in the region since the 1780s.

Haydn S. Pearson ("The Grange Votes Down Automobiles") grew up on Glenrose Farm in Hancock before and during World War I. He reminisced about his mischievous boyhood and country life in a syndicated newspaper column and in many books, including *Country Flavor* (McGraw-Hill, 1945), *Success on the Small Farm* (McGraw-Hill, 1946), *That Darned Minister's Son* (Doubleday, 1950), and *The New England Year* (W. W. Norton, 1966). After a teaching career, he retired to a farm in Greenfield.

Mortimer Peebles ("Lost Ski Areas" and "Recollections: Marion Davis, Cattle Drover") is writing a book about the metaphysics of toast.

Dawn Powell ("And Not So Well for Others") was buried in an unmarked grave in New York's Potter's Field. At her death, at age 69, in 1965, all her books were out of print. In 1987, Gore Vidal's essay on "our best comic novelist" sparked a revival. Powell was born in a small Ohio town and lived her adult life in New York, "a permanent visitor" in Greenwich Village, she said. Her sharp-eyed, satirical novels and stories capture both places. (It was Powell "who really says the funny things for which Dorothy Parker gets credit," said Diana Trilling.) Twelve of Powell's novels have now been reissued, including two volumes in the Library of America, along with editions of her plays, diaries, letters, and short stories. Vidal says there's a reason for her rediscovery: "We are finally catching up to her."

Raphael Pumpelly ("How to Build a House") was a pioneering geologist. He was famous for his scientific expeditions surveying China, Mongolia, and Japan in the 1860s. Pumpelly was a "great, blue-eyed giant, with a long, flowing beard" and a wanderlust that never abated. At age 70 he explored prehistoric civilizations in Turkestan (1903 and 1904).

Janisse Ray ("Mr. Roy's Market") is the author of *Ecology of a Cracker Childhood* (Milkweed Editions, 1999), *Wild Card Quilt: Taking a Chance on Home* (Milkweed Editions, 2003), and *Pinhook: Manifesto of Possibility and Hope* (Chelsea Green, 2005). She currently lives in Brattleboro, Vt., with her husband, Raven Burchard, and son, Silas.

Alan F. Rumrill ("The Last 113 People") is the executive director of the Historical Society of Cheshire County and a life-long resident of Stoddard. He is the author of *J. A. French's Cheshire County* (Arcadia, 1998).

Peter Sauer ("The Disorderly Origins of the Granite State") writes about landscapes, history, and politics for *Orion* magazine from his home in an upstate New York county that was surveyed and mapped in the 1760s as West New Hampshire. He serves on the Monadnock Institute's Advisory Board.

Jonathan Schach ("The Green Army of Camp Annett" and "Pisgah, a Place Apart") provided research assistance for the anthology and serves as a member of the Monadnock Institute's Executive Committee and a member of the faculty at Franklin Pierce College. He received a master's degree in environmental studies from Antioch New England Graduate School.

David Stewart-Smith ("Phineas Stevens") is of Scottish and Pennacook ancestry and has specialized in the New England frontier and Abenaki history over the past 12 years. He holds a doctorate in interdisciplinary studies (history, ethnology, and archaeology) from Union Institute. He teaches history and cultural studies at Vermont College and lives in Webster, N.H.

Roger B. Swain ("Blueberry Planet") has served as science editor of *Horticulture* magazine since the 1970s. He was a host of PBS's *Victory Garden*. He has written *The Practical Gardener: Mastering the Elements of Good Growing* (Budget Book Service, 1998), *Earthly Pleasures: Tales from a Biologist's Garden* (Lyons Press, 1994), *Field Days: Journal of an Itinerant Biologist* (Lyons Press, 1994), *Groundwork: A Gardener's Ecology* (Houghton-Mifflin, 1994), and *Saving Graces: Sojourns of a Backyard Biologist* (Little, Brown, 1991).

Newton F. Tolman ("Confessions of a Part-Time Squire") was an independent spirit. He was an outdoorsman, a musician, and a writer. At contra dances, Newt played pennywhistle, flute, and occasionally the saxophone. He coedited a collection of traditional contra dance music and wrote several books, including *North of Monadnock* (Little, Brown, 1961) and *Our Loons Are Always Laughing* (I. Washburn, 1963). He was an early skier, learning in Austria and returning home to make his own skis and to help start one of the first rope-tow ski runs in New England. In the fall he set aside music to hunt. He and his wife, Janet, were professional hunting guides. He loved a good party and enjoyed playing practical jokes. He was a man who made his own rules. Newt Tolman was an American original.

Tom Wessels ("Parables of Place") is the author of *Reading the Forested Landscape: A Natural History of New England* (Countryman Press, 1997) and *The Granite Landscape: A Natural History of America's Mountain Domes from Acadia to Yosemite* (Countryman Press, 2001). He is an ecologist in the Department of Environmental Studies at Antioch New England Graduate School. He also chairs the Robert and Patricia Switzer Foundation, which fosters environmental leadership through graduate fellowships and organizational grants.

ILLUSTRATION CREDITS AND ACKNOWLEDGMENTS

Illustration Credits & Acknowledgments

Page 91	Harold Larro Collection.
Page 91	Harold Larro Collection.
Page 93	Shedd Free Library.
Page 93	Shedd Free Library.
Page 98	Shedd Free Library.
Page 100	Photograph by Jane Lauber, Antrim, N.H.
Page 102	New England Aerial Photography.
Page 103	Historic Harrisville.
Page 105	Historic Harrisville.
Page 107	Historic Harrisville.
Page 108	Historic Harrisville.
Page 110	Peterborough Historical Society Collections.
Page 113	Photo by Richard C. Johnson.
Page 119	Michael Moore.
Page 123	Hancock Historical Society.
Page 125	Freer Gallery of Art, Smithsonian Institution, Washington, D.C.: Gift of Charles Lang Freer, F1913.93a. Detail.
Page 126	Collection of Historical Society of Cheshire County, Keene, N.H.
Page 128	Collection of Historical Society of Cheshire County, Keene, N.H.
Page 128	Collection of Historical Society of Cheshire County, Keene, N.H.
Page 129	Stoddard Historical Society.
Page 130	Stoddard Historical Society.
Page 130	Collection of Historical Society of Cheshire County, Keene, N.H.
Page 131	Collection of Historical Society of Cheshire County, Keene, N.H.
Page 131	Collection of Historical Society of Cheshire County, Keene, N.H
Page 132	Stoddard Historical Society.
Page 133	Stoddard Historical Society.
Page 134	Stoddard Historical Society.
Page 135	Collection of Historical Society of Cheshire County, Keene, N.H.
Page 135	Collection of Historical Society of Cheshire County, Keene, N.H.
Page 136	Collection of Historical Society of Cheshire County, Keene, N.H.
Page 138	Drawing by Guillermo Nuñez.
Page 143	Drawing by Guillermo Nuñez.
Page 146	Drawing by Guillermo Nuñez.
Page 149	Drawing by Guillermo Nuñez.
Page 150	Drawing by Guillermo Nuñez.
Page 153	© Pamela Stagg.
Page 160	Collection of Historical Society of Cheshire County, Keene, N.H.
Page 162	From The Collection of Marie Royce Ruffle.
Page 164	From The Collection of Marie Royce Ruffle.
Page 165	From private collection.
Page 166	From The Collection of Marie Royce Ruffle.
Page 167	From The Collection of Marie Royce Ruffle.
Page 172	Cheshire County Commission report.
Page 172	Collection of Historical Society of Cheshire County, Keene, N.H.
Page 173	Collection of Historical Society of Cheshire County, Keene, N.H.
Page 175	Collection of Historical Society of Cheshire County, Keene, N.H.
Page 178	From the Archives of the National Association of Civilian Conservation Corps Alumni (NACCCA).
Page 179	From the Archives of the National Association of Civilian Conservation Corps Alumni (NACCCA).

Page 179   From the Archives of the National Association of Civilian Conservation
           Corps Alumni (NACCCA).

Page 180   From the Archives of the National Association of Civilian Conservation
           Corps Alumni (NACCCA).

Page 181   New England Lost Ski Areas Project.

Page 182   Collection of Historical Society of Cheshire County, Keene, N.H.

Page 189   From The Collection of Marie Royce Ruffle. Detail.

Page 190   Collection of Historical Society of Cheshire County, Keene, N.H.

Page 195   Corcoran Gallery of Art, Washington, D.C., Museum Purchase, Anna E.
           Clark Fund.

Page 197   *Gladys Thayer's sleeping hut, ca. 1901.* Image is courtesy of the Abbott Hand-
           erson Thayer and Thayer family papers, 1861–1944 in the Archives of Amer-
           ican Art, Smithsonian Institution.

Page 197   *Abbott Handerson Thayer and family in Dublin, New Hampshire, ca. 1903.*
           Image is courtesy of the Nelson and Henry C. White research material,
           1898–1978 in the Archives of American Art, Smithsonian Institution.

Page 199   Abbott H. Thayer (1849–1921), *Monadnock Angel,* 1920–21, oil on canvas,
           91 ⅛ x 60 in., 1930.17. Addison Gallery of American Art, Phillips Academy,
           Andover, Massachusetts. All Rights Reserved.

Page 200   Smithsonian American Art Museum, Gift of William T. Evans.

Page 201   Mr. & Mrs. Thomas A. Rosse.

Page 202   Freer Gallery of Art, Smithsonian Institution, Washington, D.C.: Gift of
           Charles Lang Freer, F1913.93a.

Page 205   Bettmann/Corbis.

Page 209   Photograph from Allison Glass Plate Negative Collection. Courtesy of the
           Dublin Public Library.

Page 210   Elise Pumpelly Cabot.

Page 211   Archives and Special Collections, University of Nebraska–Lincoln Libraries.

Page 213   Collection of Historical Society of Cheshire County, Keene, N.H.

Page 215   John R. Harris.

Page 217   Collection of Nancy Hayden.

Page 218   Collection of Nancy Hayden.

Page 220   From private collection.

Page 221   From private collection.

Page 223   From private collection.

Page 227   Wood engraving by Randy Miller. From Richard Nevell, *A Time to Dance:
           American Country Dancing from Hornpipes to Hot Hash.* St. Martin's Press,
           1977.

Page 228   Milne Special Collections and Archives Department, University of New
           Hampshire Library, Durham, N.H. Photograph by Charles L. Hanson, Jr.

Page 229   Milne Special Collections and Archives Department, University of New
           Hampshire Library, Durham, N.H. Photograph by Charles L. Hanson, Jr.

Page 231   Photo by Allen Mendelson.

Page 233   Collection of Doolittle family.

Page 236   Elizabeth Wright Getchell.

Page 239   Collection of the Winchester Historical Society.

Page 240   Collection of Historical Society of Cheshire County, Keene, N.H.

Page 240   Harvard Forest Archives.

Page 241   Collection of the Winchester Historical Society.

Page 242   Collection of the Winchester Historical Society.

Page 243   Photo by Richard C. Johnson.

Illustration Credits & Acknowledgments

Page 246	Collection of Historical Society of Cheshire County, Keene, N.H.
Page 247	Original line etching by J. Ann Eldridge.
Page 249	Original line etching by J. Ann Eldridge.
Page 251	Mr. & Mrs. Thomas A. Rosse. Detail.
Page 252	John R. Harris.
Page 253	John R. Harris.
Page 256	Ernest Hebert.
Page 262	DiTullio family.
Page 264	Photo provided by Ann (DiGiulio) Eastman, Keene, N.H.
Page 266	Photo provided by Caroline Dintino, Keene, N.H.
Page 271	Courtesy of Monadnock Paper Mills, Inc.
Page 271	John R. Harris.
Page 273	Courtesy of Monadnock Paper Mills, Inc.
Page 274	Courtesy of Monadnock Paper Mills, Inc.
Page 274	Courtesy of Monadnock Paper Mills, Inc.
Page 277	Marlborough Historical Society.
Page 277	Marlborough Historical Society.
Page 279	Collection of the Winchester Historical Society.
Page 280	Collection of the Winchester Historical Society.
Page 282	Photo by Brendan Tapley/courtesy of The MacDowell Colony.
Page 287	Collection of Historical Society of Cheshire County, Keene, N.H.
Page 290	Michael Moore.
Page 293	Collection of Historical Society of Cheshire County, Keene, N.H.
Page 294	Collection of Historical Society of Cheshire County, Keene, N.H.
Page 295	Collection of Historical Society of Cheshire County, Keene, N.H.
Page 296	John R. Harris.
Page 297	Rindge Historical Society.
Page 298	Jeffrey B. Porter, Southwest Region Planning Commission.
Page 299	Jeffrey B. Porter, Southwest Region Planning Commission.
Page 300	Rindge Historical Society.
Page 306	Sawyer family.
Page 307	Sawyer family.
Page 309	Sawyer family.
Page 311	Ann Sawyer.
Page 314	Sawyer family.
Page 314	Sawyer family.
Page 319	Carole Allen.

EDITOR'S NOTE

Where the Mountain Stands Alone began when John Harris, director of the Monadnock Institute of Nature, Place and Culture, called a group together in 1997. John had been following the work of other institutes dedicated to studying the making and unmaking of a sense of place. The discussions were lively and enjoyable. Those who gave their time were Jane Brox, Gerald Burns, Meredith Martin, John Hanson Mitchell, Christine Salem, Peter Sauer, and myself. However, that first effort did not succeed. We were not satisfied with the book that was emerging.

This anthology owes its existence to the tireless interest of John Harris and Christine, who were determined to create a book worthy of the region. They revived the project in 2002 and we began again—or, as we joked, entered our second century working on the same book.

John is the book's all-around advocate, grants writer, story adviser, and photo researcher. Christine, who first suggested the project, has worked as a story adviser, photo detective, and—her official role—the book's marketer. For the last four years we have brainstormed stories, debated the book's shape, and reviewed contributions in day-long conferences, a steady barrage of e-mail, and many conference calls.

Amy McIntyre, administrative manager for the Community Scholarship Consortium at Franklin Pierce College, has provided essential office and computer support. Jonathan Schach, Katrina Yeager, Susan Peery, Meredith Martin, and Amy Mitchell helped with photo research.

Where the Mountain Stands Alone has benefited from the Institute's oral history project. "Story Circles" have been held in half a dozen towns, aided by a grant from the New Hampshire Humanities Council. The Story Circles have been festive evenings, and have given us a rich harvest of firsthand experience. Jonathan Schach and Elizabeth Getchell collected, edited, and augmented these stories with historic photographs and documents for the website (www.monadnockstories.org).

Alan Rumrill, director of the Historical Society of Cheshire County, was invaluable in locating photos and critiquing the colonial history. Michelle Stahl, director, Peterborough Historical Society, fielded numerous inquires. Constance A. Hall generously shared her long interview with Marion Davis. Kevin Gardner helped select the White Pine Blister Rust Maps in the New Hampshire State Archives. Cheryl Cavanaugh, operations director, The Fort at No. 4, was a helpful guide to the fort's historic artifacts. Richard Murray, senior art historian, Smithsonian American Art Museum, helped identify, select, and secure permission to reproduce paintings by Abbott Thayer. Dawn Powell's letter is reprinted by permission of the Estate of Dawn Powell. Jeremy Davis, founder of the New England Lost Ski Areas Project (www.nelspa.org), provided the Fitzwilliam ski logo. "Our Town" by Tim Clark is reprinted with permission of *Yankee Magazine*, March 1994, p. 98, "Unchanging New England." "How Did It Go Today?" is reprinted by permission of Martha Weinman Lear. This article first appeared in *The New York Times Book Review*, March 6, 1988. Mark Twain's letter is reprinted by permission of the Mark Twain Foundation.

Edie Clark, Jim Collins, Paul Hertneky, Robert M. Oksner, Sy Montgomery, Elizabeth Marshall Thomas, and Willard Williams reviewed an early version of the contents, offering good suggestions. Bill Nuñez's careful work and sharp observation have brought the landscapes in his art to life. He has been a pleasure to work with.

We also received help from Jerry Adams, Helen Bastedo, Richard Butler, Jack Calhoun, Chick Colony, William Derry, Fred and Dorothy Doolittle, Tony Dubois, Nancy Hayden, Deborah Porter Hayes, Patty Hoffman, Robert and George Graves, Marsha Griffin, Stephen Johnson, Harold Larro, June Elliott Lester, Elizabeth Poole, Jeff Porter, Amy Raymond, Charles Royce, Dale Russell, Peter and Ann Sawyer, Brendan Tapley, Barry and Renn Tolman, Alan Williams, Douglas Whynott, and JoEllen Wright.

About the Cover

Nancy Hayden kindly allowed us to reproduce this painting by Alexander James. She recalls:

When Aleck James painted the view from my grandparents' farm, I was very small and happened to be visiting. I remember only his easel and the brightly colored paints.

The story was that Aleck had had a heart attack the previous fall, and was afraid he might never paint again. He had slumped into a deep depression. My grandmother was a good friend of his and his wife Freddie's. She urged him to paint her view of Monadnock, just for fun, free of pressure.

Somehow he was persuaded—perhaps because it was such a different subject than his usual portraits, perhaps because people did not easily say "no" to my grandmother. And he responded by using a far freer, looser, more impressionistic style and a warmer, brighter palette. At a recent exhibit of his works at the Thorne-Sagendorph Art Gallery at Keene State College, this painting seemed almost to be the work of a different artist.

A Special Thanks to Our Donors

The Monadnock Institute acknowledges with gratitude the generous support of these donors who made publication of this book possible: Institute of Museum and Library Services, New Hampshire Humanities Council, and the National Endowment for the Humanties. And:

Founders
Ruth and James Ewing Fund for the Monadnock Community Foundation of the
    New Hampshire Charitable Foundation
Putnam Foundation

Benefactors
Stan and Cheri Fry
William and Maryann Harper
Dr. Arthur and Martha Pappas

Donors
Margaret A. Harris, M.D.
Andrew P. Kordalewski
David and Janice Liddell
Gilbert Verney Foundation

Supporters

Robert P. Bass, Jr.

Linda and Russell Bastedo

Faulkner Family Fund

Mr. and Mrs. Robert L. Forbes

Joslin Kimball Frank

Mr. and Mrs. John W. Harris

John and Jean Hoffman

Carl and Ann Jacobs

Paul M. Kotila

Stephen and Colleen Krause

Barbara and Walter Lacey

Ambassador and Mrs. Joseph C. Petrone

Robert and Harriet Sorensen

Story and Tom Wright

About the Monadnock Institute of Nature, Place and Culture

In 1996 the Monadnock Institute of Nature, Place and Culture was founded at Franklin Pierce College by faculty and staff in the humanities, natural sciences, social sciences, and library who were interested in the theme of place. The study of place seemed ideal for connecting interdisciplinary education, academic research, and outreach to the local community. These three goals continue to define the work of the Monadnock Institute today.

The Institute has run workshops for elementary, middle, and high school teachers since 1997. With the support of a grant from the National Endowment for the Humanities in 2001, the Monadnock Institute has undertaken an ambitious collaboration with Keene High School and the Historical Society of Cheshire County. Secondary school teachers are learning how to design place-based lessons that emphasize community memory and use digital technology.

The Institute's workshops and Story Circles have been featured in the *New York Times*, *Christian Science Monitor*, *Orion* magazine, the *Keene Sentinel*, and on the TV magazine *Chronicle* and New Hampshire Public Radio.

In 2002 the New Hampshire Humanities Council provided two grants for the Monadnock Institute to conduct eight Story Circles, informal opportunities for local residents to share memories and anecdotes of life and work in the community.

Other projects by the Monadnock Institute have received support from the New Hampshire Charitable Foundation, the Monadnock Community Foundation, the Henry Luce Foundation, the Monadnock Millennium Group, and the Faulkner Foundation.

At annual conferences the Institute has welcomed Sy Montgomery and David M. Carroll (2003), Marge Bruchac (2002), Scott Russell Sanders, Ernest Hebert, and Howard Mansfield (2001), David W. Orr (2000), William Vitek and Brian Donahue (1999), and John Elder, Robert Finch, and Jane Brox (1998).

The Monadnock Institute publishes an annual newsletter and maintains a website at www.fpc.edu/monadnockinstitute. More than six hundred individuals are members of the Institute.

INDEX

Page numbers followed by "f" indicate illustrations.

Index

Index